The Exam Class Tookit

Also available from Continuum:

100 Ideas for Essential Teaching Skills – Johannes Ahrenfelt and Neal Watkin

Innovate with ICT – Johannes Ahrenfelt and Neal Watkin

The Exam Class Toolkit

How to Create Engaging Lessons that Ensure Progression and Results

JOHANNES AHRENFELT
and NEAL WATKIN

continuum

Continuum International Publishing Group

The Tower Building
11 York Road
SE1 7NX

80 Maiden Lane, Suite 704
New York,
NY 10038

www.continuumbooks.com

British Library Cataloguing-in-Publication Data
A catalogue record for this book is available from the British Library.

ISBN: 9781441180476 (paperback)

Library of Congress Cataloging-in-Publication Data
Ahrenfelt, Johannes.
  The exam class toolkit: how to create engaging lessons that ensure progression and results/Johannes Ahrenfelt and Neal Watkin.
      p. cm.
    Includes bibliographical references.
    ISBN 978-1-4411-8047-6 (pbk.: alk. paper)
  1. Curriculum planning–Great Britain. 2. Educational tests and measurements–Great Britain. 3. Education, Secondary–Great Britain. I. Watkin, Neal. II. Title.

  LB2806.15.A37 2010
  373.126–dc22

2009014964

Typeset by BookEns Ltd, Royston, Hertfordshire
Printed and bound in Great Britain by Bell & Bain Ltd, Glasgow

Contents

List of Abbreviations

AfL	Assessment for Learning
AST	Advanced Skills Teacher
G. & T.	Gifted and Talented
MFL	Modern Foreign Languages
NQT	Newly Qualified Teacher
PGCE	Postgraduate Certificate of Education
RSS	Really Simple Syndication
TASC	Thinking Actively in a Social Context
TEEP	Teacher Effectiveness Enhancement Programme

About the Authors

Johannes Ahrenfelt is County Adviser for Learning and Teaching with ICT.

Neil Watkin is an AST in History and Lead Practitioner in Gifted and Talented Education.

1 | Design the course

The pain

Why can't exam boards or government agencies leave courses alone? There are few years when no changes need to be made and you can enjoy the teaching of a specification safe in the knowledge that it is comfortable and familiar. Change, though, does provide us with a chance to reassess what we are doing, and to some extent we have a licence to start again from the beginning and design a course that is more inviting and exciting.

Designing a new course can be daunting, but the main complaint we have heard about exam teaching is that it is dull. Teachers look at the specification, take out the contents list and use it as the basis for a scheme. We feel pressured into this approach, because exam boards know best – after all, they are the ones who set the exams.

Another problem is letting go. There are many good reasons to play it safe when it comes to designing a course. The main one we hear is pressure. Teachers feel that they are responsible for delivering good results, and that the best way to ensure this is methodically to go through the specification content. Faced with scrutiny from above and, increasingly, the expectations of students, teachers quite often resort to traditional and comfortable ways of teaching.

We spoke with a psychology teacher who said that the closer the exams got, the more didactic she became. This is a perfectly reasonable response. Faced with any pressure situation, especially one where we do not control all the variables, it is natural to try to create a safety-net. Teaching from the front and hitting students with lots of content makes us feel confident that they are definitely getting down what they need to know – after all, it is there for all to see, in black and white. This approach allows teachers to pass some of the responsibility back to students: they have given them all they need to know and so it is now up to them to pass the exams, and no one can come back to the teacher and say that parts of the course were not delivered.

This position might give some comfort, but we would argue that it misses a fundamental part of pedagogy: engagement creates better and more memorable learning. Being didactic may give students knowledge, but it does not provide a good environment for long-term learning. The majority of students will forget what they have learned minutes after they have walked out the door, and those that retain something will struggle to recall most of what was said.

We need to find better ways of making everyone feel secure, and we need to employ methods that do not abandon sound pedagogical practice but rather embrace and enhance it. So what else can we do? Well first, we can be creative and purposeful. Good learning is not found in the specification breakdown; rather, it comes from an engaging and challenging question. Starting with a list of content will hamper thinking and make your planning go stale – you will end up with a content-driven scheme that hasn't got the legs to see students through to the end.

The Big Idea: overviews

So if we abandon the specifications (for a little while anyway), where do we start? The answer is, with an overview. We believe that overviews are fundamental to creating a clear understanding of expectations and setting the tone of what is to follow for students. Overviews should be shared across a department and with students as soon as possible.

There are five key ingredients in an overview:

1. an overarching question
2. mini-enquiries that draw on themes and factors (not a plod through content)
3. an introductory task and big-picture activity
4. a creative outcome
5. a list of skills needed for the exam and specific opportunities to practise them.

Take a look at the following example for a GCSE course in the history of the American West.

We believe that this approach can work for any unit at GCSE or A Level and in any subject. Any unit contains a body of knowledge that has been specifically selected because it falls within certain boundaries. Where you have a body of knowledge within parameters you must

Should the US Government apologise for the 'genocide' of the Native Americans?

A Cunning Plan

As cunning as a fox that used to be Professor of Cunning at Oxford University, but has moved on and is working for the U.N. at the High Commission of International Cunning Planning.

Enquiry 1

What is genocide and why does it happen?
- What is genocide?
- What do the genocides in Rwanda, Cambodia and the Holocaust have in common?
- What views have the US expressed about genocide?
- Overview/chronology of American West?
- Key Assessment: *What is genocide - Explanation*

Enquiry 2

Why was Native American life so alien to White Settlers?
- What was Europe like in 1840s?
- How did Native Americans organise their daily lives?
- What were their key beliefs? Were they warlike?
- What did the first visitors to the Plains report back?
- Key Assessment: *Warfare on the Plains - description*

Enquiry 3

How powerful was the idea of 'Manifest Destiny'?
- Were the mountain men a threat to Native American life?
- Why were so many wagons crossing the Plains?
- Is the Mormon story one of persecution or triumph?
- How did the gold rush change America?
- Key Assessment: *Gold and the West - Significance*

Enquiry 4

Who was most responsible for the growth of ranching and farming on the Plains?
- Why did homesteaders begin to farm on the Plains?
- How did ranchers use the Plains? Did this change?
- Did ranchers or homesteaders have the hardest life?
- Did settlers hate each other more than Plains Indians?
- Key Assessment: *Homesteaders – Cause + Result*

Enquiry 5

How was the Native American way of life destroyed?
- How did the railroad change the Plains?
- Were reservations the only option for Native Americans?
- How similar were Custer and Crazy Horse?
- Why were the Indians defeated?
- Key Assessment: *reservations – change and continuity*

Enquiry 6

Should the US government apologise for the 'genocide' of the Native Americans?
- Overview, drawing conclusions
- Main characters of the story and genocide
- Are the characteristics the same for all genocides?
- Presentation for American Embassy – apologise?

Imagine a situation where the German Government tried to deny that the extermination of the Jewish people in the Holocaust was not genocide and should not be seen as an attempt to wipe out a whole nation... Many countries, including America, would rightly condemn their words. So why is it that the USA has never admitted to and will not discuss the 'genocide' of the Native Americans? Is this right?

Skills:
- Comparison of time periods
- Change and continuity
- Cause and result
- Significance
- Explanation

have a story (a reason why it sits within those parameters), and if you have a story you can have a question and a series of enquiries to drive students through to a logical endpoint. Each element of the overview is there for a very good reason:

◆ The question provides meaning and purpose – something to drive the learning on.
◆ The mini-enquiries break down the learning into more manageable parts – essential for understanding and, later on, revision.
◆ The introduction and big picture at the beginning help students to understand the whole picture – they know where they are heading and how they are going to get there.
◆ The creative outcome (definitely not an assessment) will bring together all elements of the course in an exciting and engaging way – helping to develop understanding and thinking.
◆ The skills needed for the exam and specific opportunities to practise them ensure that essential exam technique is catered for and delivered regularly – it is important to punctuate the fun with a good dose of exam reality.

Designing the course

Our journey into crime

In 2008 we had to design a new scheme of work for a unit about crime and punishment in Britain from 1300 to the present day. At first we struggled to find something that would fit the enquiry approach we wanted and give students something to think about. We tried lots of questions like 'What was the biggest turning-point in the history of crime and punishment?' The question itself is a valid one to ask, but it does not inspire students to want to know the answer, nor does it generate excitement. We tried a lot of different scenarios, like putting in a specific time period, 'Were medieval times the most lawless?', but we had hit a brick wall.

We went to London to do some research and after a day of hard reading we went to see a Banksy exhibition. What struck us was the way that he blended text and images to challenge stereotypes and myths about the world around us, with phrases like, 'People who get up early in the morning cause war, death and famine' and the genius image of the monkey with the tabard reading, 'Laugh now but one day we'll be in charge.' We were so impressed that on the way to the station we bought Banksy's book,[1] and within minutes our question hunt had ended.

We wanted to challenge some modern myths about crime and punishment, for example: the world is violent and out of control, we should bring back hanging. Also, we wanted students to start making informed choices about their views, and from this the question came: 'Is Britain more violent and crime-ridden than it has ever been?'

We now had a starting-point and a place of reference. We could build a scheme starting with creating hypotheses about the state of Britain today. Students could cut out articles and images and make mood boards about crime and punishment now. They could then write a paragraph outlining their views about the state of Britain, maybe even including some personal experiences. We could then look at some of the myths about Britain being safer in the past and people leaving their doors open. After this, students could look at a number of themes (law and order, crime, punishment, protest) and decide for each case when it was at its worst within our time-frame.

We now had our scheme in outline, but had to build in a range of assessments and a final activity. We took the key skills for the module and looked at opportunities where they might fit in well. Finally, we produced a grid that highlighted where each skill would be the main focus. We tweaked this until we were regularly hitting each skill with activities.

Student voice and good design

OK, 'student voice' is one the latest buzz-words in education and there are already signs of it getting into the wrong hands and out of control. Like every other initiative, it comes from solid research and with the best intentions. The work of the Special Schools and Academies Trust outlines a sensible programme of measures that could be undertaken to develop this area, if it is something you wish to pursue.

For now, we want to say just two things – a 'do' and a 'don't'. *Do* use student voices as a way of finding out what students are into and what they like and dislike about their current learning. Neal has completed a great deal of motivation and behaviour research since 2006 and firmly believes that questionnaires are less effective than face-to-face interviews. Here, you can question and, more importantly, listen to what students are saying. If you do not have time to conduct interviews, we suggest trying the 'living-graph' method. Give students a list of the lessons in a unit they have just been through and get them to plot their feelings about them against an axis of + 5 to −5. If you have time, you can get them to traffic-light the lessons for understanding (green for total, amber for partial and red for no understanding). In this way you can judge which lessons they felt were interesting and which they found useful. With a little 'tweaking' here and there, you could start to plan an excellent course that goes some way to addressing student needs and preferences. Now the don't: *don't* get student opinion on what lessons should and should not be taught. Teachers are the trained professionals and should be able to reflect on practice in the classroom. You are in a much better position to judge what is effective learning than they are. Giving them options about what task to do, or looking at what they enjoyed once it has happened is different and a good use of student voice; taking control of pedagogy is beyond the scope of students.

In summary, consult students about what they like and dislike in lessons and you could have a recipe for success for the scheme you are designing. Ask them about how it should be taught and how a lesson should be structured and you are heading for trouble.

Designing a good question

Good questions are not easy to create – it takes time. The overall aim is to create a question that students will want to answer and can live with for a while (most units are going to last for at least 12 weeks). We believe that a good question should have four characteristics:

1. *Have a problem to solve* – There is no point having a question unless it involves an issue that will need resolving. This is crucial for three reasons: it allows an enquiry to happen (where students can research and investigate); it provides a logical structure for the unit with students looking at different elements of the problem and then bringing them back together; it helps to engage them in the learning.
2. *Make it thought-provoking* – A good question will make students think about the topic. It is not there as a title, but as a way of stimulating discussion and debate. Debate is very important, as it is the only way to ensure that the question lives as long as the unit. Also, it should be possible to use the question in most of your plenaries without running short of ideas. The idea of regularly revisiting the key question in lessons is a powerful one, as it helps students to make sense of the learning. It gives them a central idea to fit their learning around.
3. *Make it relevant* – Have a question that means something to the students, that connects with an issue or concept they will have an

opinion about. There has been a lot of debate in the educational world about how far we should make learning relevant. Some people say that the integrity of the learning should be enough and that focusing on relevance distorts the subject knowledge. It is a bit like dumbing down and forgetting what is intrinsically interesting about our subject matter. On some levels we agree with this, it is always important to present information and learning that stands by itself – there has to be a reason why you are teaching the topic, otherwise it would not appear in the specifications. However, our subject matter is new and can leave students alienated from the lesson: as the teacher, you are the one with the knowledge and the students must learn some of it *before they can contribute* anything of worth. We know that this is not ideal, most learning structures, like TEEP and Accelerated Learning[2] stress the importance of engaging students the minute they walk through the door. The same applies to enquiries and questions for units: we want to grab students from the beginning and make them feel as if they can contribute. Having a relevant question does this: it allows students to make a connection and start contributing immediately, rather than simply being passive in the process (see the media studies case-study below).

4. *Make it real* – Over the last six years we have been involved in a number of big educational projects, but the most successful have been the ones that have real outcomes. The learning is not done primarily with the exam in mind, or the completing of the unit: it works towards a final piece that is tangible and has worth. Here is an example: Neal teaches a unit of work about pioneers in the American West. Students are asked to produce a film poster and a synopsis based around 'mountain men' – early travellers of the West. When they are completed, Neal gives the work to a local cinema, which judges the entries and awards the best group a free cinema ticket each. With this work, it would be quite easy to stop with the creation of the posters and synopsis and mark it. However, the fact that someone 'real' sees the work and judges it gives the learning an edge. The commitment levels rise and the students take pride in their work – the learning becomes memorable. This is easily worth the cost of four cinema tickets per teaching group.

Case-study: Design technology competition

We met a head of department who had given a Year 11 scheme a new dimension by changing the focus of the work. Mike decided that he needed to develop a more exciting start to the year, so he introduced the work as a design competition. The class was divided into groups and each group given a real design problem to work on. To make even more impact, Mike invited the leaders of each business to come in and launch the problem in person. Each problem was unique, but provided students with the opportunity to work collaboratively and go through the eight stages of the design process that were outlined on his wall. For example, a local skate shop had just sponsored a professional skateboarder and wanted to raise his profile but also exploit the link to make money. The students then had to look carefully at the design brief and conduct market research into the possibilities. They prototyped designs for a range of products and then tested them, before creating a professional pitch to deliver to an audience. Another group had to design a free gift for a metalwork company to give away with orders.

The whole competition was a great success – we were lucky enough to be invited to the final presentations that were delivered in front of the business leaders and the local mayor. The best part of the evening was seeing the confidence of students grow as their pitch went on. The group that won were not Mike's most academic or talented students, but this approach had given them the boost they needed to move beyond their normal level and create something special. Their design for an electronics company wanting to move into the children's market was superb: a soft toy that timed how long children brush their teeth.

Mike had built a fascinating enquiry that was thought-provoking from beginning to end. It was relevant to students, giving them an insight into the world of work and was about as real as a school project can be. Most of all, students were working on solving problems, real problems. There was didactic teaching but no interference; just students – being facilitated by a teacher – working things out for themselves.

cont. →

When those Year 11s look back on their school experience, we are sure this will be one of their highlights. It demonstrates what can be achieved in a school environment when the teacher has the imagination and creativity to reinvent what it means to be in a classroom.

If we employ all four elements of a good question then we get something that reads like the one in the overview shown earlier: 'Should the US government apologize for the 'genocide' of the Native Americans?' (p. 3).

◆ *Problem* There are two things implicit in this question: was there a 'genocide' of Native Americans? and, if so, should the US government apologize?
◆ *Thought-provoking* Genocide is still happening around the world and understanding why it might occur and how that links to government and choices leads to serious discussion.
◆ *Relevant* Asking students whether the US government should now apologize makes this relevant, as does the inclusion of genocide as a topic. It is something students can understand, because they have seen examples of it on the news and learned about in other lessons.
◆ *Real* In this unit the final task is to produce a letter and presentation to be sent off to the American Embassy with their findings. We encourage them to be active citizens and to stand up for their rights.

Case-study: Shalim in media studies

When Neal first started teaching he had a student in his GCSE class who was really struggling. At the time he was teaching two units about the Industrial Revolution and they were having no resonance with one young man called Shalim. His work lacked depth and his verbal responses were single words. Despite attempts to structure his talking and several sessions on connectives and linking ideas, the results were no better. Then came the time for Year 10 reports and Neal had to fill in

cont. →

the box that predicts the end-of-course grade. Reluctantly, he entered F, because he could see no way that Shalim was going to move beyond basic responses.

Some weeks later the spreadsheet of predicted grades was sent to all staff and Neal was surprised to find that one subject had predicted Shalim a grade C. The subject was media studies and it was the only one in which Shalim was given anything higher than an E grade. Neal wanted to know if there was anything that he could be doing that could make Shalim a C-grade candidate in history, so he arranged to observe the media studies teacher, taking her Year 10 lesson.

What he saw was interesting: from the first moment Shalim had his hand up and was answering questions. He was fully engaged and, yes, his work was insightful and detailed – enough to get him a C. The structure and pace of the lesson were very similar to the ones Neal had been teaching and, like him, the media studies teacher believed in active learning and student collaboration. So, why the big difference in performance?

After a discussion with the media studies teacher, it became clear: 'He feels he has something to say, because he knows something about soap operas. In fact', the media studies teacher continued, 'they all do. It gives them a way in. Everyone has seen a soap opera and can say something about it.'

Neal has taken this on board and now tries to link each topic and lesson he teaches to something that students will have an opinion about.

Creating and using overviews

Once you have the perfect question for your unit you will need to plan a sequence of mini-enquiries to help break up the learning. This serves two purposes:

◆ It is difficult to sustain interest in one single enquiry for a long period of time and an exam unit is usually quite lengthy. The development of mini-enquiries introduces a new problem for students to focus on every few lessons and helps to sustain the interest, as well as assist with memory (smaller chunks are easier to remember).

◆ It helps to prepare for the exams. Looking back over past papers will help to establish what topics appear in the exams. Some papers continually hit areas of content, while others develop themes. If you investigate and find out what are the crucial areas for the exam you can make each one the focus of a mini-enquiry.

We believe that overviews are fundamental to creating a clear understanding of expectations and setting the tone of what is to follow for students. They should be shared across a department and with students as soon as is possible.

This approach can work for any unit at GCSE or A Level and in any subject. Take another look at the overview for the American West course that we outlined earlier. You will see that there are six mini-enquiries. Each one serves a clear purpose, linked to students achieving in the final exam, because it deals with a key skill and focuses on a body of knowledge that will form an exam question:

◆ *Enquiry 1* establishes the question and gets students thinking about the topic. In this case we look comments and actions of American officials who have tried to stop the story of Native Americans being linked with the word genocide. Next, we look at what genocide is and how it occurs. We might do this by comparing events in Germany, Rwanda and Cambodia. From this we draw a set of criteria about why genocides occur. Finally, in the mini-enquiry, we complete an overview task by sorting a range of images related to the course and create a narrative to go with them (see the section on overviews below). This task, with the help of a living graph, becomes a key assessment based around the key skill of change and continuity.

◆ *Enquiry 2* You can see that the title helps students to answer the main enquiry question, but also provides a good basis for exploring the topic in hand. It engages students by giving them something to research and investigate, while bringing them closer to the answer to the Big Question. The assessment focus here is on *source skills*, i.e. it is different to the first mini-enquiry.

◆ *Enquiry 3* At this stage it is possible to revisit the criteria for genocide created earlier by the students. This enquiry starts to look at how many criteria are being met by regular contact between settlers and Native Americans. The main point is that this enquiry moves students significantly closer to the end product. Note again that the key assessment hits a different exam skill.

◆ *Enquiries 4 and 5* At this point we are introducing alternatives to the explanation in the question. We are asking students: What if the government was not responsible? What if it was the army, or the settlers acting independently? The point of doing this is to create doubt and complexity. This might sound a little mean, but it works. You are giving them a problem to solve. Without the problem it would just become a glorified march through the content and this is to be avoided at any cost. So, this throwing of new ideas into the mix is actually a device to sustain interest and make students think.

◆ *Enquiry 6* This contains a summary of the learning and of the evidence students have collected about the question. It also involves a creative outcome: a project that gets them working collaboratively to answer the big question. In this case, students create presentations for the American Embassy, looking at whether they should apologize and for what. You will see that there is no assessment listed for this module: this is intentional. We believe that the end product should be creative and exciting – engaging students at this stage of the enquiry is essential, just like having a great plenary for your lessons. Assessment, especially written assessment, clouds the issue and takes the edge off the learning. If you really need to assess their understanding, devise a few 'hinge' questions to ask over a number of lessons (see Chapter 3, pp. 92–4).

What we are left with is a set of key ingredients for a successful overview:

◆ a big question
◆ five or six mini-enquiries each with their own question
◆ an overview which enables students to make sense of the entire course
◆ four or five assessment pieces put in the most appropriate places
◆ a creative outcome (not an assessment) to end the topic.

Following the points above will give your unit of work a boost, but it will take time to devise. The positive side to this is that you get to be creative and that will benefit you and your students. Teachers should see themselves as creative professionals and embrace this set of skills more openly. For more ideas about being creative, see Tom Kelley's book, *The Ten Faces of Innovation*.[3]

Introductory tasks and overviews

In the film *The Sound of Music*, when teaching the von Trapp children to sing, Maria says, 'Let's start at the very beginning, a very good place to start . . .' Well, we think there might be a better place: the end. It is much easier for students to see where they are going if they know the whole picture. Providing this at the beginning of the unit is a great way of ensuring students see what is coming and are mentally prepared for it. This does not mean that you have to give away all the suprises, but you will have to outline the key points in the course. The question is, how do you do this without giving them a dry and boring list of content and talking them through it?

Overview tasks should develop a story that covers the whole content of the course. It should be quite visual and allow students to explore the major strands of the course and make links. We prefer the following method:

1. Find images that represent the various elements of the course and make them into sorting cards.
2. Give students the cards and ask them to sequence them into the most logical order (stress that since they have no prior knowledge, there is no right or wrong answer).
3. Get the students to develop a commentary that explains why they have ordered the pictures in that way and to tell a story about them (it is almost like a storyboard, using your images and their text).
4. Finally, display the results and encourage students to make amendments as the course unfolds. This final step was suggested to me by an English teacher called Katy Williams (there are more of her ideas in Chapter 4).

I have seen variations of this: a science teacher called Anne put 15 key images for a topic into Photo Story[4] and made a memory game. Students first tried to recall the images and then tried to connect them to the question for the unit. She used the images throughout the unit to make the learning more 'sticky' (see Chapter 2). She would start with questions like, 'Do you remember the image of the mice? What did we think they had to do with drugs?' She could then go on and develop a whole lesson around the original hypothesis of the students. This technique is very effective and we have adapted it to use in our own classrooms. The level of student engagement is very high and it helps them to start making connections between various elements of the course.

We have debated the merit of these activities with teachers at some of our seminars. There is an opinion that they are unnecessary and difficult, because students do not have the knowledge to construct a meaningful answer. We believe this misses the point. Any good sequence of learning will familiarize students with the content as soon as possible and help to 'flag up' what is coming. This approach, when coupled with an overview and a big question, can do just that. The question makes students think and intrigues them, the overview sheet (with the mini-enquiries) spells out what is going to be learned and the introductory task gives them some visuals to put to the words. We are preparing students for what is to come and doing it through as many of the senses as we can.

Using specifications and mark-schemes

So far we have been rather scathing about specifications and mark-schemes. We know that they are indispensable if you want to do a good job and that anyone who fails to look at them is going to fail their students. We are not asking you to ignore them, but to use them sparingly. Below are three reasons why they should be used less often, and attached to each reason is a course of action connected to the point:

1. The list of content for a unit is a guide. If you start planning a scheme of work by matching content to lessons, then you will end up with content-driven lessons. Look at the content to help you form a question and then bend the learning to the question. Use the list of content at the end to check that everything has been covered. If there is a little bit extra in your scheme, then great! – it shows that you have thought about what will get the message across and engage students. Also, sticking to the list means you are missing out on good stories that may help create meaning in the unit for your students. For example, there is no mention of Magda Goebbels in the contents for a history unit on the Nazi state, but her story covers so many elements of the course: anti-Semitism, family values, the inner circle, Hitler's leadership and propaganda.

2. Exam questions provide good practice for the exam, but do not engage students in their learning. It took us a good few years to

learn this lesson, but past questions should not form the Big Question, or the mini-enquiry questions. They should help you to build in your key assessment pieces (four or five across the unit), but that is all. Remember to think about the four rules for creating a question and save the exam questions for the timed essays and homework.

3. Mark-schemes are not an answer in themselves. We once talked to a teacher who could not understand why his students were missing their target grades. 'After all', he said, 'I give them the mark-scheme with every essay.' When we asked him what he did with it, he said, 'Nothing', – he just gave it to them so that they could refer to it when writing. This is not a bad idea, but like everything else, mark-schemes need to be taught. Try cutting them up into individual phrases and asking students which ones are Level 1, 2, 3 or 4. Also, encourage peer- and self-assessment. Start in a very formal way and build up until it becomes second nature.

What mark-schemes can do is help us identify the key skills that need to be the focus of our lessons. This will take a little time and we always find it easier if it is done with another teacher. Discuss what skills are being used and at what level. Try to cross-reference different question types to see if the same skills are being tested. We aim to have no more than five core skills, but sometimes this is just not possible. What is clear though, is that thinking increases as the mark-scheme levels go up. Therefore, it should be possible to create a kind of ladder on which to fit your core skills.

Progression charts

As well as designing good-quality lessons that excite and engage, we need to keep in mind that we are working for another purpose too: students need to pass their exams. Most courses last two years, and it can be a daunting task to take on the responsibility of moving students on, so that they reach their target grades and fulfil their potential.

We believe that the best way to build in progression is to create a planning chart at the beginning of the planning process. Get your big question in place, decide on your mini-enquiries, and then turn to creating your progression chart. We always complete a progression chart before starting to put in lesson content. In this way, you can blend the content around the skills that you need to teach. Take a look at the AS-level progression chart below:

Skills	→ Progression in skills →			
	Level 1 (describe)	Level 2 (explain)	Level 3 (analyse)	Level 4 (evaluate)
Use of Source Material	Sources will be used at face value, and answers will show a predominantly literal understanding of the evidence.	Balanced use of some or all of the sources in order to answer the question.	The evidence will be interrogated with confidence and discrimination to reach substantiated conclusions.	The evidence will be interrogated with confidence and discrimination, and the weight it can carry considered.
Relevant knowledge	Some relevant knowledge will be present, but there will be little or no analytical focus.	Judgements about the value of evidence in a given historical situation will be made.	The issues under discussion will be known about in some detail and the analysis will be supported by accurate and precise knowledge.	Relevant knowledge will be appropriately selected and deployed to produce a developed evaluation of these issues throughout the answer.

Figure 1.1 AS-level progression chart

These statements have been taken straight from a set of specifications. The only thing we have added is the reference to Bloom's Taxonomy under the titles. This was added to make it clear the type of thinking called for. Mark-scheme levels do step up in terms of thinking and can be used plan and to judge student progression.

In terms of designing learning, a progression chart allows you to see how skills can be stepped up over the course of a scheme of work. For example, you might hit a basic level for a particular skill in lesson 1, progress to Level 2 in lesson 4 and move to Level 3 in lesson 7. The main thing is that you are matching exam skills to the lessons you are teaching. By using a progression chart you are making it explicit to yourself that each lesson has a focus and a purpose. If you are doing this in your planning then it will be far easier to get this message across to your students. If you fully prepare to do exam skills right the way through the course, then there will be no mad dash at the end to get them practised. Also, integrating the core skills into lessons, alongside good-quality learning makes for a much better relationship between students and staff. Some teachers can come across as nagging, and hold exam grades over students as a method of control. In our experience, saying that a task has to be done because it is for the exam does not motivate students – they need something else. So a good-quality activity that is engaging and fun, but linked to an exam skill, is going to make more impact.

Case-study: Cereal-packet family

We recently saw an excellent sociology lesson that delivered a perfect balance between exam practice and engaging learning. The teacher, Leanne, started off with a short quiz using music as a timer. Then she looked at the content of the previous lesson and linked it to some exam questions from a past paper. At the end of the exam paper was a question about family – and guess what the topic of this lesson was going to be.

Using their knowledge of how to structure exam answers, students began to speculate what might go into this answer. Then, they started to get the new information: a series of adverts from TV were used to look at how families were portrayed and defined. Leanne reinforced the learning by getting students to create diagrams of the cereal-packet family using actual cereal packets. Once this was done, students returned to the exam question and began to plan.

This lesson showed us how effectively exam skills can be blended with exam practice. The planning was meticulous, but came from a deep understanding of the content, the exam process and how to engage students at AS level. This was an absolute master-class, and all from a NQT.

Course guides

Course guides are a great idea. They build on the ideas we have explained in this chapter and support the work done by the Big Question and overview. The aim of the course guide should be to support and extend learning, and should be given to students as soon as the unit is launched.

We have seen lots of course guides in the last few years, and to be honest, most of them were awful. They lack any shape or structure and are definitely not 'sticky' (see Chapter 2, pp. 26–7).

We believe that each section of a successful course guide should have five elements:

1. An interesting breakdown of the core information that shows where the section fits within the overview. It should incorporate stories and questions that challenge and engage – not just passive reading. Also, make sure that it contains images.
2. A short article or passage that *extends and strengthens knowledge* of the topic. This should be accompanied by an activity designed to raise questions and curiosity.
3. A *thinking skills activity* that forces students to use information and manipulate it – for example, a concept map.
4. *Exam question practice.* Here, you can include mark-schemes and hints about answering succesfully. Sometimes you might expect a full answer; others might be planning activities. Heads of department might want to develop core-assessment tasks through this route, so that they can monitor progress.
5. *A link back to a key question or an overview activity.* This may be as simple as creating a mindmap of the course, or as complex as an ongoing debate that requires careful management.

This may seem like a lot of work, but it means that students have a comprehensive reference point and something concrete to revise from. We were inspired to start making this kind of resource back in 2000 when we first came across a brilliant website from the history department at Passmores School in Essex. Here, all learning resources and lesson activities are available online so that students can access them whenever they like. Allowing students access to materials upfront means they can explore new avenues and shape their learning to suit their individual needs.

Sometimes, you get students who, through no fault of their own, are away for long periods. You then have to set work for them, and usually at short notice. Preparing this before your unit begins means that you do not have to do this. And making it available online means that no one has the excuse of losing it.[5]

These guides can be a powerful learning tool in lessons, for homework and during revision time.

Case-study: Blog entry by Donald Clark (Plan B)

Why questions matter
Questions really do matter in learning.

Questions and curiosity
First, they stimulate curiosity. Almost all of my learning as an adult has this dynamic. Something intrigues me and I follow it up as I'm curious to find the answer. This is the great joy of having the internet as a resource. It has made this type of enquiry and research possible.

Questions and diagnosis
Good questions diagnose your strengths and weaknesses. You don't know what you don't know and questions uncover the often uncomfortable truth that you know less than you thought you knew.

Questions and improvement
Questions and searching for answers are fundamental to the process of learning. Roger Schank has been using this apporach in all sorts of contexts, and this truly structured Socratic approach works well when used by a skilled practitioner.

Questions and motivation
To create the conditions for learning, as opposed to just delivering content, questions are the true stimulus.

Summary

We have covered a lot in this chapter and so it is useful to summarize the planning process we advocate into ten easy steps:

1. Create a *Big Question* that is thought-provoking, contains a problem, is relevant and real.
2. Divide the content up into chunks and make *mini-enquiry questions* to guide students through each one.
3. Do some *student-voice* analysis on what they like and dislike and what they see as relevant in your current schemes.
4. Design an *introductory task* that establishes the big picture for the unit and gives students some visual clues about what to expect.
5. Design a *creative outcome* (not an assessed piece) to end the unit. Make it exciting and active so that students will remember it. Make sure it sums up the learning within the unit.
6. Use the mark-scheme and specifications to identify the *core skills* needed in the unit you are covering. Be thorough and cross-reference different question types. Aim for five skills or less.
7. Make a *progression chart* so that you can track the skills you are using across the scheme. Make sure that you lead students upwards in the skills and that all skills are covered somewhere in the unit.
8. Start to plan out the content of the individual lessons, all the time referring to your progression chart and the Big Question.
9. Go back to the specification and check that you have included all the content that you need to and that all the core skills have been covered.
10. Create a course guide that has some interesting content, a thinking-skills activity, an exam question and a link back to the key question in every section.

This is a highly creative process, and when it is over I guarantee that you will feel an immense sense of achievement. After all, you will have created something relevant and real, something that has made you think and was a genuine problem needing to be solved.

Now it is time to look at another aspect of our work: getting in the classroom and teaching. This is where the real fun begins.

Notes

1. Banksy, *Wall and Piece* (London: Century, 2006).
2. See the websites for these two bodies: www.gtep.co.uk for TEEP and www.alite.co.uk for accelerated learning.
3. Tom Kelley, *The Ten Faces of Innovation: Strategies for Heightening Creativity* (London: Profile Books, 2008).
4. Photo Story is a Microsoft program that can be downloaded free from their website. For ideas about how to use it in lessons, see J. Ahrenfelt and N. Watkin, *Innovate with ICT: Enhancing Learning Across the Curriculum* (London: Continuum, 2008), pp. 29–32.
5. For more information about using the internet to present lesson resources, see ibid., pp. 49–53 and 64–8.

2 | Deliver the learning

The pain

This section is all about how to construct and deliver lessons. We have talked to many teachers on our travels and the same issues about exam lessons come up time and again. One teacher, Liam, whom we met in Leeds, summed it up:

◆ too much content
◆ too little time
◆ shortage of resources
◆ lack of interest
◆ unable to work independently.

We couldn't agree more. Teaching is demanding at the best of times and with added pressures of imposed specifications, a limit on time and minimal access to ICT it can be a daunting prospect to walk into a GCSE or A-level room.

There is also the pressure to deliver results, and this can affect the way you approach lessons. Neal was at a two-day seminar in January 2009 talking to an experienced teacher about a creative teaching project they are both working on. He said, 'I started off really well and for five or six weeks I was trying out lots of new things and enjoying it. But as the exams got closer I panicked and wasn't creative at all. I wanted to make sure they got the notes and I covered everything properly.'

This is a familiar scenario. We have observed many teachers and seen some outstanding lessons (some of which you will read about in our case-studies), but every teacher has moments when they haven't got the time to plan meticulously and develop stunning learning resources. When teachers are rushed or stressed they revert to an easiest mode of teaching. It is usually didactic and involves lots of silence. Silence is good for feeling in control – the teacher is able to 'get through' the lesson and feel OK about it. We all have our default settings for teaching. This chapter will help you to outline what yours should be if you want to create quality learning experiences.

Let's start with an activity. Imagine that you are given £100 in a vibrant city centre, and told to go and spend it. You have two hours' shopping time and you have to come back with goods or the money. What will you buy? Which shops will you hit first?

If a research company were trying to find out what was 'hot' with off-duty teachers (although I have no idea why they would really want to) this would be a perfect way to find out. The idea is discussed in a fascinating book by Tom Kelley, *The Ten Faces of Innovation*.[1] Tom helps to run a global design and innovations company called IDEO and they regularly take kids shopping to see what they are into right now.

We have tried this with our teaching groups at KS3, GCSE and A level, and the results are extremely interesting. We gave students a piece of paper and asked them to outline what they would spend £100 on if they had to in the next two hours. We emphasized that they had to spend the money or return it – no quick visits to the bank or bookies.

In Year 7 the majority of slips came back with leisure activities as a focus: football boots; console games; equipment for dancing or accessories for MP3 players and mobile phones. What this revealed was a desire to be active and involved. At this point, Year 7 was concerned with their own personal interests and trying to make their leisure experience better.

Step up to Year 10 and the results switch dramatically. Almost 80 per cent of the results centred around clothes or appearance.[2] The second most popular option was CDs and DVDs. Considering that the groups differed in ability and outlook and were spread across two schools with divergent demographics, the colouration was staggering.

So what does this reveal? Talk to Year 10 students and they will tell you that appearance matters to them – how something looks and its design is crucial. They will also tell you that they love a good story. Listen to them talk about *X Factor* and they will always refer to the back story of the contestant and never their ability to sing or perform. Why is that? Teenagers are engaged by stories.

Moving on to Years 12 and 13, another change occurred. More than half of the replies were concerned with social events:

'I would treat my close friends to a nice meal.'
'I could take 20 people to the cinema and buy them drinks
   and popcorn.'
'I would buy a decent tent so that I could go camping with
   three mates.'

It all sounds very wholesome and idealistic, but the results were once again consistent across four teaching groups in two separate schools. So, our A-level students are motivated by collaboration and social time – they like talking and interacting with others.

If we simplify this a little, we can pull out three Big Ideas from the exercise: students in exam classes want to experience:

Design
Stories
Collaboration.

Of course, this is not the most scientific way of finding out about student preferences for lessons,[3] but it does provide us with an easy and fun method for identifying student desires.

It is important to listen and engage with students in order to create a positive learning experience. One IDEO employee, designer Kate Burch, has come up with seven pointers for working with young people:

1. Ask them about their shoes – Almost every kid has an opinion about their shoes.
2. Offer something about yourself – it will make you seem more human and help open new lines of communication.
3. Ask them to invite their best friend along to talk – sometimes best friends will launch into an absorbing conversation on a subject and ignore you completely.
4. Remind them (only if it's true) that the project is top secret – it underlines the fact that you believe their ideas are important.
5. Ask for a house tour – they'll jump from the macro tour of their home to the micro focus on their room in five minutes or less.
6. Ask kids what they would buy with ten dollars. Or a hundred – what they'd buy is what's current, what's cool, what's top-of-mind for kids of that age.
7. Make them laugh – kids having fun have more to say.[4]

As teachers we can take a lot from this list. Here is our attempt to rewrite Kate's insightful work for delivering lessons:

1. *Engage* students by creating discussions around issues that are relevant and topical for them. If you want them to evaluate information, ask them about TV detectives and what they do, how they solve the crime. Then launch into the lesson.

2. There is no substitute for building *relationships*. With some classes it takes a couple of weeks, with others the best part of two years, but they need to know they can trust you and that you are there for them at that moment when you teach them.
3. *Collaborative learning* is an essential ingredient in any lesson. Group work and discovery with others will enrich the learning.
4. Make the *outcomes* as *real* as you can. Students are more likely to 'buy in' to the process if they know the work will be used as something or by someone.
5. Make the learning *relevant*. Try to bend the experience so that it fits in with the ways they like to learn and what they perceive as important (look at the £100 test results above).
6. Use all kinds of *creative resources* to draw them in. Spend time on presentation, digress occasionally and use ICT. Think about what is enjoyable and not just what needs to be covered.
7. You do not have to tell jokes, but a little light-hearted *fun* can go a long way. Get physical and make things; go on trips. Do whatever you can to bring *variety* to your classroom.

What we want to show in this chapter is how to create a whole package for learning without having to kill yourself with preparation.

The Big Idea: make it sticky!

(**Sticky** = understandable, memorable and effective in changing thought or behaviour.)

Two big questions need to be addressed by teachers each lesson:

> **What's the point of the lesson?**
> **Why should it matter to the students?**

It may seem obvious to you, why your lesson is important, but it can be easy to forget when you have taught the same topic for several years. Why should your students care that Victor Frankl lost his manuscript on psychological well-being; that a bag of butter popcorn contains 37 grams of fat; that Einstein's theory of relativity *does not mean that everything is relative*; or that the skills of *communication* and *synthesis* are probably the most important skills students need in life? It is a fair question. If you cannot provide a good enough explanation then what is the point?

Some lessons seem to 'stick' in students' memories more than others. Why? If we think about it, some information, facts, 'knowledge' is inherently interesting, whilst some is inherently uninteresting. The million-dollar question is, of course, how we can ensure that all (or at least most – let's be realistic!) lessons stick. For example, how do we get students to care about being healthy; to relate to life in the Warsaw ghetto in 1943; to understand the notion of a mathematical function?

The brothers Chip and Dan Heath have explored the idea why some messages stick and why some disappear. They argue that the main reason why people, such as teachers, fail to create effective and memorable 'sticky' lessons is because of what they call 'The Curse of Knowledge'.[5] This refers to the notion that educators and presenters of information sometimes fail to see that abstractions, the wealth of knowledge which they have and which makes sense to them, may not make sense to the students. If you try playing the *'tappers and listeners'* game you will quickly see how this problem could make it difficult to teach students:

Think of a tune, say 'Penny Lane', then tap the song using your hands on a table to another person – the 'listener'. They now have to guess which tune you have in your head based on the rhythm being tapped.

If you tried this with another person you will see that they cannot guess what song you were tapping. Research at Stanford University, CA, discovered that *tappers* predicted that 50 per cent of *listeners* would be successful in guessing their tune. In fact, only 2.5 per cent of *listeners* guessed correctly. Why did this happen? According to the Heath brothers, *'the problem is that tappers have been given knowledge (the song title) that makes it impossible for them to know what it is like to lack that knowledge'*,[6] so the isolated taps that are so clear to the *tapper* make little sense to the *listener*. As teachers we are particularly good at combating this problem, and we do so every day. However, there are still aspects of this challenge, areas of our subjects, which we may find difficult to deal with so that students can conceptualize, comprehend or be able to retain what we teach them. If we are to ensure that our lessons become memorable and therefore 'sticky', according to the authors, we need to consider six simple principles:

◆ simplicity
◆ unexpectedness

- concreteness
- credibility
- emotions
- stories.

Some of these may seem fairly obvious. However, it is worth examining them in detail. Let us take a look at a few examples.

Simplicity
What is the core that students need to understand, the *golden nugget*, and how can you ensure they understand it? If you think about the topic, *Titanic*, issues such as inequalities, poverty and social despair might surface. However, if you start a series of lessons investigating the socioeconomic problems of the late Victorian period, you might see the enthusiastic spark disappear in many of the students' faces. The core is, of course, social inequalities, but how will you reach the students? The *Titanic* sank two hours and forty minutes after setting sail and 1,517 people died, most of them from the working class. Why? Simple.

Unexpected
This one seems fairly obvious. Suppose you shock your students with a terrifying story or image … that is unexpected, but it does not give them the key ingredient which they seek: insight. Instead, get the students' interest by stimulating their curiosity through showing them there *is a gap in their knowledge* – how will it turn out? What is the answer? Using Thinking Skills mysteries in the classroom will achieve just that. There are lots of excellent examples of how effective these can be, some of which are mentioned in this book (see p. 64 for an example of how they can be used in modern foreign languages) and some which are published online.[7]

Concrete
Students' experience of education can become abstract, particularly during transition phases such as the beginning of their GCSE and A Level, or when new units of work commence. Therefore, it is crucial that we make our message, why it matters, clear to our students. In 1992 Art Silverman came across a situation where he had to make a seemingly abstract problem concrete in a way that the general public would understand and remember. He worked for a charity which sought to educate the public about nutrition. He had been asked to inform people about the dangers of eating traditional cinema popcorn

as a medium-sized bag contained 37 grams of saturated fat. Such a statement would obviously change people's cinema habits no doubt – *'no more popcorn for me!'* The reality was of course very different. Eating this amount of fat is clearly very bad for you, but the message was not concrete enough for anyone really to understand that it was dangerous. Silverman had a light-bulb moment. The charity called a press conference in which he explained: 'A medium-sized "butter" popcorn at a typical neighbourhood movie theatre contains more artery-clogging fat than a bacon and eggs breakfast, a Big Mac and fries for lunch, and a steak dinner with all the trimmings-combined!'[8]

Credibility

Making sure that students believe what you tell them is generally not a problem. Some research has suggested, however, that students more readily trust online material before teachers.[9] Therefore, testing hypothesis is an important part of exam classes learning so they understand that 'facts' vary from source to source. If you asked students to decide which source of information is the most trustworthy, which one would they choose: *The Encyclopaedia Britannica* or Wikipedia? Would they even trust information from Wikipedia? Research was carried out which compared the validity, the credibility, of *The Encyclopaedia Britannica* (which costs to subscribe to) and Wikipedia (which is free). Interestingly, there was very little difference in the content both resources provided.[10] By giving them the challenge to test a problem, students are more ready to believe, as they are in fact assessing its credibility and making an internal judgement about its trustworthiness.

Emotions

If we had time, we could customize every example we gave to ensure students relate to our messages: e.g. adding their names and names of their friends to maths examples. This would of course be next to impossible. Instead we need to try to give them more general examples without losing the opportunity for them to care. History teachers in Britain have to, and rightly should, teach about the Holocaust. This is an example of how one school started the unit:

Question 1: How many Jews were murdered by the Nazis between 1939 and 1945?

(a)   one million
(b)   four million
(c)   six million
(d)   nineteen million.

How far do you think students were able to relate to this tragic period in history? Not far. In fact, how could they relate to the deaths of more than six million Jews at all? Here is another example:

Fill a page with dots (full stops size 20, bold) and you will have approximately 600 dots. Photocopy it ten times. Give students a small piece of paper (no more than 2 x 2 cm) and ask them to draw one small dot for every person they know. Explain that most people probably have between 15 and 30 people they know including classmates, neighbours, family and friends, and that as a class you have about 600 people you know. If you put together everyone from school you will probably have several thousands. Now scatter the A4 sheets across the classroom, nonchalantly, and explain that these sheets contain 6,000 dots (names of people) and that in order to get the full extent of the number of people murdered you need to multiply this by a thousand. The penny tends to drop after that.

Stories

We have come to know man as he really is. After all, man is that being who invented the gas chambers of Auschwitz; however, he is also that being who entered those gas chambers upright, with the Lord's prayer or the *Shema Yisrael* on his lips.[11]

Do you remember what Victor Frankl lost, which was mentioned at the start of this section? Maybe; possibly not. If we had told you the following story then you probably would have remembered:

Victor Frankl and his wife were arrested together with hundreds of other Jews in 1942, in Vienna, Austria. Unbeknown to many, Frankl had developed a new theory of psychological well-being. Both he and his wife had anticipated what would happen to them so they had sewn the manuscript of the book he was writing into the lining of his coat. Victor and his wife Tilly were later transported to Auschwitz and the manuscript was eventually found and destroyed. Frankl began
cont.→

> rewriting his work from scratch, on bits of paper, and he had to endure the death of his entire family – his wife, brother, mother and father all died in the concentration camps. When the Allies liberated his camp in 1946 he had completed what was to become, according to the *New York Times*, one of the most influential books of all time: *A Man's Search for Meaning*.[12]

We know that planning all lessons based on a series of principles may not be possible all the time. However, by considering these ideas, coupled with lashings of our own creativity, we can produce powerful, purposeful lessons which contain enriching tasks that will ensure skills and learning progression for all classes.

Create meaning

Deciding on a structure for your lessons is not as easy as it might first appear. There are many strategies that compete for your attention and whole packages that you can buy into. However, we believe it is possible to outline a few points that a basic exam lesson should have.

1. *Hook* them as they come into the room. Get students thinking about the topic or the key issue by presenting them with a puzzle or unusual event, so that they are focused on the learning.
2. Give them a *question* for the lesson. As a great PGCE tutor told us in Cambridge: 'Without the puzzle, there is no learning.' What you are trying to do is to give students a picture of what the lesson will look like and how it fits in to the overview.
3. *Model* any products or outcomes for students and agree with them the purpose of the work. Avoid saying, 'We are doing this for the exam' – it will have no impact. Have a real reason for doing this work right now.
4. Maximize time for students to *work collaboratively* with the materials you give them.
5. Have a *mini-review* and use Assessment for Learning strategies like peer- and self-assessment after planning is complete and before you move on to any presentations.
6. Get students to *present* their work in a variety of ways and to a

variety of audiences: sometimes with one other student, sometimes formally to the whole class.

7. *Review* the learning and go back to the outcomes of the lesson. Talk about what has been achieved and how it has been done. Focus on knowledge and skills. Lead students into the next lesson with a preview that links to the learning from this lesson.

Health warning: All this is easier to achieve if you have an overview and a Big Question – they are essential tools (see Chapter 1).

We believe in this approach[13] and know that it works in a range of subjects. It is not too different from other models that you might see out there, except maybe in one respect: the big question. We have had this approach for many years and believe it to be an essential part of learning. The learning flows and from it you can bring in AfL with greater ease and have a basis for quality review.

Good questions take time to create (see 'Our Journey into Crime' in Chapter 1), but it is worth the effort. Each learning episode deserves a question, and it will spark instant curiosity in your students. Questions help to deliver meaning more than anything else by setting up a challenge that students can overcome. The sense of achievement can be high when students come up with the answer and present it to you or the class. Having the answer and wanting to share it is the essence of creating meaning.

What's the story?

Beyond lesson-planning and structure, having a good story to hang the learning on is vital for creating meaning. Think of stories as a clothes hanger ...

The wire coat-hanger that we know and love was inspired by a clothes-hook patented in 1869 by O.A. North of Connecticut. Albert J. Parkhouse, an employee of Timberlake Wire and Novelty Company in Michigan, created a coat-hanger in 1903, in response to co-workers' complaints that there were too few coat-hooks. He bent a piece of wire into two ovals with the ends twisted together to form a hook. Although an incredibly simple invention, it is well thought-out. Not only does it fulfil a function of hanging clothes but it also helps garments to keep their shape.

Take this a metaphor: your subject content is an item of clothing, stories are coat-hangers. Let us explain …

E.M. Forster, in *Aspects of a Novel*, wrote that 'A fact is "The queen died and the king died." A story is "The queen died and the king died of a broken heart." ' Which one is the more memorable do you think – fact or story? Stories are a part of life for human beings from the day we were told fairy-tales by parents or other loved ones, or when playground buddies shared their latest feats, through to wedding speeches explaining how the bride and groom fell in love, to granddad sharing his fishing-tales. Think back to your own schooling: what do you remember the most, the ph value of blood, the fundamentals of trigonometry, how to deconstruct text, or when a teacher told you that in 1943 a British bomber navigated to the wrong country and only realized that he was in fact flying over Stockholm after he had dropped his first cluster of bombs (no one was injured, a church wall and statue did regrettably not make it, however). Maybe you would be more inclined to remember all the above, if you start believing in the principle that there is a story there somewhere.

The more cynical of us would probably say that stories are just narratives that provide nothing more than fleeting memories, however lovely, but not essential facts. Yet facts will become more powerful and more memorable if they are placed in context and delivered with emotional impact.[14] Using stories encourages memory because we remember through stories. D. Norman's brilliant book *Things that Make us Smart* points out that 'stories are important cognitive events, for they encapsulate, into one compact package, information, knowledge, context and emotion'.[15]

The following story was emailed to us recently. At first it may seem just like a funny story, but if you read between the lines, it raises several interesting questions. Can you spot them?

Maori story

An old Maori man lived alone at his family home out in Ruatoria. He wanted to dig his kumara garden, but it was very hard work. His only son, Hone, who used to help him, was in Paremoremo prison. The man wrote a letter to his son and described his predicament:

cont. →

Kia ora e Hone,
I am feeling pretty bad because it looks like I won't be able to plant my kumara garden this year. I'm just getting too old to be digging up a garden plot.
  If you were here, all my troubles would be over. I know you would dig the plot for me.
Aroha nui,
Papa

A few days later he received a letter from his son:

E Pa,
For God's sake! Don't dig up that garden, that's where I buried the BODIES.
Love,
Hone

At 4 a.m. the next morning, Gisborne CIB and the local police showed up with a search warrant and dug up the entire area without finding any bodies. They apologized to the old man and left. That same day the man received another letter from his son.

E Pa,
Go ahead and plant the Kumara.
That's the best I could do under the circumstances.
Love,
Hone

When we received this story we were thrilled and used it immediately. It has so much potential for the classroom; you could use it to investigate the power of language and its uses, to look at motive, to understand character, or reactions (human or chemical). Think about how powerful this story would be as a starter in a lesson.

Beyond this, stories can illustrate something facts cannot and help us to create meaning by way of connection: 'Narrative imagining – story – is the fundamental instrument of thought. Rational capacities depend on it. It is our chief means of looking into the future, of predicting, of planning and of explaining ... Most of our experience, our knowledge and our thinking is organised as stories.'[16]

For our students, story is a vital part of their cultural lives. Television, music and video games are all structured around story. Using stories in teaching provides us with the potential to explore not only conceptual understanding but also to focus students on such skills as analysis, evaluation and synthesis.[17]

Mini-saga

Writing a story can give students this opportunity, but sometimes it is better to write less in order to achieve more – what about a complete story in 50 words? These are called mini-sagas. Invented by science-fiction writer Brain Aldiss, these are very, very brief stories which still have the same construct as a standard story, i.e. a beginning, middle and an end. There is a catch: each mini-saga must have exactly 50 words, excluding the title which can have 15. Here is an example:

Beginning, middle and end

It was lonely at the very beginning, but suddenly, in one large blast, everything appeared. Things moved around, linked up, slid into place. That was when they met, migrated north and made new friends. They learned new languages. In the end, they couldn't cope living together so they fought. Forever.

Any idea which story it is?

The following story was written by one of our A-level students after the end of a unit on Russian history:

The Georgian

Once upon a time there was a boy named Djugashvili. A quiet little chap who dreamt of heroic tales. Became religious, revolutionary, killed lots of soldiers. Then became rather famous. Killed lots of farmers, produced lots of tractors, maybe won WII, built large wall, built many statues, killed lots. Died.

As you can imagine, it requires great skill to be able to evaluate what needs to be included to make the mini-saga come alive: you have to analyse the relationships within and between individuals and events, as well as sequence of events, dialogues or other matters needed to synthesize a whole topic area and then fit it within the framework of the mini-saga.

Mini-sagas are most successful if you stick to two basic ideas:

◆ keep them obvious
◆ keep them cryptic.

Students can then read each other's mini-sagas, or perhaps a selection which has been chosen by the teacher. We ask students to

◆ guess who is involved
◆ what the story might refer to, e.g. a particular event, topic or theme, etc.
◆ evaluate what else could be included; perhaps something has been left out?

Try writing some mini-sagas in your subject to introduce a new topic or find a story that provides an interesting social commentary for something you are teaching.

Create clever resources

We both worked in the same department for a few years when Neal was subject leader and Johannes was a newly qualified teacher. Johannes took on an academically challenging GCSE group with several gifted and talented students. Because he was new to teaching he would quiz people about effective approaches to different units or how to tackle particular skills, and he placed a lot of emphasis on making the subject engaging while at the same time covering a demanding syllabus: a conflict we all face. One particular teacher, a very seasoned practitioner, commented that 'there's no time to do role-plays or any other silly things with exam classes. Get them to take notes, notes, notes. No notes – no revision material.' This brief conversation would knock any new teacher's enthusiasm for the profession. Surprisingly, this teacher has inspired us both to work hard at challenging students to want to learn through stimulating tasks and, hopefully, innovative teaching approaches. We both have the philosophy that good learning stems from good teaching and great results will follow. Many teachers feel the pressures of targets, results and the difficulties in covering the syllabus, and believe that there is no time to be innovative and try new ideas. John Dunford, General Secretary of the Secondary Heads' Association, tries to explain that OFSTED actually seeks to encourage innovative teaching:

> teachers ... often have more freedom than they think. We have got into a very defensive culture based on fear of Ofsted. But Ofsted has always recognized good teaching as good teaching, and good exam results as good exam results. Innovation is an important part of good teaching and it does in the end bring better exam results if more imaginative approaches are used.[18]

In 1997 a survey conducted in a school asked all the students which sources of information they trusted the most. The vast majority listed textbooks as the number one choice. Teachers came far down the list. Interestingly, students' views changed very little over the five years of secondary school.[19]

Rank the following according to how much you trust in what they say:

1. School textbooks
2. CD-ROMS
3. The internet
4. Non-fiction books
5. Teacher
6. Television
7. Radio
8. Newspapers

Many are bound to textbooks, as they provide a basis for discussion and for information-gathering. It is therefore important that we educate students to use these tools for learning effectively, and perhaps challenge them to be critical of what they read. As fixed sources of information, textbooks are inevitably imperfect guides to a subject. Textbooks have been around for a while now, and even with the advent of CD/DVD-ROM and interactive learning, they are useful as they provide a base for content and research. The eternal question is how to make them less boring. How many times have students turned to a page to answer the questions in the activity box?

14-year-old: 'I'm working on a history paper about how the Holocaust never happened.'
(*Long pause*) 'Zack, where did you hear that the Holocaust didn't happen?'
'The internet. It's on a web page at North-western University.'[20]

Harold Macmillan once stated that the main benefit of a good education is to know when somebody is talking nonsense.[21] How often do you hear students, *and teachers*, mutter something like 'Find it on the net', or 'Just do a Google search'? We all face the same dilemma of how to use the world wide web effectively and wisely. A discussion is needed about how teachers access and use the web in lessons, for homework and for useful extension tasks. There are good websites out there which can enrich learning, excite students and challenge them to think. What effective online tools[22] are available to teachers and how do you know that they are trustworthy or accurate?

Many students access and use material from online encyclopaedias such as Wikipedia and some schools subscribe to *The Encyclopaedia Britannica*. Should we be concerned about the content of these websites? If you asked them to look up the word '*Barbie*' on both Wikipedia and *Encyclopaedia Britannica*, they would discover an article on a Nazi war criminal on the latter and an article on a '*fashion model manufactured by . . .*'[23] on Wikipedia. The BBC acknowledged that Wikipedia's account of the 7 July 2005 terrorist bombings in London was as good as its own. *Britannica* has 44 million words of content and Wikipedia 250,000 million. So which one is the more accurate? All publishers can make mistakes; the question is more about how serious these mistakes are.

58 per cent of academic library assistants in the US regard Wikipedia as a credible source of information.[24]

A rigorous survey conducted by *Nature* magazine asked expert reviewers to compare 42 articles on Wikipedia with corresponding entries on *Britannica*. These were their findings:

	Serious errors	Factual errors/Misleading statements/Omissions
Wikipedia	8	162
The Encyclopaedia Britannica	4	123

Nature magazine concluded that there were no significant differences between the two resources in terms of accuracy. *Britannica* noted, however, that they were 30 per cent more accurate than Wikipedia. This is of course a point worth noting. Nevertheless, Wikipedia contains six million free articles and Britannica does not. To quote C. Leadbeater: 'Wikipedia is a good place to start ... but rarely provides the final word'.[25]

Opinions about using Wikipedia in the classroom or for research purposes varies amongst teachers, lecturers and professors from blaming the website for mistakes students make, to demanding that it is blocked entirely in schools, colleges and universities. There are opportunities to assess the accuracy of Wikipedia. Researchers at the University of California, Santa Cruz, have produced a WikiTrust for assessing every word on Wikipedia. It highlights text added by content authors according to their past editing reputation. As this works with a cached copy of Wikipedia it means that it will not be entirely up to date. Text on white background is fully trusted text and the more orange the background, the lower the value of trust.[26] This is a very useful tool for teachers and students to evaluate the credibility of some articles. More disconcerting, one could argue, is some of the recent research on the use of social media such as blogs and video clips. Universal McCann[27] set out to measure consumer usage, attitudes and interests in adopting social media platforms in 2006 and have since then involved 29 countries and 17,000 internet users up to 2008.

◆ Blogs are a mainstream media worldwide and as a collective rival any traditional media – 77 per cent of internet users have read a blog.[28]
◆ Video clips are the quickest growing platform, increasing from 31 per cent watching video clips in 2006 to 82 per cent in 2008.[29]

Blocking, banning or blaming Wikipedia or any other online resources[30] can only lead to limiting the flow of collaboration and, most significantly, the opportunity to teach students about the need to judge the reliability and validity of information that is not printed in books.

T. Haydn, Senior Reader in Education at the University of East Anglia, states that

Research evidence is emerging to suggest that pupils are starting to opt for courses where ICT is skilfully and regularly deployed. In some cases it has become apparent that, skilfully used, ICT can enhance pupil motivation, and provide pupils with a broader range of learning activities than those made possible by textbooks and worksheets.[31]

If you want to involve students actively in their learning,[32] challenge them to think about how they learn, provide a fresh approach to flexible learning while covering lots of course content or overviews for revision, then getting them involved in creating podcasts could help do just that. D.J. Malan contends that the true value of podcasting lies in its 'potential not necessarily to educate better, *but to educate further*'.[33] Other research concluded that although podcasting 'does not contain any inherent value. It is only valuable inasmuch as it helps the [teacher] and students reach their educational goals, by facilitating thoughtful, engaging learning activities that are designed to work in support of those goals.'[34] A. Rasmden, head of e-learning at Bath University, found that getting students to create their own podcasts was highly effective in involving them in their learning and moving away from teacher-led lessons. We have used various tools of ICT with many exam groups, both GCSE and A Level, and we have found that when students use ICT themselves, e.g. creating movies or creating podcasts such as radio shows or audio revision notes, they have benefited greatly from the process of creating learning content as well as evaluating each other's work (see pp. 45–9 for an example of using podcasts with sixth-form students).

Does all of this mean that textbooks are on the way out? Probably not, but although they may have been the most trustworthy source of information amongst young adults in 1997 this could now be changing. As a source of information textbooks are useful, but we still need to ensure that they are used in interesting and engaging ways, so that we continue to challenge students rather than spoonfeeding them information.

How to make textbooks less boring

There are a number of ways in which we can make good use of these iconic features of the teaching profession. This way of using textbooks simply adds another dimension to the way exam groups use the book. We will take a history example, but the technique can be modified for most classes.

Certain historical characters need to be 'dissected' fully in order for students to understand how their minds worked. Students as well as teachers sometimes leave the complexities of individuals out, as they are not part of the syllabus. However, in order to grasp the bigger picture and remember these wider issues in the exam, tackling issues such as identity and personal transformation can actually benefit these two elements of exam teaching. How could students really understand Malcolm X's hatred of white people and sudden change of heart at the end of his life without examining how his character evolved as a consequence of his dealing with external factors? Or how could the story of Jesse Owens help to deconstruct attitudes of white America in the 1930s? The following activity seeks to challenge students to 'think big' and analyse how an individual's personality or identity can impact on the way we understand the past.

We had just finished an overview of Russia from 1905 to 1924, and were about to start examining the power struggle after the death of Lenin. If students could gain some understanding of Stalin's complex persona then they might be able to analyse the reasons for many of his actions and policies.

The students were split into two groups: Group A who became Joseph Stalin and Group B who all became psychologists. Discussion started about what defines a person and how their actions can be seen as an echo of the past (e.g. their childhood). It was explained to the class that they would role-play a conversation between Stalin and the psychologist after they had completed a mini-fact-sheet about Stalin, the content of which also needed to be revised. A strict time-limit was set. Finally the classroom was changed into a 'clinic' – imagination can change a lot, so if you have an old sofa available ... Stalin was then asked to come into the office and take a seat in front of the psychologist. Each psychologist was given a psychological assessment sheet[35] to use during their diagnosis of Joseph, who answered each question as far as he could.

It was interesting to see how hard they worked during the research phase and, after speaking to students afterwards about the task, most of them mentioned that they felt that the textbook had been used with a real purpose in mind, even if it was make-believe.

This type of activity could easily be adapted for different subjects, so for example in English students could assess how Holden experienced his problems as a teenager in *The Catcher in the Rye*; while in geography you could have a dialogue about how a famous trainer brand has experienced globalization.

Challenge the textbook

Whatever the subject you may teach, there will be issues, topics, data, problems and text that can be open to debate. For example, bring in newspapers or magazine articles that raise similar issues and compare the content and message. Explore these questions:

◆ Which sets of statistics are correct? How do you know?
◆ Why do authors seem to disagree and come up with different results or different hypotheses?
◆ How do views change?[36]

Another useful way of involving the class in the best use of textbooks is to get them to ask questions about the topic studied and investigate how far the author is correct. There are many topics that change over time, especially cutting-edge subjects such as biology and technology, but there are also less tangible changes, for instance, in attitudes perceptions and tastes. Setting these developments against their own textbook really challenges them to consider issues about research, validity and bias, and can also provoke good discussion regarding what they have to think about when planning their own writing. Of course we do not wish to make them think that what they read is always inaccurate, far from it: we want them to become critical and creative in the way they gather information, research and demonstrate understanding about various subjects. In this way they begin to consider how other subjects face the same challenges; that knowledge is not static, like a textbook, but fluid and constantly evolving.

What does ... it sound like?

Open any stationery or book cupboard and you'll find a myriad of textbooks dating from the 1950s to fairly recently. Some people advocate that these are tools of the past and that WEB 2.0 has already taken their place. We disagree somewhat with this assumption. None of us is about to spend the entire capitation on digital equipment, particularly as most teachers in most departments work in 'standard' classrooms and do not have access to a computer room every day. Therefore, textbooks become part-and-parcel of daily lessons even if they are just dipped into once in a while. There are ways in which textbooks can be used in an engaging and effective way with a little bit of help from a mini-digital voice recorder.[37] The following is a history example, but you can adapt this to most other activity subjects.

Johannes wanted to get students thinking about how the Cold War started and also make them interested in this period. By the end of three lessons the class were to create a conversation between the Big Three (Churchill, Roosevelt and Stalin) using sound and the images supplied. They had to be able to explain how their relationship had deteriorated from the (apparently) cheerful first photo to the second one, which appears to indicate that Churchill and Roosevelt are closer than Stalin might prefer. The catch was that they had to imagine what each of the personalities would have wanted to say – in the accent and dialect of each leader!

The students investigated the background to the Big Three meeting and noted why the relationship changed over time. It was surprising how quickly students got into reading and taking notes from textbooks without being reminded or prompted to do so. When they had completed their background reading we returned to the two images and they identified reasons why Stalin could be interpreted as 'alone' in the East. The class was then given the instructions that they were to add a narrative to the two different images while considering the following questions:

◆ What did the three leaders really want to say? How confident was Stalin? Were the USA and Britain really all that friendly with each other?
◆ What would their accents have sounded like?
◆ How would the leaders have been affected by their personal circumstances? For example, Roosevelt was not well and did not have long to live; would this have altered the tone of his voice?

In the end, many students asked if they could create a mini-movie as well rather than only create sound, so they either used Movie Maker and a microphone, or a digital voice recorder to create a brief conversation between the Big Three. The results of the students' movies were impressive and they enjoyed this way of researching as their efforts led to something concrete other than an essay.

This method could easily be modified for other subjects:

◆ Dealing with conflict in GCSE **citizenship**: students investigate murals of 'the Troubles' in Northern Ireland and voice-over to a series of representations.
◆ Disease and resistance in GCSE **science:** students explore the relationship between pathogens and the immune system where the class creates a conversation between what the body can do to protect itself in various ways.

◆ Comparing a theme between a selection of poems in **English**: students compare how the idea of death is presented in a selection of poems (e.g. 'Cold Knap Break', by Gillian Clarke, and 'The Affliction of Margaret', by Wordsworth). They will become 'death' and explain how it differs in the different poems.

Use video clips well

Some topics may be regarded as, let's face it, rather dull by some students. Faced with such a dilemma we need to think hard to get the students remotely interested before asking them to start preparing notes, speech-writing or essays. One tool which can help to cover valuable content as well as developing students' skills further is to encourage them to create their own mini-movies. This is particularly useful in demonstrating an understanding of end-of-unit themes in modern foreign languages, explaining turning-points in history or comparing and contrasting a film with a book in English. Microsoft Movie Maker is a free and very simple video-editing software and is an ideal tool to help turn the pressure up in the classroom. It does not take long to produce a video clip.[38]

Johannes wanted to wake up a particularly quiet sixth-form class and really get them communicating with each other. They were studying the Russian five-year plans under Stalin, but they did not seem to really get into the topic. Johannes wanted to cover the content but at the same time try to get them more enthusiastic and make them see the significance of the five-year plans at the time. It became a straightforward research lesson with a twist.[39]

The main lesson objectives were to encourage research, relevance and maybe even excite students about Russian economic policies in the 1930s. (Tricky as you can imagine!) Students were informed that

◆ Targets set during the first five-year-plan had been too high and factories were unable to meet them.
◆ Their (i.e. the students') job was to prepare a speech explaining to Stalin what they had done to meet targets and why they had failed.
◆ Their speeches would be rated according to 'chance of survival' after delivering their explanations.

The class was now given time to research about the problems facing factory workers and managers. The material used was very challenging for this group[40] and students had no more than 15 minutes to complete their case-files. They were eventually told that Stalin himself was actually visiting the factory today and they would have to present their findings (explain why their factory was failing) in front of the great leader. A 15-minute deadline was set and students began working harder than ever before. When the time was up, a video started playing on the interactive whiteboard which introduced Stalin to roaring applause. The video had been edited so it appeared that Stalin was looking at them, patiently, while sipping a glass of water (or vodka). It was amazing to see how nervous this group became, but at the same time determined to face the leader and explain how difficult it had been to meet the targets. Some bottled out and started making excuses! One of them was a very confident 17-year-old whose hands suddenly started shaking and said: 'why am I so nervous it's just a silly movie?' He made his speech (very well it must be said), but the class only rated his chance of survival as very slim ...

It took approximately ten minutes to download and edit the clip,[41] but the results were excellent. Students initially treated the task as a straightforward note-taking activity, but after a few hints that they would have to stand up a couple of metres from the interactive whiteboard, speaking to Stalin, the task suddenly became very important to them. By the end of the lesson this class had used challenging statistical data, analysed a range of different sources and communicated their understanding in front of their peers.

Movie Maker can be used in various ways, from starters to main tasks and plenaries (which this particular task actually became).This resource has been used by the whole department for a few years now as it is a simple yet effective way of getting students to work extra hard. They will do that when we make our tasks matter.

Ipods in the classroom

Alex: It works because you have to really think about the topic as a whole, not only goof-around, but actually plan and consider all your key points. Because we talked about how to structure the podcast and about, like, pitfalls, we knew that we had to make it 'visual' and tell a story so people remembered our show.

Harriet: When we had learnt the technical bits then it was great. I thought it was difficult to speak into a mic though, because I felt a bit silly. I was concerned about what other people would think. The best thing about recording was that we created the content and we had to think about our message as well as where our topic fitted in with the rest of the course. That was challenging.

(Sixth-form students discussing a podcast project in March 2009)

Gimmicky? Perhaps, but at the same time this is also an opportunity to encourage students to use their MP3 players for more than simply listening to music – they could be learning at the same time! Podcasts are useful, and hopefully this example will show you how simple they are to set up with the help of online tools and how effective they can be to stimulate learning with exam classes.

You have probably gathered that podcasting is more than simply creating an MP3 file and uploading it online; that it enables you to set a channel using RSS[42] to share your creations with anyone who subscribes and who will receive all the updates automatically when they connect. Gcast.com is a free service where you focus solely on creating the content, e.g. discussions, monologues, interviews, jokes, poems and music, and Gcast.com finalizes all the technical issues. Another great thing about this site is that it also has a music website, Garageband.com, which seamlessly integrates with Gcast.com, which means that you can import music into your podcast at the click of a button. The music you store on 'MyPlaylist' can be accessed on both sites – simple!

In a nutshell:

◆ register with Gcast.com
◆ register with Garageband.com
◆ upload your creative MP3 files or record content via phone (yes, you can do that; it's great for 'Last-Minute Ideas' channel!)
◆ select the order of tracks including music added from Garage band.com
◆ click 'create podcast'.

Case-study: Making overviews engaging in the history A-level classroom

This example was used with an AS class (16–17-year-olds) of 18 students, a mixed ability group ranging from target grades A to D. The students were used to different approaches to teaching: e.g. creating movies, presentations, teaching mini-lessons and using peculiar 'games' for improving communication skills.[43] They had just completed the first half of a history course, and the intention behind creating a podcast – in fact a radio show – was to encourage them to consider what they had been taught over the past couple of months. They were

cont. →

divided into seven groups – the same number of key questions from the syllabus.

Lesson 1: Criteria and research

The initial lesson focused on the outcome of the podcast, namely that they were to create a radio show, maximum six minutes long. They had to include music taken from Garageband.com as tracks can be transferred seamlessly to Gcast.com[44] and, this is the best bit, they are royalty-free and can be downloaded. The class then had to consider what the challenges could be when presenting potentially 'heavy' material on the radio, and a discussion ensued about the challenges of audio versus visual material and the need somehow to provide listeners with a mental image of what was talked about, and that the message had to be clear.

We agreed on a number of criteria that they had to achieve to ensure a successful and purposeful podcast. Also the students were a assigned to a 'mentor group' which would listen to the podcast and evaluate it based on the agreed criteria:

Criteria	1 Excellent	2 Good	3 Room for improvement	Comments
Historical accuracy				
Historical relevance				
'Stickiness' (will you remember the key points?)				
Clarity				
Engagement/entertainment				

While students commenced their initial research, we created the podcast channel so that it would be quicker to finalize the work in later lessons. Gcast.com provides step-by-step instructions on how to set up a channel. Homework was also set in this lesson: students had to listen to a range of different radio shows on various frequencies in order to gain a fuller under-

cont. →

standing of some of the 'features' that presenters have on their shows like quizzes, call-ins, interviews, and so on.

Lesson 2: Further research and planning the radio show

The class spent an hour or so finalizing their research and structuring their radio shows. Students shared ideas for 'features', and it was agreed that three 'featurettes' were needed to create a good flow in the show.

Lesson 3: Recording

The groups made use of a number of microphones/headsets and two voice recorders[45] to record their interviews, fake call-ins and other 'featurettes'. After a bit of tweaking, all groups were practising their lines, while others were planning which part of a song they should use. It is important to give students a limit as to how long a piece of music can be so that the radio programme does not become too long. We agreed that 45 seconds was just enough to capture the moment or set the scene.

Lesson 4: Putting it together

There are different ways to piece together a podcast, but most groups choose either to import all different components, e.g. music, interviews, call-ins and main presenting, into Audacity[46] and save as a main MP3 file, but many simply uploaded their different sections into the Playlist on Gcast.com and organized the final podcast online. Either way is simple and does not require much technical understanding. It is very straightforward. After all the files had been uploaded we transferred them to the podcast channel which had been set up in lesson 1.

When everything had been completed and files uploaded we listened and evaluated the programmes. The class found it very exciting and rewarding. Some commented that it would be easier to remember different parts of the syllabus as they could relate much of the content to examples in the radio show. Once group who had focused on Nazi racial policy used the story of a fictional young girl to explain life in Nazi Germany during 1939–42. We followed her traumatic experiences from early segregation, to the Warsaw ghetto and finally to the concentration camp.

Ideas for future podcasts

◆ Case-studies in geography: students create radio shows about one case-study each.

◆ Last-minute revision: the teacher uploads mini-ideas (two to three minutes max) which emphasize a key point or idea.

◆ Revise (your topic): fact-based radio documentary with interviews and debates, similar to an ordinary radio programme.

◆ Tomorrow's world: the class creates an entire show together about how issues in, for example, history and geography will impact on the future (terrorism, global warming, fair trade and globalization).

◆ The movie vault: students analyse the relationship between book and film.

◆ How to ... write the perfect essay: students share their ideas and examples on introductions, structuring arguments, etc.

◆ How to ... work independently: students explain what they do to work well in groups as well as how to use realistic targets.

◆ How to ... get an A* grade: groups provide concrete ideas for exam and revision techniques.

Make skills matter

Students must prepare themselves for an emerging labour market that has evolved from a knowledge-based sphere of linear thinking, analytical and calculating skills to a new sphere where, among other things, they will need the ability to detect patterns and opportunities. If the former were the skills of the Information Age, then synthesis will become the core skill of the twenty-first century, where students are required to grasp the bigger picture and to combine contrasting elements into a new impressive whole. Welcome to the Conceptual Age.

During the last few years, the value of measuring and testing intelligence has been fiercely debated in the press, particularly around the time of GCSE and A-level results. Arguments vary from suggesting that exams are becoming easier to saying that they no longer serve any purpose.

The number of exams is not as important as what those exams are. Pure regurgitation of facts is not as useful as being forced to use your reasoning skills under pressure. In my work, remembering things is important, but many of those things can be looked up if I can't recall immediately. The important thing is being able to use those facts well, quickly and under pressure. That is what exams should demonstrate.[47]

A similar debate was the focus of a series of articles in *Time Magazine* in 2003, in the USA, about the SAT reasoning test, a standardized test for college admissions. A year later, in 2004, the journal reported on a new method of testing students. Robert Sternberg created a number of tasks that, in his view, would challenge students beyond linear and analytical thinking. For example, students were presented with various scenarios which they had to solve, such as arriving at a party where they did not know anyone, to persuading friends to help move furniture. These seemingly unorthodox activities are designed to measure the creative and practical skills that Sternberg says are crucial to success in college and in life, but which are ignored by the typical pencil-and-paper exam:

> The traditional theory of IQ deals with a very important part of intelligence, namely, memory and analytical skills, and that's what [our exams] measure. Those skills are important for success in school and in life. But what I discovered over the years ... is that some students were very gifted in traditional memory and analytical skills, but never good at making ideas of their own. They were good if you told them the paper topic, if you told them what exactly would be on the test. There were other students who were creative, but not necessarily as analytical as the first group. They tended to be imaginative, to have new ideas, to discover things, to invent things, but they were not necessarily the ones who are going to the best in standardized tests or going to excel in a typical class.[48]

Daniel Goleman carried out research to measure how much IQ accounted for career success. Which one do you think is the correct option?

- 50–60 per cent
- 35–45 per cent
- 23–29 per cent
- 15–20 per cent

In fact, Goleman discovered that only 4–10 per cent of IQ accounted for career success.[49] Interestingly, research carried out by the

University of Surrey's Skills Project[50] found that out of the 12 employers they interviewed (including Lloyds TSB, British Aerospace and several national consultancy firms) nearly 70 per cent of employers defined key skills they sought in prospective employees to be communication and interpersonal skills such as 'two-way communication, sharing information openly, encouraging others to speak and listening to their views'. Only 25 per cent regarded skills of analysis to be a significant skill. The vast majority of employers used some form of test to assess the suitability of the potential employee. Case-studies were the most commonly used technique to gauge problem-solving and negotiation skills. The research also concluded that the vast majority of companies were also concerned with wider skills such as *understanding the bigger picture* and adjustment to new cultures and environments. Teachers have the opportunity to prepare students with these essential skills needed for the Conceptual Age.

Teaching should be about exploration, implementation and reflection. It is when these aspects blend together that we, the teachers, have the opportunity to observe real student progress. Let us not forget why we are here and what the purpose of teaching actually is: to train a generation of children to become mature, level-headed individuals, professionals who will eventually lead our companies, run our country and, most significantly, teach our children and take care of us when we grow older. Students can lose sight of what education is for, and quickly forget the point of it all. If we do not remind them then we have failed. Should we not stimulate students into becoming critical learners, who are confident and independent – engaged learners, who can gain a sense of ownership of the taught knowledge and understand that the skills they learn in school matter? If we can achieve that, then we have succeeded.

Any good teacher conveys the outcome(s) of the lesson to students early so they know what to expect and what they will learn. Most students actually want to know this even though they may not be jumping in their seats with joy. Explaining that they will improve their communication, evaluation and synthesis skills by the end of the lesson may not be that important to many students ... unless we make it matter. How can we ensure that students really understand that the skills we teach them will matter in their lives? That the skills are relevant to them? By considering carefully how they will develop their skills in lessons, across a series of lessons and across Key Stages we can map out a clear skills progression chart that hopefully will enable students to reach the level at which you feel they should be working (see p. 16, Figure 1.1 AS-level Progression Chart and the discussion in Chapter 1, pp. 15–16. It is also crucial that students feel they are developing skills, so we need to make it concrete and provide them with tasks that give them the opportunity to test the skills you have been focusing on as a class.

Communication: the forgotten skill?

Can you pass the Lift Test?

This activity gets students thinking very carefully about their argument; the core of a message and the 'so what?' This will encourage them to consider which skills they can develop which will become essential in whatever they choose to do. It will also highlight the importance of your subject and that they can learn skills for life. Here is an English example:

Lift Test

You have written a book on John Steinbeck and have been given the opportunity to pitch your idea to a publisher in London. You have been granted five minutes of her time. Your focus for the pitch will be why some people find that *Of Mice and Men* is a sad book. (Students create their brief in this section.)

You arrive at the publishing house's foyer in good time so you even have a chance to calm yourself down, have a glass of water and maybe even glance over your main points.

Suddenly, the publisher appears in her coat and briefcase in hand and says, 'Sorry something's come up, give me the low-down on the way to my car.' You now have 45 seconds to pitch your idea as you join her in the lift down to the car park.

Students to do their presentation.

This activity works well because it provides students with something concrete, an event that could happen to them (although a publisher would allow them more time in reality!) and then the unexpected occurs when they are asked to think on their feet – quickly! This task is easily modified for a number of scenarios, for example:

◆ identifying arguments and stories in articles
◆ ecosystems
◆ turning-points in Russian history.

The two-minute talk

Terry Haydn, Senior Reader in Education at the University of East Anglia, always asks his trainees to prepare a two-minute talk. This mini-presentation can be done on any topic, but needs to be exactly two minutes. The aim is to get people used to presenting to an audience and under some sort of pressure, namely time. This may seem like an easy challenge to some, but most PGCE students who trained under Terry Haydn and both authors of this book did tend to disagree.

Two-minute presentation (Johannes)

I decided to give my presentation on the Black Panther Party, as I had done my university dissertation on the same topic, so felt confident that I could do a decent job. I wrote up the piece fairly quickly and rehearsed a few times in front of a mirror – basic preparation. When the workshop started the following day many of us were quite nervous. One brave soul, Gareth, stood up and volunteered to do his two-minute talk first. It is always hard to go first as we had never done anything like this before. He must have been petrified, poor man. Or perhaps not ... his presentation was brilliant. He confidently explained that by the end of the presentation we would learn x, y and z, and he then cracked a joke which made all of us laugh. He even managed to bring us down to a serious level and eventually left us wanting more. Simply fantastic! I was next. I stood up and looked around the room – they looked hopeful, anticipating another great presentation. After all, we were going to do this for a living so all presentations would probably be at this level, if not better. I grabbed my scrap of paper, trembling, and cleared my throat, trying to ignore that I was sweating like some sort of farm animal. Then suddenly it was over. I pulled through. Just. It was not a memorable performance but I had done it.

This may not seem like an activity worth unleashing on your poor students. Students tend to present in pairs or in smaller groups, so giving them the opportunity to talk in front of their peers for this brief amount of time will boost their confidence immensely. In fact, they will ask if they can do another one. When we use Terry Haydn's two-minute talk idea we do it twice:

◆   The first time gets them used to the format, the expectations and facing peers, and they get a quick confidence boost.
◆   The second time we ask them to present without notes. The presentation is still two minutes, but this time they can only have images to support their topic. Whether they only use one image, e.g. a painting or photograph, that will be their choice, but they must use visuals.

Although this activity was originally designed to be used with trainee teachers, adults who may have some experience of speaking to an audience because of experience from industry or university, it is a formidable activity to use with exam groups. The two-minute talk will also help develop students' skills in:

◆   communicating an important message in a concise manner
◆   analysing and contrasting the main factors of a topic or theme
◆   evaluating the main points and emphasizing the 'golden nugget'.

In essence, they are making it 'sticky'.

Case-study: Improving communication in modern foreign languages (Sara French, Assistant Head Teacher and Jeremy Moyle, Director of Language College)

In an attempt to increase pupils' success in the modern language oral examination, Dereham Neatherd High School[51] in Norfolk introduced a system common to all classes which they called 'secrétaire' (secretary). It is a very simple but effective concept which rewards students for all oral input in lessons. Each lesson one pupil acts as a secretary and records all student responses in the target language on a grid designed

cont. →

especially for this.[52] The teacher decides how many points pupils' sentences are worth, based upon length and difficulty. Students receive greater and greater rewards the further on the grid they get. At the beginning of every language lesson, five to ten minutes are set aside for students to answer questions they prepare throughout the year. These are listed on a question grid for each year group and are designed to improve students' oral fluency.[53]

Many students take this opportunity to pick up 'secrétaire' points. The questions differ for each year group, building upon the previous year and based on what students study at KS3. The list of questions for each year group is stuck in students' books for reference, and they tick them off when they can answer them confidently. The idea is that by KS4 they are not fazed by answering questions about themselves on a variety of topics.

This way of developing oral skills in modern foreign languages has had a great impact on the department's results, and oral pass rates have jumped from 42 to 72 per cent at best over a three-year period. As long as all staff are consistent in their approach and students are rewarded for their efforts, speaking a language in the artificial environment of the classroom can become meaningful and fun.

Synthesis: making it matter

When students synthesize information, they bring together contrasting pieces of knowledge that they have gathered and construct something new with it. There are lots of different ways in which you can help develop students' synthesis skills as long as they have the opportunity to revisit and practise using it regularly.

Activities where students do any of the following tend to enhance these skills:

♦ arrange
♦ combine
♦ rearrange
♦ create
♦ design
♦ invent
♦ what if?
♦ substitute.

Deconstruct the thinking

Provide the class with an image that contains a number of different parts and ask them what you can see in the image. Take ideas and add them to the board then deconstruct how they came to these conclusions. For example, an image of a fish jumping from a small fish-bowl to a larger one:

Image of	Fish	Freedom?
a fish in	Small bowl	Independence?
a fish-bowl	Large bowl	On your own?
	Water	Uncertainty?
⟶	Jumping ⟶	Courage?

Explain that they have 'synthesized' by deconstructing what they can see, then reconstructing the information so that it shows something new. This is a higher level skill which is very challenging.[54]

Mathematics: what is the HCF?

What is the highest common factor (HCF) of 24, 48 and 56? How can you use synthesis to work out what the HCF actually is?

FACTOR: We begin by establishing that factors are those numbers that divide exactly into the given number. Let us make a list of the factors of each one:

24	1, 2, 3, 4, 6, 8, 12, 24
48	1, 2, 3, 4, 6, 8, 12, 24, 48
56	1, 2, 4, 7, 8, 14, 28, 56

COMMON: Now we need to find those factors which are common: i.e. those numbers which appear in all three lists:

24	**1**, **2**, 3, **4**, 6, **8**, 12, 24
48	**1**, **2**, 3, **4**, 6, **8**, 12, 24, 48
56	**1, 2, 4**, 7, **8**, 14, 28, 56

Therefore the common factors are: 1, 2, 4, 8

HIGHEST: We finally need to assess which is the highest of our common factors:

1, 2, 4, 8

By using the skill of synthesis, students can see that the HCF of 24, 48 and 56 is in fact 8.

Business studies or economics: stock market research
You have been asked to recommend that an investor buys a firm's stock or lends a firm money. Using statistics and data from a selection of different sources students have to come up with a proposal to the client. In order to be able to do this they have to use a range of different skills including:

◆ evaluating the various possibilities
◆ using their skills of application, as they cannot make an investment decision without applying general financial principles to their specific firm
◆ focusing on synthesizing information by investigating patterns among the financial ratios and deciding which one would be the most suitable for their client.

English: what can we find out about To Kill a Mockingbird?
These quick-fire activities work particularly well after students have explored the whole text but can also be used for different segments.

◆ Imagine that you are Scout Finch. Produce a scrapbook of her memories of the summer.
  – What would she remember the most?
  – What would she have missed the most?
  – What would she have hated?
  Decorate the scrapbook with photos or illustrations that would represent special moments to her and include captions and annotations to your photos and illustrations. Then compare scrapbooks with other students and discuss which elements they have in common and which are different. Why is that?
◆ In groups of two or three, piece together a speech Atticus might have given to his neighbours describing his attitudes towards racial prejudice.
  – Which three key points would you want to emphasize to the neighbour?
  – Consider the reasons for those choices.
◆ Each member of the group will take on the roles of
  – speaker (works closely together with the writer to pick out the tone and pace of the presentation).

    – writer (needs to consider how to phrase certain elements so that some stand out while others remain low-key yet important).
    – designer (creates visual aids that represent each key point).

◆ Students present their speeches to the class. The classmates will then discuss if they agree that those were the most significant key points that Atticus would have discussed.

Student-centred learning

Thinking skills

Business guru, Guy Kawasaki, said, 'Eat like a bird and poop like an elephant.' Birds eat up to 50 per cent of their own body weight and elephants can get rid of 75 kg per day! If we are going to make learning interesting then we need to bring in tales and stories that capture interest and engage students, but the only way to find those stories is to read – *lots*.

If we apply this to teaching exam groups then we end up with a teacher armed with great subject knowledge that has great anecdotes. Students get more excitement and teachers might start to enjoy the yearly trawl through the specifications a little more. Reading and discovering new stories that encapsulate or enhance a part of the course is essential for adding interest to exam teaching. There is no substitute for this – it is time-consuming, but it will greatly improve the whole-exam-group experience.

Telling stories is one thing when faced with a Year 7 class, but quite another when coming up against Year 11 on a miserable Friday afternoon. How do we use stories without resorting to a desktop version of circle time?

One strategy is to turn that tale into a mystery. Break the story into small chunks and place them on cards. Have a central question that students can answer and let them work out what has happened. This technique works well when there is a personal story (i.e. someone's experiences) and a context. Below is an example of a mystery that is a summary of a whole on the American West. It uses a story and supports it with background information about why the events were happening. The information is on cards and can be moved around by the students and placed in different contexts.

The questions are 'Why was W.L. Couch murdered?' and 'Who was to blame?'

The statements are:

1. After 1825 the Great Indian nations had been removed from their lands and taken to live on reservations.
2. Many people who raced quickly from the starting line found that the Town Company had already set up its markers on good land.
3. People disappeared from the waiting camps and went into the forbidden land the night before. They illegally occupied good land.
4. Couch had always dreamed of building a large homestead on good land.
5. The Santa Fé Railroad ran right through the heart of the country to be opened to settlement.
6. Many gambling dens opened up quickly and were very popular.
7. New settlers were allowed to stake out 160 acres of land for themselves.
8. Many of the people who cheated and took land early were old 'boomers' (early settlers).
9. W.L. Couch had been involved in a long-running dispute over land claims.
10. Couch helped to set up a Town Company that built the first administrative buildings and stores in Oklahoma.
11. On 23 March 1889 President Harrison announced that two million acres in Indian territory would soon be opened to settlers.
12. Couch had an enemy called J.C. Adams. He was contesting Couch's claim to land and wished to see Couch out of Oklahoma.
13. There was opposition to settlement from the big cattle interests and from some of the leaders of the Indian tribes, and also from some whites who had made it their special mission to protect Indian rights.
14. The idea of manifest destiny had become so popular that people were willing to go to extraordinary lengths to acquire good land.
15. The US government provided $4 million for the purchase of Oklahoma.
16. The Town Company owned some of the richest and most prized lands in the county.
17. From 1884, Couch had led a party of 'boomers' who lived on the Oklahoma lands before they were officially sold to the government.
18. Settlers had to register a claim with the authorities and wait until 22 April when the frontier would be opened and people would race across to find land.
19. The Creek Indians and Seminoles felt that they had little choice but to sell their land and move to reservations.

20. Many people thought that Couch was a bad mayor who looked after the Town Company more than the people of Oklahoma.
21. The 'boomers' pressured the government to open up Oklahoma and officially recognize it as a white settlement.
22. W.L. Couch was elected the first mayor of Oklahoma.
23. There were few lawmen in the new state. The army had to be called to keep control.
24. Although town companies had been set up in many places, they were meant to race for land just like everyone else.
25. Many settlers felt unsafe and carried weapons around all day.

The structure of the lesson is crucial to the success of the activity: time is needed to establish the right level of challenge, to build in short- and long-term memory, to make the process of thinking visible and to debrief the skills used and look at transfer of those skills. The following points should help you to establish a really good thinking-skills lesson:

◆ Start with an example or reference that is very much part of the students' *own experience* and allow them to be drawn into the lesson. For example, whenever we start a mystery activity we ask students to name TV detectives and then tell us what they do in these shows. This leads on to a discussion about what skills they use and why. In this way, everyone in the class can contribute and feels part of the learning, but also you have warmed up the brain for the thinking that is to follow.[55]

◆ Pitch activities to challenge students, but give them some familiar anchors to hold on to. It is important to have some *recognizable material* in each thinking skills activity, so that students can lay the foundations before imagining what might happen to the rest of the information. Tasks like 'Odd One Out' or mystery picture (where you put an image outside the room and get students to recreate that image from memory) are simple ways to begin.

◆ Make all activities *collaborative*. The process works best when students are talking to each other, justifying their choices and debating theories.

◆ Make the activity *interactive*. Cards or movement will add a dimension to thinking skills (as in the mystery above) that is engaging and stimulating. There is less fear of failure with kinaesthetic activities, because answers can easily be hidden and new ones constructed.

◆ Allow plenty of time to *review* the learning and talk through how the students arrived at their answers as well as what the answer was. This will encourage them to explore methodologies and they will slowly begin to understand what they are doing and why. Link the process to the exams and show how the techniques they demonstrated will be useful for gaining good grades.

Case-study: Thinking skills mystery in MFL (Jo, second in department)

I used this lesson with an AS French class when revising for the unit 'La Santé'. Students were expected to have covered and be prepared to discuss a variety of topics within the unit, including learning about the French health system, the dangers of drinking, smoking and taking drugs, and so on. This lesson focused on the issue of drink-driving, and instead of using the somewhat dated articles from the textbook, I wanted to encourage students to be fully immersed in the issue, exploring real, up-to-date situations. From carrying out some research myself, I came across the emotional story of Jacqueline Saburido: a young girl who was involved in a horrific car accident caused by a drink driver. Jacqueline suffered over 60 per cent burns and is now campaigning internationally against drink-driving. At the time of the lesson, drink-driving was an issue prevalent in the French media as new breathalyzers were being introduced in France in clubs and pubs and also installed in cars.

The lesson started with a picture on the interactive whiteboard of Jacqueline, prior to the accident. She is smiling, at home with her parents, celebrating her 16th birthday. Having no prior knowledge to the incident, students were asked to guess the identity of this girl and encouraged to be as creative as possible. The next slides gradually provided additional photos and eventually an identity card, encouraging students to reassess the girl's identity. (Students were encouraged to use imperfect tense structures at this stage: 'I thought that she was ... but she is in fact ...') A high level of thinking was promoted through encouraging students to create the identity of an individual and adapt this as more

cont.→

clues were presented. At this point, the students were approaching the task with an element of humour, creating amusing stories surrounding this individual. Their light-hearted stance on the character was then shattered however, when the next photo to be displayed was the shocking image of the destroyed cars from the accident. Immediately, the students were hooked. They wanted to know the true identity of the girl and exactly what had happened.

The following activity involved students accessing a rather complex extended text, taken directly from an article in a French newspaper. Usually, when the students are presented with an unfamiliar text of this length, it can be off-putting. However, as mentioned above, the students this time were engrossed in the issue and genuinely wanted to know the full details. Reading strategies at this point were discussed and a mini-reading-skills activity was presented in order to encourage students to scan the text rather than become hindered by complex vocabulary and unfamiliar language structures – an approach which would be essential to apply in the AS Module 1 exam.

Once the students understood the text, the next task was presented, and students were requested to prepare and host a chat show or *débat télévisé*. The different roles were allocated and students had to prepare their character in depth in order to present themselves and their situation to the audience, and to predict and be prepared to answer any associated questions. Roles included:

◆ The presenter (who would have to introduce the whole situation on drink-driving, presenting current facts and statistics, and describe Jacqueline's story)
◆ Jacqueline herself
◆ the drink-driver (who would talk about what happened on the day of the incident and describe his time in prison)
◆ the French Ministère de l'écologie, Jean-Louis Borloo (who would talk about the new campaign for reducing drink-driving in France)
◆ an individual who admitted to drink-driving on occasions

cont.→

◆ a police officer
◆ various members of the audience (who were directed to produce questions for each guest).

Before commencing the task, students were provided with fact-sheets in French for their specific roles, and again, reading skills were applied when students had to sift through the information and decide which parts were relevant or not. Students were also reminded of key discussion and debate phrases and phrases for referring to statistics – all useful for approaching the oral exam with confidence in spontaneity. The chat show was presented in the following lesson.

This lesson worked particularly well. Students were engrossed from the start and enjoyed the challenge of preparing for the chat show. The lesson supported the mixture of abilities – many of the activities allowed for differentiation through outcome. Also, I could choose the roles depending on ability (a student on the Gifted and Talented register was allocated the more challenging role of Ministère de l'écologie for example). Follow-up lessons also clearly demonstrated that students were more informed when talking about issues associated with drink-driving and spoke with greater confidence, spontaneity and fluency.[56]

There are many examples of thinking skills lessons available, but the MFL example by Jo is one of the best we have seen. Not only does it provide an opportunity for higher-level thinking and true engagement but it does so in an original way. As we said at the start of this section, there is no substitute for reading around when it comes to finding good stories.

Independent and Active Learning

D. Souza found that the most common teaching method in both secondary and higher education was speaking or lecturing without dialogue even 'in the face of overwhelming evidence that it produces the lowest degree of retention for most learners'.[57]

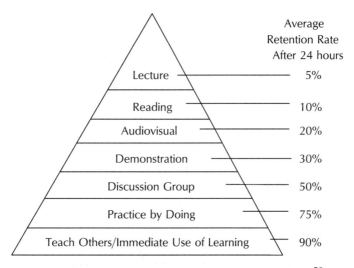

Average
Retention Rate
After 24 hours

Lecture	5%
Reading	10%
Audiovisual	20%
Demonstration	30%
Discussion Group	50%
Practice by Doing	75%
Teach Others/Immediate Use of Learning	90%

Figure 2.1 Retention varies with teaching method[58]

If you think back to the discussion on how to make your lessons 'sticky', which raised the point that students learn less from listening and most from using their learning in some way, then Bruner's ideas on learning[59] help to elucidate this information even further. Bruner argued that if teachers structure the material in the same way as we learn a language, by using words and piecing words together, so that the student can test out and use the information in a practical way, students will learn more quickly and retain the information for a longer period. Perhaps the best way to think of active learning in the classroom is to focus on learning *processes* rather than on learning *products*. The Brazilian educator Paulo Freire argued that many of us teach according to the 'banking system', whereby teachers deposit knowledge into students' brains for them to dispense at exam time in the same way that we deposit money into a savings account.[60] According to Freire, students need time to question and try out their learning in order to learn and remember.

J. Hattie investigated 253 studies on active learning in the classroom and found that those students who had been taught using active learning techniques (the experimental group) would on average achieve a grade 1.5 times higher than those students who were taught by the traditional methods (the control group).[61] Other research suggests that by saying less, students learn more. In a study by Ruhl,

Hughes and Schloss,[62] lecturers were told to pause for two minutes on three occasions during each of five lecturers, each interval lasting for about 12–18 minutes. Students did not interact with the lecturers during this time and instead reworked notes or discussed with a partner. When each lecture finished, students spent three minutes writing down everything they could remember from the lecture. After 12 weeks they were given a multiple-choice test to measure long-term retention. At the same time, a control group was given the same lectures but without the two-minute pause. The group of students who had been given a two-minute pause did significantly better on the recall and comprehension tests, achieving up to two grades higher than the other group.

Independent learning

Can you envisage a situation where a task is set, for example:

> **Produce a piece of audio-visual media that explains the rock cycle and create an A4 revision guide on the topic.**

After you have given these instructions students move into groups and begin to research and respond creatively? Maybe, sometimes, never?

There are two main reasons why students find it difficult to work independently:

◆ They are used to being spoon-fed information. They cannot work on their own unless step-by-step plans have been laid out for them.
◆ Many teachers believe they are under pressure to deliver content and so revert to a style of teaching that minimizes thinking and maximizes output.[63]

Carl Rogers investigated the relationship between teachers and students and found that approximately 25–30 per cent of students are self-directing; the rest will just do what they are supposed to do. He recognized two types of learning: (1) cognitive, the memorization of different things; and (2) experiential, the applied knowledge that comes from doing, for example active enquiry and problem-based learning.[64] This is why the role of the teacher becomes crucial. Rogers saw the role of the teacher to be one of facilitator – a person who creates an environment for learning in which:

- students participate, control and direct the learning process
- self-evaluation is used to assess student learning
- experiential learning is fostered.

It is challenging to be able to gauge how much guidance is needed for a certain group or individual student without giving them too much direction. Too much direction moves away from their sense of ownership of the learning journey. So, to follow in the spirit of Carl Rogers, teachers need to find the right balance and provide enough direction as facilitators so that the learners can identify and tackle areas of difficulty on their own.

Ensure progression of independent learning skills

D. Boud investigated autonomous learning in higher education, and he lists a range of things that students need to do in order to become independent learners:

- Identify learning needs
- Set goals
- Plan learning activities
- Find learning resources
- Work collaboratively
- Use teachers as guides and counsellors rather than instructors
- Create problems to tackle and select learning projects
- Choose where and when to learn
- Apply determining criteria to their work
- Engage in self-assessment
- Undertake to do additional non-teacher-directed learning
- Learn outside the confines of the educational institution and decide when learning is complete
- Reflect on their learning process.

How can we teach students to achieve these qualities? Most students do not know how to work independently, so we need to show them how they can. It takes a lot of practice to work well on your own, but with some guidance and models to follow students quickly learn to become more autonomous.[65] The Quality Improvement Agency for Lifelong Learning (QIA) recommends the following ideas for encouraging students to become independent learners:[66]

Reflection	Encourage your learners to think about what learning strategies work for them and what progress they are making. Provide pro formas for learners to record this.
Sharing ideas	Create opportunities for group and paired work, and for mutual support. Encourage learners to share stories and strategies, and seek ideas from other people in the group so that the teacher is not the only source of support.
Questions	Develop a learning atmosphere and exercises that encourage learners to ask questions. Use problem-solving techniques rather than finding right and wrong answers to closed questions.
Learner voice	Learners tend to become more confident when they know that their views will be taken seriously, so provide opportunities for learners to express their needs and concerns.
Catch confidence	Provide a framework for recognizing and recording progress and achievement. Include constructive comments from peers as well as teacher and learner feedback.
Create opportunities for independent learning	Do not be afraid to leave your students to tackle questions on their own or as part of a group exercise. Create plenty of opportunities for learners to practise their skills outside the classroom.
Learners centre stage	Encourage learners to demonstrate what they have learned; this helps to reinforce their learning. Ask them to explain points to others in their group.
Support learners to develop their study skills	Build study support into your courses. Identify which literacy, language or numeracy skills learners need in order to cope with their subjects.
Progression	Encourage students to identify their goals from the start of their journey with you. Discuss with them the learning that will help them reach those goals. Find out whether they need support with developing their literacy, language, numeracy and speaking skills.

We have a lot of experience of working with exam groups on developing their skills of working independently and we have found that as long as you begin by providing some basic structure, such as TASC wheel, and maintain close discussions with students at the start and during their learning projects, then they become more confident and ready to take risks in their learning. Kolb's reflective learning cycle[67] provides a good overarching structure for teachers helping to develop students' independent learning skills.

Once the work flow has been tried and established with the group, we explore using action plans,[68] so that the students can plan their work effectively and begin to set their own targets (see Independent Learning Progression Chart for KS4–5, p. 69). When you examine the chart you will soon discover that teachers support students to some extent in Year 10, that there is a focus on teaching them how to use online resources effectively and there is the opportunity to 'book the teacher'. This is a simple booking sheet which breaks down each lesson into ten-minute slots for the duration of the project: where a spokesperson from each group can make an appointment with the teacher to discuss their project (not to be confused with learning conversations that take place after the independent learning project is finished). Support is then gradually taken away as students enter into Year 11 and beyond, and there is a greater emphasis on teaching the class about research skills and using online material (including discussing referencing, reliability and so forth). It is important to note

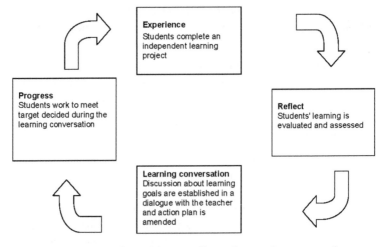

Figure 2.2 Adapted from Kolb's reflective learning cycle

History example	Year 10	Year 11	Year 12	Year 13
Topic	Crime and Punishment	Life in Germany 1919–45	Germany/Appeasement	Civil Rights
Independent learning support	GCSE action plans 'How to use the internet well' (lesson plan + document) Teacher-booking sheet	GCSE action plans 'How to make the most out of online material' (lesson plan + document) Teacher-booking sheet	AS action plans 'How to make the most out of the library and online material' (lesson plan + document) Teacher-booking sheet	A2 action plans 'How to make the most out of the library and online material' (lesson plan + document) Teacher-booking sheet
Target-setting	Students set their own targets after discussion with teacher	Students set their own targets	Students set their own targets after discussion with teacher	Students set their own targets
Criteria	Students construct their own enquiry questions together	Students construct their own enquiry questions	Students support their work with evidence/references	Students support their work with evidence/references
Check points /evaluation	See GCSE check point and evaluation sheet	See GCSE check point and evaluation sheet	See AS check point and evaluation sheet	See A2 check point and evaluation sheet
Learning conversation	Discussion with whole class and groups; targets for next projects set together with students	Discussion with whole class and group; targets for next projects set by students	Discussion with group and face-to-face chat; targets for next projects set by students	Discussion with group and face-to-face chat; targets for next projects set by students

Figure 2.3 Independent Learning Progression Chart

that for an independent learning project to work we, the teachers, must learn to take a step back and allow students to learn from their mistakes. The process is crucial to developing autonomy. We will, however, make good use of starters and plenaries to aid in this process, particularly at the beginning of a project. The aim of 'stepping away' from the class is to encourage students to approach the teacher, and this can take some time for them to get used to. When the project is complete and the learning is assessed and evaluated, after students present their results to the class, for example, then the learning conversation and target-setting become imperative to ensure progression of both independent learning skills and understanding.

Working on developing students' independent learning skills is a long process and requiring you, the teacher, to think carefully about when your help is needed, when to encourage groups and when to keep your distance. You may find that leading a brief discussion at the start of each lesson, a sort of best-practice opportunity, helps many groups to develop more quickly. Equally, allowing students to spend the first ten minutes reviewing and amending their targets, and then sharing their thoughts with each other, can really push the most able to think more deeply about their work while helping the lower-attaining students.

Case-study: Students as teachers in the history classroom

Encouraging independent learning with exam classes is hard. There is not time, they may not do the work and there is not enough time … time … It does take a while for students to learn to work on their own and it requires a lot of practice in KS3 for it to work effectively. However, the biggest problem is not really time but that that we do not trust students to do the work properly. If we set them a task which listens to what they have to say; encourages what they wish to achieve and provides them with enough space and time then the results will follow. The following activity took around six lessons and we only focused on the topic of 'witchcraft' as part of a GCSE Crime and Punishment development study. Witchcraft accounts for only 15 marks of the exam. We spent six hours, plus three hours' homework. It worked.

> *Teacher*: What do you think of their choice of question?
> *Connor*: Well, it's kind of 'big', you can infer things, you can analyse … it's a very good question. It is! There's not like one simple answer, just like a knowledge question 'who did what, when …', you can like expand on this one and take it further.

This is a brief summary of what we did with some of our Year 10 groups. We have used this exact approach with students from Year 9 through to Year 13, and it works every time.

The students were given these criteria to follow:

- The learning would be identified during the question-and-answer session, including the plenary.
- They need to engage the class
- They need to create and employ resources (including the use of the interactive whiteboard) in a functional and imaginative way.

Lesson 1: Questioning and the perfect lesson

During the initial lesson two students interviewed each other about a recent holiday:

Sophie: Where did you go on holiday then?
Ben: Spain.
Sophie: How long did you go for?
Ben: One week.
Sophie: Was it good?
Ben: Yeah.

We wanted them to gain awareness of the difficulty in building an enquiry question which was both challenging but also gave students the opportunity to analyse and evaluate historical issues. The class quickly realized the problems with the questions posed, and a discussion ensued about what was needed to extend Ben's one-word answers to explanations.

Groups were split into threes and fours, and students were asked to list the main topics in their books:

1. Life in the 1600s (including major events).
2. Origins of witchcraft as a crime.
3. Escalation.
4. The end of persecution.
5. Matthew Hopkins in East Anglia.
6. Persecution of witches 1400–1600.

We then discussed Bloom's taxonomy of how thinking evolves in different stages, and how they can learn to progress on their own. Examples were given about how their thinking might move from, e.g.

knowledge, to comprehension, to application and *analysis*. The main issues about the topic of witchcraft were handed out and students had to decide which topic they wanted to examine, rather than the teacher giving out topics. This way the groups got to study what they really wanted. If there were duplicates of topics chosen then those groups had to discuss the possibility of changing to another topic.

The groups were given ten minutes to think of a number of questions (approximately three to five), one of which could become a potential Key Question, using Bloom's Taxonomy as guidance. Discussion ensued about the type of questions they had written down and what characterized a challenging question. Groups commented on the suitability and limitations of some of the examples given. One student noted that 'if you ask a *'when'* question then it's difficult to move away from simply listing ideas' and that 'we should all be focusing on questions which get us to *analyse'*. Groups then went back to their original questions, modified these if necessary, and decided on one key question to use for their lesson. By the end of the lesson students had come up with the following questions:

◆ Why did people in the Middle Ages believe in witchcraft?
◆ Matthew Hopkins terrified and destroyed East Anglia. Discuss.
◆ How far has the perception of women changed since the 1600s?
◆ Why did the crime of witchcraft appear and then disappear?

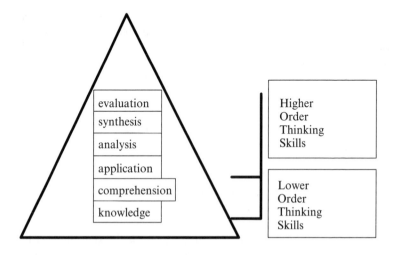

Figure 2.3 Bloom's taxonomy of the cognitive domain

The structure of lessons

One week earlier we had given students a challenge to write down their thoughts about a lesson they felt was 'good' and explain why (without mentioning names of teachers). We discussed what they had discovered and why they felt a certain lesson was good. Students were then given an explanation and shown concrete examples of the structure of a lesson including use of objectives, 'hooks', starters, main task(s) and plenary. The class was given clear guidance about each of the lesson components. We then discussed what they considered to be a good lesson, what made them interested, even inspired. We annotated students' responses on a flip-chart and then in their groups they had to compile a list: *Five essential components for the perfect lesson*, with ideas about what they would like to see in an ideal lesson. Suitability of outcome(s) was then discussed and it was agreed that some tasks were better than others (e.g. quizzes do not tend to challenge students and taking notes from PowerPoint presentations does not encourage learning). Groups then started writing down ideas for what they wanted their co-students to learn in the lesson and how they were going to ensure this learning took place.

Lesson 2: Research

We started by discussing their action plans, and some students gave examples of some of the issues they wanted to look into and what sort of targets they had set themselves. A few students commented that they wanted to spend a fair amount of time planning the activities, while others commented that they needed to do rigorous research before they were expert in their given topic. Groups then researched their topics. Our groups are used to working independently and making use of either TASC wheel or work-plans to structure their work. We decided to use the school library for this lesson to give them a good environment to do their research. Groups were encouraged to set their own homework by dividing the research into smaller parts which were then assigned to the various team members.

Lesson 3: Final research

This was the final preparation lesson and included groups completing their lessons, creating resources, setting up and producing relevant material for the interactive whiteboard. The class was now informed that during every mini-lesson each group would be assigned to another one and would have to write a critical appraisal of that group. This way, they not only had the opportunity to evaluate another group's lesson but were also reflecting on their own learning and execution of the lesson.

Lesson 4/5: Let's teach!

Groups taught their lessons. At the end of each lesson the class gave their new teacher immediate feedback commenting on what they had learnt, the way they had been taught and how engaged they had been.

Lesson 6: Plenary

We spent the final lesson discussing the outcomes of the project and what the students thought about delivering their own mini-lessons. Points were also raised about what they had learnt from this experience. Several commented that they had gained complete ownership of their work; that they had become specialists in their given topics and felt they could help others to gain a fuller understanding. Most importantly, many students made it clear that they felt respected and trusted by their peers as well as their teacher.

This approach made it clear that if learning is to be effective then making it relevant, keeping it interesting and providing a challenge are all essential components that need to be addressed. We have used this way of collaborating with students from different year groups and in various topics, and each time the students have had similar positive experiences. Handing over the board-pen to a class can be daunting at first, but if planned carefully it can be a truly rewarding endeavour.

Giving students the trust, effort and time will ensure they know that their work matters. Even better, they will use the following skills, which are crucial to their learning:

◆ communication
◆ analysis
◆ evaluation
◆ synthesis.

The only difference was that this time they actually used them in a situation where they were able to see the results in their fellow classmates – and they were in charge of their learning.

Active learning

Many teachers say active learning would be great 'if they had the time'. But the research shows that if you *make* the time for effective active learning by doing less didactic teaching, then your students will do better. It may seem strange not to be able to say everything you know about the topic you are teaching, but it won't help if you do. You know too much!

(G. Petty)[69]

There are many different ways of using active learning techniques, and some work better than others depending on the group you are teaching, the time of day and your relationship with the group. It is important to note, however, it does not matter if you have never used active learning in your lessons, although you may feel a bit silly at first when you explain to the students that they are going to use the Talking Knot or create a human mind-map. The main thing is that students very quickly get used to standing up, moving around, talking, acting or whatever else you need them to do to understand a difficult concept or topic.

Example: Discuss the grey matter: continuums

Continuums are, according to Wikipedia: 'anything that goes through a gradual transition from one condition, to a different condition, without any abrupt changes.'[70] Using physical continuums are excellent for showing classes that many things are not black and white, that some questions have several answers or that a concept can be evaluated in many ways. Take a look at this history example: the Protest Continuum.[71]

Instructions for using continuums

The rationale behind this activity was to allow students time to reflect about the nature of protest and consider where each one would go on a continuum from extremely violent to peaceful.

- Hand out one card/sheet per student.
- Explain the task/question.
- Inform them that they must place themselves on the continuum.

Simple! Students spend some time discussing whether or not an item (e.g. hunger-strike) ought to be peaceful as it will have an impact on the person's health as well as the immediate surrounding (family members, etc.). Allow them time to organize themselves and then ask each one (or pick a few, depending on the size of the continuum) to explain their choice.

There are lots of different examples of how to use this active learning technique. You could, for instance, set up a continuum of

Agree–Disagree and then play the class a selection of video clips which they have to respond to; or read a passage from a book after which students have to decide how the key characters have been portrayed by the author. Physical continuums are excellent tools as they challenge students to think on their feet, collaborate, argue their case and evaluate difficult issues.

Model answers (**Blue Peter**-style)
We are big fans of visual approaches to learning and this technique uses it to excellent effect.

When you have completed a unit, get students to create a 3D model to represent the topic. The idea is to create the shape and fill it with words and phrases to help make sense of the topic. The beauty of a 3D model is that it has sides and surfaces that can mean different things. For example, a physics unit on 'Producing Electricity' could be represented by a model of a battery (without a bottom). You could write about types of current on the inside and ways of making electricity on the outside.

If you require a set of information and then a layer underneath, use flaps. For example, if you are doing a character study in English literature and want to show two views (e.g. good and bad side of Frankenstein) then layer two images one on top of the other and add a set of words to each one, adding symbols and images to aid the memory. The idea is to connect a process and creativity (i.e. thinking) with knowledge. This helps students to remember and make sense of a topic.

Example: Thinking about concepts – 'active mind-mapping'
Some groups find it very hard to understand how concepts/events, etc. link together. You can explain, show them and get them to write about them, but there is still no real understanding. Allowing a class *physically to feel* how things might connect – how they 'slot in' – makes your message more 'sticky' and they will more easily recall and grasp what you want them to learn. Mind-mapping[72] is a useful way of doing this.

The rationale behind mind-mapping is for students visually to give an answer to the question. This can be achieved in many different ways and some groups may not choose to create a mind-map. However, most groups will see that some events and concepts connect and that some belong in the same category. By the end of the activity, groups should have a large display which they then need to explain.

Instructions for mind-mapping
◆ Split the class into small groups, say, three to four students in each.
◆ Give them a copy of the handout.
◆ Explain that they will have to work together to answer the question visually and be able to explain their choices.
◆ They need to create a large mind-map.

Whatever the subject, the results are the same. Groups will first begin to discuss/disagree where each 'bubble' should go, then they will start to see some links but may still argue over what connects with which element and how they could group others together. Eventually they come to (some sort of) an arrangement where all parties are happy and they can easily explain their answer.

You may ask, why not just get them to draw up a mind-map in their books? The answer is that by creating a physical mind-map together on the floor, the activity tends to generate a lot of heated discussion, which they later remember. Moreover, the fact that they physically move pieces around (sometimes string could also be used to link things more obviously – groups find all sorts of ways to solve problems) helps them to see more clearly how concepts/events, etc. connect and how the relationships between these affect each other. Finally, it is also easier to compare other student's mind-maps and even suggest alternatives by moving individual elements (or bubbles) around.

This is also a good way of getting them to work on the 'bigger picture' – see Chapters 1 and 3 (pp. 0 and 00) on using overviews and reviews for more ideas.

Example: Create 'interactive' diagrams with your students
Teachers are generally very good at planning for a range of learning styles. It is, however, sometimes difficult to cater for the kinaesthetic learner effectively. *Kinaesthetic* learning is more than simply 'getting them out of their seats', isn't it? How could we ensure that this learning style is the focus and what type of activities are there which are genuinely physical? We have already discussed how to make mind-maps more active and how continuums can be made kinaesthetic, but there are also other methods which can be applied that will enhance learning. The examples listed below have been used with all abilities across KS4 and KS5 and they work well.

Venn diagrams

Although the following is a history example, the idea can easily be used in other subjects.

We had just finished looking at the problems facing the Weimar Republic in the 1920s and we wanted the class to assess how well the new republic dealt with the issues of the time. We created a (very) large triple Venn diagram using toilet paper (although a more sophisticated way would have been to have used a large piece of string) in the middle of the room). The diagram used socioeconomics, politics and foreign policy as the key factors. Each student was given a statement, which they placed on the Venn diagram and explained their reason to the rest of the group. The discussion worked well and the students could literally see how some of the problems were linked to several factors. When they later sat a mock exam and a similar question came up, they remembered the issues we had discussed from the lesson (they could even remember where they stood) and did rather well.

String them along

For us, the point of active learning is to make thinking and skills visible to the learner: it is not something that happens inside their heads, but can be seen and manipulated right in front of them.

A crucial skill in any subject is the ability to link ideas or data. Take the following level descriptor for business studies GCSE: 'For 4 marks [out of 4] the role of the Competition Commission and how it can prevent abuses of power will be described fully, with clear use of terminology and links between ideas within the thought process'.

There is no better way of teaching the skill of linking than making physical links with string. Split the class into smaller groups and give them an element of a topic to look at. They should be supplied with a banner or headline text and an information sheet. Once students have gained an understanding of the concept or section they are looking at, get out the string.

Students must now physically link themselves to another concept, with the string acting as the connection. Another member of the group can loop a piece of paper over the string to say what the link is. Within minutes the class will have created a physical representation of the topic. Use a camera to capture the moment and then back up understanding with a concept map afterwards – simple, but effective.

Summary

There is a lot to consider in this chapter about how students learn and how to construct and deliver lessons that 'stick' with our learners, so here's a list of our most valuable tips:

1. Creative learning experiences are possible to maintain without burning out by focusing on what students like, want and are already familiar with in their lives, e.g. stories and social relationships.

2. Consider the core, the 'golden nugget' of your lesson(s) and the Scheme of Learning. Are you communicating this message to students? Could you make it even clearer?

3. Certain lessons 'stick' in students' memories more than others because some information or *knowledge* is inherently interesting while some is inherently uninteresting. Teachers can ensure content which is traditionally dry also becomes memorable by broadly following key principles in their planning, e.g. keeping the core simple, unexpected, concrete, credible, emotional and using stories to create meaning.

4. Good learning stems from good teaching and great results will follow – make time to be innovative, OFSTED wants you to! What can you do to make those dusty old textbooks come alive again? Could technology help out perhaps?

5. Make skills matter to students. Make skills relevant, so students know that communication and synthesis skills can actually help them today as well as in ten years when they leave education.

6. Use a variety of teaching tools, for example, Thinking Skills and Active Learning to challenge students regularly. Plan these activities into Schemes of Learning so they matter and are not 'bolted on' when a resource suddenly becomes available.

7. Create progression charts for key skills throughout Key Stages 4 and 5 as well as one for any independent learning.

8. Allow students time, even six to seven lessons, to immerse themselves in an independent learning project – the benefits are tremendous and there is time. Yes, really.

Notes

1. Tom Kelley, *The Ten Faces of Innovation: Strategies for Heightening Creativity* (London: Profile Books, 2008).

2. In total, 170 students were given the £100 test (60 Year 7 (11–12 years old), 75 Year 10 (14–15 years old), 35 Year 12–13 (16–18 years old)).
3. There is a wealth of research on student voice on the internet. Start with the Specialist Schools and Academies Trust website, www.specialistschools.org.uk
4. Kelley, *The Ten Faces of Innovation*, pp. 30–31.
5. C. Heath and D. Heath, *Made to Stick* (London: Random House, 2008).
6. Ibid., p. 20.
7. For great thinking skills activities see http://www.innovativeict.net/examples
8. C. Heath and D. Heath, 'Sticking to it', Association Now, February 2007.
9. T. Haydn and C. Counsell, *History, ICT and Learning* (London: RoutledgeFalmer, 2004) p. 00.
10. See Chapter 2, p. 00–00 for a more detailed look at using online material and a further discussion on the comparison between *The Encyclopaedia Britannica* and Wikipedia.
11. V. Frankl, *A Man's Search for Meaning* (London: Beacon Press, 2000).
12. M. Scully, 'Viktor Frankl at Ninety: An Interview', www.First Things.com (April 1995).
13. Our ideas for planning lessons are outlined fully in W. Watkin and J. Ahrenfelt, *100 Ideas for Essential Teaching Skills* (London: Continuum, 2006). Sections 2, 3 and 4 are most relevant.
14. Podcasting is one way of creating stories which contain both elements. See http://www.staffroomproject.com/?q = ipod-in-the-classroom.html for more information.
15. D. Norman, *Things that Make us Smart* (New York: Perseus Books, 1994).
16. Mark Turner, *The Literary Mind: The Origins of Thought and Language* (Oxford: Oxford University Press, 1996), p. 4.
17. See Watkin and Ahrenfelt, *101 Ideas for Essential Teaching Skills*, p. 16 and http://www.educationforum.co.uk/HA/bloom.htm for an interesting review and links.
18. Diana Hinds, 'If we Don't Innovate, we Won't Raise Standards', *Guardian* online, education supplement: http://education.guardian.co.uk/therisktakers/story/0,,1777940,00.html
19. M. Howe, cited in T. Haydn and C. Counsell (eds), *History, ICT and Learning* (London: RoutledgeFalmer, 2004), p. 200.

20. A. November, 'Teaching Zack to think', November Learning: http://novemberlearning.com/resources/archive-of-articles/teaching-zack-to-think/, 1998.
21. Haydn and Counsell (eds), *History, ICT and Learning*, p. 200.
22. See http://www.staffroomproject.com/?q = deliver-learning.html for a list of great websites we find useful for our teaching.
23. http://en.wikipedia.org/wiki/Barbie
24. A. Harvey, 'The Use of Wikipedia in Libraries: Research in an Era of Decentralized Authority', 28th Charleston Conference, 8 November 2008.
25. C. Leadbeater, *We −Think* (London: Profile Books, 2008), p. 18.
26. The WikiTrust at http://wiki-trust.cse.ucsc.edu/index.php/Main_Page
27. 'McCann's Comparative Study on Social Media Trends', April 2008, www.universalmccann.com
28. McCann's Comparative Study on Social Media Trends, April 2008, p. 18, www.universalmccann.com
29. Ibid., p. 12.
30. Assuming these do not contain material that could offend anyone and do not have any criminal content.
31. T. Haydn, cited in J. Ahrenfelt and N. Watkin, *Innovate with ICT − Enhancing Learning across the Curriculum* (London: Continuum, 2008).
32. For actual active learning ideas please see pp. 2, 88, 97.
33. D.J. Malan, 'Podcasting Computer Science E-1.', in *Proceedings of the 38th SIGCSE Technical Symposium on Computer Science Education*, ACM SIGCSE Bulletin, 39.1 (March 2007): 389–93.
34. A. Daley, 'Teaching with Technology White Paper: Podcasting', Office of Technology for Education and Eberly Center for Teaching Excellence, Carnegie Mellon University, Pittsburgh, PA, 6 April 2007.
35. Available here: www.staffroomproject.com/?q = resources.html
36. Montage-a-Google was set up by Grant Robinson, a digital designer, and can be found on his site: http://grant.robinson.name/projects/montage-a-google/
37. Voice recorders are fairly cheap nowadays and many MP3 players and mobile phones come with voice recorders as standard. See our reviews of recent MP3 quality voice recorders at: www.innovative ict.net/voicerecorders
38. If you are unsure how to use it, take interactive tutorial http://www.innovativeict.net/powerpoint
39. Download the lesson plan plus resources from http://www.staff roomproject.com/?q = resources.html

40. We gave them sections from C. Corin and T. Fiehn, *Communist Russia under Lenin and Stalin* (London: Hodder/Murray, 2002).

41. The video clip can be found at http://www.staffroomproject.com/?q = engage-alevel-students.html

42. Visit our website for videos about RSS and podcasting: www.staffroomproject.com/?q = ipod-in-the-classroom.html

43. Many resources can be found on the main website, www.staff roomproject.com/?q = resources.html, but we have also included a range of tutorials and interactive resources on our ICT website: www.innovativeict.net

44. www.gcast.com and www.garageband.com work seamlessly together.

45. Voice-recorders are great as they can be placed on a table and will pick up students' discussions and record in digital quality, unlike simple microphones which tend to record poor audio quality. They are not expensive, visit www.innovativeict.net/voicerecorders for examples of voice-recorders we like to use.

46. Audacity is a free audio recording software which can compile and save audio into different formats. Go to your favourite search engine and download it today – it's simple to use.

47. BBC News Online, Talking Point, Are Exams a Waste of Time?, http://news.bbc.co.uk/1/hi/talking_point/1979407.stm

48. Robert Sternberg, *The Yale Herald*, 38.13 (3 December 2004).

49. D. Goleman, *Emotional Intelligence – Why it can Matter More than IQ* (London: Bantam, 1995).

50. C. Moorcroft and P. Burden, University of Surrey Skills Project Employer Research Report, July 1999.

51. See mfl.neatherd.org for more details of this system.

52. See Appendix 1 for the secretaire grid.

53. Visit www.staffroomproject.com/?q = resources.html to download these oral question grids.

54. See www.staffroomproject.com/?q = synthesize-making-it-matter for an example of the image we used in class.

55. The origin idea for how to 'launch' a mystery appears in one of our favourite teacher resources, the 'Thinking through' series, edited by Fisher and Leat and published by Chris Kington. All their subject-specific books are crammed full of great ideas for thinking skills.

56. For all Jo's resources see www.staffroomproject.com/?q = resources. html

57. D. Sousa, *How the Brain Learns* (New York: Corwin Press, 2004).

58. Ibid.

59. J. Bruner, *The Process of Education* (Cambridge, MA: Harvard University Press, 1977).

60. P. Freire, *The Politics of Education* (New York: Bergin & Garvey, 1987).

61. J. Hattie, cited from Quality Improvement Agency, Gold Dust Resources' Active Learning Information sheet; http://excellence.qia.org.uk/Golddust/activelearning/activelearning.html.

62. Ruhl *et al.*, 'Using the Pause Procedure to Enhance Lecture Recall', *Teacher Education and Special Education*, 10 (Winter 1987): 14–18.

63. Watkin and Ahrenfelt, *100 Ideas for Essential Teaching Skills*.

64. C. Rogers, *Freedom to Learn* (London: HarperCollins, 1969).

65. There are many approaches to guiding students to become more independent; we will give examples of some of the techniques we use. We have also made use of other methods such as Belle Wallace's Thinking Actively in a Social Context (TASC) wheel (www.nace.co.uk/tasc/tasc_home.htm) follows a problem-solving structure which works very well with students.

66. The Quality Improvement Agency for Lifelong Learning Teaching and Learning Programme, *Developing the Expert Learner*, pp. 2–3 (see www.gia.org.uk).

67. This cycle has been adapted from D. Kolb, *Experiential Learning: Experience as the Source of Learning and Development* (Camden, WJ: Pearson Education, 1984).

68. See Appendix 1.

69. Cited from www.geoffpetty.com/activelearning.html

70. http://en.wikipedia.org/wiki/Continuum

71. Documents can be downloaded from www.staffroomproject.com/?q = resources.html. This idea has been adapted from an excellent activity by Terry Haydn. For more ideas from this teaching guru, see his website: http://www.uea.ac.uk/%7Em242/historypgce/welcome.htm

72. Active mind-map can be found at: www.staffroomproject.com/?q = resources.html

3 | Review to Learn

The pain

We level and grade anything that moves.
(Angela, subject leader)

This section focuses on reviewing and assessing learning. We have worked with a range of different teachers over the past few years and we have discovered that many feel that it is difficult to find the right balance between teaching engaging and challenging lessons while ensuring that content is covered and learning is established and assessed at regular intervals. The second problem for teachers is how to make reviewing and assessing *useful* to students and more than just a grade for them or for the school's administration. We have a lot of experience in both of these areas and have worked with many inspiring teachers; some of their thoughts and ideas have been included in this chapter.

It's difficult to set engaging assessments, but I guess that's not the point?
(Tom, NQT)

If you think back to the discussion about the ways in which students are taught and how they learn best in Chapter 2,[1] it may come as no surprise to you that most students' experience of school is one of silence and listening. We conducted a survey where approximately 300 GCSE and A-Level students were asked about common teaching methods. Which do you think were the two most common teaching tools?

- ◆ PowerPoint
- ◆ teacher talking
- ◆ CD-ROM
- ◆ video/DVD

- internet (where you use websites which contain activities)
- paired work (e.g. card-sorting)
- textbooks

Teacher talking and PowerPoint scored the highest. Surprised? Of course this doesn't have to be a major cause for concern; however, if research is correct then students learn more through active engagement in the lesson.[2] So, if they are listening, writing and answering questions, what are they not doing? We have to be persistent in checking what students have learnt to ensure that they progress through good review activities and good assessment. We now come back to the original problem to ensure we assess students for the right reasons so that our teaching does not become, as a workshop delegate said to Johannes in 2009, 'assessment driven, and there's always another one for them to take so I can check progress'. We hope that this chapter will help to solve, or at least move towards, useful and purposeful assessment, where students understand what they need to do to progress.

The Big Idea: make learning purposeful, memorable and powerful

In his book *A Whole New Mind*, Daniel Pink explains that

> ... the future belongs to a very different kind of person with a very different kind of mind — creators and empathizers, pattern recognizers and meaning makers. These people — artists, inventors, designers, storytellers, caregivers, consolers, big picture thinkers — will now reap society's richest rewards and share its greatest joys.[3]

This distinctly new group of people will offer more than linear, logical thinking and they will view their environment, workplace and life from a more holistic perspective, aware of the changing world around them. The educational system must meet that challenge.

Teachers in the UK are facing difficult challenges when it comes to assessing students' understanding. In April 2002 a parliamentary report revealed that the average grades achieved by A-level candidates have been rising steadily for the past 25 years.[4] The government and teaching institutions uphold that the enhanced grades symbolize higher levels of achievement due to improved and more experienced teaching methods, but many academics and particularly mass media claim that the change is due to grade inflation and tests and exams are getting easier.[5] Others argue that as schools are put under pressure to achieve good results, students are being trained to pass specific examinations, at the expense of a general understanding of their subjects.[6] As we discussed in the first section of this chapter (p. 84) and in Chapter 2 (p. 26) teachers need to find a balance between teaching to enhance students' skills and learning, and raising attainment. We believe that if students are to gain more than just a grade after some 11–13 years of study we must think carefully about our planning, assessing and delivery of the curriculum. The exam is one thing. What about our country's future? How profound, the cynic amongst us would argue, but let's consider Dylan Wiliam:

> ... there is no doubt that the higher the education level you have, the more you earn during your life, the longer you live and the better quality of life. For society, there are lower criminal justice costs, by increasing the level of education, you reduce the amount of money spent on incarcerating people. It reduces the cost of healthcare because people take care of themselves better ... there is no alternative but to keep on raising levels of educational achievement.[7]

Read the following question and then choose one of the options:

When do I assess my students?

(a)   at the start of a unit
(b)   in the middle of a unit
(c)   at the end of a unit
(d)   all the time

What's your answer? If you answered either c or d then you belong to the majority of educators out there. You teach the unit or course, then you assess. If you are a science teacher at KS4 or KS5 then you might assess as in the (d) option because many of your courses require that. Or do they? Perhaps you could not choose? Has your department considered why you assess when you do? Perhaps because it is at the end of the unit and that's what you are supposed to, or maybe you have decided to assess them in the middle when they have practised a certain skill?

We believe the key to good assessment is when it is

- *Purposeful*: Remember the story, your schemes of learning, the unit, the idea – set their learning in context. If this is achieved well then students can clearly see that there is a reason to assess and they feel it moves them forward and is not just giving them a grade.
- *Regular*: Assessments are handed back promptly and students have a chance to meet their targets immediately, i.e. they do not have to wait weeks between assessment 1 and 2 – how will they remember what to do to meet the target you set? Assessment for learning is used to ensure progression.
- *Varied*: How do you assess their learning? Do they ever have the opportunity to communicate their understanding verbally or do they always write? Even A-level classes benefit from face-to-face assessments or open discussion. Can they demonstrate their understanding in a range of different ways? For instance, can they
  - construct something
  - present to the class
  - compile a case file with evidence about a topic based on criteria set by you?
- *Skills-based*: Assessment is made after they have worked on particular skills or used to test a key skill, e.g. evaluation or synthesis.
- *Powerful*: They have learnt something they feel could be used, or they experience a 'light-bulb' moment. If they see that they can progress both within a lesson and across, then they are more likely to want to do well.

Review to learn

Teacher: Morning all. OK, write down three things that you remember about the character of Elizabeth Bennet in *Pride and Prejudice* from the last lesson.

Class looks puzzled; some begin to write.

Teacher: Right, what can you tell me about Elizabeth?

Two students raise their hands.

Most teachers have experienced this situation at some time, and finding out that the majority of the class has forgotten what they taught them the previous lesson can be frustrating. But should we not expect students at some point to forget the information we cram into

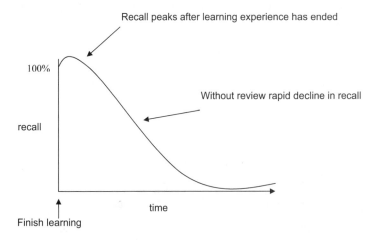

Figure 3.1 Reviews

their heads? In fact, according to M. Hughes, we should expect it, as if we do not review the information is forgotten almost instantly. The graph above explains that only after 24 hours of a lesson ending almost 80 per cent of what was taught has been lost.[8] So, if you taught the lesson a week earlier, without reviewing, students are even less likely to remember.

Mike Hughes, in his book *Closing the Learning Gap*[9] states 'Trying to learn without reviewing is like trying to fill the bath without putting the plug in'. This may seem like an interesting comment, particularly as at the end of a lesson students' retention rates are at their lowest as their brains begin to process the newly acquired information. This is why plenaries are so important, to enable students to remember what you have taught them. However, we must review their learning more than at the end or at the start of a lesson. If students are to remember the key points of the lesson, the 'golden nugget', we need to provide them with a clear overview at the start of the course so they know what to expect and what to look out for. We also need to plan carefully regular review points in schemes of learning, so classes have the opportunity to revisit key issues and concepts and students will also be able to see that reviewing makes them remember and understand. When time allows, especially during independent learning projects, use learning conversations with individual groups or students to discuss issues raised in class. These conversations are effective as they provide 'thinking time' for students and they do not have the peer or time pressures of a standard lesson.

Encourage retention and understanding of key issues and concepts[10]

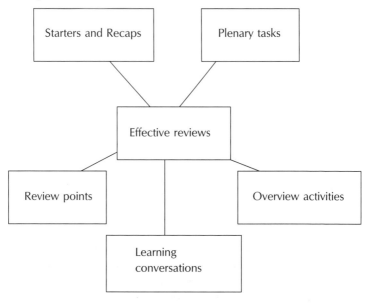

Figure 3.2 Effective learning

Assessment forms part of the review process and will help in moving students forward as well as inform planning. The key to effective progression of students' learning is the dialogue between them and you so the feedback provided needs to be clear, consistent and matter to their learning. If assessment feedback is to be valuable in guiding learning it needs to focus on 'growth rather than grading',[11] encouraging and advancing student learning. Research has shown that educators often regard assessment as providing only a grade or brief comments to their students, yet expect improvement as a result. According to D. Sadler, students seem to fall into either 'active' or 'passive' learners. Their level of engagement with written assessment feedback appears to be variable, with some students at either end of a spectrum. While many students *actively* make use of the feedback and are very keen to learn from it and develop academically, others lack motivation and under-standing. The latter group can show a distinct lack of purpose in learning or give the impression that the grade is their ultimate goal.[12] This group can be moulded to understand the importance of assessment if we ensure they grasp the feedback given to them.

Making feedback matter

Student use of feedback is a skill which requires investment on the part of the teacher to develop properly.[13] We need to prepare students to connect with their feedback, otherwise they might show little evidence of progress or intrinsic motivation to learn.[14] Most students want clear, constructive and informative comments that can be easily understood, and let us not forget that they particularly value feedback that gives them positive encouragement. This may seem obvious, but in the drive to assess, some of us may become too focused on target-setting and may forget to pass on a few words of encouragement.

In 2006 D. Nicol and D. Mackfarlane-Dick investigated what students sought from feedback. They discovered that the vast majority expressed a need to engage with the teacher in face-to-face dialogue to discuss their feedback as well as sharing experiences with their peers.[15] Similarly, S. Pitts found that students also wanted to build an understanding of the feedback messages received by the teacher 'through dialogue'[16] to further their learning.

Go through the requirements of the assessment so that the class understands what they need to do	Ensure students are clear about the assessment criteria before they commence their assessment	Give them the opportunity to peer-mark so they can see how other students write and have the possibility to use the mark scheme on a deeper level so they feel part of the process
Provide concrete instruction on how to make best use of the feedback they receive. Give them an example so they can see how to improve; ask them to redraft a part of the assessment so they can meet the target immediately	Try to engage in a *learning conversation* with the students particularly if it is their first assessment with you as their teacher	

Keep the structure of assessment and feedback simple, consistent and clear: (for an excellent example of using Assessment for Learning see p. 94, Example: Assessment for Learning made Easy)

Assessment: an expert view

One of the leading authorities on assessment, and a big influence on us, is Dylan Wiliam. In a 2007 lecture, he made the following comments about assessment:

… we cannot predict what it is that children will learn as a result of our teaching. So we cannot have quality assurance in learning. We have to have quality control. We have to keep on checking on what it is the kids have actually learned, because we cannot predict it. You cannot have perfect teaching ... The important thing is that what gets learned as a result of a particular sequence of instruction activities is impossible to predict, but student errors are not random. Those are the two most important insights in twentieth-century psychology.[17]

This deceptively simple insight should have a massive impact on our classrooms. If errors are not random and based on a level of reasoning – however basic – then as teachers we need to structure assessment so that it gets to grips with this. The key is creating good questions.

Good questions are ones designed to check different levels of student understanding, so that as a teacher you can alter your teaching to respond to the results. Below is a physics example given by Dylan Wiliam:

The ball sitting on the table is not moving. It is not moving because:

(a) No forces are pushing or pulling on the ball.
(b) Gravity is pulling down, but the table is in the way.
(c) The table pushes up with the same force that gravity pulls down.
(d) Gravity is holding it onto the table.
(e) There is a force inside the ball keeping it from rolling off the table.

This question does a number of things: it provides a number of plausible alternatives (there are no essentially 'wrong' answers); it challenges students to think carefully about a key concept; it holds within it different levels of understanding. Williams calls these 'hinge' questions, because they test understanding of a core concept within a course.

Theory into practice
Applying this to exam groups and assessment at KS4 and 5 is easy and powerful. You can develop questions that match up to the levels in your mark-scheme. For example, here is a question we devised about a key concept in a history module 'The American West':

Why did ranching change on the plains?

(a) Changes to profits meant there was a decline of cattle drives and open ranges.

(b) Demand for beef led to conflict over land and conflict helped in the decline.

(c) The blizzards killed cattle. Demand for beef fell.

(d) Railroads and longhorn cattle made it easier to set up ranches.

Neal trialled this with two Year 10 groups after they had been involved in teaching each other lessons on ranchers. The ideas was to test levels of understanding and try to see what kind of score they might get in an exam, if they were to take it right now. The results were really surprising. There was a significant match between the prior attainment data of students and the answers they selected. Option c was based on a Level 1 history response (simple statements) and was chosen by four students in our sample of 50. Interestingly, these students had the lowest prior attainment scores across the two groups. Option a was based on a Level 4 response (sustained argument) and was the most popular choice, with 27 votes. This suggests that around half of each understood the complexities of this key concept. The really powerful part of the process is that you get to assess an entire class (and their levels of understanding) really quickly. There is nowhere to hide and students have to get involved.

After the 'hinge' question, the next step was to develop a strategy about what to do next. It was clear that the next lesson needed to be thought about carefully and activities tailored to move students on. I devised four activities based around the same topic. For example, students who selected option C were given an activity to move them on to Level 2 (in this case a card-sorting exercise that developed into a display piece, focusing on the use of connectives like 'because').

This follow-up activity is absolutely essential if we are going to get our students to prepare fully for the exams. The following chart about effective feedback in higher education illustrates why it is so vital.

Effect of formative assessment (HE)

Table 3.1 Revised values

	Number	Effect
Weaker feedback only (giving results)	31	0.14
Feedback only (giving results and correct answers)	48	0.36
Weaker formative assessment (some explanation given)	49	0.26
Moderate formative assessment (specific actions given to close the gap)	41	0.39
Strong formative assessment (comment and activity to close the gap)	16	0.56

Source: Based on Nyquist

Nyquist, along with several other leading experts in the field, concluded that the most effective form of feedback is giving speedy response in the form of an activity to move students forward. This may well be good practice and going on in many classrooms across the country, but it is worth a reminder – especially when the students in question are sitting external exams. This approach of next-steps activities linked to exam-board levels is a powerful model for improvement. So, in summary, an assessment sequence might look something like the model below:

Table 3.2 Assessment sequence

Step 1:	Step 2:	Step 3:	Step 4:
Create a learning experience based around a key concept.	Review understanding by giving the whole class a 'hinge' question where there are no wrong answers and choices are set against exam criteria. Record student answers.	Follow up the assessment with a set of activities designed to move students to the next level (e.g. from Level 2 to Level 3 of the exam-board mark-scheme).	Ask another 'hinge' question that will tell you if students are moving on.

Well-thought-out formal assessment

The idea of next-step activities can be applied to more formal exam practice as well. Using mark-schemes and model answers with students has become standard practice in schools, but it can leave students cold and far from engaged. Looking at the 'learning journey' students go through when completing an assessment can yield some powerful changes to the process. You need to observe where your students are hitting difficulties and why. With this information you can devise a better process that fully supports students and gets them closer to quality exam answers.

Case-study: One small step

Recently we talked to an experienced teacher called Rob, who had changed the way that he did assessment at GCSE. After attending one of our INSET sessions, he looked at how he constructed assessment pieces and made a significant addition: a thinking-skills activity. He told us that there was too much of a mental leap for his students to make with assessments. He was giving out stimulus material, mark-schemes and the questions, but students were still complaining that they did not know where to begin. At first, he answered them with that great teacher cliché 'Sit and think about it for a while', but he then decided to support this class with an activity. He now adds a concept map, 'Odd One Out', or sorting activity to all assessments. He gives the class the question and material, goes through the mark-scheme and then gives students 20 minutes to complete the thinking-skills task together. After this, the students were ready to launch into the writing and were happier about what needed to be written.

What we liked about Rob's thinking-skills approach is that it recognized a particular need the students had and found a way to address it. Also, it brought an element of fun and engagement into assessment – something seriously lacking in most cases.

Assessment for Learning made easy

Students become very nervous and frightened by the mere term 'assessment'. Although some students will rise to the pressure, a large number may actually underperform because it is deemed an assessment.

(Tom, NQT)

The example below shows how simple Assessment for Learning (AfL) techniques can make students more focused and confident about how to improve. This approach will enable the class to see concrete progress within the lesson as well as across lessons. This is a history example, but can easily be modified for any subject.

Johannes was teaching a mixed-ability Year 10 class about protest through history. This particular lesson investigated the key question: 'What impact did [different protests] ... have on law-making and law-enforcement in England?'[18] Some of the protests included Poll Tax riots and Conscientious Objection during the Second World War.

Assessment for Learning: history example

Starter

First, students assessed the severity of some protests using an *active protest continuum*.[19] After discussing the outcome of the task, the class moved straight to the assessment task which involved analysing a range of historical sources. The students first discussed the source material together as a class, and then explored what they needed to do to answer the question successfully. Students annotated the sources in pairs, after which an exemplar answer was given to them.

Task 1: Speed AfL

Students faced each other in pairs, and were told to mark the exemplar answer using the criteria/mark-scheme. The first to find one of the top levels would win. We then discussed students' responses and they highlighted where the 'exemplar student' had achieved a certain level on the interactive whiteboard. There were some disagreements about how the answer moved up the levels.

cont. →

Task 2: Towards progress

The class now moved to a more challenging question and the skill had also changed. We treated this question in the same manner as the previous one and then compared the differences between the two questions. As a class we then analysed the mark-scheme for question 4 and what they would need to do in order to reach a high level.

Students then answered question 4 on their own and a time limit was set. Students then marked their answers in pairs, using the criteria/mark-scheme. Students discussed how their partners had reached a certain level and what they thought was particularly good about their answer as well as setting them a target for improvement. We then examined an answer, which was quickly scanned for students to see, and comments were made about the strengths and weaknesses of this particular response. Questions were taken in to mark for the next lesson.

At the start of the following lesson the class peer-assessed, using mark-schemes, three responses from grades A–C, starting with grade C. After discussing the answers, assessments were handed back and students were asked to read the teacher's comments and to try to meet their targets – examples of meeting the target were either given by the teacher or the student's answer showed evidence so this area was highlighted.

This way of using assessments is simple, structured and engaging, as students feel they can move forward in that lesson and beyond. When a class has experienced this process they enjoy assessments because they know that improvement will be concrete and real.

Example: using visual assessment

Using active learning techniques benefits students greatly (see introduction to this chapter), and creating opportunities for using this method with assessment really does produce excellent results. Students who work with assessments on this level eventually gain a concrete understanding about

- the various components of an answer
- how to build an ideal solution to a problem/question
- how/where they 'hit' each level
- different versions of an answer to the same question
- exploring links/categorizations, themes and trends.

Build the answer

Type up an answer in your favourite word processor and place each paragraph on a separate page with the size big enough to be able to read from a few metres away. (You could use sentences in the same way, of course.) You could use an ideal answer, but in order to show them how they could improve, we use a C or D grade. Discuss the question with the class and what they think they ought to include in an ideal answer, and note ideas down on the board.

Split the class into groups of three and give them the (laminated) jumbled answer. Now inform them that they are to construct or piece together an answer using the available material. Students place the answer on the floor and move the various components around until they have reached a possible answer. Discuss students' ideas and, this is crucial, ask them what they could do to improve the answer. Allow them a few minutes to return to their answer and give them some sheets of paper for details. Finally, get one group to show the rest of the class their example, and discuss it.

An alternative to the example above is to involve the whole class (depending on size — a maximum of 20 works well). 'Extras' can play examiners. Give some a piece of the answer (about 12–15 students need to be involved here), and give others possible headings or factor/theme cards (4–5 students) and another group GCSE-level or A-level criteria cards. Get them to construct the answer together as a group. This generally creates a lot of discussion and it might be easier if the teacher leads this together with the students. When the answer has been laid out on the floor, or ask the 'factors/heading' students to decide which factor is discussed in which paragraph. The final step is for the last group to level the piece.

It is important at this stage to ensure that the class is familiar with peer-marking and comfortable with GCSE-level or A-level criteria. Get them to decide as a group where each level ought to be placed. When they have completed their marking ask them to justify their decisions and then get feedback from the rest of the class. Some students may disagree with the judgements of the marking group, so allow the changes to be made if necessary.

Review

Example: Pecha-Kucha – using images to review a whole topic

Making students see the bigger picture is difficult but crucial. Using overviews early in the course, say, when you introduce a new topic or unit is an ideal way of getting them thinking about the 'story' of what you're doing. Revisiting these overviews is also important so students can see where they are heading, particularly if you are teaching a thematic or synoptic approach. For example, how will students grasp why peasants during the period 1855–1956 link with the Russian 'empire' or 'nationalities'? Overviews are also useful in individual topics such as electricity in chemistry, marketing in business studies or human relationships in religious studies.

We work hard at creating activities that make overviews matter to students, getting them thinking about how the smaller picture fits in with the bigger picture. Here's an example of encouraging them to consider just that.

Pecha-Kucha, or 'chatter' is a method of presenting using visuals, which was first introduced in 2003 by two Australian architects who sought to keep presentations tight and focused.

The rules are simple:

◆ Create a PowerPoint presentation, or using Keynote, with 20 images lasting for 20 seconds, as you tell the story in sync with the pictures – it must be timed.
◆ Your presentation will only last for exactly *six minutes and 40 seconds*. Slides will play automatically (panic!) so when the last slide has been shown it's all over ... Nice and simple!

Give the students a good topic or theme which requires them to think about the bigger picture. They then have to use 20 images which demonstrate their understanding. Of course, it is easy to adapt the number of slides and reduce the time for the whole presentation. For a first attempt with students we recommend five or six slides for 20 seconds each.

Pecha-Kucha is an excellent way of making it difficult for students to 'go deep' in their presentations – they will have to do that during their research. Also, the audience will have to 'dig deep' by asking challenging questions in order for them to see the bigger picture. The whole class will therefore improve their skills.

> **Pecha-Kucha about:**
>
> The importance of the 'beast' in *Lord of the Flies*?

> **Pecha-Kucha about:**
>
> How desertification can be reduced.

> **Pecha-Kucha about:**
>
> Energy for the home.

> **Pecha-Kucha about:**
>
> The Romantic period 1810–1910 in music

The limitations imposed on them will enable them to focus on:

- evaluating the theme
- selecting and ranking which elements are most significant to the question
- demonstrating clear judgement on broad questions
- communicating their own understanding to their peers.

It takes practice to do Pecha-Kucha well, but once an exam group has had the opportunity to do a presentation, both they and you will discover what a great challenge it can be. If you plan to do Pecha-Kucha, you might wish to provide students with a collection of images from which they have to select the most suitable ones for their presentation. This will not only save time, especially as some students spend hours searching for images, but it also requires them to be selective and to consider carefully which images are the most suitable or most conducive to their work.

Case-study: Using comic strips to make geography case-studies 'stick' (Tom Stafford, geography teacher)

GCSE and A-level geography require students to look at numerous case-studies. There is a real need within the subject to make these more engaging and appealing. In the past I have done this by a variety of means, including podcasting, webpages, role-plays, decision-making exercises and using Microsoft Movie Maker.

This particular lesson was used with a GCSE class for a unit on Water. Students were required to give an example of how human influence has affected a water supply. The lesson focused on the issue of pollution and the environmental degradation of the Aral Sea. The class had spent a previous lesson solving the mystery of 'What happened to the Aral Sea?', so entered the classroom with sound prior knowledge of the causes, effects and responses. This activity was used to review knowledge and understanding of the case-study's key components.

The object of the lesson was for students to design a comic strip to illustrate the story of the pollution and destruction of the Aral Sea. This was done using an online comic-strip generator (www.pixton.com). The website enables learners to create a comic without actually having to draw – a task students often find problematic. Pixton also allows a teacher to create the opening scenes of a comic strip, and then any number of users can add their own slides to conclude the story. Thus the class was directed to the part of the site[20] where the opening sketches of the comic had already been designed. The advantage of this structured approach is that the characters have been created and it gives the students a platform to work from. Students spent the rest of the lesson completing their comic strips.

The value of using comic strips within geography is that it demands that students prioritize the key components of a case-study. This lesson required students to use application and higher-order synthesis by using previous knowledge and understanding to construct a cartoon representation of a case-study.

This approach allows all students to access a case-study through an alternative route. For some students it may just be the method which will allow material to stick. Finished comics can be easily embedded within a website or a virtual learning environment.[21]

The above is a good example of how online tools such as Pixton.com can provide teachers with an opportunity to engage and challenge students, while at the same time ensuring that they progress. These type of websites also allow exam groups to think about audience, purpose, context and argument. There are similar websites available, such as ToonDoo.com. This particular website allows the user to register quickly and then produce high-quality and varied comics in only a few minutes. Although there are very few differences between Pixton.com and ToonDoo.com, the latter offers more in terms of usability, graphics and sleekness. We have used both sites with both GCSE and A-level groups with great results.[22]

Jigsaw and cooperative learning in the classroom

Most *cooperative learning* approaches have one great thing in common: the traditionally passive classroom becomes an active, thinking classroom. One such example which works well with exam groups is *Jigsaw*. Professor Aronson invented the Jigsaw strategy in 1971 'as a matter of absolute necessity to help defuse an explosive situation'[23] and since then this approach has been shown to increase students' self-esteem, confidence and academic improvement both in terms of knowledge and understanding but also in skills such as recollection, comprehension, communication and independent learning. Although cooperative learning activities lend themselves brilliantly to activating classes, they are also great tools for review and overview activities.

1. Divide the class into groups of five to six students. Make sure each group is diverse in terms of gender, ethnicity, race and ability (where applicable). Inform them that this is their 'team' and that by the end of the lesson they will need each other to compete for the glory of the quiz – the lesson plenary.
2. Divide the lesson into five to six topics. For example, if you are investigating human biology then split the topic into (a) Defending against infection (b) Diet and Exercise (c) Drugs and health (d) Hormones (e) The nervous system.
3. Explain that each student needs to learn one topic. Ensure that students have only access to their topics.
4. Allow them time to read their topic at least twice and become familiar with it. They do not need to memorize it.
5. Create provisional 'expert groups' by having one student from each jigsaw group join other students assigned to the same topics. Give students in these expert groups time to discuss the main

points of their topics and to rehearse the presentations they will make to their jigsaw group. This is an important element of the task as they will begin to communicate their understanding of the topic. This is also an opportunity to clarify main issues that they might have forgotten and misunderstood.

6. Students then return to their jigsaw groups.
7. Students present their topic to the rest of the group. Encourage fellow students to ask questions for clarification. Remind them to place handouts (or the resource they used in the expert groups) on the floor or away from them.
8. This is where you have the opportunity to walk around the room to act as facilitator, if needed. Intervene where necessary, for example if one student is dominating the sharing of information.
9. At the end of the lesson, make sure that you test students (e.g. using a quiz) on the material they have used, so that they realize that this activity is not just fun and games but actually works.[24]
10. Try to re-emphasize the key skills of the lesson: active listening, communication and, of course, recollection and comprehension.

Jigsaw mathematics

In this maths example each group member becomes an expert on a different concept or procedure, and they will ultimately teach their concept to the group. Try using this approach when covering factoring of polynomials, where the coefficient of the first term is 1. There are four unique cases. Create base groups of four students, each one counts off from one to four, and then distribute an activity sheet for each case. The activity sheets have five sample polynomials that you have made up for the students to factor, plus a space for each student, to make up five problems. Students create new groups by combining with other students who have been assigned the same case number, again four to a group. They now work together to decide what is unique about their cases. They are, in fact, becoming experts in the case to which they have been allocated.

The final steps involve students developing a teaching strategy to take back to their base groups. They now make up their own problems. Each student practises his or her explanation with the case group.

Jigsaw history

We use cooperative learning with a lot of our classes. It helps to cover content, provides exam groups with a solid overview at the start of a unit, and can also be used to consolidate and review work at the end of a long unit or course. Johannes' A-level group were studying Russian dictatorships 1855–1956, but were finding it difficult to see the bigger picture of the different themes and how they linked together.

The class was divided into five jigsaw groups of five students.[25] Each student was given the instruction to become an expert on a particular 'leader' on the theme of 'Rule and Government'. The 'leaders' were:

1. Alexander II
2. Alexander III
3. Nicholas II
4. Lenin and the Bolshevik Party
5. Stalin
6. Khrushchev.

Students were instructed to read their fact-file twice and were then asked to move into their 'expert' groups. They now shared what they had learnt about their respective leaders and spent about four to five minutes doing so. Students then rejoined their original jigsaw groups and had to present information they had gathered during the lesson. Johannes finally quizzed the class and students were competing in their jigsaw groups. They loved it.

Example: One-Lesson movie – consolidate learning in any subject

This approach works best at the beginning or end of a unit or course and develops the students' ability to:

◆ find links between issues and factors
◆ consider where a particular study 'slots into' a unit
◆ argue their point of view.

Split the class in groups (about four to five students) and give them a set of images that represents a theme within a unit. For example:

History:

Medieval
1. Kingship
2. Hobbies and Sport
3. Transport
4. Jobs and work
5. Buildings
6. Health and medicine

Religious studies:

Prejudice and discrimination
1. Christian
2. Hinduism
3. Islam
4. Judaism
5. Sikhism

Ensure that the images contain a number of contradictions and they cause debate, for example, both women and men are included in the work section, or town, country and castles all appear under buildings in the history example.

Once students have been given their pack of five images, they must think about and then decide which most represent the theme they have. This should generate a lot of discussion with students trying to argue for a favourite image to be included. If discussion is slow within a group, allocate one image to each student and get them to make a case for it to be included.

Once the two images have been chosen, students must write a short commentary to go with their images. This should include what the images reveal about the theme and why they chose them, and should be formally written up into a 20–30 second script.

The communication is slowly built up throughout this activity. Firstly, images are sorted and discussed within small groups. Then, a formal script is created – bringing together the group's ideas. Only at this point is it shared with the wider world. Going straight in with a microphone could be quite daunting for some pupils, but building up the process slowly brings many more students into the task and allows them to make more effective contributions.[26]

Using Movie Maker and a simple microphone, create a movie with the class. Each group sends a representative to the front of the room and they select their images and place them on the timeline (see separate Movie Maker sheets). They then click the 'narrate' button and start to record their commentary. When each group has done this, you will end up with a class movie that can be shown, edited and added to at a later date.

Debrief the learning and as well as looking at the finished movie, ask students about the way their groups functioned and how they completed the task. Ask how they decided on their images and what processes they went through. Try to get them thinking about where else these techniques might be used.

Summary

Assessment is a massive topic that can fill whole books. Here is our attempt to bring it down to five easy steps:

1.   Decide when and what to assess. Focus on skills and try to assess where that skill naturally occurs in the work and not just at the end

of the unit or topic. Whatever you choose, make sure that assessment and feedback are regular.

2. Create a learning experience around a key concept and assess students with a carefully worded question. Remember that it does not have to be followed with a formal written response – keep assessment varied and engaging.

3. Involve students in the process and make assessment simple, clear and constructive. Set clear criteria and make sure they are fully understood by students. If students are involved, make sure that you help them to understand what quality feedback looks like.

4. Remember that assessment should ultimately be about growth rather than grading. Feedback needs to help students take the next step. Student errors are not random, and with careful planning we can use mark-schemes and examples to help them move on.

5. Follow up assessments with an activity that assists students in their quest to move on. Make sure that they have reflection time and can physically see what the next step looks like.

Notes

1. See Chapter 2, pp. 23–6.
2. D. Sousa, *How the Brain Learns* (London: Corwin Press, 2004).
3. Daniel H. Pink, *A Whole New Mind – Why Right-brainers Will Rule the Future* (New York: Riverhead Books, 2008).
4. Parliamentary Select Committee on Education and Skills, Third Report   www.publications.parliament.uk/pa/cm200203/cmselect/cmeduski/153/15303.htm
5. So are A levels getting easier? BBC News Online, Thursday, 16 August 2001, http://news.bbc.co.uk/1/hi/education/1495184.stm
6. BBC News Online Monday, 15 August 2005 http://news.bbc.co.uk/1/hi/education/4153816.stm
7. D. Wiliam, cited in S. Clarke, *Active Learning through Formative Assessment* (London: Hodder Education, 2008).
8. M. Hughes *Closing the Learning Gap* (Stafford: Network Educational Press, 2003).
9. Ibid., p. 53.
10. For more discussion and ideas about learning and retention see Chapter 2, pp. 63–5.
11. D. Sadler, 'Evaluation and Improvement of Academic Learning', *Journal of Higher Education* 54.1 (1983): 60–79.

12. Ibid., p. 61.
13. P. Orsmond, S. Merry, K. Reiling, 'Biology Students' Utilization of Tutors' Formative Feedback:A Qualitative Interview Study', *Assessment and Evaluation in Higher Education* 30.4 (2005): 369–86.
14. A. Mutch, 'Exploring the Practice of Feedback to Students', *Active Learning in Higher Education* 4.1 (2003): 24–38.
15. D. Nicol and D. Macfarlane-Dick, 'Formative Assessment and Self-Regulated Learning: A Model and Seven Principles of Good Feedback Practice', *Studies in Higher Education* 31.2 (2006): 199–218.
16. S. Pitts, '"Testing,Testing …" How Do Students Use Written Feedback?', *Active Learning in Higher Education* 6.3 (2005): 218–29.
17. Dylan Wiliam, Association for Learning Conference, Nottingham, September 2007.
18. Lesson plan and resources can be downloaded from www.
19. staffroomproject.com/?q = resources.html, scroll down to Chapter 3.
20. See Chapter 2, pp. 74–8 to read more about using active learning techniques with exam groups.
21. See http://pixton.com/uk/comic/wtoxiffs
22. See http://innovativeict.blogspot.com/2009/03/using-comix-strips-in-teaching.html for examples of how Pixton.com has been used in the classroom.
23. See www.innovativeict.net/comics for examples of students' as well as teachers' contributions: www.jigsaw.org/history.htm
24. These steps have been adapted from Elliot Aronson's website: www.jigsaw.org/steps.htm
25. It is easy to cut group numbers by combining two topics/leaders/ concepts as most A-level classes are relatively small. For example, in this activity we actually removed one 'leader', namely the Provisional Government.
26. J. Ahrenfelt and N. Watkin, *Innovate with ICT – Enhancing Learning across the Curriculum* (London: Continuum, 2008).

4 | Revision and exam skills

The pain

Let's take a step back for a minute. You have designed the perfect course with a Big Question and exciting enquiries. You have introduced the unit visually and created some fascinating lessons, using stories and getting students to investigate issues for themselves. You have reviewed the learning at regular intervals and built in quality assessment through 'hinge' questions in plenaries and by targeting core skills through mock exam questions. How could this fail to get your students the top grades?

Actually, there are still two important elements that we need to go through with our students to get them through exams. These are revision and exam skills. These are problematic for many reasons, which we will discuss one at a time.

Revision is the perennial problem. We know that students need to do it and they need to start early. Also, we know that most students are bad at it. The problem is compounded by study leave, when you have no control over what students do. There are some really good revision sites out there, the BBC's Bitesize being the most comprehensive, but they only cover part of what needs to be learned – they deal only with the content. This book has consistently pushed the message that content alone is not enough to engage or get students through the exam process. So, that means it is down to the class teacher to ensure that all the areas are covered: skills and content. Also, you might be covering material that students last encountered nearly two years before. They say a week is a long time in politics, two years in the life of a teenager is an epoch. Revision is hard. It is hard for the students and it is hard for the teacher to make exciting. How do you make something exciting when you have already done it once? How do you offer something new and exciting that at the same time reinforces the key content and the core skills? Hopefully, this chapter will have some of the answers.

Exam skills are difficult to cater for. As subject leaders, we have seen a rise in the number of students who are opting out of papers when they hit a barrier. This is a serious problem. You can equip students with lots of skills and knowledge to tackle different styles of question, but if they won't even read it, then what can you do? Luckily, most students will try their best to answer the questions in front of them, but how do you ensure that they make the most of their time and don't forget everything they have learned? How can you help them to prepare and keep calm under the pressure of a lengthy exam? There are answers to these points and we will explore them later.

The Big Idea: let them hear the 'symphony'

Just as we did with thinking and overviews, the best way to deal with revision and exam skills is to teach them explicitly and make them visible. In the classroom you can see more moments of epiphany when the task or skill has been visualized than through the spoken word or reading. Preparation for the final examination is no different. Students need to be able to see – on a piece of paper, right in front of them – how revision works, and how to prepare themselves with essential exam skills.

Students need to see past all the 'stuff' they have to learn and concentrate on the whole. It is, as Daniel Pink calls it, the skill of symphony:

> Symphony, as I call this aptitude, is the ability to put together the pieces. It is the capacity to synthesize rather than analyze; to see the relationships between seemingly unrelated fields; to detect broad patterns rather than to deliver specific answers ... Symphonic thinking is a signature ability of composers and conductors, whose jobs involve corralling a diverse group of notes, instruments and performers and producing a unified and pleasing sound. Entrepreneurs and inventors have long relied on this ability. But today Symphony is becoming an essential aptitude for a much wider swathe of the population.[1]

This requires a whole new set of skills from the one needed to answer the exam questions successfully, and this is what makes it important. It is vital to know what to do with the questions in the exam, but it won't matter what you do, if you cannot manage the revision and find a route through the paper. Therefore you have to help students understand the importance of these two elements in their preparation.

Emotional intelligence guru Daniel Goleman writes:

> People tend to differ in the general degree to which they have hope ... Some typically think of themselves as able to get out of a jam or find ways to solve problems, while others simply do not see themselves as having the energy, ability, or means to accomplish their goals. People with high levels of hope ... share certain traits, among them being able to motivate themselves, feeling resourceful enough to find ways to accomplish their objectives, reassuring themselves when in a tight spot that things will get better, being flexible enough to find different ways to get to their goals ... and having the sense to break down a formidable task into smaller, manageable pieces.[2]

Here is the nature of the task: we have to teach students to be resilient and resourceful, to think for themselves and keep that big picture in their minds. Nothing to worry about then (this is us being hopeful!) ...

Make revision stick

Good revision should ensure that students remember essential facts, feel confident about the structure of an ideal answer, grasp how issues link together in a 'bigger picture' and understand relationships between factors, events, individuals, values, and so on. It is our job to see that all of these elements are achieved. What makes all of these elements of learning stick? If we have thought carefully about what we want them to learn, made our aims/objectives clear, revisited sections regularly so that classes gain insight into wider issues surrounding our subjects and started to think critically and creatively about how we do this (as discussed in Chapter 1) then students will benefit and their own revision will become easier and more purposeful.

Excellent revision requires thorough planning and engaging ideas. We have extensive experience in working with exam groups and have achieved excellent results in both KS4 and KS5 for many years. We would like to share our ideas about revision in this section, both for GCSE and A-level students.

Many students, even at the end of their studies, can still be ill-equipped with study skills, so it is essential that we provide them with a basic framework from which to work. A good starting-point is to provide them with student versions of the syllabus, a sort of 'annotated tick-list'[3] where they can go through the entire course and tick off the sections they feel they need to revise further. The second step is to give them a range of overview activities so they can revisit and review the bigger picture and map out ideas about each segment, keeping in mind the overview (see the history example Crime and Punishment, where we have mapped out key points in their learning). The third step is to use active learning techniques of various kinds[4] to make the learners see how issues, concepts and factors link together as a group. The final method we use regularly is the group-mapping and four-way mapping. These two activities get students collaborating on a common topic and building up their ideas and revision notes as a group.

In summary:

Step 1: The annotated tick-list
Step 2: Overview
Step 3: Active learning techniques
Step 4: Collaborative mapping.

Make recollection interesting: flash-cards with a difference

Let's face it: students also have to remember stuff. One way of encouraging them to work hard at remembering facts, is to introduce a competitive element to their revision.

Flash-cards have been around for a while: you read out a key word/concept/fact and see what you remember. Hopefully the following ideas of using flash-cards will make them more exciting.

1: Post-It!

Students place the flash-cards on their foreheads without looking at them before (this is crucial!). In pairs, students ask the other person yes and no questions which guide them to the item on their foreheads. For example, 'Treaty of Versailles' might appear on the card, so the student has to ask questions such as 'Did this event happen during the First World War?', 'Did it involve several countries?', etc. When the student finally figures out which word is on her forehead she has to recall as much as she can about that particular topic. Students love this game.

2: Tick each other off

Create a set of straightforward flash-cards, but add a blank box next to each key fact:[5]

Question/Key Word:

Munich Putsch

Answers:

- ☐ 1923 Beer Hall Putsch.
- ☐ Hitler's attempt to exploit the crisis of 1923.
- ☐ Hitler firmly believed in passive resistance as it fought against the conditions of the Treaty of Versailles – reparations.
- ☐ March on Munich (like Mussolini's march on Rome).

Causes:
- ☐ (a) Weimar weaknesses: the failing economy, previous uprisings and the fact that many people now hated the government enabled the Putsch to happen.
- ☐ (b) The Nazi Party was growing from 6,000 to 55,000.
- ☐ (c) Hitler hoped that the Munich Putsch would force others to rebel.

Results:
- ☐ Blocked by armed police and soldiers – 16 Nazis and three policemen were killed.
- ☐ Army never helped Hitler – stayed loyal to government.
- ☐ Hitler realized: ballot v. bullet.
- ☐ Showed that the extreme right had become organized.
- ☐ Trial turned Hitler into a national hero, and laid the foundation of his future success.

Explain that they will work with a 'study-buddy' who will tick off each piece of information they get correct. The study-buddy is allowed to give them five hints during the whole flash-card activity. Students then swap and do the same thing again for the other person. When the cycle is complete students compare and see who got the most ticks! This activity can lead to some bickering about certain answers, particularly when they have done this revision technique a few times – nobody likes to lose!

Case-study: Voluntary extra lessons (Terry Haydn, Senior Reader in Education at the University of East Anglia)

I taught in an inner-city comprehensive where many of the pupils were not particularly driven or scholarly.

Initially I offered one lesson in the middle of the pre-exam holiday to my A-level pupils, partly because I thought it would be good for morale, and partly as I thought it would nudge them into working together with each other to revise outside the session. Nearly all of them turned up and there was a good mood to the session, and they appreciated that I had given up a bit of my spare time.

This led me to experiment with offering an 'early start' lesson to my GCSE group on the morning of the exam. It was open to anyone who wanted to come, whether they were in my set or not. 'Voluntary: come whenever you want any time after 7.45 a.m.' (exams all started at 9.30 a.m.).The idea was that I would just run through some things for an hour and a half or so, in the hope that if we had gone through it just before the exam, they would probably remember it.

I was surprised how may pupils turned up. Even pupils who had been fairly regular truants came (although not necessarily at 7.45 a.m. I don't know what difference it made in terms of their grades. I guess that in some cases it might have just made a grade difference. But it did seem to make a difference to many pupils' attitudes. I am aware that teachers' holidays are precious, but of all the things I ever did (I used to take teams, run clubs, etc.), this was probably the thing that I got most out of in terms of return on time invested.

'Email bursts' (simple and effective)

It can be difficult to motivate students to revise before exams so getting them to practise exam skills at home might be an even greater challenge. But if we give them more bite-sized portions to work on at regular intervals, say 15 minutes, then it seems achievable without being too taxing for them.

Once such way is to put a class, or a series of classes, on a 'group list' in your email client. Then email students tasks or activities lasting about 15 minutes. If you want to ensure that your workload does not increase then using 'flash-card' activities where students get the correct or ideal answer could be a solution. Assessment for Learning is also a tremendous tool for these shorter tasks. Try sending them a question with some guidelines, and a peer mark-sheet for them to tackle first. Then, when they have completed the question, send them an 'ideal' answer so that they can compare their answers.

Feedback from our students on this idea was good, and the vast majority signed up for the 'email bursts'. Some students liked the idea that doing these mini-tasks meant that they were doing something extra, whereas other students felt that they were doing some work before the exam which they might not have done otherwise. Also, many thought that teachers had provided them with a more personalized approach to their studies with consideration of their academic needs. It really does not take long to discuss the various groups together as a department and then get individual teachers specializing on a particular need, e.g. moving between levels 3–4, A* or Gifted and Talented, or a certain skill or section of your exam.

The key to a successful email campaign is for it to be regular and consistent right up until the exam. What do students wish to focus on? What do they feel are their weaknesses? Starting with a quick review/questionnaire will provide you with a clear idea of the sort of skills and activities appropriate for the emails.

Four-way mapping

In groups of four, students get an A3 sheet (or sugar paper) with the key questions or topic they are about to study in the middle. They will then take a corner of the sheet each and spend two to three minutes noting down their thoughts on this particular topic or question. By allowing them to think on their own and then engage with their group you give them space; most students find this way of mapping calming as they have something to fall back on once the discussion begins. After two to three minutes, students share their ideas with the rest of the group, and common trends and thoughts are added to the middle of the sheet around the key word/questions.

Case-study: Collaborative mapping in modern foreign languages (Jo Baldwin, modern foreign languages department)

I wanted to get a rather reserved Year 11 class to communicate with each other as well as work together to produce a revision package which they could all use later on. The exercise was straightforward and the outcome proved very successful.

I organized the room into several stations and each one had a flipchart paper blutacked to the wall with an image in the middle of one of the GCSE topics that they had studied:
I used the following exam-board topics:

Travel and tourism
Health and fitness
Leisure and free time
Education.

The class was split into five groups with five students in each. The aim of the task was for students to find synonyms as well as associated words and phrases from each of the main topics. This is a key skill in the language GCSE listening and reading paper.

Step 1: Each group sat down by one of the stations and had 60 seconds to map as many things they could spot in the image, without adding any associations or synonyms. These notes were added by the image.
Step 2: Groups were given two minutes to map as many words and phrases they knew about the topic on the flipchart. These notes were written anywhere on the flipchart paper and in a different colour.
Step 3: Groups now shifted between each station spending a maximum of 45 seconds on each topic. This was done until all groups had been to every station once.

cont. →

The class found this way of working to be a very creative process as they first had the opportunity to 'wake up' their brains with the initial mapping task before having to think quickly about the issues surrounding the topic. When they visited other stations they had first to spend a few seconds reading what other students had come up with and then map their own ideas.

Students always like this activity as it gives them the opportunity to practise what they have learnt, challenge themselves and gain new ideas, words and phrases from their fellow classmates. What is particularly good about this task is the fact that you can display students' work around the room and use their posters as revision.

Exam skills

Start with a real brainstorm

We know what you are thinking: brainstorming is old — so old that people have started to come up with names like 'mind showers' and 'thought-drops' to make it sound more exciting. Despite these feeble attempts to breathe new life into the technique, we would like to show you a better brainstorm — how it was originally intended to be carried out. It is worth trying this, because it parallels the techniques needed to do well in an exam.[6]

1. Divide the class into groups of four and get them around a common space (e.g. a square of tables or on the floor).
2. Provide them with a big piece of paper and a range of writing materials. Now give out very general topics connected with the part of the course you are about to revise and practise their exam skills.
3. Allow each group four minutes silently to brainstorm everything they can remember about that topic (associated words or phrases are allowed). Encourage students to use images as well as text, but stress the importance of remaining silent and getting down as many ideas as possible. Quantity is definitely the aim — to achieve this, you could get students to number their ideas and have a competition to see who can think of the most.

4. When the four minutes are up, each person in the group takes it in turn to guide the others through their thoughts. At this stage there are no bad ideas and everyone should listen carefully to what is being said without interrupting. When the person talking has finished, others can ask questions, as long as they don't make negative comments about ideas.

5. Next, give students a focused exam question based on their ideas. Ask them to write down all the relevant points from their big sheet on to Post-It notes.

6. Stick the Post-It notes on a wall and start, as a group, to plan an essay.

7. Present the essay plan to the rest of the group. The same listening rules apply as in the group stage.

What we like about this approach is that it allows people to contribute before they collaborate. Each group member can potentially come up with a valid point.

In terms of exam skills, this activity is good for helping with recall and also assists students to develop their selection of relevant information. If they are faced with a large array of information in the exam, or are stuck about what to write, this technique can help.

Preparing students mentally for the exam

We have become more and more aware of the needs of a certain group of students. Up until now we have concentrated on exam technique as a way of preparing students with an arsenal for tackling the exam. The rest of this section will give you plenty of ideas about how this can be done and why it is so vital. However, in 2007 we taught a group of students who could, by the end of May, quote every technique back without a moment's hesitation – they understood the need to create multi-part answers and to explain fully; they knew that not all the content required was visible in the question (see the section 'watch out for icebergs', p. 119) and how to cope with this. And yet they still underperformed to a significant degree in their mock exams.

After careful analysis of the papers we discovered a worrying trend. Several students had attempted the first couple of questions and no more, or had not even put pen to paper. Some might put this down to a lack of revision and the apathy that mock exams can create. But we strongly believe that there are deeper issues involved.

After student-voice sessions with those students affected we came to realize that they were missing one crucial technique: they did not know how to think their way through an exam. They knew how to tackle individual questions, but not how to solve issues as they arose. Faced with this seemingly insurmountable problem, they simply gave up and did nothing more. Just as Daniel Goleman said, those without hope tend to lack the resources to find a route through.

We ran a series of sessions for these students to help them to learn to cope with the exam situation. We took them out of normal lessons and tried to show them how they could make the most of the situation if they came across a few questions that they could not answer. The two-hour session was broken into four parts; these went as follows:

◆ *Word trees*: Students start with a key word in the question and think of two words that are associated with it. Each of those words is then taken on and two new words are made from them. This continues until they have run out of words. The purpose of this is to show students that a little bit of thinking can give them a whole vocabulary to use.

◆ *TASC wheel*: This is an eight-part process designed to help students work through issues. Although it is meant for group activity, we felt it had an impact as students were able to attach their situation to a programme and work through it. We got students to look at this in relation to sitting an exam paper and getting stuck. Below are the stages in the TASC wheel and what we got students to think about and act upon.

  – *What do I know about this?* (Students put down any prior knowledge, supported by Five W-questions plus a How sheet.)
  – *What is the task?* (Students analyse the question and write down what kind of answer the examiner is expecting, e.g. 'This starts with "Why" so that means you need to explain and use factors'.)
  – *How many ideas can I think of?* (Students try to fit their knowledge into categories, using some of the techniques for language, like the word-tree.)
  – *Which is the best idea?* (They decide on a plan and jot it down.)
  – *Let's do it!* (They transfer the plan to the top of the answer booklet and make sure that it will answer the question.)
  – *How well did I do?* (Using self-assessment, they judge how good they think the answer will be and then make any last-minute changes.)
  – *Let's tell someone!* (Students write their responses and develop an answer.)

  – *What have I learned?* (Students reflect immediately on the process and then move on to the next question.).

◆ *Three-panel vision*: We gave each student three pieces of paper and got them to condense content, techniques and problem-solving skills, so that they each occupied a piece. We then placed the panels in front of them so they were staring straight at them, and got them to memorize the panels. They then helped test each other. We then took them to the exam hall and asked them to visualize the panels. This produced a great response in students.

◆ *Question walks*: For this game we prepared a set of questions about one topic and put the answers on the back. Students were given one each and had to walk around the room asking the question of others. They had to listen to the reply and give them the right answer. This continued until all students felt that they were visiting people and getting all the answers right. We tested their knowledge and saw their confidence rise. We then showed them how to take a topic and reduce it down to manageable levels before trying to learn it.

These techniques gave them more confidence and the ability to sit an exam. They resat the paper and we saw a marked improvement in their results – something close to their target grades. Above all, participation levels were up and students were starting to see that they could achieve something in the exam.

Students in charge of exam preparation

A good way to involve students in their own exam preparation is to get them to create resources, such as revision notes, which they can share with others online. Students enjoy taking responsibility for their own learning, and giving them the opportunity to discuss, write and share what they know about exams and revision is always appreciated as it shows them that we trust their judgement about the subject or topic.

Students can create their own movies, which they then upload to Vimeo.com or Youtube.com. For example their movies could be about

◆ how to write the perfect answer to a cross-referencing question for a history Paper 2
◆ what to think about when preparing for a GCSE oral exam
◆ the most effective way to read a text and take notes.

If you don't want to go down the geeky route, then try getting students to make their own exam papers. Give them the number of questions that need to be included and the marks that need to be given (we prefer to print these elements out for them so that they are fixed) and some old exam papers. Then split the class into groups and give each one a different topic area to look at. You can take this activity as far as you like: for example, getting students to produce resources to go with their questions and even mark-schemes. They can swap papers and try to answer them, critiquing the quality as they go. We have found that any work connected to creating questions has a positive effect on motivation and increases the ability of students to answer them successfully.

Case-study: Visualizing answers in English

The problem with many exam skills is that they are difficult to 'see'. Students know that they need to adapt what they are saying to suit particular answers, but they cannot visualize exactly what this looks like.

Katy, an English Advanced Skills Teacher, has been working with her exam classes to turn explanations of various concepts into visual images. The process is simple: students have to make a representation using toys or paper creations to explain a language concept. The result is that creating explanations (a key exam skill in English) is turned into a physical act and one that is highly memorable.

This approach works for any subject. We have seen the same approach used in science to explain key concepts and we use it in history to show change over time (before and after shots). It is like drawing a cartoon strip, but the physical element of creating the characters and taking the photos works better, because it gets students collaborating and is more engaging.

A variation on this approach is to create puppet shows. Here the action is live and the scenery can take on real significance: it can explain context or importance.

Watch out for icebergs

In an exam there will be different types of questions that require a specific response. We have just completed a range of templates for history students that take these question types and provide a visual

Figure 4.1 Photos of student explanation

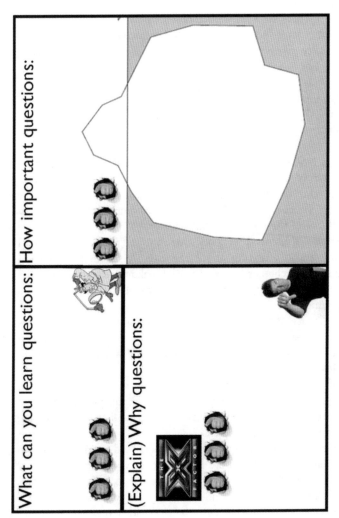

Figure 4.2 Questions

framework to prompt students (see the image on p. 121 for some examples). This maybe something as simple as showing a pointing finger to symbolize how many points need to be made in an answer to score well, or something more complex.

Below is a strategy we first saw being used by a humanities adviser, Dale Banham. There are a substantial number of questions that require a large amount of knowledge not mentioned in the question. This type of question usually involves a degree of evaluation or a judgement needs to be made. For example:

> How important was ...?
> How far ...?
> Is it fair to say that ...?

One way of tackling this type of question is to use the analogy of an iceberg. One of an iceberg's main features is that most of it is underwater and therefore not seen. For our purposes – and we apologize to the geographers for a gross over-simplification – we say that two-thirds of the iceberg is under water.

This shows students that only one-third of the potential total marks goes towards writing about the issue raised in the question (check your mark-schemes for exact mark breakdowns). The rest of the marks come from supplying other information that provides a counterargument.

Drawing an iceberg outline and using it to plan means that students become familiar with the process and start to use it. They can put key points about the topic in the question above the water-line and other points below.

One of our favourite sounds during revision is the unprompted voice saying, 'Is this an iceberg question, Sir?' At this point, you know that exam technique is starting to get through and that students are really starting to get somewhere.

You need to look closely at past papers and mark-schemes to discover what question types are most used in your subject area and what skills are needed. For example, we looked at a business studies GCSE specification for edexcel and saw 'inference' was a significant skill in several questions. In this case, you could work on 'inference diagrams' with students (see the example overleaf).

The purpose of this work is to get students as familiar with the style of the exam as possible before they sit it.

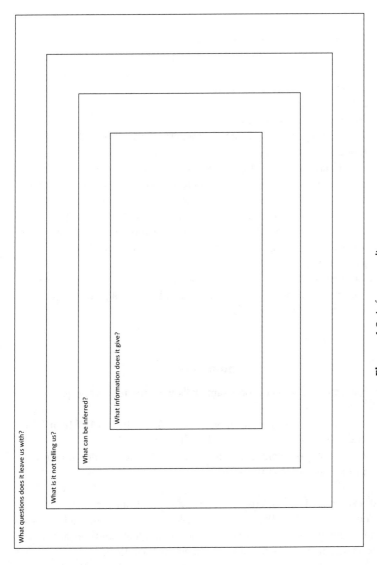

What questions does it leave us with?

What is it not telling us?

What can be inferred?

What information does it give?

Figure 4.3 Inference diagram

The exam: final tips

Below are five pieces of advice that we give to students about how to tackle an exam paper:

1. Read everything once before you start writing. It is better to know what is ahead of you; it will reduce panic if you get to a difficult question if you have already seen it once before. Also, you might get ideas about the difficult topic while you are writing answers to other questions.
2. Read each question three times: (1) for the topic; (2) for the question type; (3) for any parameters placed on the answer. Underline all of these.
3. If you have 'reduced down' your revision (gone from notes, to key phrases, to key words) you should be able to jot down the key words before you write. Allow yourself a few moments to plan.
4. Always have a structure and focus. It is better to write with a goal or argument in mind. However, the structure and length of your answer will change according to the type of question and how many marks it is worth.
5. Try to read through answers at the end of the exam. You might be able to add in some additional comments to clarify your argument and score a few extra marks.

Summary

We started our discussion on exam skills with the following questions:

◆   How do you ensure that your students make the most of their time and don't forget everything they have learned?
◆   How can you help them to prepare and keep calm under the pressure of a lengthy exam?

The examples in this chapter work on the principle that getting students to visualize their learning makes it more memorable. Also, good technique for the paper and each individual question are vital. This should help them to make the most of their time.

Showing students how to think through a paper is essential. You can model this with problem-solving techniques such as brainstorming and using the TASC wheel. Try the techniques above for getting students to think about how to tackle challenging questions.

Above all, give them hope. We talked to a head of sixth form called Esther: she believes that the single most important factor in improving results is the human touch. She commented, 'If students like their teacher and get on with them, then they will work for them and want to do well for them. It is a shame not all teachers realize this.' Good teachers will make students feel ready to succeed with a mixture of clever learning and praise, but also with warmth and humour.

Now, bring on the exams!

Notes

1. Daniel Pink, *A Whole New Mind: Why Right-Brainers Will Rule the Future* (London: Marshall Cavendish, 2008), p. 130.
2. Daniel Goleman, *Emotional Intelligence: Why it Matters More than IQ* (London: Bloomsbury, 1996), p. 84.
3. Download the example from www.staffroomproject.com/?q = resources.html
4. See Chapter 3, pp. 107–18, for activities that will help revision.
5. See: www.staffroomproject.com/?q = resources.html, for examples of flash-cards.
6. We would like to thank Deb Khan, who works with companies on creativity, for introducing us to this technique. We now use it all the time in our teaching and the impact is tremendous. See Deb's blog 'Creative Inspiration', at http://debkhan.typepad.com

Bibliography

Books

Ahrenfelt, J. and Watkin, N., *Innovate with ICT: Enhancing Learning across the Curriculum* (London: Continuum, 2008).

Banksy, *Wall and Piece* (London: Century, 2006).

Bruner, J., *The Process of Education* (Cambridge, MA: Harvard University Press, 1977).

Clarke, J., *Active Learning through Formative Assessment* (London: Hodder Education, 2008).

Frankl, V., *A Man's Search for Meaning* (London: Beacon Press, 2000).

Freire, P., *The Politics of Education* (New York: Bergin & Garvey, 1985).

Goleman, D., *Emotional Intelligence – Why it can Matter More than IQ* (London: Bantam, 1995).

Haydn, T. and Counsell, C., *History, ICT and Learning* (London: Routledge, 2004).

Heath, C. and Heath, D., *Made to Stick* (London: Arrow Books, 2008).

Hughes, M. *Closing the Learning Gap* (Stafford: Network Educational Press, 2003).

Kelley, T., *The Ten Faces of Innovation: Strategies for Heightening Creativity* (London: Profile Books, 2008).

Kolb, D., *Experiential Learning: Experience as the Source of Learning and Development* (London: Financial Times, 1984).

Leadbeater, C., *We –Think* (London: Profile Books, 2008).

Norman, D., *Things that Make us Smart* (New York: Perseus Books, 1994).

Pink, D., *A Whole New Mind – Why Right-brainers Will Rule the Future* (New York: Riverhead Books, 2008).

Rogers, C., *Freedom to Learn* (London: HarperCollins, 1969).

Souza, D., *How the Brain Learns* (London: Corwin Press, 2004).

Turner, M., *The Literary Mind: The Origins of Thought and Language* (Oxford: Oxford University Press, 1996).

Watkin, N. and Ahrenfelt, J., *100 Ideas for Essential Teaching Skills* (London: Continuum, 2006).

Journals and online documents

Daley, A., 'Teaching with Technology', White Paper: Podcasting, 6 April 2007, Office of Technology for Education and Eberly Center for Teaching Excellence Carnegie Mellon University.

Harvey, A., 'The Use of Wikipedia in Libraries: Research in an Era of Decentralized Authority', 27th Charleston Conference, 8 November, 2008.

Hattie, J., 'Quality Improvement Agency, Gold Dust Resources', Active Learning Information sheet http://excellence.qia.org.uk/Golddust/ activelearning/activelearning.html

Malan, D.J., 'Podcasting Computer Science E-1', in *Proceedings of the 38th SIGCSE Technical Symposium on Computer Science Education, ACM SIGCSE Bulletin*, 39.1 (March 2007): 389–93.

Moorcroft, C. and Burden, P., *University of Surrey Skills Project Employer Research Report*, University of Surrey, July 1999.

Mutch, A., 'Exploring the Practice of Feedback to Students', *Active Learning in Higher Education*, 4.1 (2003): 24–38.

Nicol, D. and Macfarlane-Dick, D., 'Formative Assessment and Self-Regulated Learning: A Model and Seven Principles of Good Feedback Practice', *Studies in Higher Education*, 31.2 (2006): 199–218.

Orsmond, P., Merry, S., Reiling, K., 'Biology Students' Utilization of Tutors' Formative Feedback: A Qualitative Interview Study', *Assessment and Evaluation in Higher Education*, 30.4 (2005): 369–86.

Parliamentary Select Committee on Education and Skills, Third Report www.publications.parliament.uk/pa/cm200203/cmselect/cmeduski/ 153/15303.htm

Pitts, S., ' "Testing, Testing ..." How Do Students Use Written Feedback?', *Active Learning in Higher Education*, 6.3 (2005): 218–29.

Quality Improvement Agency for Lifelong Learning Teaching and Learning Programme, *Developing the Expert Learner*, 2008.

Ruhl, K.L., Hughes, C.A. and Schloss, P.J., 'Using the Pause Procedure to Enhance Lecture Recall, *Teacher Education and Special Education*, 10 (winter 1987): 14–18.

Sadler, D., 'Evaluation and Improvement of Academic Learning', *Journal of Higher Education*, 54.1 (1983): 60–79.

Wiliam, Dylan, 'Assessment, learning and technology: prospects at the periphery of control', Association for Learning Conference, Nottingham, September 2007.

Websites

www.gtep.co.uk (for TEEP)
www.staffroomproject.com
www.alite.co.uk (for accelerated learning)
www.innovativeict.net
www.geoffpetty.com
http://debkhan.typepad.com
www.specialistschools.org.uk
http://www.uea.ac.uk/%7Em242/historypgce/welcome.htm
www.FirstThings.com
www.nace.co.uk
www.pixton.com
www.jigsaw.org
http://www.educationforum.co.uk/HA/bloom.htm
www.novemberlearning.com
www.universalmccann.com
www.gcast.com
www.garageband.com
http://grant.robinson.name/projects/montage-a-google/

Appendix
Secrétaire grid

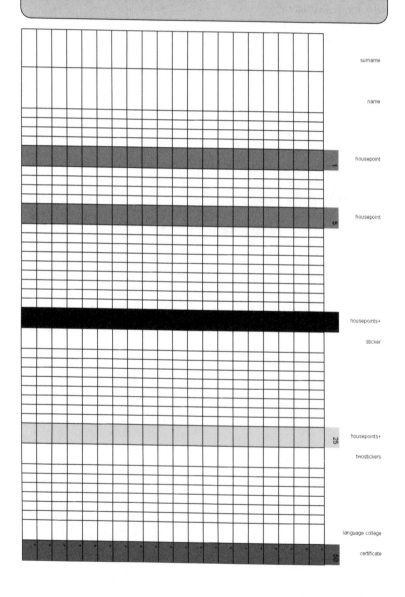

Index

NB: page numbers in italic indicate figures or tables

DAVID HUME
'Sirius of the Scottish Enlightenment'

Philosopher; Historian; Essayist; Extrovert; Executive Chef; *bon viveur*
Friend to: Benjamin Franklin and Adam Smith
Foe to: Autocracy, Oligarchy and religious Bigotry
Francophile: Student in Anjou, Diplomat in Paris
Advocated: Freedom of Trade, Speech and the Press
Supporter of Independence for the Americans
Believer in God, but not in Miracles or Prophecy
Admired by: Einstein, Voltaire and Kant
Citizen of Edinburgh's New Town and Saviour of Princes Street...

In this book you will find David Hume's thought and arguments unaltered – but with his mellifluous prose now attired in 21st century dress. Take him home and, as he suggests, apportion your belief solely to the evidence presented. Above all, follow his lifelong fight with superstition and ignorance – but NB ignore his *hallux aureus*.*

DAVID W PURDIE was born privately in Prestwick and educated publicly at Ayr Academy and Glasgow University. He is a Professor Emeritus of Hull University and is presently an Hon. Fellow of the Institute for Advanced Studies in the Humanities of the University of Edinburgh, where his field is the history and philosophy of the 18th century. David is Editor-in-Chief of *The Burns Encyclopaedia*, which covers the life and work of the poet Robert Burns, and editor of Sir Walter Scott's *Ivanhoe* and *The Heart of Midlothian*, both adapted for the modern reader. He is a former Chairman of the Sir Walter Scott Club. In non-academic mode, he is the co-author of *The Ancyent & Healthfulle Exercyse*, a history of golf, and of *The Dean's Diaries*, an exposé of the goings-on at the (fictional) St Andrew's College in Edinburgh.

PETER S FOSL is Professor of Philosophy at Transylvania University in Lexington, Kentucky, where he chairs the PPE program. Fosl is co-editor of the *Dictionary of Literary Biography* volumes on the history of British

---

* golden big toe!

Philosophy, co-author with Julian Baggini of *The Philosopher's Toolkit* and *Ethics Toolkit*, and he is author of *Hume's Scepticism: Pyrrhonian and Academic* (forthcoming with Edinburgh University Press). Fosl has published numerous articles on the history of philosophy and on popular culture. He was a Fulbright student in Edinburgh and the David Hume Fellow of the University of Edinburgh's Institute for Advanced Studies in the Humanities (IASH) during the 2013–4 academic year.

David Hume on God

Selected Works Newly Adapted
for the Modern Reader

Edited by
DAVID W PURDIE and PETER S FOSL

Luath Press Limited
EDINBURGH
www.luath.co.uk

First published 2019

ISBN: 978-1-913025-49-6

The paper used in this book is recyclable. It is made from low
chlorine pulps produced in a low energy, low emission manner from
renewable forests.

Printed and bound by Bell & Bain Ltd., Glasgow

Typeset in 11 point Sabon by Lapiz

Contents

David Hume: Timeline and Publications

1711   Born in Edinburgh

1721–5   Studies at the University of Edinburgh

1735–7   Studies at Collège La Flèche, Anjou, France

1739–40   *A Treatise of Human Nature* (3 Vols.)

1741–2   *Essays Moral and Political* (2 Vols.)

1745   Fails to gain the Chair of Moral Philosophy, Edinburgh

1745–6   Tutor to Marquis of Annandale

1746–7   Secretary to Gen. James St Clair. Assault on Lorient

1748   Secretary of St Clair's embassy to Vienna and Turin

            An Enquiry Concerning Human Understanding

            A True Account of the Behaviour of Archd. Stewart Esq.

1749–51   At family seat of Ninewells, Scottish Borders

1751   *An Enquiry Concerning the Principles of Morals*

1752–3   Riddle's Land, Lawnmarket, Edinburgh

1752–7   Keeper of the Advocates' Library

1753–62   Resident in Jack's Land, Canongate, Edinburgh

1752   *Political Discourses*

1753   *Essays and Treatises on Several Subjects*. 4 Vols.

1754–62   *The History of Great Britain*: 4 Vols.

1757   *The Natural History of Religion*. In: *Four Dissertations*

1762–71   Resident in James's Court, Lawnmarket. Edinburgh

1763–6   Secretary, then Chargé d'Affaires, British Embassy, Paris

1766   Escorts Jean-Jacques Rousseau to England

1767–8   Under-Secretary of State, Northern Department

1769   Retirement to Edinburgh

1771–6   Resident at St Andrew Sq., New Town, Edinburgh

1776   Death of David Hume

1777   *My Own Life*

1779   *Dialogues Concerning Natural Religion*

1783   *Of Suicide* and *Of the Immortality of the Soul*

Editors' Preface

DAVID HUME was a massive figure of the Enlightenment, both intellectually and physically. This brightest star in that constellation of genius was described in Bertrand Russell's magisterial *History of Western Philosophy* as the greatest philosopher ever to write in the English language.

A true polymath, Hume was also an historian, an essayist on economics and politics, a diplomat and senior civil servant, who often entertained friends and neighbours in Scotland, Paris and London. A jovial host and *chef de cuisine*, he spread the best table and kept the finest wine cellar in Edinburgh's elegant New Town. Here he received guests such as the economist Adam Smith, the jurist Lord Kames and the first American polymath Ben Franklin. They were regaled with wit, anecdote, philosophy and *Soupe à la Reine*, its recipe a present from Hume's French ladyfriend Marie-Charlotte Hyppolyte de Campet de Saujon, Comtesse de Boufflers-Rouverel, no less.

Born in 1711 into a family of minor Border gentry whose estate of Ninewells lay close to the Berwickshire town of Chirnside, Hume was educated privately and then at the University of Edinburgh. Rejecting the law as a profession, he decamped to Paris, Rheims and finally to the Loire valley in Anjou. There, after several years of study at the Collège Royal de La Flèche he published in 1739, still aged only 28, *A Treatise of Human Nature* his first great work of philosophy. This was an attempt to introduce into human affairs the then evolving empirical methods of scientific enquiry pioneered in England by Francis Bacon, John Locke and Isaac Newton.

There followed a series of Essays on moral and political and subjects and then his two great *Enquiries*. The first, *An Enquiry Concerning Human Understanding* (1748) was a revision of Part I of his original *Treatise* while his revision of Part II, *An Enquiry into the Principals of Morals* (1751) was, in his own words, 'of all my works, unquestionably the best.' It was while the latter *Enquiry* was in press that Hume completed drafts of the two books on religion which are at the core of the present work. Hume carried out a major critique of religious theory and practice on two broad fronts and in two major works: first, in the *Natural History of Religion* (1757), he examined the origin of religious beliefs and observances in human societies. In his subsequent *Dialogues Concerning Natural Religion*, published posthumously in 1779, he enquired: do such beliefs and behaviours have a foundation in Reason?

In Section x of his *Enquiry Concerning Human Understanding* (1748) which was entitled *Of Miracles*, Hume had examined the phenomenon of miraculous occurrences, while in Section xi, entitled *Of a Particular Providence and of a Future State*, he addressed the question of the existence of a definable and executive Deity and of an afterlife. In *Four Dissertations* (1757), his *Natural History of Religion* was published alongside three Essays: *On the Passions*, *On Tragedy* and *On the Standard of Taste*. His initial intention had been to publish five essays, including *On Suicide* and *On the Immortality of the Soul*, but when advance copies of this work provoked considerable alarm among his friends as well as his publisher, Andrew Millar, Hume had them removed. An allegation that Hume considered the soul to be mortal, ie to perish at death, had been one of the six 'Remonstrances' mounted by the Kirk, successfully, against his 1745 application for the Chair of Moral Philosophy at the University of Edinburgh.

The central issue of whether religious belief has a logical foundation was addressed by Hume in his *Dialogues concerning Natural Religion* (1779). It takes the form of a report, by an observer, of the dialogue between three fictional discussants examining the question of the existence and, in particular, the nature of a Deity.

Loosely based on Cicero's celebrated *De Natura Deorum* (On the Nature of the Gods), Hume's participants in the *Dialogues* are:

Demea, an orthodox believer who advances arguments *a priori*;
Cleanthes, advocating the 'Argument by Design' ie *a posteriori*;
Philo, a sceptic whose positions are generally close to those of Hume.

Considered too sensitive for publication in his lifetime, the MS was consigned to his literary executor Adam Smith who likewise withheld it from the public. In 1779, some three years after Hume's death it was finally published by his advocate nephew and namesake, later Professor of Scots Law at the University of Edinburgh.

Hume kept his central religious positions to himself. He was no theist, but no atheist either. Most likely he was a mitigated deist, believing as do many scientists today, that some as yet undetermined agency triggered the massive detonation and subsequent inflation of the 'singularity', popularly the Big Bang, which produced the Universe around us.

In 1763, the perceptive Sir James MacDonald of Sleat, Baronet, wrote home from Paris where his friend '*le bon David*' Hume was Secretary to our Embassy, saying,

> poor Hume, who on your side of the water was thought to have too little religion, is here thought to have too much...

As always, Hume was the personification of his own 'just man, who proportions belief to the evidence.' That evidence is set out in this work on all aspects of religious belief and activity. Hume invites you to be just – ie just that!

Introduction

A CENTRAL PROBLEM for the non-specialist reader over the works of Hume today is that his mellifluous 18th century prose appears strange to our eyes and ears in terms of syntax, grammar and punctuation. Sentences can be very long; commas terminate each phrase; sentences often end with the verb, as in German, while main and subordinate clauses jockey with each other for precedence. These difficulties are relatively minor and may be obviated without disturbing in any way the majestic flow of the man's thought and argument. There is, however, a much more serious problem: the very meaning of the words deployed by Hume.

We may be clear on the contemporary 18th century meanings of all Hume's terms through Samuel Johnson's *Dictionary of the English Language* (1755) published two years before *The Natural History of Religion* (NHR) and available through the Advocates Library in Edinburgh of which Hume was the Keeper.

Johnson's title page proclaims the *Dictionary* to be a work:,

In which the WORDS are deduced from their ORIGINALS

    AND

ILLUSTRATED in their DIFFERENT SIGNIFICATIONS

Johnson was unwittingly stating the present problem. Hume's texts illustrate the different significations of words between his day and ours. The lapse of two and a half centuries has brought some dramatic and many subtle changes in the precise meaning of many of Hume's substantives, verbs, adjectives and adverbs. To remain true to his intent, the modern reader's attention requires to be drawn to shifts in meaning *significant* enough (NB the word's own shift) to derail the flow of argument.

Finally, it is clear both from his letters to his London publisher William Strahan and from his repeated revisions to his texts that Hume himself was much concerned with enhancing the lucidity of his work. We have sought to continue that process by the following dual approach.

It is worth pointing out that Hume himself edited the texts of others. In Section XIII of the *Natural History*, an extract from Vol. II of Chevalier Ramsay's *Philosophical Principles of Natural and Revealed Religion* has been altered both stylistically and to a lesser degree in substance.

TL Beauchamp, editor of the Clarendon Edition of Hume's works, states that his editing was 'progressive' over the eight editions of the *Natural History of Religion* which appeared in his lifetime.

The problem of modernising a classic text for a modern readership is not new. It was articulated 22 centuries ago by Cicero, one of whose dialogues, *De natura deorum* (On the Nature of the Gods), served as one of Hume's models for his own *Dialogues*. In his *Brutus*, a history of Greek and Roman oratory Cicero says:

> Why must the works of Lysias and Hyperides[1] be so fondly courted, while Cato[2] is overlooked? His language indeed has an antiquated air... but that was the language of his time. If we change and modernise it, add improvements of number and cadence, give an easier turn to his sentences and regulate the structure and connection of his words... you will discover no-one who can claim the preference to Cato...[3]

Throughout his life, David Hume continually revised his works to enhance their lucidity as described by his fellow philosopher and economist Adam Smith, also his literary executor. Here, Smith writes to Hume's publisher William Strahan in London just after the philosopher's death in the summer of 1776:

> Upon his return to Edinburgh... he continued to divert himself, as usual, with correcting his works for a new Edition. He felt that satisfaction so sensibly when reading, a few days before, Lucian's Νεκρικοι διαλογοι [Dialogues of the Dead]. Among all the excuses to Charon for not entering his boat, he could not find one that fitted him...

> He diverted himself with inventing jocular excuses he might make to Charon, and with imagining the surly answers.

> 'Good Charon, I have been correcting my works for a new edition. Allow me a little time, that I may see how the public receives the alterations.' But Charon would answer,

> 'When you have seen the effect of these, you will be for making other alterations. There will be no end of such excuses; Step into the boat!'

---

1 Two of the ten celebrated Greek 'Attic Orators' of the 5th and 4th centuries BCE.
2 M. Porcius Cato (The elder) 234–149 BCE. Statesman, moralist and orator.
3 M. Tullius Cicero, *Brutus*, 67.

To paraphrase Hume's subtitle to his *Treatise of Human Nature*,[1] this work is an attempt to introduce an experimental method of redaction into Humean subjects.

Primary revisions were proposed by a grammarian (David Purdie). Each revision was then critically examined by a professional philosopher and Hume scholar (Peter Fosl) charged with ensuring that Hume's original intention and flow of argument are undisturbed. Emendation was kept to the absolute minimum required for restoration of clarity. For example, italicisation was used solely to maintain fidelity to the argument. We thus present a translation of his works on religion into modern English, while conserving the streaming and precision of Hume's original thought. Also conserved, we trust, is the eloquence and lucidity of the original, together with the literary context of the neo-classical era of its composition. To this end, footnotes accompany those terms whose meaning has shifted since Hume put quill to parchment. Virtually all footnoted references to shifts of meaning, represented by asterisks throughout, cite Samuel Johnson's *Dictionary of the English Language* (SJ).

The project underlying this book was stimulated by an exchange during the Press Conference at the Hume Tercentenary Colloquium in 2011 at the University of Edinburgh. A journalist asked why Hume's works were little read now by the general public for whom he wrote. He was told that although Hume wrote with great clarity, he did so in the language of the mid-18th century. Subsequent evolution in English grammar, syntax and punctuation plus alterations in meaning and purposive expression, had veiled his works from modern eyes. Undeterred, the journalist then asked what was being done about this. To this there was no answer.

What follows, therefore, is what the present editors did about it. The central purpose is to open to Hume's original target audience his writings on religious affairs; a subject which was of central importance to him – and which remains of perennial interest to humankind.

---

1 An Attempt to Introduce the Experimental Method of Reasoning into Moral Subjects.

The Natural History of Religion

EDITORS' NOTE: The text of David Hume's dedication of this work to his friend and cousin[1] is unaltered. In the interests of clarity, some footnotes have been provided.

TO: The Reverend Mr Hume,

Author of Douglas, a Tragedy.

My Dear Sir,

It was the practice of the antients to address their compositions only to friends and equals, and to render their dedications monuments of regard and affection, not of servility and flattery. In those days of ingenious and candid liberty, a dedication did honour to the person to whom it was addressed, without degrading the author. If any particular appeared towards the patron, it was at least the partiality of friendship and affection.

Another instance of true liberty, of which antient times can alone afford us an example, is the liberty of thought that engaged men of letters, however different in their abstract opinions, to maintain a mutual friendship and regard; and never to quarrel about principles, while they agreed in inclinations and manners. Science was often the subject of disputation, never of animosity. *Cicero*, an Academic,[2] addressed his philosophical treatises, sometimes to his close friends *Brutus*, a Stoic;[3] or to *Atticus*, an Epicurean.

---

1 Rev John Home (1722–1808), minister of Athelstaneford, E. Lothian and cousin of David Hume. His play, *Douglas: a Tragedy*, opened successfully in Edinburgh in 1756, to the pious and vociferous outrage of the conservative wing of the Kirk.

2 The term 'academic' in Hume's time had acquired the connotation of 'sceptic'. Here, 'academic' associates Cicero with the philosophers of Plato's Academy in Athens who had taken a sceptical direction. These: Philo of Larissa (c.154–c.84 BCE), a teacher of Cicero's; Clitomachus (187–110 BCE); Carneades (c.214–c.129 BCE) and Arcesilaus (c.315–240 BCE) before him. Cicero, more eclectic than sceptic, was, however, strongly influenced by scepticism. Hume was an avid reader of Cicero.

3 A follower of the philosopher Zeno of Citium (c.334–c.262 BCE).

I have been seized with a strong desire of renewing these laudable practices of antiquity, by addressing the following dissertations to you, my good friend: For such I will ever call and esteem you, notwithstanding the opposition, which prevails between us, with regard to many of our speculative tenets. These differences of opinion I have only found to enliven our conversation; while our common passion for science and letters served as a cement to our friendship. I still admired your genius, even when I imagined, that you lay under the influence of prejudice; and you sometimes told me, that you excused my errors, on account of the candour and sincerity, which, you thought, accompanied them.

But to tell truth, it is less my admiration of your fine genius, which has engaged me to make this address to you, than my esteem of your character and my affection to your person. That generosity of mind which ever accompanies you; that cordiality of friendship, that spirited honour and integrity, have long interested me strongly in your behalf, and have made me desirous, that a monument of our mutual amity should be publicly erected, and, if possible, be preserved to posterity.

I own too, that I have the ambition to be the first who shall in public express his admiration of your noble tragedy of *Douglas*; one of the most interesting and pathetic pieces that was ever exhibited on any theatre.

Should I give it preference to the *Merope* of Maffei,[1] and to that of Voltaire,[2] which it resembles in its subject; should I affirm, that it contained more fire and spirit than the former, more tenderness and simplicity than the latter; I might be accused of partiality: And how could I entirely acquit myself, after the professions of friendship, which I have made you? But the unfeigned tears which flowed from every eye, in the numerous representations which were made of it on this theatre; the unparalleled command, which you appeared to have over every affection of the human breast: These are incontestable proofs, that you possess the true theatrical genius of *Shakespeare* and *Otway*,[3] refined from the unhappy barbarism of the one, and licentiousness of the other.

---

1 Francesco Scipione Marchese di Maffei, Italian dramatist and classical scholar. His verse tragedy *Merope* was staged at Modena in 1713.
2 Voltaire's play *Mérope* appeared in 1743. In Greek mythology, Merope was a Queen of Messenia, in the Peloponnese.
3 Thomas Otway (1652–85) Restoration dramatist. His most celebrated work was *Venice Preserv'd* (1682).

My enemies, you know, and, I own, even sometimes my friends, have reproached me with the love of paradoxes and singular opinions; and I expect to be exposed to the same imputation, on account of the character, which I have here given of your *Douglas*. I shall be told, no doubt, that I had artfully chosen the only time, when this high esteem of that piece could be regarded as a paradox, to wit, before its publication; and that not being able to contradict in this particular the sentiments of the public, I have, at least, resolved to go before them. But I shall be amply compensated for all these pleasantries, if you accept this testimony of my regard, and believe me to be, with the greatest sincerity,

Dear Sir,

Your most affectionate Friend & humble Servant,

David Hume.   Edinburgh, 3 Jan. 1757

INTRODUCTION

While every enquiry regarding religion is of the utmost importance, there are two questions in particular that challenge our attention: the question of religion's foundation in reason; and the question of its origin in human nature. Happily, the first and most important question is also provided with the most obvious, or at least the clearest, solution. The whole fabric of Nature attests an intelligent Author. After serious reflection, no rational enquirer can suspend belief for a moment in the primary principles* of genuine theism[1] and religion.

But the second question, concerning the *origin* of religion in human nature, presents greater difficulty. Belief in invisible, intelligent power is diffused generally among humanity at all places and in all ages.[2] However, it has neither been so universal as to preclude exceptions, nor has it been to any degree uniform in the ideas that it has suggested. If travellers and historians may be believed, some nations have been discovered that actually

---

* Principles: *Primordial substance; original cause.* SJ
1 The belief in a single, universal, creative Deity, actively engaged in human affairs.
2 Commonly known as the '*consensus gentium*' (consensus of the people) argument for the existence of God.

entertain no sentiments* of religion.¹ Furthermore, no two nations – and scarcely any two people – have ever found their beliefs on the subject to agree precisely.

It would appear, therefore, that religious sentiment does not spring from an original instinct or *primary* impression of human nature, such as that giving rise to self-love, affection between the sexes, love of progeny and gratitude or resentment. This is because every one of this class of instincts has been found to be *absolutely* universal in all nations and ages, as well as being invariably found in inflexible pursuit of a precisely determined objective.

The most basic religious principles must thus be *secondary*. As such, they may easily be perverted by various accidents** and causes. Also, their operation may be entirely prevented in some cases by an extraordinary concurrence of circumstances. What those principles are that give *rise* to original religious belief and what are those accidents and causes that *direct* its operation, is the subject of our present enquiry.

SECTION I:

That Polytheism was the primary Religion.

It appears to me that if we consider the improvement of human society from its rude beginnings to states of greater perfection, polytheism, or idolatry, was and necessarily must have been, the first religion of humanity.² This opinion I shall attempt to confirm by the following arguments.

It is an incontestable matter of fact that 1,700 years ago, all humankind were polytheists.³ The doubtful and sceptical principles of a few philosophers, or the theism (a none too pure theism) of one or two nations, form no objection worth regarding. Behold then, the clear testimony of history. The farther we move back into antiquity, the more we find humanity plunged

---

* Sentiment: *Thought; Notion; Opinion.* SJ
** Accident: *That which happens unforeseen; by chance.* SJ
1 Hume and John Locke were aware of the religion-free 'Topinamboues', properly the Tupinamba people of coastal Brazil, described by the German explorer Hans Staden in his *Wahrhaftige Historia*, or True History (1557).
2 Hume sometimes uses polytheism and idolatry synonymously. However, he consistently regards polytheism as idolatrous, but not idolatry as invariably polytheistic; eg in his *History of England*, he reports that the Mass in general and the alleged transubstantiation of bread and wine in the Eucharist are held by Protestants to be 'idolatry'.
3 Probably an underestimate. Many scholars place the era of the biblical patriarchs: Abraham, Isaac and Jacob, in the Intermediate Bronze Age, c.2200–1800 BCE.

into polytheism. There are no marks or symptoms of any more perfect*
religion. The most ancient records of the human race present us with the
polytheistic system as the popular and established creed. The north, the
south, the east and the west give unanimous testimony to the fact. Can there
be any opposition to such comprehensive evidence?

As far back as writing or history reaches, humankind in ancient times
appears universally to have been polytheistic. Shall we assert that in still
more ancient times, before the knowledge of letters or the discovery of any
art or science, people entertained the principles of pure theism?[1] In other
words, shall we assert that, while still ignorant and barbarous, they discovered truth, but fell into error as soon as they acquired learning and polite-
ness? Such an assertion contradicts all appearances not only of probability,
but also our present experience concerning the principles and opinions of
barbarous nations. The native tribes of America, Africa and Asia are all
idolaters. There is not a single exception to this rule.

Indeed, let a traveller visit any unknown region and find its inhabitants
cultivated in the arts and sciences. While on that account there would still be
odds against their being theists, the point could not be established without
further inquiry. However, were the inhabitants found to be ignorant and
barbarous, then without *any* religious enquiry the traveller might declare
them idolaters with scarcely the possibility of error.

It seems certain that according to the natural progression of human
thought, people must first entertain a grovelling, familiar notion of superior
powers *before* advancing to the concept of one perfect Being who bestowed
order on the whole frame** of Nature. We may just as reasonably imagine
that people inhabited palaces before huts, or studied geometry before agriculture; as assert that the Deity appeared to them a pure spirit, omniscient,
omnipotent and omnipresent, *before* being conceived as a powerful, though
limited, Being with *human* passions***, appetites, limbs and organs. The
mind ascends gradually from inferior to superior. By abstracting from what
is imperfect, it forms an idea of perfection. Slowly distinguishing the nobler
parts of its own frame from the grosser, it learns to transfer only the *former*
parts, now much elevated and refined, to its Divinity.

---

* Perfect: *Finished; complete; consummate.* NB also *fully informed.* SJ
** Frame: *Fabric; System; Order.* SJ
*** Passions: *Any of the affections* [emotions] *of human nature: Love; Fear; Joy; Sorrow.* SJ
1 ie Monotheism.

Nothing could disturb this natural progress of thought, except some obvious and invincible argument that might lead the mind *straight* to the pure principles of theism by making it leap over, at one bound, the vast gulf between the human and the divine nature. I accept that the order and frame of the Universe affords just such an argument when accurately examined. However, I cannot believe that this consideration could have influenced humankind when forming its first crude notions of religion.

The origins of objects familiar to us never strike our attention or curiosity. However extraordinary or surprising these objects may be in themselves, they are passed over by the raw and uneducated multitude with little examination or enquiry. Adam, as described by Milton,[1] rising suddenly in Paradise in the full perfection of his faculties, would naturally be astonished at the glorious appearance of Nature: the heavens; the air; the earth; his own organs and members*. He would be moved to ask: from whence had this wonderful world arisen?

Barbarous and impoverished humanity, however, had no time to admire the *regular*** face of Nature at the first emergence of society. Oppressed by numerous wants and passions, they had no time to enquire into the origins of objects to which they had been gradually accustoming from infancy.

On the contrary, the more regular and uniform, ie the more perfect that Nature appears, the more are people familiarised to it and the less inclined to scrutinise and examine it. In contrast, the birth of an abnormal infant excites people's curiosity and is deemed a prodigy.[2] Its novelty alarms them and immediately sets them a-trembling, sacrificing and praying. But an animal complete in all its limbs and organs is to them an *ordinary* spectacle. It produces no religious opinion or affection. Ask whence that animal arose, and you will be told: from the copulation of its parents. And whence came these parents? From the copulation of *theirs*. A few removes satisfy popular curiosity, setting the objects at such a distance that people lose sight of them entirely. Do not imagine that they will so much as ask whence came the *first* animal – much less, whence the whole system or united fabric of the Universe? Or, if you were to put such a question to

---

* Members: *Limbs; any part appended to the body.* SJ. Lat. *membrum*, a limb.
** Regular: *Initiated and formed according to established rules or discipline.* SJ.
  Implying a primary Ruler.
1 John Milton, *Paradise Lost*, VIII. 250–82.
2 Prodigies in Hume's time were still generally reckoned to be omens or portents.

people generally, do not expect that they will employ their minds with any anxiety upon a subject so remote, so uninteresting and so greatly beyond the limit of their abilities.

Furthermore, if by reasoning from the model supplied by Nature, people were *first* led into the belief of one supreme Being, they would never have abandoned that belief in order to embrace polytheism. Indeed, those same principles of reason that had first produced and then diffused so magnificent an opinion over humankind would have been easily capable of preserving it. The initial discovery and proof of any doctrine is much more difficult than the subsequent supporting and retaining of it.

Just as there is a great difference between historical facts and speculative opinions, so the knowledge of the one is not propagated in the same manner as the other.[1] An historical fact, passed down by oral tradition[2] from the initial eye-witnesses and contemporaries, is progressively disguised* by every successive narration and may eventually retain very little, if any, resemblance to its original truth.

Such human factors as the frailty of memories; love of exaggeration and supine carelessness** soon pervert accounts of historical events, unless corrected by books and writing. Here, argument or reasoning has little or no place, never recalling truth once it has escaped from those narrations. It is thus that the fables of Hercules[3] Theseus[4] and Bacchus[5] are believed to have been originally true history, corrupted thereafter in transmission.

But with regard to *speculative* opinions, the case is far different. If these opinions are founded on arguments so clear and obvious that they convince the generality of humankind, then those very arguments that first diffused them will still preserve their original purity. If the arguments are more abstruse and more remote from common understanding, then the opinions they support will remain confined to a few persons. Consequently, as soon as people abandon the contemplation of the arguments, their opinions will immediately be lost and buried in oblivion.

---

* To Disguise: *to disfigure; to alter or change in form.* SJ
** Carelessness: *Inattention; negligence.* SJ
1 This was relevant to Hume's other great work of the period: *The History of England, from the Invasion of Julius Cæsar to the Revolution in 1688*; 4 Vols. (London: Andrew Millar, 1754–62).
2 Used in the sense of transmission. Lat. *tradere*, to hand on.
3 Greek demi-god and hero of the Twelve Labours.
4 Mythical founder-king of Athens, son of Poseidon and friend of Hercules.
5 Latin alternative name for Dionysus, Greek god of wine, ecstasy and drama.

Whichever side of this dilemma we take, it appears impossible that theism could, through the exercise of reason, have been the *primary* religion of the human race; only afterwards, through corruption of that reason, giving birth to polytheism and the varied superstitions[1] of the heathen world.

Reason, when self-evident, prevents these corruptions. When abstruse, however, it keeps its principles entirely beyond the knowledge of the commonality who alone are liable to corrupt any principle or opinion.

SECTION II:

Origin of Polytheism.

If we wish to indulge our curiosity by enquiring into the origins of religion, we must turn our thoughts towards polytheism as the primitive* religion of uninstructed humanity.

Were people led into the apprehension** of an invisible, intelligent Power by a contemplation of the works of Nature, they could never possibly entertain any conception other than that of one *single* Being who bestowed both existence and order on the Universe, adjusting its parts according to a regular plan or connected system. To persons of a certain turn of mind, it may not appear altogether absurd that *several* independent beings endowed with superior wisdom might collaborate in the development and execution of one regular plan. This, however, is an arbitrary supposition. Even if accepted as possible, it is admittedly unsupported by probability nor necessity. All things in the Universe are evidently integral; everything is adjusted to everything else; one design prevails throughout. This uniformity leads the mind to acknowledge *one* Author because the idea of different authors, with no distinction between attributes or operations, only perplexes the imagination while bestowing no satisfaction on the understanding.

---

* Primitive: *Ancient; Original; Established from the beginning.* SJ
** Apprehension: A conception in the mind. SJ. Lat. *apprehendere*, to lay hold on.
1 To Hume, superstition was belief, usually religious unfounded on reason, together with practices arising from such beliefs.

The statue of Laocoön[1] was, as we learn from Pliny, the work of three artists.[2] If not told this, however, we should certainly never have imagined that such a group of figures, cut from one stone and united in one plan, was not the contrivance and work of a single sculptor. It is surely not a natural and obvious supposition to ascribe a single effect to a combination of several causes.

On the other hand, if we leave the works of Nature and trace the footsteps of invisible power in the various and contrary events of human life, we are necessarily led into polytheism and to the acknowledgment of *several* limited and imperfect deities. Storms and tempests ruin what is nourished by the sun. The sun destroys what is fostered by the dews and rains. War may be favourable to a nation afflicted with famine through the inclemency of the seasons. Illness and plague may depopulate a kingdom amidst the most profuse plenty. The same nation is not, at the same time, equally successful at sea and on land. Currently triumphant over its foes, a nation may later have to submit to the military success of those enemies. In short, the behaviour of events, or what we call the *plan* of a particular Providence,[3] is full of variety and uncertainty. Thus, if we suppose it to be directly controlled by any intelligent beings, we must acknowledge a contrariety* in their designs and intentions. We must also accept a constant combat of opposite powers and, within the same power, a repentance or change of intention arising either from impotence or from levity. **

Each nation has its tutelary *** deity with each element being subjected to its invisible power or agency. Not only is the province of each god separate from that of another, but also the operations of the same god are not always certain and invariable. Today it protects; tomorrow it abandons us. Prayers and sacrifices, rites and ceremonies, well or ill-performed, are the sources of favour or enmity and produce all the good or ill-fortune of humankind.

---

* Contrariety: *Inconsistency*. SJ
** Levity: *Inconstancy, changeableness*. SJ
*** Tutelary: Protective; defensive. SJ. Lat. *tutus*, safe.
1 Trojan prince, uncle of Aeneas and priest of Apollo. Killed with his two sons by serpents sent by Athena for his famous warning about the Trojan Horse: *Timeo danaos et dona ferentes* (I fear Greeks, even when bearing gifts.) Virgil, Aeneid 2. 49.
2 Gaius Plinius Secundus (23–79 CE) Known as Pliny the Elder. Roman natural historian killed by the eruption of Vesuvius, which buried Pompeii. He claimed that The *Laocoön* (now in the Vatican museum) was the work of the Rhodian sculptors Athenodoros, Agesander and Polydoros. Pliny, *Historia Naturalis* 36. 37.
3 Hume's term for a specific provider Deity or deities, active in human affairs.

We may conclude, therefore, that in all nations that have embraced polytheism, the first ideas of religion arose not from a contemplation of Nature, but from concern for the events of life and from the incessant hopes and fears that actuate the human mind. Accordingly, we find that idolaters separate the provinces of their deities. They then have recourse to that particular invisible agent to whose authority they are currently and directly subjected and whose province is to superintend the actions upon which they are immediately engaged. Thus Juno[1] superscript tis invoked at marriages; Lucina at births[2]; Neptune receives the prayers of mariners, Mars those of warriors.

The farmer cultivates his fields under the protection of Ceres while the merchant acknowledges the authority of Mercury.[3] Each natural event is believed governed by some intelligent agent. Nothing prosperous or adverse can happen in life without that agent being the subject of specific prayers or thanksgivings.[4]

It must be accepted that in order to sustain people's attention beyond the present course of events, or to lead them to infer *invisible* intelligent power, they must be actuated by some motive. This must be one that prompts thought and reflection, thus provoking their first enquiry. But to what motive, or passion, shall we turn in order to explain an effect of such mighty consequence? Not speculative curiosity surely, or the pure love of truth. Such motives are far too refined for such gross conceptions. They would lead to enquiries concerning the fabric and construction of Nature, a subject too large and comprehensive for their then narrow capacities. No passions, therefore, can be supposed to work upon barbarous peoples except the *ordinary* emotions of human life: anxious concern for happiness and dread of future misery; terror of death; thirst for revenge; appetite for food and other necessaries. Agitated by such hopes and fears and especially the latter, it is with a trembling curiosity that people scrutinize the evolution

---

1 The wife of Jupiter, Juno was the Roman counterpart of Hera, the Greek goddess of marriage and fertility.

2 'The Light-bringer' (to the child). Lucina was Juno in the context of childbirth.

3 Ceres: Roman goddess of agriculture. Mercury: The messenger of the gods, Hermes in the Greek pantheon. He doubled as the Roman god of trade (Lat. *Merx*).

4 [Hume's note.] As early as Hesiod's time [*c.*700 BCE] there were 30,000 deities, but the tasks to be performed by these still seems too great for their number. The provinces of the deities were so subdivided, that there was even a god of *sneezing*. See Aristotle, *Problemata physica*, 33.7. The province of copulation, suitable to the importance and dignity of it, was divided among several deities. Hesiod, *Works and Days*, II. 252–5.

of future situations and examine the various and contrary events of human life. It is in this disordered scene, with eyes still *more* disordered and astonished, that they perceive the first faint traces of Divinity.

The same Subject continued.

We are placed in this world as if in a great theatre where the true sources and causes of every event are entirely concealed from us. Neither do we have either sufficient wisdom to foresee – or power to prevent – those ills with which we are continually threatened. We hang in perpetual suspense between life and death, health and sickness, plenty and want. These are distributed amongst the human species by secret and unknown causes whose operation is often unexpected and always inexplicable. These unknown causes then become the constant object of our hopes and fears. The emotions being kept in perpetual alarm by an anxious anticipation of events, the imagination is equally employed in forming ideas of those powers upon which we are entirely dependent.

Suppose people could dissect Nature according to the most probable, or at least the most intelligible philosophy. They would then find that these unknown causes are nothing other than the particular fabric and structure of minute parts of their own bodies and of external objects. They would also discover that all the events about which they are so much concerned are produced by regulated and constant machinery. However, such understanding exceeds the comprehension of the uneducated, who can only conceive of the unknown causes in a general and confused manner. However, since their imagination is perpetually employed on the subject, it naturally labours to form some particularly distinct idea of them. The more they consider these unknown causes themselves, together with the uncertainty of their operation, the less satisfying are their enquiries. However unwillingly, they would have had to abandon such an arduous attempt at understanding, were it not for the propensity of human nature to lead to a system that gives them at least some satisfaction.

There is a universal tendency among human beings to conceive all *other* beings to be like themselves. Furthermore, they tend to transfer to every object those qualities with which they are familiar and of which they are intimately conscious. Thus do we find human faces on the Moon and armies in the clouds. We also have a natural propensity, if not corrected by experience and reflection, to ascribe everything that hurts or pleases us, to malice or to goodwill respectively. Hence the frequency and beauty of *prosopopoeia*[1] in poetry, where trees, mountains and streams are personified, and the inanimate parts of Nature acquire sentiment[2] and passion. Although these poetical figures and expressions do not inspire actual belief, they serve at least to illustrate a certain tendency in the imagination, without which they could neither be beautiful nor natural. Nor is a river-god or a Hamadryad[3] always taken for a merely poetical or imaginary personage. It may sometimes enter the real creed of the uneducated multitude, while each grove or field is held to be possessed of a particular *genius* or invisible power that inhabits and protects it.[4] Indeed, philosophers cannot entirely exempt themselves from this natural frailty, having often ascribed to inanimate matter the *horror* of a vacuum, together with sympathies, antipathies and other natural human emotions. The absurdity is not less when we cast our eyes upwards. Transferring human passions and infirmities to the Deity (as is too common) we represent it as jealous and revengeful, capricious and partial, in short like a wicked and foolish person in every respect, except in superior power and authority.

No wonder then that humankind, absolutely ignorant of causes yet anxious concerning future outcomes, should acknowledge dependence on invisible powers possessing sentiment and intelligence. Those unknown causes continually engaging their thoughts are all perceived to be of the same kindred, or species.[5] Nor is it long before we ascribe to them thought, reason, emotion and sometimes even human limbs and figures, in order to give them a greater resemblance to ourselves.

Superstition increases proportionately to the degree to which the course of a person's life is governed by the unexpected. This is particularly observed in gamesters and sailors. These most abound in frivolous[6] and superstitious beliefs despite being the least capable of all regarding serious reflection.

---

1 A figure of speech in which either non-human living things, inanimate objects or abstract ideas are represented as having human qualities. Also known as personification.
2 In Hume's usage, a 'sentiment' is either an emotion, a judgement or an opinion.
3 A type of Dryad, or mythical tree nymph. Hamadryads were bonded to a particular species of tree, each living only as long as the tree itself. Dryads punished humans who harmed trees. River-gods were rivers personified.
4 What is called in Latin the *genius loci* ('spirit of the place'); the local protecting deity.
5 ie the same species as human beings; *Homo sapiens*.
6 *Slight; trifling; of no moment.* SJ

The gods, says Coriolanus in Dionysius,[1] have an influence in every affair, but above all in war where the outcome is so uncertain. However, all human life is subject to fortuitous accidents, especially before the institution of order and good government. It is therefore natural that superstition should have prevailed everywhere in barbarous ages, making people enquire concerning those invisible powers controlling their happiness or misery. Superstitious people, ignorant of astronomy and the anatomy of plants and animals, are not curious[2] enough to observe the admirable adjustment of ultimate causes. They remain unacquainted with a first and supreme Creator, that infinitely perfect Spirit who, alone and by almighty will, bestowed order on the whole system of Nature. Such a magnificent idea is too big for their narrow conceptions which are neither able to observe the beauty of the work, nor to comprehend the grandeur of its Author. They conceive their deities, however potent and invisible, to be a species of *human* creatures, perhaps elevated from among common humanity, but retaining human passions and appetites, together with corporeal limbs and organs. Such *limited* beings, although masters of human fate, are hence incapable of extending their influence everywhere. They thus require to be vastly multiplied to cover the sheer variety of events happening over the whole face of Nature, every place being stored with a crowd of local deities. It is thus that polytheism has prevailed – and still prevails – among the greatest part of uninstructed humankind.

The following lines of Euripides are so much to the present purpose that I cannot forbear quoting them:

> There is nothing secure in the world; no glory, no prosperity. The gods throw all life into confusion... so that all of us, from ignorance and uncertainty, may pay them the more worship and reverence.[3]

Any of the human emotions may lead us into the notion of invisible, intelligent power. Hope will do this as well as fear; gratitude as well as affliction. However, if we examine our own hearts or observe what passes around us, we shall find that people are much oftener thrown on

---

1 Cn. Marcius Coriolanus, Roman general of the 5th century BCE. See Plutarch, *Parallel Lives: Coriolanus*, X.I. Shakespeare's play derived from Plutarch, whose source was Dionysius of Halicarnassus (fl. *c.*30 BCE), Greek *rhetor* (orator) and historian of Rome. See Dionysius, *Antiquitates Romanae*, 8.33.

2 Desirous of information; 'Be not curious in unnecessary matters...' Eccles. 3.23.

3 Hecuba (956–60). The three great tragedians of classical Greece were Aeschylus, Sophocles and Euripides (*c.*480–406 BCE). The latter's *Hecuba* depicts the of the queen of Troy in the wake of the deaths of her husband King Priam and their children amidst the carnage of the Greek sack of the city.

their knees by the melancholy than by the pleasant passions. Prosperity is calmly received as our due and few questions are asked concerning its cause or author. It begets cheerfulness, activity, alacrity and a lively enjoyment of every social and sensual pleasure. While in this state of mind, individuals have little leisure[1] or inclination to think of the unknown, invisible regions. On the other hand, each disastrous accident alarms them and starts them enquiring into the principles whence it arose. Apprehensions spring up with regard to futurity. The mind, now sunk into apathy, terror and melancholy, has recourse to every method of appeasing those secret intelligent powers upon whom our fortunes are entirely supposed to depend.

No subject matter is more frequent with all popular[2] divines than the advantages of affliction in bringing people to a due sense of religion. This they do by subduing that confidence and sensuality* which, in times of prosperity, make them forgetful of a divine providence. Nor is this topic confined to modern religions; the ancients also employed it. Thus the Greek historian Diodorus:

> Fortune has never liberally and without envy bestowed an unmixed happiness on humankind. With all her gifts she has always conjoined some disastrous circumstance, in order to chastise people into a reverence for the gods whom, in a continued course of prosperity, they are apt to neglect and forget.[3]

What age or period of life is the most addicted to superstition? The weaker and more timid. Which sex? The same answer must be given. Thus Strabo writes:[4]

> The leaders and examples of every kind of superstition are the women. These excite the supplications and the observance of religious days. It is rare to meet with one that lives apart from the females, yet is addicted to such practices. Nothing can, for this reason, be more improbable than the

---

* Sensuality: *Addiction to corporal pleasures.* SJ
1 'Leisure' was synonymous with 'time available' in Hume's day.
2 Those who address the common people.
3 Diodorus Siculus. *Bibliotheca historica* 3.47. A Sicilian Greek, (fl. *c*.60–30 BCE) His *Historical Library* is a world history in 40 books, centred on Rome. He had a euhemerist view of the gods, ie treating their mythology as symbolic accounts originating from historical fact, as discussed by Hume.
4 Strabo. *Geographia*, 6. 297. Greek geographer (64 BCE – *post* 24 CE) from Amasia in Pontus. A Stoic, his 17-book *Geography* was a school text until the Middle Ages.

account given of an order of men among the Getes who practised celibacy and were, notwithstanding, the most religious fanatics.[1]

This is a process of reasoning that would lead us to entertain a bad idea of the devotion of monks. However, we know by experience, perhaps not so common in Strabo's day, that one may practise celibacy and profess chastity and yet maintain the closest connections and most entire sympathy with that timorous and pious sex.

SECTION IV:

Deities not considered as Creators or Formers of the world.

The only point of theology where we shall find almost universal agreement is that there exists in the world, invisible, intelligent *power*. In popular systems of theology, however, there is the widest difference as to whether this power is supreme or subordinate; and whether confined to one Being or distributed among several. There is further disagreement as to what attributes, qualities, associations and principles of action are ascribable to such beings on all of these points.

Before the revival of letters,[2] our ancestors in Europe believed – as we do at present – that there was one supreme God, the author of Nature. Its power, though in itself uncontrollable, was however often exerted by the interposition of angels and subordinate ministers who executed its sacred purposes. However, our ancestors believed that all Nature was also full of *other* invisible powers such as fairies, goblins, elves and sprites. These beings were stronger and mightier than people, though much inferior to the celestial beings who surrounded the throne of God.

Now, suppose that in those ages, anyone were to deny the existence of God and the angels. Would not this impiety have justly deserved the appellation of atheism,[3] even though they still accepted, by some odd capricious reasoning, that the popular stories of elves and fairies were

---

1 The Getes were the tribes known to the Romans as the Dacii. Inhabiting Dacia, modern Romania and part of Bulgaria, they were praised by Herodotus for their bravery and law-abiding ways. Hume's quotation and its uneasy relationship to the remark that follows seems calculated to question the probability of both monastic vows of celibacy and religious beliefs being faithfully maintained.

2 Presumably the Renaissance, originating in 14th century Italy.

3 'Atheist' in Hume's time was extended to errant believers such as those deviating from orthodoxy by denying the afterlife, original sin, providence, the trinity etc.

accurate and well-grounded? The difference between such a person and a genuine theist is infinitely greater than that between him and someone who absolutely denies *all* invisible intelligent power. It is a fallacy to place, through the casual resemblance of names, such opposite opinions under the same denomination, when unaccompanied by any conformity of meaning.

To anyone who considers the matter fairly, it will appear that all the gods of polytheists are no better than the elves or fairies of our ancestors, equally undeserving of pious worship or veneration. Polytheists, as pretended* religionists, are thus really a species of superstitious atheists. They acknowledge no being that corresponds to our idea of the Deity; no *first* principle of mind or thought; no *supreme* government and administration; no *divine* construction or intention in the fabric of the world.

The Chinese beat their idols when their prayers are not answered.[1] The deities of the Laplanders are any large stones of extraordinary shape with which they meet.[2] Egyptian mythologists, in order to account for animal worship, said that the gods, pursued by the violence of Earth-born humans who were their enemies, had been obliged to disguise themselves as beasts.[3] The Caunii, a nation in Asia Minor, having resolved to admit no strange** gods, would regularly assemble fully armed and beat the air with their lances. They proceeded in that manner to their frontiers in order, they said, to expel foreign deities.[4] 'Not even the immortal gods,' said some German nations to Caesar, 'are a match for the Suevi.'[5]

---

* To pretend: *to claim, falsely or truly. Seldom used without a shade of censure.* SJ
** Strange: *Of another country,* SJ; cf Fr. *étrange,* foreign.
1 Louis Daniel, Père le Comte SJ, *Memoirs and observations… made on a late journey through the Empire of China* (1696).
2 Jean-François Regnard (1655–1709). *Voyage de Laponie* (Lapland journey), 1731. He describes the customs of the Saami people of Lapland.
3 Diodorus Siculus, op.cit, 1.86. Lucian, *On Sacrifices,* 14. Ovid refers to this tradition, *Metamorphoses,* 5. 21ff. See also Manilius, *Astronomica,* 4. 580 & 800.
4 Herodotus, *History,* 1. 172. The Caunii took part in the Mithridatic massacre of Romans in Asia in 88 BCE. See Appian of Alexandria, *The Mithridatic Wars,* 4. 22.
5 C. Julius Caesar, *De Bello Gallico* (On the Gallic War) 4.7. The Suevi were a bellicose German group of large Rhineland tribes encountered by Caesar in his campaign against Ariovistus in 58 BCE. They were a thorn in Rome's flesh until the very end of the Western Empire in the 5th century CE.

In Homer, Dione says to Venus, wounded by Diomedes:

Many ills, my daughter, have the gods inflicted on people – and many ills, in return, have people inflicted on the gods.[1]

We only have to open any classic author to meet with these gross representations of the deities. Longinus observes with reason that such ideas of the divine nature, if literally taken, contain a true atheism.[2]

Some writers have expressed surprise that the impieties of Aristophanes should have been tolerated, indeed publicly acted and applauded by the Athenians.[3] The latter were a people so superstitious and so fiercely protective of their public religion that, at the same time, they were executing Socrates for his imagined incredulity. These writers, however, do not believe that Aristophanes' ludicrously familiar images of the gods appeared impious, or were the genuine lights by which the ancients conceived their divinities.

What conduct can be more criminal, or mean, than that of Jupiter in the *Amphitryon*?[4] Yet that play, representing his gallant* exploits, was imagined so *agreeable* to him that it was always acted in Rome by public authority when the State was threatened with pestilence, famine, or any general calamity.[5] The Romans supposed that, like all old lechers, he would be highly pleased with this recital of his former feats of prowess and vigour and that there was no more appropriate topic upon which to flatter his vanity.

Xenophon[6] says that in wartime the Lacedaemonians always put up their petitions to the gods *very* early in the morning. This was in order to be ahead of their enemies by being the first of the day's petitioners, thus pre-engaging the gods in their favour. We gather from Seneca the Younger that

---

* Gallant: *lewd; debauched.* SJ

1 Homer, *The Iliad* v. 382. Dione was the consort of Zeus and, by him, mother of Aphrodite (Venus). The latter was wounded at Troy by Diomede, a fearsome Greek warrior and leader of the men of Argos and Tiryns in the Peloponnese.

2 Longinus, *On the Sublime*, 9.7. Longinus (first century, CE) has never been positively identified. It has been suggested that a better title is 'On Sublimity'

3 Aristophanes, (*c.*445–*c.*385 BCE) Athenian writer of comedies. A merciless critic of militaristic civic policy and a potent satirist of political and intellectual bombast.

4 *Amphitryon* is a Latin play by T. Maccius Plautus (*c.*250–184 BCE) set in Thebes. While Amphitryon was away from Thebes at war, Jupiter seduced his virtuous wife, Alcmena, by appearing to her in the guise of her husband. She was not amused.

5 Arnobius, *Seven Books Against the Heathen*, 8. 33. Arnobius of Sicca, in modern Tunisia, was an orator and a Christian apologist of the early 3rd Century CE.

6 Xenophon, (*c.*428–*c.*354 BCE) *The Constitution of the Lacedaemonians*, XIII. 2–5. An Athenian soldier, military historian and disciple of Socrates. Banished from Athens, he served in Lacedaemon (Sparta).

it was usual for worshippers in the temples to try to influence the beadle or sexton so as to obtain a seat near the image of the deity. This was in order to be best heard in their prayers and applications to it.[1]

The people of Tyre, besieged by Alexander, threw chains over their statue of Hercules to prevent that deity from deserting to the enemy.[2] Augustus, having twice lost his fleet in storms, forbad the carrying of Neptune in processions with the other gods, reckoning that he had thus sufficiently revenged himself.[3] After the death of Germanicus the people were so enraged at their gods that they stoned them in their temples and openly renounced all allegiance to them.[4]

To ascribe the *origin* and fabric of the Universe to these imperfect beings never enters into the imagination of any polytheist or idolater. Hesiod, whose writings together with those of Homer contained the canonical system of the heathens, supposes both gods and people to have sprung equally from the unknown powers of Nature. Throughout the whole of Hesiod's *Theogony*, Pandora[5] is the only instance of a *creation*, a voluntary production, formed by the gods merely to despite* Prometheus who presented humankind with stolen celestial fire. Indeed, ancient mythologists seem to have always embraced the idea of birth *out* of something else,[6] rather than a full-blown creation or formation. Thus they accounted for the origin of the Universe.

Ovid lived in a learned age and had been instructed by philosophers in the principles of a divine creation, or formation of the world. Finding that such an idea would not agree with the popular mythology of his writings he left it, as it were, loose and detached from his system. *Quisquis fuit ille*

---

* To despite: *To vex; affront with malice.* SJ
1 L. Annaeus Seneca (*c.*4 BCE–65 CE) *Epistolae Morales* (Moral Letters) No.41. Roman Stoic philosopher. The 124 Letters were addressed to his friend Lucilius, Governor of Sicily.
2 Q. Curtius Rufus, *Historiae Alexandri Magni*, 4.3. Curtius (fl. first century CE) wrote his *Histories of Alexander the Great* in ten books. In 332 BCE Tyre, in modern Lebanon, fell after a seven-month siege to Alexander, who promptly slaughtered the entire garrison.
3 Gaius Suetonius, *De vita caesarum*; *Vita Divi Augusti.*, 16.
4 Suetonius, *De Vita C. Caligulae Caesaris*, 5. Germanicus Julius Caesar (15 BCE–19 CE), adoptive son and heir of the Emperor Tiberius and father of Caligula. The popular Roman general's death in Antioch is thought to have been by poison on the orders of Tiberius.
5 Hesiod, *Theogony*, 1. 570. Pandora, (Πανδορα 'the all-giving') was the first woman. She was crafted from earth by Hephaestus as a daughter to Zeus and bride to Epimetheus, brother of Prometheus, humanity's fire-bringer. Pandora's Box, opened, released all evils. Pandora is also a moon of Saturn – and the planet mined for its riches in the 2009 movie *Avatar*.
6 ie from an existing source;

deorum[1] says he, dissipated the chaos and introduced order. He knew it could neither be Saturn, nor Jupiter, nor Neptune, nor any of the *received**deities of paganism. His theological system had taught him nothing upon that score and he leaves the matter equally undetermined.

Diodorus Siculus, beginning his historical work by enumerating the most reasonable opinions concerning the origin of the world, makes no mention of a Deity or intelligent Mind.[2]

However, it is evident from his *History* that he was much more prone to superstition than to irreligion. Talking of the Ichthyophagi,[3] a nation in India, he says that there being such great difficulty in accounting for their descent, we must conclude them to be *aborigines*[4] They have thus no beginning to their descent, having propagated their race from all eternity, as some physiologers[5] have justly observed in their works on the origin of Nature.[6]

Diodorus adds:

> But in such subjects as these, that exceed all human capacity, it may well happen that those who discourse the most, know the least. They reach a specious appearance of truth in their reasonings while extremely wide of the real truth and matters of fact.[7]

To our eyes, this is a strange sentiment to be embraced by a professed and zealous religionist. The same author, who can thus account for the origin of the world without a Deity, esteems it *impious* to explain the common accidents of life from physical causes! Earthquakes, inundations and tempests he devoutly ascribes to the anger of Jupiter or Neptune; plain proof of whence he derived his ideas of religion.

But it was merely by accident that, in ancient times, the question of world *origins* ever entered into religious systems, or was examined by theologians. Philosophers alone professed to deliver such systems, but it was also pretty late before even they came to the notion of a Mind or supreme

---

* Received: *Generally allowed*. SJ; ie broadly accepted.
1 'Whichever of the gods it was.' Ovid, *Metamorphoses*, 1.1.32. P. Ovidius Naso (43 BCE – 18 CE), anglicised to Ovid. With Vergil and Horace, he was one of the three canonical poets of Latin literature.
2 Diodorus Siculus, *Bibliotheca Historica*, 1.6.
3 Greek. Literally 'Fish-eaters'.
4 Lat. *Ab origine*; 'from the origin' – of the Earth.
5 Practitioners of natural philosophy, ie physics. From Gk. φυσεοσ, Nature.
6 Diodorus Siculus Ibid., 3.20.
7 Ibid. 15.48.

Intelligence as the first Cause of all. To account for the origin of things *without* a Deity was so far from impiety in those days that Thales, Anaximenes, Heraclitus and others who embraced that system of universal origins, did so unchallenged. Indeed, Anaxagoras, the first undoubted theist among the philosophers, was perhaps also the first ever to be accused of atheism.[1] It will be easy to give a reason why Thales, Anaximander and those early philosophers – who really *were* atheists – might be orthodox in the pagan creed; and why Anaxagoras and Socrates, though real theists, must have naturally been reckoned impious in ancient times.

The blind, unguided powers of Nature, if they could produce humankind, might also produce such beings as Jupiter and Neptune. These beings, the most powerful and intelligent in the world, would be proper objects of worship. But where a *supreme* Intelligence is admitted as the first Cause of all, these capricious beings – if existing at all – must appear highly subordinate and dependent. Consequently, they must be excluded from the ranks of deities. Plato[2] assigns this reason for the imputation* thrown at Anaxagoras, namely his denying the divinity of the stars, planets and other *created* objects.

We are told by Sextus Empiricus[3] that Epicurus, when a boy, was reading with his tutor these lines of Hesiod:

> Eldest of beings, Chaos first arose;
> Next Earth, wide – stretch'd, the seat of all…[4]

The young scholar first displayed his inquisitive genius, by asking, 'And whence Chaos?' – only to be told that he must turn to philosophers for a solution to such questions. After this hint, Epicurus abandoned philology** – and indeed all other studies – in order to devote himself to the study of philosophy. Here alone he could anticipate satisfaction in dealing with such sublime subjects.

---

* Imputation: *Censure; reproach*. SJ
** Philology: *Studies philological are History, Grammar, Rhetoric, Poesy and Language*. SJ
1 Anaxagoras was accused of 'atheism' or 'impiety' by Cleon for suggesting the αρχη (*arché*) or originative principle of the Cosmos was νους (*nous*) 'mind or intelligence' thus relegating the Greek gods from the premier division of deities. He also said the sun and moon were physical, not divine. Pericles, his former pupil, is said to have appeared in court for the defence. See Diogenes Laertius, *Lives*, 2.12.
2 *The Laws* 10. Socrates cited this event to account for his own prosecution; Plato, *Apology* 26d.
3 Sextus Empiricus, (fl. 3rd century CE), Greek philosopher-historian and perhaps physician, author of a comprehensive account of Greek Pyrrhonian scepticism. Hume quotes from his treatise *Against the Physicists*, 2.18–19; aka *Adversus mathematicos*.
4 *Theogony* 2. 116–7

With philologists and mythologists scarcely ever displaying much penetration, the common run of humanity were never likely to push their researches far, or to derive their systems of religion from reason. Even the philosophers who discoursed on such topics readily assented to the grossest theories, accepting the joint origin of gods and people from: night; chaos; fire; water; air, or from whatever they had established to be the ruling element.

Nor was it only in respect of their *first* origin, that the gods were supposed dependent on the powers of Nature. Throughout the whole period of their existence they were subjected to the dominion of fate or destiny.

Think of the force of necessity,' says Agrippa to the Roman people, 'that force to which even the gods must submit.'[1]

The younger Pliny, conforming to this way of thinking, tells us that amidst the darkness, horror, and confusion of the first eruption of Vesuvius, several individuals concluded that all Nature was going to wrack, with both gods and humans perishing together in one common ruin.[2]

It would be a great complaisance* indeed, were we to dignify with the name of religion such an imperfect system of theology as polytheism, putting it on a level with later systems founded on more just and sublime principles.

> For my part, I can scarcely accept that the principles of even Marcus Aurelius, Plutarch and certain other Stoics and Academics are worthy of the honourable appellation of theism, despite being much more refined than pagan superstition. For if heathen mythology resembles the ancient European system of spiritual beings, *excluding* God and angels and leaving only fairies and sprites; so the creed of these philosophers may equally and fairly be said to exclude a Deity – and to leave us *with* only angels and fairies.

---

* Complaisance: *A desire to please; an act of adulation.* SJ

1 Dionysius of Halicarnassus, *Antiquitates Romanae* 6.54. Not to be confused with the Marcus Agrippa who commissioned the Roman Pantheon and served as Augustus's Admiral. This was Agrippa Menenius, Consul of the Republic in 503 BCE.

2 G. Plinius Caecilius Secundus, *Epistolae,* 6. The 'younger' Pliny (61–113 CE), Roman administrator, correspondent of Trajan and nephew of the naturalist 'elder' Pliny, killed in that very Vesuvian eruption of 79 CE.

SECTION V:

Various Forms of Polytheism: Allegory, Hero-Worship

Our present business is chiefly to consider the gross polytheism of common humanity and to trace[1] its various appearances in the principles of
human nature whence they are derived. Whoever learns[2] by argument of the
existence of invisible intelligent power is reasoning from the admirable construction of natural objects and regards the world as the workmanship of
that divine Being, the original Cause of all things. The common polytheist,
however, is so far from accepting that idea, that he deifies *every* part of the
Universe, conceiving all conspicuous productions of Nature to be *themselves*
real divinities. The sun, moon, and stars are all gods according to this system. Fountains are inhabited by nymphs, and trees by Hamadryads.[3] Even
monkeys, dogs, cats and other animals may become sacred and generate
religious veneration. Hence, however strong the *propensity* to believe in an
invisible, intelligent power in Nature, polytheists have an equally strong tendency to focus their attention on sensible* and visible objects. It is in order
to reconcile these opposite inclinations that they unite the invisible power
with some visible object.

Furthermore, the distribution of distinct areas of responsibility to the
various deities results in the entry of allegory, both physical and moral, into
the common systems of polytheism. Thus the god of war will naturally be
represented as furious, cruel, and impetuous; the god of poetry as elegant,
polite, and amiable and the god of merchandise, especially in early times, as
thievish and deceitful.

The allegories conjectured by Homer and other mythologists have,
I accept, often been so strained that people of sense tend to reject them
as entirely imaginary, the conceptions of critics and commentators. On
the slightest reflection, however, it is undeniable that allegory really has
a place in heathen mythology: Cupid is the son of Venus; the Muses are

---

* Sensible: Perceptible. That which can be *sensed*.
1 *To follow with exactness;* [and] *to mark out.* SJ
2 Learn: *The word signifies both to learn and to teach; to both gain and impart knowledge.* SJ
3 In Greek mythology, there were, according to Anatheus, some eight dryad nymphs called
  hamadryads, daughters of the forest divinity, Oxylos. *Vide* Section III.

the daughters of Memory; Prometheus is the wise brother and Epimetheus the foolish[1] Hygeia, goddess of health, is the daughter of Aesculapius, god of medicine. Who cannot but observe allegory in these and in many other instances?

When a god is supposed to preside over any passion, event, or system of actions, it is almost unavoidable to give it a genealogy. It is also supplied with attributes and adventures appropriate to its supposed powers and influence, thus carrying on that human similarity and comparison so natural to the human mind. We ought not to expect perfect allegories to be produced by ignorance and superstition. This is because there is no work of genius that requires a finer hand, or has been executed more rarely with success. That *Fear* and *Terror* are the sons of Mars is appropriate – but why are they mothered by Venus? That *Harmon* is the daughter of Venus seems reasonable – but why by Mars?[2] That *Sleep* is the brother of *Death* is suitable, but why describe him as enamoured of one of the Graces?[3] Since the ancient mythologists fall into such gross and palpable mistakes, we surely have no reason to expect such refined and complex allegories as some have deduced from their fictions.

Lucretius[4] was plainly seduced by the strong appearance of allegory observable in pagan fictions. He first addresses himself to Venus as the generating power that animates, renews and beautifies the Universe. However, he is soon betrayed into incoherencies by mythology, praying to the allegorical Venus to appease the fury of her lover Mars. This is an idea drawn not from allegory but from the popular religion that Lucretius, as an Epicurean, could not consistently accept.

The deities of the common people are only marginally superior to human creatures. Hence where they are affected with strong sentiments of veneration or gratitude for any hero or public benefactor, nothing can be more natural than conversion into a god. They thus fill the heavens with continual recruits from among humankind.

---

1 Prometheus and Epimetheus were sons of the Titan Iapetus. The former was smart, the latter dim. Prometheus ('fore-thinker' in Greek) took a spark of heavenly fire and donated it to humanity. Zeus chained him to a rock in the Caucasus where an eagle fed daily upon his liver.
2 Hume means *Harmonia*, daughter of Venus, goddess of love – and Mars, god of war.
3 Homer, *Iliad*, XIV. 267. The three Graces, daughters of Zeus and the nymph Eurynome were: Aglaia (Splendour), Euphrosyne (Mirth) and Thalia (Good Cheer).
4 Titus Lucretius Carus (*c.*99–*c.*55 BCE) Roman exponent of the philosophy of Epicurus in his 7,400-line poem, *De Rerum Natura* (On the Nature of the Universe).

Most of the divinities of the ancient world are supposed to have once been human, their *apotheosis** being due to the admiration and affection of the people. The actual history of their adventures, corrupted by tradition[1] and elevated by marvels, becomes a plentiful source of fable. This is especially when passing through the hands of poets, allegorists and priests who successively augment the wonder and astonishment of the ignorant multitude.

Painters and sculptors also came in for profit from the sacred mysteries. By furnishing people with visible representations of their divinities, whom they clothed in human figures, they greatly increased the public devotion and defined its object. It was probably due to a *lack* of these arts in rude, barbarous former ages that people deified plants, animals and even brute unorganised matter. Rather than be without a perceptible object of worship, they affixed divinity to such ungainly forms. If any statuary** of Syria had carved an accurate figure of Apollo, the conic stone Heliogabalus would never have received such profound adoration as a representation of that solar deity.[2] Jupiter Ammon is represented by Curtius as a deity of the same kind.[3] The Arabians and Persinuntians [*sic*] also adored shapeless unformed stones as their deity.[4] Thus did their folly exceed that of the Egyptians.

---

* Apotheosis: Deification.
** Statuary: *A sculptor. One that practises, or possesses, the art of making statues.* SJ
1 This is tradition in the original sense; ie of being handed down to successive generations. Lat. *tradere* to hand over.
2 Herodian of Syria, *History of the Empire from the Death of Marcus* 5.3.10.
  A Roman civil servant, Herodian (*c.*170–240 CE) wrote history in Greek, covering 180 to 238 CE. The Emperor Elagabalus (204–222 CE) had the Romans worshipping the sun in the shape of *El-Gabal*, a black conical meteorite from Emesa in Syria.
3 Q. Curtius Rufus. *History of Alexander the Great*. 4.7.23 *Quo pro deo colitur...umbilico maxime similis est.* (What they worship as the god is very like a navel.) The temple of Zeus Ammon, at Siwa in Egypt, was visited by Alexander (and part of his army) whereupon the oracle immediately declared him the son of Zeus.
4 Arnobius of Sicca, *Adversus Gentes*, 6.11. The Arabians worshipped an unformed stone, while the people of Pessinunte, in modern Turkey, where there was a cult of the mother goddess Cybele, worshipped a *silex*; Lat. flint.

Stilpo was banished by the council of Areopagus for affirming that the Minerva in the citadel was no divinity, but instead the workmanship of the sculptor Phidias.[1] What degree of reason must we expect in the religious belief of the commonality in other nations when *Athenians* and *Areopagites* could entertain such gross conceptions?

These then are the general principles of polytheism. They are founded on human nature and little, or not at all, dependent on caprice and accident. Since the *causes* of human happiness or misery are very little known and very uncertain, we anxiously endeavour to attain a definitive idea of them. However, we find no better expedient than to represent them as intelligent voluntary agents like ourselves, only somewhat superior in power and wisdom.

The limited influence of these agents, and their great propensity for human weakness, introduces the varied distribution and divisions of their authority and thereby gives rise to allegory. The same principles naturally also deify *mortals* superior in power, courage or understanding. They produce hero-worship clothed with a fictional history and a mythological tradition in all its wild and unaccountable forms. Since an invisible spiritual Intelligence[2] is an object too subtle for common understanding, people naturally affix it to some *perceptible* representation. This may be drawn from conspicuous elements of Nature, or from the statues, images and pictures with which a later, more refined age represents its divinities.

Almost all idolaters, of whatever age or country, concur in these general principles and conceptions. Even the particular characters and areas of activity that they assign to their deities are not so very different. Greeks and Romans, whether arriving as travellers or conquerors, found their own deities everywhere without much difficulty, saying: *This is Mercury; that is Venus; this Mars; that Neptune,* whatever might be the title by which the

---

1 Diogenes Laertius *op.cit.* 2.116. Stilpo, properly Στιλπον, or Stilpon (c.360–c.280 BCE) was a Greek moral philosopher and teacher of Zeno of Citium, founder of Stoicism. The Areopagus, 'Hill of Ares', a rocky outcrop below the Acropolis, was the ancient site of the Athenian assembly. Aeschylus, in the *Oresteia*, has it as the place under which the Furies reside. Phidias sculpted the great chryselephantine Athena *parthenos* (virgin) in the central *cella* (chamber) of the Parthenon.

2 *Cf.* the λογοσ (Logos) of John 1.1–3 and identified as God. Logos is defined as 'immanent cosmic rationality; pure intelligence' Lampe, GWH, *A patristic Greek Lexicon* (Oxford: OUP, 1961)

strange god was denominated.[1] According to Tacitus, the goddess Hertha[2] of our Saxon ancestors seems to be none other than the *Mater Tellus*[3] of the Romans – and his conjecture was evidently correct.

SECTION VI:

Origin of Theism from Polytheism.

The doctrine of one supreme Deity as the author of Nature is very ancient. It has spread over great and populous nations and is embraced by persons of all ranks and conditions. However, whoever thinks that its success is due to the force of the invincible *reasons* upon which it is founded, is little acquainted with the ignorance and stupidity of the generality of humankind. Such a person is also clearly unaware of the incurable prejudices of humans in favour of their particular superstitions.

Even today in Europe, ask the general public why they believe in an omnipotent Creator. They will never mention the beauty of *ultimate* causes, for of these they are wholly ignorant. They will not hold out their hands, bidding you contemplate the suppleness and variety of the joints in their fingers bending all one way, with counterpoise from the opposable thumb. They will not cite the softness and the fleshy parts of the inside of their hands, with all the other circumstances fitting them for the purpose for which they were destined. Long accustomed to these, they behold them with inaction and unconcern.

They will, however, tell you of the sudden and unexpected death of a person; of the fall and bruise of another; the excessive drought of this season; the cold and rains of another. These they ascribe to the direct operation of Providence. Such events, to rational thinkers the chief *difficulties* in admitting a supreme Intelligence, are to them the sole arguments *for* it.

---

1 Caesar, *De Bello Gallico*, 6.17. The Romans identified the ancient British goddess Sula with Minerva at their *Aquae Sulis* (the Waters of Sula), modern Bath.

2 Hertha was an alternative name for Nertha, from *der erde* (the earth) a Germanic fertility and Earth goddess. It, or rather she, is also an asteroid.

3 Tacitus, *de moribus germanorum*, 40. *Mater tellus* was a Roman goddess; literally 'Earth mother'.

Many theists, even the most zealous and refined, have denied an identifiable or *corporate*[A] Providence. They assert that the Sovereign Mind, or first Principle of all things, having fixed the general laws by which Nature is governed, gives free and uninterrupted course to these laws.[1] The Mind does not disturb this settled order of events by acts of will. Its adherents say that it is from the beautiful integration and rigid observance of established rules that we draw the chief argument for theism – and that it is from those same principles that we are enabled to counter the principal objections to it.

However, this is so little understood by the generality of humankind that wherever they observe anyone ascribing *all* events to natural causes and removing the *particular* interposition of a Deity, they are apt to suspect the grossest infidelity. Says my Lord Bacon, 'A little philosophy makes men atheists: a great deal reconciles them to religion.'[2] People are taught by superstitious prejudices to lay the stress on the wrong place. When that fails them, and they discover, by a little reflection, that the course of Nature is actually regular and uniform, their faith totters and falls into ruin. However, being taught by further reflection that this very regularity and uniformity is the strongest *proof* of design and of a supreme Intelligence, they return to their former belief, able now to establish it on a firmer and more durable foundation.

Convulsions in Nature, disorders, prodigies, miracles, though most contradictory to the plan of a wise Superintendent, impress humanity with the strongest sentiments of religion. This is because it is in such circumstances that the causes of events seem the most unknowable and unaccountable. Madness, fury, rage and an inflamed imagination sink people closest to the level of beasts. For similar reasons, these situations are often supposed to be the only ones where we can have any communication with the Deity *without* an intermediary. In nations that have embraced the doctrine of theism, we may therefore generally conclude

---

1 This is a concise definition of Deism, in which Providence is seen as operating generally, ie through the laws of Nature, as opposed to a Particular or interventional Providence. See Hume, *An Enquiry Concerning Human Understanding*, Section xi.

2 Lord Francis Bacon, 'Of Atheism', in *Essayes or Counsels, Civill and Morall* (1625). Properly: 'A little *Philosophy* inclineth man's mind to *Atheisme*, but depth in *Philosophy* bringeth men's minds about [ie back] to religion.'Bacon (1561–1626), English statesman, scientist, philosopher and author, was one of the principal theorists of early modern scientific method and a proponent of the idea that Nature is governed by regular natural laws.

that, since the common people still build it upon irrationality and superstition, they are never led to that doctrine by any process of argument.
They arrive only by a train of thinking more suitable to their intelligence
and ability.

In an idolatrous[1] nation it may readily happen that although the people admit the existence of *several* limited deities, there is however one god
whom they make the particular object of their worship and adoration.[2]
On the one hand, they may suppose that in the distribution of power and
territory among the gods, their nation was placed under the jurisdiction
of that particular deity. On the other hand, by reducing heavenly objects
to the model of things below, they may represent one god as the prince, or
supreme magistrate,[3] over the rest. Though of the same *nature*, it rules the
other gods with the authority exercised by earthly sovereigns over their
subjects and vassals. Hence, whether this god is considered as *their* peculiar patron, or as the *general*[4] sovereign of heaven, its worshippers will
endeavour by every art to insinuate themselves into its favour. Imagining
it to be pleased by praise and flattery like themselves, no eulogy or exaggeration will be spared in their addresses to it. As the fears or distresses of
the people become more urgent, new strains of adulation continue to be
invented in proportion. The individual outdoing a predecessor in swelling
the titles of their Deity, is sure to be outdone by a successor with yet newer
and more pompous epithets of praise.

Thus they proceed till at last they arrive at Infinity itself, beyond which
there is no farther progress. In striving to get farther and to portray a magnificent *simplicity*, they are fortunate if they do not run into inexplicable
mystery, thus destroying the Deity's intelligent nature upon which, alone,
rational worship can be founded. While they confine themselves to the
notion of a perfect Being and the Creator of the world they are coinciding,
by chance, with the principles of reason and true philosophy. However they
are not guided to that notion by reason – of which they are largely incapable – but by the adulation and fears of the most basic superstition. We
often find amongst barbarous nations – and even sometimes amongst the
civilized – that when every strain of flattery has been exhausted towards

---

1 ie polytheistic.
2 This form of religion is otherwise known as 'monolatry.' It is the form of religion Voltaire
   would argue characterized early religion in the article, 'Religion' in his 1764 *Dictionnaire
   philosophique* or Philosophical Dictionary.
3 'A person invested with authority; a governor.' SJ
4 As an adjective: 'Comprising the whole.' SJ. ie overall.

arbitrary* princes whose every *human* quality has been applauded to the utmost, their servile courtiers finally represent them as real divinities. They are then presented as such to the people as objects of adoration. How much more natural, therefore, that a limited *deity*, first supposed to be only the immediate author of particular goods and ills in life, should be represented finally as sovereign Maker and modifier of the Universe?

Even where the notion of a supreme Deity is already established; if a nation recognizes a *subordinate* tutelary divinity, saint, or angel, their addresses to it gradually rise and encroach on their supreme Deity, whose adoration ought naturally to *lessen* every other worship and abase every other object of reverence. The Virgin Mary thus proceeded from being merely a good woman to the usurpation of many attributes of the Almighty, before being checked by the Reformation.

God and St Nicholas go hand in hand, in all the prayers and petitions of the Muscovites.[1] It was thus that the deity who, from lust, converted himself into a bull in order to carry off Europa[2] and who from ambition dethroned his father Saturn, became the pagan *Optimus Maximus*.[3] It was thus that the Deity, whom the earliest Jews conceived *only* as the God of the patriarchs Abraham, Isaac, and Jacob, became *Jehovah*, creator of the Universe.

The Jacobins,[4] who denied the Immaculate Conception, have always been very unhappy in their doctrine, even though political reasons have kept the Roman Catholic Church from condemning it. The Cordeliers have run off with all the popularity.[5] However, we learn from Boulainvilliers,[6] that in the fifteenth century an Italian Cordelier maintained that, during the three days

---

* Arbitrary: *Despotic, absolute, capricious* SJ
1 St Nicholas is the principal patron saint of Moscow, or Muscovy, and of the Eastern or Greek Orthodox Church.
2 Europa, princess of Phoenicia, abducted to Crete by Zeus disguised as a white bull.
3 Zeus became the supreme Roman deity, titled IOM; *Iuppiter Optimus Maximus*; Jupiter, best and greatest (of the gods).
4 Jacobins; Dominican friars, founded by St Dominic de Guzman and known for their scholarly inquiry. The philosopher Thomas Aquinas was a Dominican. They are called 'Jacobins' from their first official convent, the Convent of St Jacques, near the church of St Jacques, Paris. It is today in the Latin Quarter and near the Sorbonne.
5 Cordeliers: alternative name for French monks of the Franciscan order, founded by St Francis. From their *cordelière*, a girdle of rope worn around the waist.
6 Compte Henri de Boulainvilliers (1658–1722), author of *Abrégé chronologique de l'histoire de France* and friend of the sceptic Pierre Bayle, translator of Spinoza and author of *La vie de Mahomet*.

when Christ was interred, the hypostatic union[1] was dissolved and that during that period his human nature was not a proper object of adoration. Without the art of divination, one might predict that so gross and impious a blasphemy would be anathematized by the people. It was the occasion of great insults on the part of the Jacobins who now got some recompense for their misfortunes in the war over the Immaculate Conception. Rather than relinquish this propensity to adulation, religionists in all ages have involved themselves in the greatest absurdities and contradictions. Homer, in one passage, calls Oceanus and Tethys[2] the original parents of all things, conforming to the established mythology and tradition of the Greeks. Yet, in other passages he cannot resist complimenting Zeus, the reigning deity, with that magnificent appellation. He accordingly names him the father of gods and humans.[3] He forgets that every temple was full of the ancestors, uncles, brothers, and sisters of this Zeus, who was in reality nothing but an upstart parricide and usurper. A similar contradiction is observable in Hesiod where it is even less excusable, since his professed intention was to deliver a true genealogy of the gods.[4]

Consider a religion – and we may suspect Islam of this inconsistency – that sometimes painted the Deity in the most sublime colours as the creator of heaven and earth, yet sometimes degraded it to the level of human creatures, representing it as: wrestling with a man;[5] walking in the cool of the evening;[6] showing its back parts[7] and descending from Heaven to inform itself of what passes on Earth.[8] This religion at the same time ascribes to the Deity suitable infirmities, passions, and partialities of the moral kind. Such a religion, after it was extinct, would be cited as an instance of those contradictions that arise when the gross, vulgar, natural conceptions of humanity are set against their continual propensity towards flattery and exaggeration.

Nothing indeed would prove more strongly the *divine* origin of any religion than to find – as is happily the case with Christianity – that it is free from a contradiction so incident* in human nature.

---

* Incident (as adjective): *Apt to happen.* SJ
1 Hypostasis: *The oneness of the Christ and his consubstantiality with the Father.* SJ
2 Homer, *The Iliad*, XIV. 200–4 and 301–4. In Greek myth, the Titan Oceanus was the son of Uranus (Heaven) and Gaia (Earth) and, in Homer, the parent with Tethys of all the gods.
3 Ibid: XV. 12 & 47
4 Hesiod, *Theogony*, 47–52.
5 Genesis 32.24
6 Ibid. 3.8
7 Exodus 33. 23
8 Ibid. 33.5

SECTION VII:

Confirmation of this Doctrine.

In general, it appears certain that uneducated people originally saw their Divinity as a *limited* being, only considering it the particular cause of health or sickness, plenty or want, prosperity or adversity. Yet, when more magnificent ideas are urged upon them, they reckon it dangerous to refuse their assent.

Will you say your Deity is finite and restricted in its perfections; may be overcome by a greater force; is subject to human passions, pains, and infirmities; has a beginning and may have an end? These they dare not affirm. Thinking it safest, however, to comply* with the higher encomiums[1], they try to ingratiate themselves with their Deity by an affected ravishment and devotion. As confirmation, we may observe in this case that the assent of the common people is merely verbal. They are incapable of conceiving the sublime qualities they appear to attribute to the Deity. Their actual *idea* of it, despite their pompous language, is still as poor and superficial as ever.

The Magians[2] say; original Intelligence, the first Principle of all things, reveals itself solely to the mind and the understanding *without* any intermediary. It has, however, placed the Sun as its visible image. When that bright luminary beams over the earth and the firmament, it is only a faint copy of the glory residing in the higher heavens. If you would to escape the displeasure of this divine Being, you must be careful never to set your bare foot upon the ground, nor spit into a fire or throw water upon it, even though it were consuming a city.[3]

The Moslems ask; who can express the perfections of the Almighty? Even the noblest of its *works*, when compared to *it*, are but dust and rubbish. How much more must human conception fall short of its infinite

---

* To Comply: *To be obsequious to*; SJ
1 Formal expressions of praise; panegyrics.
2 Plural of Magian, more usually 'Magi', as in the visitors to the infant Christ A Zoroastrian caste in ancient Persia associated with sacrifice, divination and astrology. Herodotus refers to them in *The Histories* 1.132 as does Xenophon in *Cyropaedia* 'The Education of Cyrus', VIII.3.11. The English term magic derives from them.
3 Hyde, *Religio Veterum Persarum*, XXIII. 306–8. Dr Thomas Hyde (1636–1703), Asian scholar and Laudian Professor of Arabic at Oxford, 1691–1703. The 'Religion of the ancient Persians' was his *magnum opus*.

perfections? Its smile and favour renders people happy forever. To obtain it for your children, the best method is to cut off from them, when infants, a little bit of skin about half the breadth of a farthing.[1]

The Roman Catholics say; take two bits of cloth, say about an inch or an inch and a half square and join them by the corners with two strings or pieces of tape about sixteen inches long. Then throw this over your head, making one of the bits of cloth lie on your breast and the other upon your back, keeping both next your skin. There is no better secret for recommending yourself to that infinite and eternal Being.[2]

The Getes,[3] commonly styled 'immortal' from their unwavering belief in the soul's immortality, were genuine theists and unitarians.[4] They affirmed Zamolxis, their Deity, to be the only true god and asserted that the worship of all other nations was being addressed to mere fictions and chimeras. But were their religious principles any more refined on account of these magnificent pretensions? Every fifth year they sacrificed a human victim whom they sent as a messenger to their Deity in order to inform it of their needs and wants.

When it thundered they were so provoked that, in order to return the defiance,[5] they let fly arrows at it, and did not decline the combat as one-sided. Such at least is the account given by Herodotus of the theism of the 'immortal' Getes.[6]

SECTION VIII:

Flux and reflux of polytheism and theism.

It is remarkable that the principles of religion have a kind of flux and reflux[7] in the human mind, people having a natural tendency to rise from idolatry to theism and then to sink back into idolatry again. The ignorant and

---

1 Hume refers to circumcision. A farthing (orig. *fourthing*) was an imperial unit of currency and one quarter of a penny. It ceased to be UK legal tender in 1960.
2 Hume here refers to the small devotional scapular (from Lat. *scapulae*, the shoulders) in contrast to the much larger monastic variety.
3 The Getae anglicised to Getes, a people who lived in Dacia, modern Romania and part of Bulgaria.
4 Unitarians believe God to be a single entity and personality; in contrast to the doctrine of the Trinity – three persons in one God.
5 Thunder and lightning were seen as intrusions by a rival god.
  Defiance. *A Challenge; an invitation to fight.* SJ
6 Herodotus, *Histories* IV. 93–97. See also Section III.
7 Ebb and flow.

uninstructed of humankind, a few excepted, never elevate their contemplation to the heavens. Neither do their disquisitions* penetrate sufficiently far into the secret** structure of animal or vegetable bodies to discover the supreme Mind, or original Providence, that bestowed *order* on Nature.

They take a more confined and selfish view of these admirable works, concluding that their own happiness and misery depends on the secret influence and unforeseen concurrence of external objects. Thus they perpetually and attentively regard the unknown causes governing all natural events, distributing pleasure and pain, good and ill, by their powerful yet silent operation.

In every emergence*** these unknown causes are appealed to, and in their general appearance or confused image, reside the perpetual objects of human hopes, fears, wishes and apprehensions. Human imagination, uneasy with its incessant *abstract* conception of objects, begins by degrees to render them more *particular*. It clothes them in shapes more suitable to its natural comprehension. It represents them as being like humankind; sentient, intelligent beings actuated by love or hatred, pliable through gifts, entreaties, prayers and sacrifices. Hence the origin of religion – and hence the origin of idolatry or polytheism.

The same anxious concern for happiness that generates the idea of these invisible, intelligent powers, does not allow humanity to long retain their first, simple conception of them as powerful, but *limited* beings; masters of human fate, yet slaves to destiny and the course of Nature. Exaggerated praises and compliments continue to swell their ideas of them. By elevating their deities to the utmost bounds of perfection, humanity finally produces the attributes of unity and infinity, simplicity and spirituality.

Such refined ideas, however, being beyond the ordinary comprehension, do not remain long in their original purity. They require to be supported by the notion of mediators or subordinate agents, interposed between humanity and the supreme Deity. These demigods or middle beings, by partaking more of *human* nature and thus more familiar to us, become the chief objects of devotion. They thus gradually resurrect the idolatry formerly banished by the ardent prayers and panegyrics of timorous, indigent mortals.

---

* Disquisitions: *Enquiries.* SJ
** Secret: *Hidden; undiscovered.* SJ
*** *Any sudden occasion.* SJ

These idolatrous religions, by subsiding progressively into grosser and more vulgar conceptions, finally destroy themselves. Furthermore, through the crude representations they form of their deities, they turn the tide again towards monotheism.

In this alternating cycle of human sentiment and belief, so great is the propensity to return to idolatry that even the utmost precaution may be unable to prevent it. Some theists, particularly Jews and Muslims, have been aware of this, as evidenced by their prohibition of all the arts of statuary and painting. Moreover, they even forbid the representation of *human* figures in marble or colour, lest the infirmity of humankind should thence produce idolatry. The feeble human understanding is incapable of conceiving their Deity as a pure Spirit and perfect Intelligence, yet their natural terrors keep them from imputing to it the least shadow of limitation and imperfection. Thus they fluctuate between these opposite beliefs. The same infirmity continually drags them downwards from an omnipotent and spiritual Deity to a limited and corporeal one; and from there to a statue or visible representation. Equally, the same endeavour at elevation continually pushes them upwards from the statue or material image to an invisible power; and from that invisible power to an infinitely perfect Deity, the creator and sovereign of the Universe.

SECTION IX:

Comparison of these Religions, with regard to
Persecution and Toleration

Polytheism or idolatrous worship, being founded entirely on primitive tradition, is subject to a great difficulty; namely that any barbarous, corrupt practice or opinion may be authorized by it. Furthermore, it gives full scope for knavery* to impose on the credulity of idolaters until morals and even humanity are expelled. At the same time, idolatry is attended by a manifest advantage. By limiting the powers and functions of its deities, it naturally admits the gods of other sects and nations to a *share* of divinity. It thus renders all the various deities, rites, ceremonies and traditions compatible with each other.

---

* Knavery: *Dishonesty; wickedness; fraud.* SJ

Marcus Verrius Flaccus, cited by Pliny,[1] affirmed that it was usual for the Romans, before they laid siege to any town, to invoke the tutelary deity of that place. By promising it equal or greater honours than those presently enjoyed, they sought to bribe it to betray its friends and adherents. For this reason, the name of the tutelary deity of Rome herself was kept a most religious mystery lest, in the same manner, enemies of the Republic attract it to their service. Without the *name*, they thought, nothing such could be practised. Pliny says that the common form of invocation was preserved up to his time in the ritual of the pontiffs. Macrobius has transmitted a copy of it[2] from the work.

Secret Things of Sammonicus Serenus.[3] Theism is the opposite in both its advantages and disadvantages. As a system supposing one sole Deity the perfection of reason and goodness, if correctly observed it should banish everything frivolous, unreasonable, or inhuman from religious worship. Thus it should set before people the most illustrious examples as well as the most commanding motives of justice and benevolence.

These mighty advantages are not negated – for that is impossible – but they are somewhat *diminished* by the inconveniencies arising from the vices and prejudices of humanity. While a sole Object of devotion is acknowledged, the worship of other deities is regarded as both absurd and impious. Indeed, this unity of the Object seems naturally to require unity of both faith and ceremonies. It thus furnishes schemers with a pretence[4] for presenting their adversaries as profane – and hence objects for divine and human vengeance.

Since each sect is positive that only its own faith and worship are entirely acceptable to the Deity, no sect can conceive it being pleased with different or opposite rites and principles. Hence the various sects descend naturally into animosity, discharging at each other that most furious and implacable of all human passions – *sacred* zeal and rancour. In both ancient and modern times, the tolerating spirit of polytheists is obvious to anyone conversant

---

1 Pliny the Elder, *Historia Naturalis*, XXVIII. 4. 18–9. M. Verrius Flaccus (55 BCE–20 CE) was a Roman grammarian of the early Empire.

2 *Saturnalia*, III.9. Macrobius, (fl.5th century CE), Roman antiquarian and historian.

3 Q. Sammonicus Serenus (?–212 CE). Roman physician, tutor to the Emperors Geta and Caracalla and murdered by the latter. Hume cites his *Res Reconditae* (secret things). His medical textbook *De Medicina Praecepta* was used until medieval times.

4 Pretence: *A claim; false or true*. SJ. Also dynastic. Prince Charles Edward Stuart, a claimant to the British throne, was styled 'The Young Pretender'.

with the writings of historians or travellers. When the oracle of Delphi was asked what rites or worship was most acceptable to the gods, it replied, 'Those that are legally established in each City.'[1]

In those times it seems that even priests could permit salvation to those of a different communion. The Romans commonly adopted the gods of conquered peoples and never disputed the attributes of those local and national deities in whose territories they resided.[2]

The religious wars and persecutions of the Egyptian idolaters are indeed an exception to this rule, but are explained by ancient authors for singular and remarkable reasons. Different species of animals were the deities of the different Egyptian sects and these deities, being continually at war, engaged their adherents in the combat. The worshippers of dogs could not long remain at peace with adorers of cats or wolves.[3] But where that contention was absent, Egyptian superstition was not as incompatible as is commonly imagined. We learn from Herodotus that very large contributions were given by Amasis towards the rebuilding of the temple of Delphi.[4] The intolerance of almost all monotheistic religions maintaining the *unity* of God, is as remarkable as the contrasting principle of polytheists. The implacably narrow spirit of the Jews is well known. Islam set out with still more bloody principles and even to this day deals out damnation – though not burning at the stake – to all other sects.

Among Christians, if the English and Dutch have embraced the principles of toleration, this singularity has resulted from the steady rise of the *secular* power, in opposition to the continued efforts of priests and bigots. The disciples of Zoroaster[5] shut the doors of heaven against all but the Magians. Nothing obstructed the progress of the Persian conquests more than their furious zeal against the sacred temples and images of the Greeks.[6]

---

1 Xenophon, *Memorabilia*, I.3
2 eg the Romans tactfully named Bath *Aquae Sulis* (The Waters of Sula) after the ancient British deity of the hot springs. The Romans identified her with their Minerva.
3 Plutarch, 'On the Worship of Isis & Osiris,' *Moralia*, LXXII.
4 *Histories*, II.180. Amasis, aka Ahmose, II (570–526 BCE) was a Pharaoh of the 26th dynasty and the last great ruler of Egypt before the Persian conquest of Cambyses II.
5 Their deity, Ahura Mazda, was unitary. Zoroastrianism was the dominant religion of Iran, until marginalised by the advent of Islam. See Hyde, op. cit.
6 Herodotus, Ιστοριαι (*History*) VIII.33–35.

After his overthrow of the Persian Empire we find Alexander, a polytheist, immediately re-establishing such worship among the Babylonians which had been abolished by their former monotheistic princes.[1] Even Alexander's blindly devoted attachment to Greek superstition did not prevent him from sacrificing according to Babylonian rites and ceremonies.

So *sociable* is polytheism that even the utmost fierceness and antipathy it encounters in a conflicting religion, is scarcely able to disgust it and keep it at a distance. Augustus praised most highly the reserve of his grandson, Gaius Caesar, when this latter prince, passing by Jerusalem, did not deign to sacrifice according to the Jewish law.[2] Why did Augustus so approve of this conduct? Because Judaism was esteemed ignoble and barbarous by polytheists.[3]

I affirm that few of the corruptions of idolatry and polytheism are more pernicious to society than is the corruption of *theism* when carried to the utmost.[4] The human sacrifices of the Carthaginians, Mexicans and many barbarous nations do not exceed the persecutions of the Holy Inquisition[5] at Rome and Madrid.[1] Most nations have fallen into this guilt of human sacrifice, although that impious superstition has never prevailed in any *civilised* nation, unless we except the Carthaginians; the Tyrians soon abolished it.

A sacrifice is conceived as a present delivered to the deity by destroying it and thus rendering it useless to men. This is done either by burning what is solid, pouring out liquid, or killing the living. For lack of a better way of doing the deity a service we do *ourselves* an injury, imagining that thereby we are at least expressing hearty goodwill and adoration. Thus our mercenary devotion deceives ourselves – while imagining it deceives the deity.

---

1 Arrian, *Anabasis*, III.16. Flavius Arrianus (*c*.85–*c*.150 CE) was a soldier, Stoic philosopher and historian of the campaigns of Alexander the Great of Macedon.
2 Suetonius, Vita Augusti, XCIII. *Gaium nepotem…apud Hierosolyma non supplicasset, conlaudavit.* Suetonius does not specify that Caligula avoided sacrificing, but merely worshipping according to the Jewish rite.
3 Ibid. Judaism is monotheistic, as are Christianity and Islam.
4 *Corruptio optima pessima* (Anon.) Corruption of what is *best* – is the worst of all.
5 The Roman Catholic agency for the investigation, detection and suppression of heresy. Since 1965 it has been styled *The Congregation for the Doctrine of the Faith*. Its sanctions, performed by the secular power, included imprisonment, torture and execution.

Apart from the Carthaginian and Mexican bloodletting being less than that of the Holy Inquisition at Rome and Madrid, the human victims of polytheism, by being chosen by lot or by some exterior signs, do not affect the rest of society. In contrast, virtue, knowledge and love of liberty are the qualities that call down the fatal vengeance of Inquisitors. These qualities when expelled from society, leave it in a most shameful state of ignorance, corruption and bondage. The illegal murder of a single individual by a tyrant is more pernicious than the death of a thousand by pestilence, famine, or any blind calamity. In the temple of Diana at Aricia, near Rome, whoever murdered the current priest was legally entitled to be installed as his successor.[1] This was a very unusual institution, since however barbarous and bloody are the common superstitions towards the laity, they usually turn to the *advantage* of the holy order.

SECTION X:

With regard to Courage or Abasement.

From the comparison of theism and polytheism, ie idolatry, we may form other observations confirming the common observation that 'the corruption of the best things gives rise to the worst.'

When the deity is represented as *infinitely* superior to humankind, this belief – though altogether just[2] – plus superstitious terror, is apt to sink the human mind to the lowest level of submission and abasement. Such a belief also describes the monkish virtues of mortification,* penance, humility and passive suffering as the only qualities acceptable to the deity.

However, where the gods are conceived to be only a *little* superior to humanity and where many are elevations from the human ranks, we are more relaxed in our addresses to them. Without profanity, we may sometimes even aspire to rival and emulate them. From hence may come activity, spirit, courage, magnanimity, love of liberty and all the virtues that aggrandize a people.

---

* Mortification: *Humiliation*. SJ
1 Strabo, *Geographica*, 5. 239. Suetonius, *Vita Caligulae* xxxv. 'The priest who slew the slayer – and shall himself be slain.'
  TB Macaulay, *Lays of Ancient Rome*; *The Battle of Lake Regillus*; x.
2 Just; *Precise; accurate.* SJ. Hence 'Altogether just' = entirely accurate.

The heroes in paganism correspond to the saints in Popery and to the holy dervishes in Islam.[1] The place of Hercules, Theseus, Hector and Romulus, is now taken by Dominic,[2] Francis,[3] Anthony[4] and Benedict.[5] Thus the former means of obtaining celestial honours among humankind: destroying monsters; subduing tyrants and defending our native land, have become whippings; fastings; cowardice; humility; abject submission and slavish obedience.

One great motivation of the pious Alexander the Great in his military expeditions was his rivalry with Hercules and Bacchus whom he justly claimed to have excelled.[6]

After Brasidas, that generous and noble Spartan, fell in battle he had Heroic honours paid him by the inhabitants of Amphipolis whose defence he had conducted.[7]

In general, all the founders of states and colonies among the Greeks were raised to this lower rank of divinity by those who reaped the benefit of their labours. This gave rise to the observation of Machiavelli that the Christian doctrines of Roman Catholicism, by recommending only *passive* courage and suffering, had subdued the spirit of humanity, fitting them only for slavery and subjection.[8] This observation would certainly be fair, were there not many other circumstances in human society that control the nature and character of a religion. Brasidas once seized a mouse and, having been bitten by it, let it go.

'There is nothing so small and feeble,' said he, 'that it cannot make shift to save its life – if it only has the courage to defend itself.'[9] Cardinal Bellarmine[10] patiently and humbly allowed fleas and other odious vermin to prey upon him, saying,

---

1 Moslem holy men, characterised by extreme poverty and austerity, broadly equivalent to the mendicant friars of Christianity or the *Sadhus* of Hinduism.
2 St Dominic (1170–1221) Founder of the Dominican Order
3 St Francis of Assisi (1181–1226) Founder of the Franciscan Order.
4 St Anthony of the Desert (fl. 3rd century CE). Founder of Christian monasticism.
5 St Benedict of Nursia (480–547 CE). Author of *The Rule* followed by Benedictines.
6 Arrian, *Anabasis, passim*, but particularly IV. 10
7 Thucydides, *The Peloponnesian War*, v.11. Brasidas (c.470–422 BCE) was a Spartan officer active during the first decade of the war. Defending Amphipolis in Thrace, he was killed in action while defeating the besieging Athenians under Cleon.
8 Niccolò Machiavelli, *Discorsi*, VI.
9 Plutarch, *Apophthegmata Laconica* (Sayings of the Spartans).
10 Cardinal Roberto Bellarmine (1542–1621). Italian Jesuit. He was the first cleric to order Galileo to renounce his heretical claim that the Earth revolved around the Sun.

We shall have Heaven to reward us for our sufferings, whereas these poor creatures have nothing but the enjoyment of the present life.[1]

Such is the difference between the maxims of a Greek hero and a Catholic saint.

SECTION XI:

With regard to Reason or Absurdity.

Here is another supportive observation together with a new proof that it is indeed the corruption of the best things that begets the worst.

If we examine, without prejudice, the ancient heathen mythology in *poetry*, we shall not discover any absurdity as monstrous as we may suspect. Where is the difficulty in conceiving that the same powers or principles – whatever they were – that formed this *visible* world of humans and animals also produced a species of gods; intelligent creatures of more refined substance and of greater authority?

That these creatures may be capricious, revengeful, passionate or voluptuous is easily conceived; for among humankind, nothing more engenders such vices than the freedom conferred by *absolute* authority.[2] In short, the whole mythological system is so natural that it seems more than probable that it has been actually carried into execution somewhere or other in the vast Universe.

The chief objection to it with regard to *this* planet, is that it is not confirmed either by reason, or by authority. Ancient tradition, insisted on by heathen priests and theologians, is a weak foundation. It also transmitted so many contradictory reports, each supported by equal authority, that it becomes absolutely impossible to fix a preference amongst them.

A few books therefore, would be sufficient to contain all the polemical *writings* of pagan priests, whose whole theology consists more of traditional stories and superstitious practices, than of philosophical argument and debate.

Things are, however, different where *theism* forms the fundamental principle of any popular religion. Theism is so conformable to sound reason that philosophy is able to incorporate itself within such a theological system. Furthermore, if the other dogmas of that system be contained in a sacred

---

1 P. Bayle, Entry 'Bellarmine' in A *General Dictionary, historical & critical*, III. 173
2 Hume anticipates William Pitt the Elder, Earl of Chatham, in the House of Lords (1770)
   'Unlimited power tends to corrupt the minds of those who possess it.'

book such as the *Alcoran*[1], or are determined by a visible authority such as the Pope, speculative thinkers naturally give their assent. They also embrace a theory instilled into them from their earliest education and that also possesses *some* degree of consistency and uniformity.

Since *all* of these appearances are bound to prove deceitful, however, philosophy will soon find herself very unevenly yoked to her new associate. Instead of *controlling* each principle as they advance together, at every turn she is perverted to *serve* the purposes of superstition. For besides the unavoidable incoherencies that need to be reconciled and adjusted, one may safely affirm that all popular theology, especially the scholastic,[2] has a penchant for absurdity and contradiction.

The doctrines of scholasticism would appear easy and familiar, if only they did not trespass beyond reason and common sense. They, however, require amazement to be engendered, mystery to be affected, darkness and obscurity to be sought. Hence, basic merit must be accorded to those devout worshippers who lack an opportunity to *subdue* their rebellious reason through belief in the most ridiculous illogicalities. Ecclesiastical history amply confirms these reflections. Whenever a controversy is started, some always claim to foretell the outcome with certainty. They say that whichever opinion is *most* contrary to plain sense is sure to prevail, even where the general interest* of the system does not require that result. Though the accusation of heresy may be bandied about for some time among the disputants, that very heresy will *invariably* come to rest on the side of reason. It is claimed that anyone with sufficient learning to know the definition of the Arian, Pelagian, Erastian, Socinian, Sabellian, Eutychian, Nestorian and Monothelite heresies, not to mention the Protestant (whose fate is still uncertain) will be convinced of the truth of this observation.[3] It is thus that a system can ultimately become the more absurd, simply from it being reasonable and philosophical at the outset.

To oppose the torrent of scholastic religion by such feeble maxims as:

> It is impossible for the same thing to be – and not to be;
> The whole is greater than a part;

---

* Interest: *Influence; importance.* SJ
1 A variant of the *Qur'an* (the Koran); in Arabic, literally 'The Reading.'
2 Scholasticism was essentially an attempt to reconcile classical philosophy with medieval Abrahamic theology. The term often connotes the medieval schools of Western Christendom. It was prominent *circa* the 10th through 15th centuries.
3 The followers of Arius denied the separate identity of the Father and the Son; Pelagians denied Original Sin; Socinians the divinity of Christ; Erastians the authority of Church over State. For the rest, see: www.roman-empire.net/religion/heresy.html

Two and three make five, is like attempting to stop the ocean's inrush with a bullrush.

You want to deploy profane *reason* against sacred mystery? Then no punishment is great enough for your impiety! Those same fires that were kindled below heretics will also serve for the destruction of philosophers – such as you.

SECTION XII:

With regard to Doubt or Conviction.

Every day we meet with people so *historically* sceptical as to assert the impossibility of any nation ever believing such absurd principles as those of Greek and Egyptian paganism. At the same time, however, they are sufficiently dogmatic to think the same absurdities are *not* to be found in other religious communions.

Cambyses entertained similar prejudices. Impiously, he ridiculed and even wounded Apis, the great god of the Egyptians who appeared to his profane senses nothing more than a large spotted bull.[1] Herodotus, however, judiciously ascribes this outburst of passion to a disorder of the brain; real madness. Otherwise, says the historian, he would never have openly affronted any established worship. On religion, he continues, each nation is best satisfied with their own, thinking they have the advantage over every other nation.

It must be admitted that the Roman Catholics are a very learned sect and that no denomination, except the Church of England, can dispute their being the most learned of all the Christian churches. However Averroes, the famous Arabian, who had no doubt heard of the Egyptian superstitions, declares that the most absurd and nonsensical of all religions is that whose adherents, having created their deity, proceed to eat him.[2] I believe, indeed, that there is no tenet in all paganism that gives so great a scope for ridicule as that of the

---

1 Cambyses, King of Persia (530–522 BCE), son of Cyrus the Great. He conquered Egypt in 525 BCE and killed the Apis Bull. As it represented the god Ptah, creator of the Universe, the bull was sacred to Egyptians. Herodotus, *Histories*, III. 29 and 30.

2 Ibn Rushd (1126–98) Anglicised to Averroes. Muslim polymath born in Cordoba and resident in Andalucía, Spain. He wrote on Islamic philosophy, medicine, jurisprudence and produced admired commentaries on Plato and Aristotle.

Roman Catholics' *Real Presence*.[1] It is so absurd that it eludes the force of all arguments. There are even humorous stories on the subject. These, though somewhat profane, are commonly told by the Catholics themselves. It is said that one day a priest inadvertently administered, instead of the Sacrament, a counter that had accidentally fallen among the holy wafers.[2] The communicant waited patiently for some time, expecting that it would dissolve on his tongue. However, finding that it still remained intact, he took it out, crying to the priest:

> I wish you had not made the mistake of giving me God the Father. He is so hard and tough, that there is no swallowing him!

A famous general in the Muscovite service, having come to Paris to recover from his wounds, brought along with him a young Turkish prisoner. Some of the teachers at the Sorbonne (who are just as fanatical as the dervishes of Constantinople) thinking it a pity that the poor Turk should be damned for lack of instruction, earnestly solicited Mustapha to turn Christian. As an encouragement, they promised him plenty of good wine in this world and paradise in the next. These allurements were too powerful to resist and so, having been well instructed and catechized, he at last agreed to receive the sacraments of baptism and the Eucharist. The priest, however, wanting to make everything sure and solid, still continued with his instructions and began the next day with the usual question,

> 'How many gods are there?'

> 'None,' replies Benedict – for that was his new name.

> 'What, none at all?'

> 'To be sure,' said the honest proselyte, 'you told me all along that there is but one God – and yesterday I ate him.'

Such are the doctrines of our Roman Catholic brethren. We are so accustomed to these doctrines that we never marvel at them, although in a future age it will probably be difficult to persuade people that anyone could ever embrace such principles. Moreover, it is a thousand to one against these nations themselves *not* having something fully as absurd in their own creed – to which they will give their most implicit religious assent.

---

1 Real Presence. The transubstantiation of the bread and wine of the Eucharist into the *actual*, rather than the (Protestant) *representational*, body and blood of the Christ. In RC doctrine, the sensory qualities of the host bread and wine are unchanged, but the 'substance' is transmuted. The priest's act of consecration replaces the substance of bread and wine with the *actual* substance of God, the 'real presence', with which the communicant is now, literally, in union.
2 A coin-shaped circular piece of wood, ivory or metal. Used in accountancy.

I lodged once in the same hotel in Paris[1] as an Ambassador from Tunis who, having passed some years in London, was on his way home. One day I observed His Moorish Excellency amusing himself on the porch by surveying the splendid equipages that drove along. There chanced to pass that way some Capuchin friars who had never seen a Tunisian while he, though accustomed to European dress, had never seen the grotesque figure of a Capuchin.[2] It is impossible to express the mutual admiration they inspired in each other. Had the chaplain of the Tunisian embassy entered into a debate with these Franciscans, their reciprocal surprise would had been of the same order. Thus does all humanity stand staring at one another; and there is no beating into their heads that the turban of the African is not just as good, or as bad, a fashion as the cowl of the European.

'He is a very honest man,' said the Prince of Sallee, speaking of de Ruyter; 'It is a pity he were a Christian.'[3]

Let us suppose an academic of the Sorbonne saying to a priest of Sais.[4]

'How can you *worship* leeks and onions?'

'If we worship them,' replies the latter, 'at least we do not at the same time *eat* them!'

'But,' says the learned academic, 'what strange objects of adoration are cats and monkeys!'

'They are at least as good as the relics or rotted bones of martyrs!' answers his equally learned antagonist.

'Are you not *mad*,' insists the Catholic, 'to cut one another's throats over the preference of a cabbage or a cucumber?'

'That I will admit,' says the pagan, 'provided *you* confess that it is still *madder* to fight over preference among volumes of spurious theological argument, ten thousand of which are not equal in value to *one* cabbage or cucumber!'

---

1 Hume was in Paris while diplomatic Secretary to Gen. St Clair in 1738 and later with Lord Hertford, British Ambassador to France, 1763–5.

2 The Friars of the Capuchin Order wore a long, pointed hood or *capuccio*. See: *Of Miracles* (*Enquiry concerning Human Understanding* 10.18).

3 Sallee, a port of western Morocco notorious for piracy. The Dutch Admiral Michiel de Ruyter (1607–77) trading there in 1641, greatly impressed the Sultan, Sidi Ali ben Mohamed ben Moussa, with his fair dealing.
    See Blok, P., *Life of Admiral de Ruyter*, pp.22–6. In 1667 he sailed up the Thames, burning three capital ships in the Battle of the Medway, as described by Pepys.

4 The Sorbonne (University of Paris) founded c.1257. In Hume's time it taught Catholic orthodoxy. Sais was an ancient city of Egypt where venerated objects included articles animal, vegetable and mineral.

It is strange that the Egyptian religion, though so absurd, should yet have borne so great a resemblance to that of the Jews, ancient writers of the greatest genius being unable to observe any difference between them. Remarkably, both Tacitus and Suetonius[1] expressly treat these religions as the same when describing the Senate's decree, in the reign of Tiberius, banishing Egyptian and Jewish proselytes from Rome. It appears that the decree itself was founded on that supposition. These wise heathens, observing the general air, genius and spirit of the two religions to be the same, reckoned the differences in their dogmas to be too frivolous* to deserve attention.

Every bystander will easily judge – but unfortunately the bystanders are few – that if any popular religious system could only be established simply by exposing the absurdities of *other* systems, then every adherent of every superstition would be able to justify the blind and bigoted attachment to the principles in which they had been educated. But even without such an extensive knowledge-based assurance – and perhaps better without it – there is no shortage of human religious zeal and faith. Diodorus Siculus gives a remarkable example of this, of which he himself was an eyewitness.[2] While Egypt lay under the greatest terror of the Roman name, the people turned with the utmost fury upon a legionary soldier guilty of the sacrilegious impiety of accidentally killing a cat. All the efforts of their Prince were unable to save him.[3]

I am persuaded that, at that time, the senate and people of Rome would not have been so delicate[4] with regard to their national deities. Shortly afterwards, they readily deified Augustus and would have dethroned every god in heaven for his sake, had he seemed to desire it.

Presens divus habebitur Augustus, says Horace.[5]

That is a very important point. In other nations and other ages, the same circumstance has not been deemed altogether innocent. When Louis XIV took upon himself the protection of the Jesuits' college of Clermont,

---

* Frivolous: *Slight; trifling.* SJ
1 Tacitus, *Annales*, II. 85. Suetonius, *Vita Tiberii*, XXXVI.
2 Diodorus Siculus, *Bibliotheca historica*, 1.83. Diodorus, a Sicilian Greek from Agira, was in Egypt during the 180th Olympiad (60–56 BCE)
3 Ptolemy XII *Auletes* 'The Flute Player.' Also known to his subjects, doubtless for good reasons, as 'The Bastard.' He was the father of the celebrated Cleopatra.
4 Consisting of *small* parts. SJ
5 *Odes*, III. 5 *Augustus shall be held to be a god on Earth.*

that Society of Jesus ordered the King's arms to be put up over the gate, taking down the cross in order to make way for it. This gave occasion to the following epigram:

Sustulit hinc Christi posuitque insignia regis
Impia gens alium nescit habere Deum.[1]

'Notwithstanding the sanctity of our holy religion,' says Cicero, 'no crime is more common with us than sacrilege.'[2] But whoever heard of an Egyptian violating the temple of a cat, an ibis or a crocodile? The same author says in another place[3] that there is no torture an Egyptian would not undergo, rather than injure an ibis, an asp, a cat, a dog or a crocodile. Thus it is strictly true, as Dryden observes:

Of whatsoe'er descent their godhead be,
    Stock, stone, or other homely pedigree,
In his defence his servants are as bold,
    As if he had been born of beaten gold.[4]

Indeed, the baser the materials of which the divinity is composed, the greater the devotion it is likely to excite in the deluded breasts of its worshippers. They exult in their shame and gain credit with their deity by braving, for its sake, all the ridicule and derision of its enemies. Ten thousand Crusaders enlist under the holy banners and even take pride openly in those parts of their religion that their adversaries regard as the most reproachful.

There occurs, I admit, a difficulty in the Egyptian system of theology. Indeed, few systems of that kind are entirely free from difficulties. It is evident from their method of procreation that a couple of cats would, in the space of fifty years, stock a whole kingdom. In twenty more, assuming they remained the subject of religious veneration, it would not only be easier to find a god than a human being in Egypt – as Petronius says was the case in some parts of Italy[5] – but also the gods would thus ultimately

---

1 'They took down the sign of Christ; put up the arms of Louis
  Impious folk. Couldn't tell God from hooey!'
2 *De Natura Deorum*, I. 29.
3 *Tusculan Disputations*, V. 27.
4 John Dryden, *Absalom and Achitophel*, 100–3.
5 Petronius, *Satyricon*, XVII. Gaius Petronius Arbiter (c.27–66 CE) was described by Tacitus as the *arbiter elegantiae* 'arbiter of taste' in Nero's Rome. His picaresque novel *Satyricon* directs Rabelaisian humour through the character Trimalchio at Nero himself. Petronius was a watchful voluptuary at Nero's court, as played by Leo Genn in *Quo Vadis* (MGM, 1951). Petronius survives as an Asteroid (No.3244) that, thankfully, does not intersect Earth's orbit.

starve the humans out, leaving themselves neither priests nor worshippers. It is therefore probable that this wise nation of Egypt, the most celebrated in antiquity for prudence and sound policy, foresaw such dangerous consequences. They then reserved all their worship for *fully-grown* divinities, using this freedom to drown the holy spawn or little sucking gods without scruple or remorse. Thus, in no way is the practice of warping tenets of religion to serve temporal interests seen to be an invention of our present later ages.

The learned and philosophical Varro,[1] when discoursing of religion, claims not to deliver anything beyond probabilities and appearances, such being his good sense and moderation. The passionate and zealous St Augustine, however, censures the noble Roman for his scepticism and reserve and professes the most thorough belief and assurance.[2] On the other hand, the heathen poet Namatianus,[3] a contemporary of Augustine, absurdly[4] believes the religious system of the saint to be so false that, says he, even the credulity of children could not induce them to believe it.

Is it strange when mistakes are so common to find everyone positive and dogmatic – their zeal often rising in proportion to the error? Spartianus says:

> *Moverunt, et ea tempestate Judaei bellum*
> *quod vetabantur mutilare genitalia.*[5]

'At this time the Jews went to war because they were forbidden the practice of genital mutilation.'[6]

---

1 Varro, *De lingua Latina*. v.10. Marcus Terentius Varro (116–27 BCE) was a soldier and man of letters of enormous output (*c.*600 volumes). *De lingua Latina* (On the Latin Language) is a valuable grammar also covering syntax and some fanciful etymologies. His religious scepticism drew the wrath of St Augustine – and the respect of Hume.

2 St Augustine of Hippo, *de civitate dei* (On the City of God), III.17. Aurelius Augustinus (354–430 CE) Christian philosopher, ex-pagan and scourge of heretics. He rebukes scepticism as sinful in his *Contra academicos*. Augustine's views on predestination (he was all for it) influenced theologians down to and including John Calvin. His '*De civitate Dei* (On the City of God)' contrasts with his *Confessions* with its memorable *da mihi castitatem et continentiam, sed noli modo* ('Give me chastity and continence – but not *just* yet').

3 Namatianus: *De reditu suo*,1.394. Rutilius Claudius Namatianus (fl. 5th century CE) Roman poet. 'On his homecoming' is a fine poem describing a voyage in 416 CE from Rome to his childhood home of Toulouse in Gaul.

4 Probably another of Hume's ironic *apologia* for conventional theism.

5 Spartianus, *Historia Augusta* XIV.2 In his *Life of Hadrian*, Aelius Spartianus describes the Jewish revolt of 132–5 CE, led by Shimon bar Kochba and Rabbi Akiva. It was brutally crushed by Hadrian.

6 ie circumcision.

If ever there were to be a nation, or a time, in which the public religion lost all authority over humankind, we might expect it to be Rome during the Ciceronian age. Then, infidelity would have openly erected its throne and Cicero himself, in every speech and action, would have been its most declared abettor. It appears, however, that whatever sceptical liberties that great man might take in his writings or in philosophical conversations, in the common conduct of life he still avoided the imputation of deism and profaneness. Even within his own family and to his wife, Terentia, whom he trusted greatly, he was willing to appear a devout religionist. A letter addressed to her survives in which Cicero earnestly requests her to sacrifice to Apollo and Aesculapius in gratitude for the recovery of his health.[1]

Pompey's devotion was much more sincere. In all his conduct during the civil wars he paid a great regard to auguries, dreams and prophesies.[2] Augustus also was tainted with superstition of every kind. Just as it was reported of John Milton that his poetical genius never flowed with such abundant ease as in the spring,[3] Augustus, in contrast, observed that in the same season his genius for dreaming was imperfect, his dreams being less *reliable* than during the rest of the year.

That great and able Emperor was also extremely uneasy when he happened to change his shoes, and put the right shoe on the left foot.[4] In short, it cannot be doubted that adherents of the established superstitions of antiquity were as numerous in every country as are those of the modern variety at present. Its influence was as universal, though not so powerful. Just as many people gave their assent to it, although that assent was seemingly not so strong, precise, or affirmative.

We may observe that, despite the dogmatic and imperious style of all superstition, the *conviction* of the religionist in all ages is more affected than real. It scarcely ever approaches, to any degree, the solid belief and persuasion governing us in the common affairs of life. People dare not

---

1 Cicero, *Epistolae ad Familiares*, xiv.7 His *Letters to his Friends* is one of the finest correspondences in all literature. The letters provide deep insight into the orator and politician himself and into the political and social life of the later Roman Republic.
2 Cicero, *de divinatione*. II. 24.
3 In his *Life of Milton* (1694), Edward Philips, the poet's nephew and one of his amanuenses, reported him as saying that, 'his vein never happily flowed, but from the autumnal equinox to the vernal' ie from mid-September to mid-March.
4 Suetonius, *De Vita Augusti*, 90–2.

acknowledge, even within their own hearts, the doubts that they entertain on such subjects. They make a merit of *implicit* faith, privately disguising their actual infidelity by the strongest assertions and by the most positive bigotry.

Nature, however, is too difficult for all their endeavours. She does not permit the obscure, glimmering light from shadowy regions to equal the strong impressions made by common sense and experience. The usual course of people's conduct belies their words, showing that their true assent in matters religious is due to some unaccountable mental operation. This lies between disbelief and conviction – though approaching much nearer to the former than to the latter.

The human mind, therefore, appears to be of such a loose and unsteady a texture that even now, when so many continually subject it to the hammer and chisel, they are unable to engrave lasting theological tenets upon it. How much more must this have been the case in ancient times, when the servants of the holy function were comparatively so much fewer?[1] No wonder that appearances were very inconsistent in those days. On some occasions people might appear determined infidels and enemies to the established religion without being so in reality – or at least without knowing their own minds in that particular.

Another cause rendering the ancient religions much looser than the modern, is that the former were *traditional* and the latter are *scriptural*, that is, derived from Scripture. Ancient religious tradition was complex, contradictory and on many occasions doubtful. Thus it could not possibly be reduced to any standard and canon, or even supply any *determinate** articles of faith. The stories of the gods were as numberless as Roman Catholic legends and although almost everyone believed some of these stories, no one could know, let alone believe, the whole. At the same time, all must have acknowledged that no one part stood on a better foundation than the rest. Furthermore, the traditions of different cities and nations were on many occasions in direct opposition and no reason could be assigned for preferring one to the other. Since there were an infinite number of stories, upon which tradition was in no way authoritative, there was thus an insensible gradation from the most fundamental articles of faith to loose and precarious fictions.

---

* Determinate: *Established; decisive; conclusive.* SJ
1 Religious operatives in ancient Greece and Rome were largely secular.

The pagan religion, therefore, seemed to vanish like a cloud whenever it was approached and examined piecemeal. It could never be ascertained by any fixed dogmas and principles. Although this did not convert the generality of humankind from so absurd a faith (for when will the people be reasonable?) yet it made them falter. It also made them more hesitant in holding to their principles and was even apt to produce certain mental attitudes that resulted in practices and opinions that had the *appearance* of determined infidelity. To this we may add that the fables of the pagan religion were themselves light, easy and familiar. They were also *without* devils, seas of brimstone, or indeed any object that could terrify the imagination.

Who could resist smiling at the thought of the loves of Mars and Venus or the amorous frolics of Jupiter and Pan? In this respect, it was a truly poetical religion, even if it had rather too much levity for the graver kinds of poetry. We find that it has been adopted by modern bards who do not talk of those old fictional gods with greater freedom and irreverence, than did the ancients themselves of those *real* objects of their devotion.

The inference is by no means valid that, just because a system of religion has made no deep impression on the minds of a people, it must therefore have been positively rejected by all those of common sense. Equally, we should not infer that *irreligious* principles were generally established by argument and reason, despite the influences of education. Indeed, the contrary may be more probable. The less importunate and demanding any species of superstition appears, the less will it provoke the people's spleen and indignation, or engage them in enquiries concerning its foundation and origin.

Meanwhile, it is obvious that the sway of all religious faith over the understanding is wavering and uncertain. It is subject to every variety of mood and dependent on the imagination being struck by present events. The difference is only one of degree. An ancient will alternate strokes of impiety with those of religion throughout a whole discourse. A modern often *thinks* in the same way, though in his *expression* he may well be more guarded. Witness this remarkable passage of Tacitus:

> Besides the manifold vicissitudes of human affairs, there were prodigies in Heaven and Earth; the warning voices of the Thunder, and other intimations of the future, auspicious, gloomy, doubtful and not to be mistaken. Never, surely, did more terrible calamities of the Roman people, or evidence

more conclusive, prove that the gods take no thought for our happiness, but only for our punishment.[1]

Augustus's quarrel with Neptune is an instance of the same kind. Had not the Emperor believed Neptune to be a real being and to have dominion over the sea, where had been the foundation of his anger? And if he *believed* it, what madness to provoke that deity still farther.[2] The same observation may be made upon Quintilian's exclamation on account of the death of his children.[3]

Lucian tells us expressly[4] that whoever disbelieved the most ridiculous fables of paganism was deemed the most profane and impious. Indeed, why would that agreeable author have employed the whole force of his wit and satire against the national religion, had it *not* been generally believed by his countrymen and contemporaries?

Livy acknowledges the common incredulity of his age just as frankly as any divine would at present, but then condemns that very incredulity just as severely.[5] And who can imagine that a national superstition that could delude so ingenious a man would not also impose itself on the generality of the people?

The Stoics bestowed many magnificent and even impious epithets on their 'Sage'[6]; that he alone was rich, free, a king and equal to the immortal gods. They forgot to add that he was not inferior in prudence and understanding to an old woman. For surely nothing can be more pitiful than the sentiments Stoics entertained with regard to religious matters. They seriously

---

1 Tacitus, *Histories*, 1.3. The year is 69 CE, 'The Year of the Four Emperors.'

2 Suetonius, *De vita Augusti*, XVI ...*exclamaverit etiam invito Neptuno victoriam se adepturum, ac die circensium proximo sollemni pompae simulacrum dei detraxerit* ([Augustus] cried that he would have victory in spite of Neptune and had the god's image removed from the sacred procession at the next Games in the Circus.

3 Quintilian, *Institutio Oratoria* VI. Preface: 'What father with a spark of proper feeling would not pardon me for having no heart to pursue my researches further, and... no other use for my voice than to rail against the gods for having suffered me to outlive all my nearest and dearest, testifying that Providence deigns not to watch over this Earth of ours?' He refers to his late wife and two sons.

4 Lucian, *Philopseudes*, III. The satirist Lucian of Samostata's *The Lover of Lies* (*c.*150 CE) is a frame story in which Tychiades, the narrator, soundly debunks a parade of allegedly supernatural events. One tale was *The Sorcerer's Apprentice*, itself the inspiration for Goethe's *Der Zauberlehrling* (1797).

5 Livy, *History of Rome*, X.40

6 The 'Sage' was the Stoic term for their ideal wise person.

agreed with the common augurs[1] that when a raven croaks from the *left* it is a good omen, but a bad omen when a noise from the same quarter is made by a rook.

Panaetius was the only Stoic among the Greeks who so much as expressed doubt with regard to auguries and divinations.[2] Marcus Antonius tells us that he himself had received many admonitions from the gods in his sleep.[3] It is true that Epictetus forbids us to regard the language of rooks and ravens, but not because they do not speak the truth. It is only because they can only foretell the breaking of our neck or the forfeiture of our estate, these being circumstances, says he *stoically*, that in no way concern us.[4] Thus the Stoics unite philosophical enthusiasm with religious superstition. The force of the Stoic mind, being directed to the field of morality, was unaffected in that of religion.

Plato represents Socrates as affirming that the accusation of impiety raised against him was owed entirely to his rejecting such fables as those of Saturn's castrating his father and the subsequent dethroning of Saturn by Uranus and Jupiter.[5] Yet, in a subsequent *Dialogue*, Socrates confesses that the doctrine of the mortality of the soul was the received opinion of the people.[6] Is there any contradiction here? Yes, surely. However, the contradiction is not in Plato; it is in the people themselves. In general, their religious principles are *always* composed of the most discordant parts, especially so in an age when superstition sat so easily and lightly upon them.

Xenophon's conduct, as related by himself,[7] is both incontestable proof of the general credulity of humankind in those ages, and of the incoherence, in *all* ages, of people's opinions in religious matters. This great captain,

---

1 Augurs: Roman religious officials who foretold events by interpreting signs and omens such as the flight and behaviour of birds and the entrails of sacrificial animals.

2 Cicero, *De Divinatione*, 1.3. Panaetius of Rhodes (c185–c110 BCE), commonly categorized along with his student Posidonius as part of the 'Middle Stoa', was the last *scholarch* of the Stoic school of philosophy in the *stoa poikile* of Athens. His principal work, *On Duties*, was a sourcebook for *De Officiis*, Cicero's work of the same title; itself an inspiration to Hume.

3 Hume is referring to the Emperor Marcus Aurelius, *Meditations*, 1.17.

4 Epictetus, *Encheiridion*, 18. He was a Greek Stoic philosopher (55–135 CE) and a freedman. He founded a school in Epirus in Greece when Domitian expelled all philosophers from Rome c.93 CE for persistent and uncontrolled thinking (though perhaps more strategically because of the nature of his political opposition).

5 Plato, *Euthyphro*, 6a–b.

6 Plato, *Phaedo*, 64a, 65a, 68b.

7 Xenophon, *Anabasis*, 'The expedition up-country'; *passim*.

philosopher and disciple of Socrates, delivered some of the most refined sentiments with regard to a deity, yet gives all the following marks of common, pagan superstition:

On Socrates' advice, he consults the oracle of Delphi, before he would engage in the expedition of Cyrus.

The night after the Greek generals are seized, he has a dream to which he pays great regard, but thinks ambiguous.

He and the whole army regard sneezing as a very lucky omen.

He has another dream when he comes to the river Centrites, to which his fellow-general, Cherosophus, also pays great regard. The Greeks, suffering from a cold north wind, sacrifice to it; and the historian observes that it immediately abates.

Xenophon consults the sacrifices in secret, before he would form any resolution with himself about settling a colony.

He was himself a skilful augur and decided, by examining the sacrificial victims, to refuse the offer of sole command of the army. The Spartan general, Cleander,[1] though very desirous of the command, refused for the same reason.

Xenophon mentions the place of Hercules's descent into hell as believing it, saying that the marks of it still remain.[2] He almost starved the army, rather than lead them to the field against the auspices.

His friend Euclides, the augur, would not believe that he had brought no money from the expedition till he, Euclides, sacrificed when he saw the matter clearly in the victim's exta.[3] Proposing a project of mines to increase of the Athenian revenues, Xenophon advises them to first consult the oracle.

That all this devotion was not a farce in order to serve a political purpose appears both from the facts themselves and from the genius of that age, when little or nothing could be gained by hypocrisy. Besides, Xenophon, as appears from his *Memorabilia*, was a kind of heretic in those times, which no *political* devotee ever is.

---

1 See Xenophon, *Anabasis* 6.2

2 The Acherusian Chersonese (peninsula) is modern Karadeniz Ereğli on the southern shore of the Black Sea in Turkey. Here, Hercules descended into Hades to abduct its three-headed canine guardian, Cerberus – his twelfth and final Labour.

3 The entrails. Abdominal organs of the victim, particularly liver; used for divination.

It is for the same reason I maintain that Newton, Locke, Clarke, etc., being *Arians* or *Socinians*,[1] were truly sincere in the creed they professed. I always deploy this argument against libertines,[2] who claim that it was impossible for these great philosophers not to have been hypocrites.

Cicero, who affected in his own family to appear a devout religionist, has no hesitation in a public court of law to treat the doctrine of an afterlife as a ridiculous fable to which nobody should pay the slightest attention.[3] In addition, Sallust describes Caesar speaking the same language openly in the Senate.[4]

Cicero, Seneca and also Juvenal maintain that there is no boy, or old woman, so ridiculous as to believe the poets in their accounts of an afterlife. Why then does Lucretius exalt Epicurus so highly for *freeing* us from these terrors? Perhaps the generality of humankind were then in the position of Cephalus in Plato[5] who could ridicule these stories while young and healthful, but when old and infirm, began to entertain apprehensions of their truth. Even at present we may observe this to be not unusual.

It is however apparent that all these freedoms did not imply total and universal infidelity and scepticism amongst the people. Although some parts of the national religion hung loosely upon the human mind, other parts adhered more closely. It was then the chief business of sceptical philosophers to show that there was no more foundation for the one than for the other. This is the artfulness of Cotta in *de natura deorum*, Cicero's dialogue concerning the nature of the gods.[6] He refutes the whole system of mythology by gradually leading the orthodox from the more momentous stories that were believed, to the more frivolous that everyone ridiculed. He moves

---

1 Arians asserted that Christ the Son was subordinate to the Father; Socinians denied the divinity of Christ.

2 *One who lives without restraint, or Law.* SJ

3 Cicero, *pro cluentio*, LXI.171. This was the orator's celebrated and successful court defence of Aulus Cluentius Habitus in 66 BCE on a charge of poisoning his stepfather.

4 Sallust, *Bellum Catilinae*, LI.16. Gaius Sallustius Crispus (86–34 BCE), Roman historian, soldier and horticulturalist. His 'Catilinarian War' dealt with the conspiracy of Catiline, thwarted by Cicero in 63 BCE.

5 *The Republic*, I, 330d

6 A debate among Velleius, an Epicurean, Balbus, a Stoic and the sceptic Cotta, at the latter's residence at Rome. C. Aurelius Cotta (*c.*124–73 BCE) was an uncle of Julius Caesar and an adherent of the philosophy of the New Academy. Cotta represents Cicero here, a role reprised by Philo for Hume in his *Dialogues*, q.v., a work modelled on that of Cicero. As Hume describes his own philosophy as Academical, Hume's description of the Academical sceptics' 'chief business' here suggests that he is also confessing something of his own motives.

from the gods to the goddesses, from the goddesses to the nymphs and from the nymphs to the fawns and satyrs. This was the same method of reasoning[1] that had been employed by Cicero's master Carneades.[2]

Overall, the greatest observable differences between a traditional, mythological religion and a systematic, scholastic one, are two:

First: the former is often less offensive to reason, consisting of only a multitude of stories that, however groundless, imply neither express absurdity nor exhibit demonstrable contradiction.

Second: they also sit so light and easy on people's minds that, although the traditional religion may be universally *received*, it makes no universal or deep impression on the emotions and understanding.

SECTION XIII:

Impious Conceptions of the divine Nature in popular Religions of both Kinds

The primary religion of humankind arises chiefly from an anxious fear of future events. It may thus be easily conceived that ideas of invisible, unknown powers will be entertained by gloomy anxious persons. Every image of divine vengeance, severity, cruelty and malice will appear, augmenting the ghastliness and horror that seizes the terrorised religionist. With the mind in panic, active imagination further multiplies the objects of terror. Meanwhile, the profound darkness or, worse, that glimmering light with which we are surrounded, portrays the most dreadful manifestations of the spectres of divinity. There is no framed concept of perverse wickedness that such terrified devotees do not unhesitatingly apply to their Deity.

This appears to be the natural state of religion when surveyed in one light.

If on the other hand, however, we consider the spirit of praise and eulogy that has a necessary place in all religions (another consequence of those very terrors) we should expect a contrary system of theology to prevail. Every virtue and every excellence must now be ascribed to the Divinity; no exaggeration being sufficient to reach the perfections with which it is

---

1 A form of *reductio ad absurdum*.
2 Sextus Empiricus (*c*.160–210 CE) *Against the Mathematicians* I. 182–90
    A philosopher and perhaps physician, his works are the most complete surviving account of Greek and Roman scepticism, chiefly of the Pyrrhonian school.

endowed. Whatever strains of panegyric can be invented are immediately embraced without reference to any arguments or phenomena. It is reckoned a sufficient justification that they give an even more magnificent idea of the divine object of worship and adoration.

Here, therefore, is a kind of contradiction between the different aspects of human nature that enter into religion. Our natural terrors present the notion of a devilish and malicious Deity, while our propensity to adulation leads us to one that is excellent and divine. The influence exerted by these opposite principles is variable and depends on the differing levels of human understanding. Among nations yet to develop sophisticated ideas of power and knowledge, worship may be paid to a Being that is agreed to be wicked and detestable. They may be reluctant, however, to pronounce this judgment in public or in the temple where the Being may be supposed to hear their reproaches.

Such rude and imperfect ideas of the Divinity long adhere to all idolaters, and it may be safely affirmed that the Greeks themselves never got rid of them entirely. Xenophon, when praising Socrates, reports that the latter disagreed with the common opinion that supposed the gods to know some things, while being ignorant of others.[1] He maintained that they knew *everything* done, said, or even thought. As this, however, was a philosophical argument far beyond the conception of its countrymen, we need not be surprised if, in their books and conversation, they criticised the deities worshipped in their temples. The ancients considered it an extraordinary philosophical paradox that the presence of the gods was not confined to the heavens but extended everywhere, as we learn from Lucian.[2]

It is also observable that Herodotus, in many of his passages, does not hesitate to ascribe *envy* to the gods,[3] a sentiment more suitable than any other to a mean and devilish nature. Pagan hymns, however, sung in public worship contained nothing but praise to the gods, even while the most barbarous and detestable actions were being ascribed to them. When the poet

---

1 Xenophon, *Memorabilia of Socrates*, 1.1. This section deals with the charges laid against the philosopher, viz that he had failed to respect the established gods, introduced new gods – and corrupted the Athenian youth. He is described as a theist.
2 Lucian of Samosata (125–180 CE), *Hermotimus, or the Rival Philosophies*, 81. Longest of Lucian's many works, it is a Platonic dialogue between Hermotimus, an old Stoic and Lycinus, who represents the author.
3 *History*, 7.46

Timotheus recited a hymn to Artemis[1] in which he enumerated, with the most fulsome eulogies, all the actions and attributes of that cruel and capricious goddess, someone present in the audience, called out:

'May your daughter become such as the Deity you celebrate'[2]

People, however, farther exalt their idea of their Divinity; it is their notion only of its power and knowledge, not of its goodness, that is increased. On the contrary, their terrors naturally increase in proportion to the supposed extent of his knowledge and authority. They believe that no secrecy can conceal them from its scrutiny, even the inmost recesses of their hearts lying open. They must then be careful not to develop any manifest sentiment of blame* and disapproval. All must be applause, ravishment and ecstasy.

While their gloomy fears make them ascribe to the god conduct that would be severely criticised in *human* creatures, they must still praise and admire such conduct in the divine object of their devotions. Thus it may safely be affirmed that, in the conception of their less critical adherents, popular religions are really a species of demonism. The higher the deity is exalted in terms of power and knowledge, the lower it sinks in goodness and benevolence, whatever the deluded praises bestowed on the god by its devotees. Among idolaters, the words used may be false and belie the actual, secret, opinion. Among more exalted religionists, however, this opinion *itself* regularises a kind of falsehood and belies the inward sentiment. The heart secretly rejects their cruel and implacable vengeance, but the outward judgment dares not pronounce them other than perfect and adorable. Additional misery from this inward struggle only aggravates the other terrors permanently haunting these unhappy victims of superstition.

Lucian observes that a young man who reads the history of the gods in Homer or Hesiod will find high celebration of their factions, wars, injustice, incest, adultery and other immoralities.[3] He is therefore much surprised to

---

* Blame: *Criticism*. SJ
1 The irascible, bow and arrow-wielding goddess of the hunt. Timotheus of Miletus (*c.*446–357 BCE) was a Greek poet and musician. Apparently he described her as θυιάδα φοιβάδα μαινάδα λυσσάδα: or 'ecstatic, Bacchic, frantic, fanatic.' Plutarch, *Moralia*; *Concerning Superstition* 10.170a-b
2 According to Plutarch, the heckler was the lyric poet Cinesias (450–390 BCE).
3 Lucian, *Menippus – or the descent into Hades*, III. Menippus of Gadara (fl. 3rd century BCE) was a Cynic and satirist. His lost works strongly influenced both Varro and Lucian. The Menippean genre of prose satire, combining a variety of targets and literary styles, is named after him. Gadara, in modern Jordan, was the home of the collectively suicidal Gadarene swine of Luke 8.32.

observe later in the real world that punishments are inflicted by law for those very actions ascribed to *superior* beings. Even stronger, perhaps, is the contradiction between the descriptions given to us by some later religions and our natural ideas of generosity, lenience, impartiality and justice. The barbarous conceptions of the divinity are increased among us in proportion to the multiplied terrors of these religions.

Bacchus, a divine being, is represented by heathen mythology as the inventor of dancing and the theatre. In ancient times, plays were a part of public worship even on the most solemn occasions and, in times of pestilence, were often employed to appease the offended deities. But they have been zealously proscribed by the godly in later ages[1] and the playhouse, according to one learned divine, is the very porch of hell.[2] We shall now establish more conclusively that a religion can represent the Divinity in a still *more* immoral and unfriendly light than that pictured by the ancients. To do this, we shall cite a long passage from an author of taste and imagination who was surely no enemy to Christianity.

This is the Chevalier Ramsay,[3] a writer who had so laudable an ambition to be orthodox that he never finds any difficulty even with the doctrines most challenged by freethinkers: the trinity, incarnation and satisfaction.[4] His humanity alone, of which he seems to have had a great stock, rebelled against the doctrines of eternal reprobation and predestination. Ramsay expresses himself thus:

> What strange ideas would an Indian or a Chinese philosopher have of our holy religion, if they judged by the accounts given of it by our modern Freethinkers and sanctimonious theologians of all sects?' According to the odious and overly *simple* system of these incredulous scoffers and credulous scribblers;

---

1 A blast clearly aimed at the Edinburgh divines, persecutors of the Rev John Hume, cousin of David and dedicatee of this work, for staging *Douglas, a Tragedy* in 1756.

2 Probably *The Absolute Unlawfulness of Stage-Entertainment* by the Rev William Law (1726). Law was tutor to the father of the historian Edward Gibbon whose *Memoirs of my Life* (1796) contains a witty demolition of Law's frenzied attack on the theatre as 'The Porch of Hell; the place of the Devil's abode.. A Play is the Devil's triumph, etc etc'.

3 Andrew Michael Ramsay (1686–1743). Son of an Ayr baker. Episcopalian and Jacobite theologian. He was the Biographer of the RC Archbishop François Fénelon and tutored the 'young pretender' Prince Charles Edward Stuart and his brother Henry. His major work was *Philosophical Principles of Natural and Revealed Religion* (1748). He befriended the young Hume in France. Ramsay's text was edited stylistically and in substance by Hume.

4 'Satisfaction' as a theological doctrine holds that the incarnation and crucifixion were necessary to 'satisfy' the offense of the world's sin. It derives from legal doctrines of redress or 'satisfaction' for injury or offense. In duelling, the challenger would cite his requirement for 'satisfaction' for a perceived insult.

the God of the Jews is a most cruel, unjust, partial and fantastical being. He created, about 6,000 years ago, a man and a woman and placed them in a fine garden of Asia, of which there are no remains. This garden was furnished with all sorts of trees, fountains and flowers. He allowed them the use of all the fruits of this beautiful garden, except one. It was planted in the midst thereof and that had in it a secret virtue of preserving them in continual health and vigour of both body and mind, of exalting their natural powers and making them wise. The Devil entered into the body of a serpent and solicited the first woman to eat of the forbidden fruit; she engaged her husband to do the same.

To punish this slight curiosity and natural desire for life and knowledge, God not only threw our first parents out of Paradise, but also condemned all their posterity to temporal misery and the greatest part of them to eternal pains. This he did, though the souls of these innocent children have no more relation to the soul of Adam than to those of Nero and Mahomet and since, according to the scholastic drivellers, fabulists, and mythologists, all souls are created pure and infused immediately into mortal bodies as soon as the foetus is formed. To accomplish the barbarous, partial decree of predestination and damnation, God abandoned all Nations to darkness, idolatry and superstition, without any saving knowledge or salutary graces, save one particular Nation whom he chose as his peculiar people. This chosen Nation was, however, the most stupid, ungrateful, rebellious and perfidious of all.

After God had thus kept the far greater part of humanity in a reprobate state for nearly 4,000 years, he changed all of a sudden and took a fancy for other nations beside the Jews. Then he sent his only begotten son to the world in human form to appease his wrath, to satisfy his vindictive justice and to die for the pardon of sin. Very few Nations, however, have heard of this gospel. All the rest, though left in invincible ignorance, are damned without exception or possibility of remission. The greatest part of those who *have* heard of it, have changed only some speculative notions about God and some external forms in worship. In other respects, the bulk of Christians have continued as corrupt as the rest of Humankind in their morals; yea, so much the more perverse and criminal, that their understanding was greater. Except for a very small select number, all other Christians will, like the Pagans, be forever damned. The great sacrifice offered up for them will become void and of no effect, and God will take delight forever in their torments and blasphemies. Although by one *fiat* he can change their hearts, yet they will remain forever unconverted and unconvertible, because he will be forever unappeasable and irreconcilable. It is true that all this makes God odious: a hater of souls rather than a lover of them; a cruel, vindictive tyrant; an impotent or wrathful demon, rather than an all-powerful, beneficent father.

Yet all this is a mystery. It has secret reasons for his conduct that are impenetrable. Though it appears unjust and barbarous, yet we must believe the contrary because what is injustice, crime, cruelty and the blackest malice in *us*, is justice, mercy and sovereign goodness in *him*.'

Incredulous Freethinkers, judaizing Christians and fatalistic theologians have thus disfigured and dishonored the sublime mysteries of our holy faith; *thus* they have confounded the nature of good and evil, and transformed the most monstrous passions into divine attributes. They have surpassed the Pagans in blasphemy, by ascribing to the eternal nature, as *perfections*, what constitute the most horrid human crimes. The grosser Pagans contented themselves with attributing lust, incest, and adultery to the deities; but the predestinarian theologians have divinized cruelty, wrath, fury, vengeance and all the blackest vices.'[1]

Ramsay asserts elsewhere that the Arminian[2] and Molinist[3] schemes serve very little to mend the matter. And having thus excluded himself from all received sects of Christianity, he is obliged to advance a system of his own. This is a kind of Origenism[4] and supposes the *pre-existence* of the souls both of humans and beasts and the eternal salvation and conversion of all people, beasts and devils. This notion, however, being peculiar to himself, we need not discuss it. I thought the opinions of this ingenious author very interesting; but I do not claim to endorse the accuracy of them.

Nothing can preserve untainted, the genuine principles of morals in our judgment of human conduct, *except* having those very principles as an absolute necessity for the existence of society.

If common conception can indulge princes in a system of ethics different from that regulating private persons, how much more does this apply to those superior beings, whose attributes, views and nature are so totally unknown to us? *Sunt superis sua jura.*[5]

'The gods have maxims of justice peculiar to themselves...'

---

1 Chevalier Ramsay, *Philosophical Principles of Natural and Revealed Religion*, II
2 Arminianism rejects predestination and affirms the freedom of the human will.
3 Molinism is a doctrine reconciling divine providence with human free will.
4 So named for Origen Adamantius (184–253 CE), early Christian theologian.
5 Ovid, *Metamorphoses*, IX. 500. This might also be construed, 'The gods are a law unto themselves.'

SECTION XIV:

Bad Influence of popular Religions on Morality.

Here I cannot resist observing a fact that may be worth the attention of students of human nature. In every religion, however sublime the *verbal* definition of its Divinity, perhaps the majority of worshippers will not seek divine favour through virtue and good morals – the *sole* requirement of a perfect Being. Rather – they will seek it by frivolous observances, intemperate zeal and rapturous ecstasies, or by belief in mysterious and absurd opinions. Precepts of morality constitute the smallest part of the Seder[1] as well as of the Pentateuch,[2] and we may also be certain that this part was always the least observed and regarded. When the old Romans faced an epidemic, they never ascribed their sufferings to their vices; never dreamed of repentance or reform. They never regarded themselves as the world's greatest robbers, a people whose ambition and avarice had desolated the earth, reducing opulent nations to destitution. They simply created a Dictator in order to drive a nail into a door, believing that they had thus sufficiently appeased their incensed Deity.[3] On the island of Aegina in Greece, a faction formed a conspiracy and barbarously and treacherously assassinated seven hundred of their fellow citizens. They carried their fury so far that, one miserable fugitive having fled to the temple, they cut off the hands by which he clung to the gates, carried him out of holy ground and murdered him. Herodotus says that it was by this *impiety* – and not by their other cruel assassinations – that they offended the gods and contracted an inexpiable guilt.[4]

Indeed, let us suppose a circumstance that seldom happens: that a popular religion were discovered expressly declaring that nothing *but* morality could gain the divine favour; that its priests inculcated this through daily sermons containing all the arts of persuasion. So inveterate are people's

---

1 The family ritual prescribed by Jewish law and based on God's command (Exodus 13.8) that Jews retell the story of the Exodus from Egypt. During Passover, families gather to share a symbolic meal and read from the *Haggadah*, an ancient work derived from the Seder service prescribed by the Mishnah, the first major codified redaction of Jewish oral traditions. Hume may also have been referring to the Sad-der, a work edited by Thomas Hyde setting out the precepts and rituals of Zoroastrianism.

2 Pentateuch; from Gk. *penta* (five) + *teukhos* (scroll), the first five books of the Old Testament, ie Genesis to Deuteronomy.

3 Livy, *The Histories*, 7.3. Every mid-September a nail was fixed into the wall of the temple of Jupiter to propitiate the god–principally for the avoidance of epidemics. The official was titled; *Dictator clavis figendae causa* or 'Nail-fixing Supremo.'

4 *History*, VI.

prejudices that, for lack of some other superstition, they would simply make the very *attendance* at these sermons the essential of religion, rather than make them the basis of virtue and good morals. The sublime *Prologue* of the Laws of Zaleucus[1] did not inspire the Locrians, as far as we understand, with any sounder notions of the measures of acceptance of the Deity than were familiar to other Greeks.

This observation then, holds universally; but one still may be somewhat at a loss to account for it. It is sufficient to observe that people everywhere degrade their deities into similarity with themselves, considering them merely a species of human creatures, albeit somewhat more potent and intelligent. This will not remove the difficulty. For no-one using natural reason is so stupid as *not* to regard virtue and honesty as one's most valuable qualities. Why not ascribe the same sentiment to the Deity? Why not make *all* religion, or at least the chief part of it, consist of these attainments?

Nor is it satisfactory to say that the practice of morality is to be rejected as more *difficult* than that of superstition. Not to mention the excessive penances of Brahmins[2] Talapoins[3] and other Buddhist monks; take the Ramadan[4] of the Turks. During this month the poor wretches abstain from eating or drinking from the rising to the setting of the sun often in the hottest month of the year in some of the world's hottest climates. It is certain that Ramadan must be more severe than the practice of any *moral* duty. The four Lents of the Muscovites[5] and the austerities of some Roman Catholics appear more disagreeable than meekness and benevolence. In short, all virtue is agreeable when people are reconciled to it, even by minimal practice. In contrast, all superstition is forever odious and burthensome.

Perhaps, the following account may be received as a true solution to the difficulty. The duties that an adult performs as a friend or parent seem to be those simply owed to one's benefactors or children. One cannot neglect these

---

1 Diodorus Siculus, *Historical Library*, XII. 20. Zaleucus, a pupil of Pythagoras, urged the Locrians to seek divine favour through just and honourable behaviour, rather than by sacrifice, or gifts to gods. Locri is in modern Reggio Calabria in southern Italy.

2 Brahmins: members of the highest caste of Hindus, comprising not only priests but also scholars, educators and jurists.

3 A Buddhist monk or priest, specifically in E. India, Sri Lanka and S. E. Asia.

4 Ramadan: one of the five defining duties, of Islam. The others are: *salat* (ritual prayer five times daily); at least one *haj* (pilgrimage to Mecca); *zakat* (charity to the poor); and *shahadah* (declaring Allah to be the only god and Muhammad to be his prophet). Muslims practice *shawm*, fasting from sunrise to sunset during Ramadan, ninth month of the Islamic calendar when the first verses of the *Qur'an* were revealed by *Jibraeel* (Gabriel) to Mohammed.

5 John Bancks, *The Life & Reign of Czar Peter the Great of Muscovy*, III (1740)

duties without breaking the ties of nature and morality. A strong inclination may prompt one to their performance, while an impulse of order and moral obligation adds its force to these natural ties. The whole person, if truly virtuous, is drawn to one's duty without any effort or endeavour. Even in respect of those virtues that are more austere and more founded on reflection, such as: public spirit; filial duty; temperance or integrity, we perceive that the moral obligation removes all pretension to *religious* merit.

Virtuous conduct is deemed no more than what we owe to society and to ourselves. In all this, however, superstitious people, find nothing actually performed for the sake of their *Deity* that can peculiarly recommend them to divine favour and protection. They do not consider that promoting the happiness of their fellow creatures is the most genuine method of serving the Deity. They continue to seek some more *direct* service to the supreme Being in order to allay those terrors by which they are haunted. They will thus more readily embrace any recommended practice that either serves no purpose in life, or offers the strongest opposition to their natural inclinations. Moreover, this will be done on account of those very circumstances that should make them absolutely *reject* it. Such a practice seems to such people more purely religious because it results from no *other* motive or consideration. If they sacrifice much of their personal ease and quiet for its sake, their claim of merit will appear to them to increase in proportion to this display of zeal and devotion. In repaying a loan or settling a debt, the Divinity is nowise indebted to them, since such acts of justice are what they were *bound* to perform. Indeed they are what many would have performed even if there were no god in the Universe.

If they fast for a day, however, or give themselves a sound whipping, this they believe to be a direct service to God. No other motive could engage them to such austerities. By such distinguishing marks of devotion they have now acquired divine favour, in recompense for which they may now expect protection and safety in this world – and eternal happiness in the next.

Hence in many instances, the greatest crimes have been found to be compatible with superstitious piety and devotion. It is also unsafe to infer favourably in respect of people's morals from the fervour or strictness of their religious exercises, even if one believes them to be sincere. Indeed, it has been observed that enormities of the blackest dye are apt to produce superstitious terrors and increase religious passion. Bomilcar,[1] having formed a conspir-

---

1 Diodorus Siculus, *Bibliotheca Historica*, xx.12 In 308 BCE, Bomilcar's attempted *coup d'état* was foiled, and he was arrested and crucified.

acy to assassinate the whole senate of Carthage and usurp the liberties of
his country, lost the opportunity through continual attention to omens and
prophecies. As an ancient historian remarked on that occasion;

> Those who undertake the most criminal and most dangerous enterprises are
> commonly the most superstitious.[1]

Their devotion and spiritual faith increase with their fears. Catiline was not
satisfied with the established deities and the received rites of the national
religion,[2] his anxious terrors making him seek new inventions of this kind.
He probably would never have dreamed of these had he remained a good
citizen and obedient to the laws of his country.

To all this we may add that *after* the commission of crimes, remorse
and secret horrors arise. These give no rest to the mind; rather, they make
it have recourse to religious rites and ceremonies as expiations of its
offences. Whatever weakens or disorders the internal frame promotes the
interests of superstition. In contrast, nothing is more destructive to superstition than a strong, steady virtue, either preserving us from disastrous,
melancholy accidents or teaching us to bear them. During such calm sunshine of the mind, superstitions, those spectres of false divinity, never make
their appearance.

On the other hand, when we abandon ourselves to the natural, undisci-
plined suggestions of our timid and anxious hearts, every kind of barbarity
is ascribed to the supreme Being from the terrors with which we are agitated.
Every kind of caprice is ascribed to the methods that we embrace in order to
appease it. We may universally observe that barbarity and caprice, however
nominally disguised, form the ruling character of the Deity in popular religions. Even priests, instead of correcting these depraved ideas of humankind,
have often been found ready to foster and encourage them.

The more tremendous the representation of the Divinity, the more
tame and submissive do people become to its ministers. The more inexplicable the measures of submission required by it, the more necessary does
it become to abandon natural reason and yield to their ghostly guidance
and direction. Thus it may be granted that although the stratagems of
human beings may aggravate our natural infirmities and follies of this

---

1 Ibid., xx.43

2 In 63 BCE, Lucius Sergius Catilina plotted a *coup d'état* against the Roman Republic but
was thwarted by the Consul Cicero and others. See Cicero, *In Catilinam*, 1.6 and Sallust,
De Bello Catilina, XXII.

kind, they never originally beget them. Their root strikes deeper into the mind and springs from the constitutional and universal properties of human nature.

SECTION XV:

General Corollary.

The stupidity* of barbarous and uneducated people is such that they may not discern a sovereign Author in the more obvious and hence familiar works of Nature. Conversely, it scarcely seems possible that those of good understanding should reject that idea when suggested to them. A purpose, an intention and a design is evident in everything. With our comprehension sufficiently enlarged to begin contemplating the origins of this visible system, we must adopt the idea of some intelligent Cause, or Author, with the strongest conviction. Where educational prejudices do not oppose so reasonable a theory, the *uniform* maxims that prevail throughout the Universe naturally, if not necessarily, lead us to conceive this Intelligence as single and undivided. Even the contradictions of Nature, by revealing themselves everywhere, become proofs of a consistent plan. They also establish one *single* purpose or intention, however currently inexplicable and incomprehensible. Good and ill are so universally intermingled that it is difficult to distinguish them: happiness and misery; wisdom and folly; virtue and vice. Nothing is pure and entirely of a piece. All advantages are attended with disadvantage. A universal balance prevails in all conditions of being and existence, and it is thus not possible for us, by our most fanciful wishes, to form the idea of an absolutely desirable station or situation.

According to Homer, the cups of life filled for us are always mixed from the vessels on either hand of Zeus. If any cup be presented altogether pure, the same poet tells us that it is drawn *only* from the left-handed vessel.[1]

---

* Stupidity: *Insensibility; sluggishness of understanding.* SJ
1 Homer, *Iliad*, XXIV. 525–30. King Priam of Troy, grieving for his slain son Hector, is told by Achilles that Zeus bestows gifts on mortals from two urns: that on the left for evils, the other for blessings. Sometimes he mixes the two, but sometimes he doles out only sorrows from the left. This, human beings must learn to endure.

The more exquisite any small specimen of good afforded us, the sharper the evil allied to it. Few exceptions are found to this uniform law of Nature. The sprightliest wit borders on madness; the highest effusions of joy produce the deepest melancholy; the most ravishing pleasures are attended with the most cruel lassitude and disgust; the most flattering hopes make way for the severest disappointments. In general, no course of life has such safety (for happiness is not to be dreamed of) as the temperate and moderate, maintaining in everything and as far as possible, mediocrity* and a kind of insensibility.** The good, the great, the sublime and the ravishing are pre-eminent in the genuine principles of theism. Hence it may be expected from the analogy of Nature that the base, the absurd, the mean and the terrifying will be equally detected in religious fictions and unfounded conceptions. The universal propensity to believe in invisible, intelligent power is, if not an original instinct, at least a general attendant of human nature. It thus may be considered as a kind of mark or stamp that the divine Artisan or Deity has set upon its work. Surely nothing can more dignify humanity than to be thus selected, from *all* other parts of creation, to bear the image or impression of the universal Creator. Examine this image, however, as it appears in the popular religions of the world. How disfigured is the Deity in our representations! What caprice, absurdity and immorality are attributed to God! How greatly is the Deity degraded below what we, in common life, would characterise as someone of sense and virtue! It is a noble privilege of human reason to attain knowledge of the supreme Being, thus enabled to infer, from the visible works of Nature, so sublime a principle as its supreme Creator.

But turn to the reverse of the medal. Survey most nations and most ages. Examine the religious principles that have in fact prevailed in the world. You will scarcely be persuaded that they are anything other than the dreams of sick people. Alternatively, you perhaps will regard them more as the playful whimsies of monkeys in human shape, rather than the serious, positive, dogmatic asseverations of a Being, that dignifies itself with the name of rational.

Hear the verbal protestations of all people. There is nothing so certain as their religious tenets. Now examine their lives. You will scarcely think that they repose the smallest confidence in those tenets. The greatest and truest zeal gives us no security against hypocrisy. The most open impiety is attended with secret dread and remorse. There are no theological absurdities

---

* Mediocrity: *A middle state between two extremes; moderation.* SJ. Hume may advert to Aristotle's Doctrine of the Mean, incised at the door of the temple of Apollo at Delphi and paraphrased as: Μεδεν Αγαν, Meden Agan, 'all things in moderation.'

** *Inability to perceive.* SJ. Mental detachment.

so glaring that they have not at times been embraced by people of the greatest and most cultivated understanding. Conversely, no religious precepts are so rigorous that they have not been adopted by the most voluptuous and most abandoned of humanity.[1] *Ignorance is the mother of Devotion* is a maxim[2] that is proverbial and confirmed by general experience. Look out for a people entirely destitute of religion. If you find them at all, be assured that they are but few degrees removed from brutes. Is there anything *so* pure as some of the morals included in theological systems? Is there anything *so* corrupt as some practices to which these systems give rise? The comfortable views exhibited by the belief in an afterlife are ravishing and delightful. But how quickly do they vanish on the appearance of its terrors, keeping as they do a firmer and more durable possession of the human mind?

The whole is a riddle, an enigma, an inexplicable mystery. Doubt, uncertainty and suspension of judgment are the only results of our most accurate scrutiny of natural religion. But such is the frailty of human reason and such the irresistible contagion of opinion, that even this deliberate doubt could scarcely be upheld unless we enlarge* our view and, by opposing one species of superstition to another, set them a-quarrelling.

Meanwhile, during their fury and contention, we ourselves may happily make our escape into the calm though obscure regions of Philosophy.[3]

---

* Enlarge: Expand; specifically *broaden*. SJ
1 Cicero, *De Divinatione*, II.58. *Nihil tam absurde dici potest quod non dicatur ab aliquo philosophorum.* 'There is nothing so absurd & sayable that some philosopher has not said it.'
2 Robert Burton; *Anatomy of Melancholy* (1621) 4.3.
3 In this paragraph one sees Hume adopting the Pyrrhonian sceptical philosophical strategies of (1) suspension of judgment, (2) the opposing of contrary positions, (3) the effort to escape controversy and the agitated emotions accompanying it and (4) in favor of peace or tranquility. *cf.* Sextus Empiricus (fl. 3rd century CE), *Outlines of Pyrrhonism*. Hume's acknowledgment of the 'frailty of human reason' marks the influence of Academic Scepticism, the other central stream of sceptical philosophy; *cf.* Cicero, *Academica*.

Dialogues Concerning Natural Religion

Introduction:

Dramatis Personae:

Pamphilus, the narrator and observer of the *Dialogues*, together with his epistolary correspondent Hermippus. They are fictional in the present context, as are the three central discussants: Philo, Cleanthes and Demea. Excepting the latter, however, individuals of these names were distinguished in antiquity.

Hermippus of Smyrna was a peripatetic philosopher and biographer of the 3rd century BCE. Pamphilus of Alexandria was a philologist, critic and editor of the 1st century CE from the school of Aristarchus of Samothrace. The extant works of both were likely known to Hume. Another Pamphilus was an obscure rhetorician mentioned by Aristotle in his *Rhetoric* 2.23.20 and derided by Cicero in *De Oratore* 3.81. A third Pamphilus was an artist.

The historical Cleanthes of Assos (in modern Turkey) was a Greek Stoic philosopher who, *c.*262 BCE, succeeded Zeno of Citium as *scholarch* (head) of the Stoic school of philosophy in Athens.

Philo of Larissa in Thessaly (158–84BCE) was the last known *scholarch* or head of Plato's Academy in Athens in its skeptical period. He taught a mitigated skepticism, a term used by Hume to describe his own overall position in his *Enquiry concerning Human Understanding*. He is best known today as the exiled teacher, in Rome *c.*88 BCE, of Cicero, whose *De Natura Deorum* (On the Nature of the Gods) diffused Academic skepticism across the Latin world.

Demea alone appears to have no classical provenance, save as one of the eponymous *dramatis personae* in Terence's play *Adelphoe* (The Brothers).

Pamphilus writes to Hermippus:

Hermippus:

It has been remarked that while ancient philosophers conveyed most of their instruction in the form of dialogues, this method of composition has been little practised in more recent times – and where it has, it has seldom suc- ceeded. The accurate and structured argument now expected of philosoph- ical enquiry, naturally dictates methodical, didactic writing. One can thus explain the point at issue immediately and, without prior preparation, go on directly to the evidence upon which it is established.

However, it hardly appears natural to illustrate a philosophical system through the medium of a conversation. By departing from the didactic style, writers of dialogue seek to give a freer air to their works by avoid- ing the appearance of Author and Reader. They are, however, apt to run into a worse inconvenience by conveying instead the image of Teacher and Pupil.

Furthermore, if they present the debate in the natural spirit of a good company, throwing in a variety of topics and preserving a proper balance, they will lose much time both in preparation and in transitions between speakers. The reader will find that all the graces of dialogue hardly compen- sate for the sacrifice of order, brevity and precision.

There are some subjects, however, to which dialogue-writing is pecu- liarly adapted, and where it is still preferable to the direct method of literary composition. Any point of doctrine so obvious as to scarcely require dis- pute, but at the same time so important that it cannot be too often repeated, seems to require handling by such a method. A conversation, by the novelty of its manner, may compensate for the unoriginality of the subject, while the sheer vivacity of dialogue may enforce the precepts. Similarly, a variety of opinions may appear lively and relevant when presented by various person- ages and characters.

Alternatively, any question of philosophy so obscure and uncertain that human reason can reach no fixed determination on it should, if it is to be treated, lead us naturally to a book in dialogue and conversation style. Rea- sonable men may be allowed to differ where no-one can reasonably be cer- tain. Opposite opinions, even without any decision being reached, afford an agreeable amusement. If the subject is interesting the book will, in a sense, take us into company. It will thus unite study and society, the two greatest and purest pleasures of human life.

Happily, these circumstances are all to be found in the subject of Natural Religion.

What truth is so obvious and so certain, as the being of God? The most ignorant ages have acknowledged this truth, for which the most refined geniuses have striven ambitiously to produce new evidence and arguments. What truth is as important as this, the ground of all our hopes, the surest foundation of morality and the firmest support of society? It is the only principle that ought never to be absent from our meditations.

However, in examining this obvious and important truth, what obscure questions arise! They concern the nature of the divine Being, its attributes, its decrees and its plan of providence. These have always been the subject of debate, yet human reason has not reached any certain conclusion. The topics are so interesting that we cannot restrain inquiry into them; yet our most accurate researches have produced nothing but doubt, uncertainty and contradiction.

I recently had occasion to observe this when, as usual, I passed part of the summer with Cleanthes and was present at his conversations with Philo and Demea, of which I gave you a rough account. You told me your curiosity was aroused and that I must present their reasoning in more exact detail and display their various accounts on the delicate subject of Natural Religion. The remarkable contrast in their characters raised your expectation still further. You contrasted the accurate philosophical turn of Cleanthes with the casual scepticism of Philo, contrasting both with the rigidly inflexible orthodoxy of Demea.

My youth rendered me a mere listener to their debates, but natural youthful curiosity also deeply imprinted in my memory the whole chain and connection of their arguments. I trust that I shall not omit or confuse any significant part of them in the account that follows.

PART I

After I joined the company, whom I found sitting in Cleanthes' library, Demea paid Cleanthes some compliments on the great care he took of my education, and on his unwearied perseverance and constancy in all his friendships.

DEMEA The father of Pamphilus here was your intimate friend, Cleanthes, while the son is your pupil. Indeed he may be regarded as your adopted son, judging by the pains you take in instructing him in every useful branch of science and literature. I believe your prudence equals your industry, so let me give you a maxim I have followed with my own children, to see how far it agrees with your practice. My method is founded on the saying of an Ancient:

'Students of Philosophy ought first to learn Logic, then Ethics, next Physics and, last of all, the nature of the Gods.'[1]

To him, natural theology was the most profound and abstruse science of all, requiring the most mature judgement from its students.[2] Thus, only a mind previously enriched with all the other sciences could safely be entrusted with it.

PHILO Are you not very late, Demea, in the teaching of religious principles to your children? Is there no danger of their neglecting, indeed rejecting altogether, opinions they have heard so little about during their education?

DEMEA It is only as a *science*, by which I mean a discipline subjected to human reasoning and disputation, that I postpone the study of natural theology. My chief care is to continually season their minds with piety through precept and instruction. Also, while they are passing through every other science, I hope to deeply imprint a habitual reverence for the *principles* of religion. I point out to them the uncertainty of each component of scientific and philosophical inquiry: the eternal disputations; the obscurity of all philosophy; the strange, indeed ridiculous, conclusions that some of the greatest geniuses have derived from the principles of mere human reason.

Having thus tamed their minds to a proper submission and self-restraint, I then have no hesitation in opening to them the greatest mysteries of religion. I *then* perceive no danger of philosophy arrogantly leading them to reject established doctrines and opinions.

PHILO Your precaution of the *early* seasoning of your children's minds with piety is certainly very reasonable; it is also necessary in this profane and irreligious age. But what I chiefly admire in your educational plan is your

---

1 Plutarch, *De repugnantiis stoicorum* (On Stoic self-contradictions) IX.1035.
   The 'Ancient' was Chrysippus (c.280–207 BCE) educated in the Academy founded by Plato. He was converted to Stoicism by the historical Cleanthes (c.331–232 BCE) whom he succeeded as *scholarch* (head) of the Stoa, Cleanthes himself having succeeded Zeno of Citium, founder of the school in the *Stoa Poikile* in Athens.
2 Natural Theology may be taken as the critical study of the origin and development of religious belief, observance and practices in human populations and societies.

method. You take advantage of those very principles of philosophy and learning that, by inspiring overconfidence and self-sufficiency in human abilities, have always been found to be so *destructive* to the principles of religion!

The less well educated, are unacquainted with science and deep inquiry. Observing the endless disputes of the learned, they commonly have a thorough contempt for philosophy. They thus rivet themselves all the more tightly to the great points of theology taught to them.

However, those entering even a little into serious study and inquiry, find many examples of the *evidence* for religious doctrines being most extraordinary. Consequently, thinking nothing too difficult for *human* reason, they presumptuously break down all fences and profane the innermost sanctuaries of the temple.

CLEANTHES I hope will agree with me that after we have abandoned ignorance (the *surest* remedy) there is one expedient left to prevent this profanity and it is this; let Demea's principles be improved and cultivated! Let us become thoroughly aware of the weakness, blindness and narrow limits of human reason. Let us consider its uncertainty and endless contrariness even in matters of common life and practice. Let the errors and deceits of our very *senses* be set before us; the insuperable difficulties attending first principles[1] in all systems; the contradictions intrinsic to the very ideas of matter, cause and effect, extension[2] and space, time and motion. In a word, *quantity* of all kinds, this being the object of mathematics; the only science that can fairly claim to any certainty of evidence.

When these topics are displayed in their full light, as they are by some philosophers and almost all divines, who can retain any confidence in this frail faculty of human reason? Who can pay *any* regard to its conclusions on points so sublime, so abstruse, and so remote from common life and experience? When the cohesion of the parts of a simple stone, or even those parts of its composition conferring *shape* – when such familiar objects are *so* inexplicable and contain circumstances *so* contradictory, with what assurance can we *possibly* decide the origin of worlds – or trace their history from eternity to eternity?

---

1 Origins. From Lat. *Principium,* beginning.
2 Dimensions of length, breadth and depth.

PAMPHILUS While Philo was thus speaking, I could observe a smile on the countenance both of Demea and Cleanthes. That of Demea implied unreserved satisfaction with the theories delivered. However, in Cleanthes I could distinguish an air of strategic calculation, as if he perceived some raillery or artificial malice[1] in the reasoning of Philo...

CLEANTHES You propose then, Philo, to erect religious faith upon a base of philosophical *scepticism*? You think that if certainty, or evidence, can be expelled from every *other* subject of inquiry, it will retreat to theological doctrines, acquiring there a superior force and authority? Whether your scepticism is as absolute and sincere as you claim, we shall learn when this company breaks up... for we shall then see whether you go out by the door – or by the *window*! We shall then see whether you *really* doubt if your body has gravity and can be injured by a fall. This is an event that *can* occur, according to popular opinion, *itself* derived of course from our fallacious senses and even more fallacious experience.[2]

This last consideration, Demea, may actually abate our ill-will towards that laughable sect, the Sceptics. For if they are thoroughly in earnest, they will not be around long to trouble the world with their doubts, cavils, and disputes. If they are only in jest, they are perhaps poor humorists but can never pose any real threat either to the state, to philosophy or to religion.

In reality, Philo, it seems certain that a person might renounce *all* beliefs and opinions in a flood of sceptical emotion after reflecting on the contradictions and imperfections of human reason. However, it would be impossible to persevere with *total* scepticism or make it govern our conduct for more than a few hours. External objects press in; passions solicit; philosophical melancholy dissipates. Even the utmost intensity of emotion will never preserve the poor appearance of scepticism. And for what reason should such violence be self-imposed? On this point it will be impossible for a person ever to be satisfied since it too is inconsistent with their sceptical principles.

---

1 That is, irony.
2 More irony. Cleanthes is referring to the absolute scepticism of Pyrrho of Elis (c.360–c.270 BCE) founder of the sect. His followers literally tracked him to protect him from trundling carts, dogs and precipices, so sceptical was he of immanent peril.

Thus, overall, nothing could be more ridiculous than the principles of the ancient Pyrrhonians[1] if, as is claimed, they tried to practice throughout life the scepticism learned in their schools. To the latter they ought to have confined them...

In this view, there appears a great resemblance between the sects of the Pyrrhonians and the Stoics. Though they are perpetual antagonists, both seem to be both founded on the erroneous maxim that what a person can perform *sometimes* in some circumstances; they can *always* perform in every circumstance.

When the Stoical mind, elevated into a sublime enthusiasm of virtue, is strongly attracted to any species of honour or public good, its high sense of duty withstands the utmost in bodily pain & suffering. By such means it is perhaps even possible to smile and exult during torture. If this is sometimes the case in *physical* reality, how much more may philosophers in their Schools, or even in the closet,[2] work up such an enthusiasm that they can endure, in their *imagination*, the most acute pain or calamitous event. But how shall they sustain this enthusiasm itself? The tautness of the mind relaxes, and cannot be recalled at pleasure. Trivial interests lead them astray. Misfortunes attack unawares – and the philosopher sinks by degrees into the plebeian.

PHILO Cleanthes, I accept your comparison between the Stoics and the Sceptics. However, at the same time you may observe that although the Stoic mind cannot support the highest flights of Philosophy, yet even when it sinks lower, it still retains something of its stoical disposition. The effects of the Stoics' reasoning will appear both in their conduct in common life – and through the whole tenor of their actions. The ancient schools, particularly that of Zeno,[3] produced examples of virtue and constancy that seem astonishing to present times.

> Vain Wisdom all and false Philosophy.
> Yet with a pleasing Sorcery could charm
> Pain, for a while, or Anguish; and excite
> Fallacious Hope, or arm the obdurate Breast
> With stubborn Patience, as with triple Steel.[4]

---

1 Followers of Pyrrho rejected true knowledge of the material world. They aimed at *ataraxia* (mental serenity), through suspension of judgement. Pyrrho travelled to India in the train of Alexander the Great and, like the Beatles, was influenced by 'Magi'.

2 'Closet' here refers to the philosopher's study, rather than to any smaller apartment.

3 Zeno of Citium (*c.*333–262 BCE) the Greek Cypriot founder, *c.*300 BCE, of the Stoic school of philosophy, so named for its location in the Στοὰ Ποικίλη, the *Stoa Poikile* (painted porch) a colonnade in the Agora of Athens.

4 Milton, *Paradise Lost*, II. 565–9. Hume has altered Milton's 'obdured' to 'obdurate.'

Similarly, if a person has become accustomed to sceptical considerations on the uncertainty and narrow limits of reason, they will not entirely forget them when attention turns to other subjects. However, in philosophical principles and reasoning – I dare not say in *common*[1] conduct – they will be found different from those who either have never formed an opinion on the matter, or have entertained sentiments more favourable to human reason.

To whatever length anyone may push speculative *principles* of scepticism, I accept that the sceptic must act, live and converse like other people. For this they are not obliged to give any reason other than the absolute *necessity* under which they lie for doing so. If they carry speculations further than the constraints of this necessity and theorizes on natural *or* moral subjects, they are allured by a certain pleasure and satisfaction found in so doing. Besides, they consider that everyone, even in everyday life, is required to possess more or less of this theory: that from earliest infancy we continually advance in forming more general principles of conduct and reasoning. The larger our acquired experience and the stronger the *reason* with which we are invested, will always render our principles more general and comprehensive. What we call philosophy is nothing but a more systematic and methodical operation of the same kind. To philosophise on such subjects is not essentially different from reasoning on daily life. We may expect greater stability, if not greater truth, from our philosophy on account of its more exact and more disciplined method of proceeding.

We would have to be free of the merest *tendency* to scepticism not to see that when we look out beyond human affairs and the properties of matter, we have exceeded the reach of our faculties. This is especially true when we carry our speculations into: the two eternities (that *before* life and that *after* life); into the present state of things and the creation and formation of the Universe; into the existence and properties of spirits and the powers and operations of one universal Spirit existing without beginning or end: omnipotent; omniscient; immutable; infinite and incomprehensible. So long as we confine our speculations to trade, morals, politics or criticism, we can always make appeal to common sense and experience. This strengthens our philosophical conclusions and at least partly removes the suspicion we rightly entertain over highly subtle and refined reasoning.

---

1 Everyday

But in *theological* reasoning we do not have this advantage. Here, we are employed upon subject matter that we realise is too large for our grasp but, more than any others, *requires* to be familiarised to our understanding. We are like foreigners in a strange country where everything seems suspicious,* and where we are in constant danger of transgressing the laws and customs of the people. We do not know how far we ought to trust our everyday methods of reasoning on such a subject. This is because even in *common* life we cannot account for them, being entirely guided by a kind of instinct or necessity in employing them.

All sceptics claim that if reason is considered in the *abstract*, it furnishes invincible arguments against itself. Thus we could never retain any conviction or assurance on any subject, were not *sceptical* reasoning so refined and subtle and thus quite unable to counterbalance the more solid and natural arguments derived from our senses and experience.

But it is equally evident that whenever our arguments run *outwith* common life and thus lose the advantage of evidence from the senses & experience, then even the most refined scepticism moves up to parity with them and is now a counterbalance. The one now has no more weight than the other. The mind must remain in suspense between them; and it is this very suspension, or balance, that is the triumph of scepticism.

CLEANTHES Philo, I see that like all speculative sceptics, your teaching and your practice are equally at variance in abstruse theory, as they are in the conduct of common life! Wherever evidence reveals itself, you adhere to it despite your claimed scepticism. I also observe that some members of your sceptical sect are just as *decisive* as those professing greater certainty and assurance. In reality, would a man not be ridiculous in claiming to reject Newton's explanation of the wonderful phenomenon of the rainbow,[1] because that very explanation gives a minute anatomy of the rays of light; a subject too refined for human comprehension? And what would you say to someone who had no *particular* objection to the arguments of Copernicus[2]

---

* *Giving reason to imagine ill, without proof.* SJ

1 Sir Isaac Newton (1643–1727) in *Optics* (London, 1704). The English polymath showed that prism-refracted sunlight displays a spectrum from long wavelengths (red) to short (violet). In 1999, he was voted by contemporary physicists one of their three greatest, together with Albert Einstein and James Clerk Maxwell.

2 Nicolaus Copernicus (1473–1543). Polish Catholic priest and Renaissance scientist. His *De revolutionibus orbium coelestrum* ('On the Revolutions of the celestial Spheres') founded modern astronomy, positing the heliocentricity of our solar system.

and Galileo[1] on the motion of the Earth, yet withheld their assent on the *general* principle that these subjects were too magnificent and remote to be explained by the narrow, fallacious *reason* of humanity?

There is indeed a kind of brutish, ignorant scepticism, as you well observed, that gives ordinary people a prejudice against anything they do not easily understand. It makes them reject every principle requiring elaborate reasoning to prove and establish it. This species of scepticism is fatal to knowledge, though *not* to religion. Those making the greatest profession of it we often find assenting not only to the great *truths* of theism and natural theology, but also to the most absurd beliefs handed down by traditional superstition. They firmly believe in witches, though they will neither believe nor even *listen* to the simplest proposition of Euclid![2]

On the other hand, refined and philosophical sceptics fall into an opposite inconsistency. They push their researches into the most abstruse corners of science where their assent, attending them at every step, is proportional to the evidence they meet. They are even obliged to acknowledge that the *most* abstruse and remote objects are those *best* explained by philosophy. Light is actually anatomised! The true *system* of the heavenly bodies is discovered and ascertained! However, the nourishment of bodies by food is still inexplicable and the cohesion of the parts of matter still incomprehensible. In every question, therefore, these sceptics are obliged to consider each particular piece of evidence separately, proportioning their assent to its precise degree. This is their practice in the natural, mathematical, moral and political sciences.

Why not the *same*, I ask, in the theological and religious field?

Here, why must conclusions be rejected *solely* on the general presumption of the insufficiency of human reason *and* without any particular discussion of the evidence? Is not such paradoxical conduct clear proof of prejudice and emotion?

Our senses you say, are fallacious and our understanding erroneous. Our ideas of the dimensions, duration and motion, even of the most familiar objects, are full of absurdities and contradictions. You challenge me to solve the difficulties or reconcile the inconsistencies you discover in them.

---

1 Galileo Galilei (1564–1642). Italian polymath. He endorsed the Copernican system for which he was threatened with torture by the Holy Inquisition and confined, *sine die*, by the Pope to his villa, *Il Gioiello* (the Jewel) near Florence. A belated apology came from Pope John Paul II in 2000, the Church now conceding heliocentrism.
2 Greek mathematician (fl. *c.*300 BCE) in Alexandria. His discipline of geometry is contained in the several books of *The Elements*, his great work on mathematics.

I have not the capacity for so great an undertaking. I have not the time to devote to it and I perceive it to be superfluous. Your own conduct, in every circumstance, refutes your principles. It shows the firmest reliance on all the accepted maxims of science, philosophy, morals, prudence and behaviour.

I shall never assent to so harsh an opinion as that of a celebrated writer[1] who says that the Sceptics are not a sect of philosophers; they are only a sect of liars. I, however, will affirm (without offence, I hope) that they are actually a sect of jesters or mockers. However, when I find myself disposed to mirth and amusement, I shall certainly choose a less perplexing and abstruse form of entertainment. A comedy, a novel, or at most a history, seems a more natural recreation than metaphysical subtleties and abstractions.

In vain would the sceptic make a distinction between science and common life, or between one science and another. The arguments employed in *all* of these, if valid, are of a similar nature and contain the same force and evidence. Or if there be any difference among them, the advantage lies entirely on the side of theology and natural religion. Many principles of mechanics are founded on very abstruse reasoning and yet no man with any pretensions to science, even the speculative sceptic, entertains the least doubt with regard to them. The Copernican system of planetary motion contains the most surprising paradox,[2] one contrary to our natural conceptions, to appearances and to our very senses. Yet even monks and inquisitors are now constrained to withdraw their opposition. And shall Philo, a man of such broad intelligence and extensive knowledge, entertain any general and non-specific scruples with regard to the religious hypothesis? It is founded on the simplest and most obvious arguments and unless it meets with *artificial* obstacles, is easily understood by the mind of Man?

DEMEA here we may observe a pretty curious circumstance in the history of the sciences. After the union of philosophy with popular religion at the first establishment of Christianity, nothing was more universal among religious teachers than declamations against reason, against the senses, in short against every principle derived from *human* research and inquiry. All the topics of the ancient academics were adopted by the Fathers of the

---

1 Antoine Arnauld (1612–94). French theologian, mathematician, philosopher and friend of René Descartes. Hume cites his *La Logique, ou l'arte de penser* (1662)

2 That the rising and setting sun is not due to its orbiting the Earth and that the solar system is heliocentric, ie sun-centred, rather than geocentric, or earth-centred.

Church[1] and were thence propagated for several ages in every school and from every pulpit in Christendom. The Protestant reformers embraced the same principles of reasoning, or rather declamation. All their panegyrics on the excellence of faith were sure to be interlarded with severe strokes of satire against natural reason. A celebrated prelate too, Monsieur Huet[2] of the Romish Communion, a man of the most extensive learning who wrote a demonstration of Christianity, has also composed a treatise containing all the baseless criticisms of the boldest and most determined Pyrrhonism.[3]

John Locke seems to have been the first Christian who ventured openly to assert that faith was nothing other than a species of reason and that religion was only a branch of philosophy. He said that a chain of argument similar to that establishing any truth in morals, politics, or physics, might always be employed in discovering all the principles of both natural and revealed theology.[4] The misuse that Pierre Bayle and other irreverent intellectuals made of the philosophical scepticism of the Fathers and first reformers, still further propagated the thoughtful judgment reached by Mr Locke.[5]

Indeed it is now avowed by all claimants to reasoning and philosophy that the terms Atheist and Sceptic are almost synonymous. And as it is certain that no-one can be in earnest when professing the latter principle, I would hope that there are as few who seriously maintain the former.

PHILO Do you not remember the excellent saying of Lord Francis Bacon on this subject?

---

1 The Fathers were the principal theologians of the early Christian church, such as St Augustine, St Ambrose and St Jerome. By no means all were saints...

2 Pierre-Daniel Huet (1630–1721). French bishop and theologian. Cleanthes refers to his *Traité philosophique de la faiblesse de l'esprit humain* (Amsterdam, 1723) For Huet, as for Pascal, reason and sense are incapable of truth with certainty. That can be done only by faith. Published posthumously like Hume's *Dialogues*, it also caused a seismic controversy.

3 The sceptical teaching associated with Pyrrho of Elis (c.360–c.270 BCE); to him is often attributed the most radical abandonment of belief.

4 John Locke (1632–1704). English physician and empiricist philosopher. He held that human ideas were not innate but were inscribed by sense perception, ie experience, on a 'void white paper', often incorrectly rendered as a *tabula rasa* (Lat. scraped tablet). In his *Reasonableness of Christianity* (1695), Locke memorably states that removing reason to make way for revelation extinguishes the light of both.

5 Pierre Bayle (1647–1706). Huguenot sceptical philosopher. Hume was thoroughly familiar with his *Dictionnaire Historique et Critique*, a vast compendium of intellectual curiosities, known as 'The Arsenal of the Enlightenment.' Bayle spent most of his productive life as a refugee in Protestant Holland.

CLEANTHES 'A little Philosophy makes a man an Atheist – a great deal converts him to religion?'[1]

PHILO A very judicious remark. But what I have in view is another passage. Bacon, having mentioned King David's fool who said in his heart 'there is no God,'[2] observes that atheists nowadays have a double share of folly. They are not content to say *in their hearts* that there is no God, but they also *utter* the impiety. They are thereby guilty of multiplied indiscretion and imprudence. I believe such people cannot be very formidable, although they never were more in earnest.

But though you should rank *me* in this class of fools, I cannot resist a remark that occurs to me from the history of the religious and irreligious scepticism with which you have entertained us.

It appears to me, that there are strong symptoms of manipulation by priests in the whole progress of this affair. During ignorant ages, such as those following the dissolution of the ancient Schools,[3] priests perceived that Atheism.

Deism,[4] indeed heresy of any kind, could only come from the presumptuous questioning of received opinions; and from a belief that human reason was equal to everything. Education then had a mighty influence over the human mind. It was almost equal in force to evidence from the senses and common understanding, by which even the most determined sceptics must admit themselves governed.

But at *present*, when the influence of education is much diminished and when, from a more open knowledge of the world, we have learned to *compare* the popular principles of different nations and ages, our sagacious divines have changed their whole system of philosophy. They now talk the language of Stoics, Platonists and Peripatetics,[5] not that of Pyrrhonians and Academics.

---

1 Francis Bacon, 1st Viscount St Albans (1561–1626). English polymath: philosopher; statesman; scientist and jurist. Lord Chancellor of Great Britain to King James I. Cleanthes prefigures his essay *On Atheism*, published in *Essays* (1597). The precise quotation is: 'It is true, that a little Philosophy inclineth Man's mind to *Atheism*; but depth in philosophy bringeth Men's minds about [back] to Religion.'

2 'The fool hath said in his heart, there is no God. They are corrupt, they have done abominable works, there is none that doeth good.' Psalms, 14.1, Authorised Version.

3 In 529 CE, the Roman Emperor Justinian closed the philosophical Schools of Athens, including the Academy founded by Plato that had operated for almost a thousand years. The professors left for Persia and the court of King Chosroes at Ctesiphon in modern Iraq.

4 Deists believe in a creator God, but one that is indifferent, ie non-interventional, both in the affairs of Nature and those of living creatures such as humanity.

5 Platonists were followers of Plato. Peripatetics followed Aristotle.

If we distrust human reason, we have now no other principle to lead us into religion. Thus, priests are sceptics in one age, dogmatists in another. Whichever, the system best suiting their purpose of gaining ascendancy over humankind, they are sure to make their favourite principle and established tenet.

CLEANTHES It is very natural for people to embrace those principles by which they can best defend their doctrines. Nor do we need to turn to priestcraft[1] to account for such a reasonable expedient. Surely *nothing* can indicate more strongly that a set of principles is true and acceptable than to observe it tending to confirm true religion *and* confounding the trivial objections of atheists, libertines and freethinkers of all denominations.

PART II

DEMEA Nothing, Cleanthes, could surprise me *more* than the light in which you put this argument. From your whole tenor, one would imagine that you were maintaining the *existence* of God against the trivial objections of atheists and infidels. You clearly felt it necessary to champion that *most* fundamental religious principle; one that I do hope is not an issue between us. I believe that no-one of common sense[2] ever entertained serious doubts about such a certain and self-evident truth.

However, the question does not concern the existence, but rather the *nature* of God. This I affirm to be incomprehensible. It is unknown to us, due to the frailty of human understanding. The essence of that supreme Mind; its attributes; the manner of its existence; the very nature of its duration; every *particular* of so divine a Being is mysterious. As finite, weak and blind creatures, we ought to humble ourselves in its august presence. Conscious of our frailties, we should silently adore its infinite perfections that 'eye hath not seen, ear hath not heard' and the human heart cannot conceive.[3] These matters are hidden from human curiosity in a deep cloud and it is *profanity*

---

1 See G. Berkeley, *Alciphron: or, the minute Philosopher.* (1732). Alciphron was a Greek writer of the 1st century CE. A 'minute philosopher' was Bishop Berkeley's dismissive term for freethinkers such as Dr Bernard Mandeville and the 3rd Earl of Shaftesbury, against whom the seven Dialogues of *Alciphron* were directed. Cleanthes echoes the assault on priests and 'priestcraft' by Alciphron in *Dialogue* 1.3

2 Probably a reference to Prof Thomas Reid of Glasgow University, a founder of the philosophical school of Common Sense and the only major philosopher to engage with, and misunderstand, Hume's *Treatise of Human Nature* in its author's lifetime.

3 Demea quotes from I Corinthians, 2.9, 'But as it is written, eye hath not seen, nor ear heard, neither have entered into the heart of man, the things which God hath prepared for them that love him.' King James.

to attempt penetration of their sacred obscurity. Indeed, second only to the impiety of denying its existence, is the temerity of prying into its nature and essence, decrees and attributes.

However, lest you think that my piety has got the better of my philosophy here, I shall bring support for my opinion, if it needs any, from a great authority. I could cite all the divines, almost from the foundation of Christianity, who have considered this, or any other theological subject. However, I shall confine myself to one person celebrated equally for piety *and* for philosophy; Father Malebranche.[1]

He says:

> One ought not so much to call God a spirit, in order to express positively what he is, as in order to signify that he is not matter. He is a Being infinitely perfect: of this we cannot doubt. But in the same manner as we ought not to imagine, even supposing him corporeal, that he is clothed with a human body, as the anthropomorphites[2] asserted, according to the view that that figure was the most perfect of any; so, neither ought we to imagine that the spirit of God has human ideas, or bears any resemblance to our spirit, according to the view that we know nothing more perfect than a human mind. We ought rather to believe, that as he comprehends the perfections of matter without being material... he comprehends also the perfections of created spirits without being spirit, in the manner we conceive spirit: That his true name is, 'He that is', or in other words, Being without restriction, all Being, the Being infinite and universal.'[3]

PHILO Demea, after citing so great an authority and a thousand more you might produce, it would be ridiculous to add my opinion or express approval of your beliefs. But surely, when reasonable people treat these subjects the question can never concern the *being*, but only the *nature* of the Deity.[4] The former truth, as you observe, is unquestionable and self-evident. Nothing exists without a cause and the original Cause of this Universe (whatever *it* be) we call God and piously ascribe to it every species of perfection. Whoever questions this fundamental truth deserves every punishment that can be inflicted among philosophers; namely, ridicule, contempt and disapproval.

---

1 Nicolas Malebranche (1638–1715) French cleric, ethicist, physicist and rationalist disciple of René Descartes.

2 From Greek Ανθροποσ (man) and μορφη (shape) ie those envisioning God in human form. 'And God created Man in his own image...' Genesis 1.27.

3 Nicolas Malebranche, *De la Recherche de la Vérité* (1674), 3.9.

4 Hume again follows *On the Nature of the Gods* where Balbus, a Stoic and colleague of the historical Cleanthes, makes this very point. Cicero, *De Natura Deorum* 2.5.

However, as all perfection is relative, we ought never to imagine that we can comprehend the *attributes* of this divine Being. Neither may we suppose that its perfections have any analogy or likeness to the perfections of a *human* being. We justly ascribe to it wisdom, thought, design and knowledge because these words are honourable among us. We have no other language or other conceptions to express our adoration. But let us beware of thinking that *our* ideas correspond in any way to *its* perfections, or that its attributes have any resemblance to these qualities among human beings. The Being, infinitely superior to both our limited view and our comprehension, was thus more the object of worship in the temple, than of disputation in the medieval schools.[1]

In reality, Cleanthes, in coming to this conclusion I have no need of the affected scepticism that so displeases you. Our ideas reach *no* further than our experience; and we have *no* experience of divine attributes and operations. I need not conclude my syllogism since you can draw the inference for yourself. And it is a pleasure to me – and I hope to you too – that both sound reasoning and sound piety concur here in the same conclusion. Both of them establish the adorably mysterious and *incomprehensible* nature of the supreme Being.

Cleanthes now addressed himself to Demea, rather than replying to Philo's pious declamations.

CLEANTHES So as not to lose time, Demea, I shall briefly explain how I conceive this matter. Look round the world. Contemplate every part of it. You will find it is nothing but one great machine, subdivided into an infinite number of lesser machines. These in turn have subdivisions to a degree beyond the ability of our human senses and faculties to trace or explain. All these various machines, down to their *minutest* parts, are adjusted to each other with an accuracy that ravishes all who contemplate them with admiration. Throughout all Nature, the remarkable adaptation of means to ends resembles, though it much exceeds, the productions of human intelligence and design. Since the *effects* so resemble each other, we are led by all the rules of analogy to infer that their *causes* must also have a resemblance. Hence, the Author of Nature is similar to the human mind, though possessing faculties much larger, proportional to the grandeur of the executed work.

---

1 In the medieval schools, Scholasticism sought to reconcile Christian theology with classical and late antiquity philosophy, particularly that of Aristotle and the Neoplatonists. Notable 'Schoolmen' included Peter Abelard, Duns Scotus and Thomas Aquinas.

By this argument *a posteriori* and by this argument *alone*, we prove both the existence of a Deity and also its similarity to the human mind and intelligence.

DEMEA Cleanthes, let me tell you that from the beginning I could not endorse your conclusion concerning the similarity of the Deity to human beings. Still less can I approve of the means by which you endeavoured to establish it. What? No demonstration of the *being* of God! No abstract arguments! No proofs *a priori*! Are these proofs, hitherto insisted on by philosophers, all fallacy, all sophism? Can we reach no further in this subject than experience and probability? This is not to turn against respectable efforts to support belief in a Deity, but by this affected candour you surely give atheists advantages unobtainable through argument and reasoning.

PHILO What I chiefly question in this subject is not so much that Cleanthes reduces all his religious arguments to *experience*, but that they appear to be not even the most certain and irrefutable of that inferior kind justification. That a stone will fall, that fire will burn, that the earth has solidity, we have observed thousands of times. Thus when any new instance is presented, we unhesitatingly draw the accustomed inference. Exact similarity of cases gives us perfect assurance of a similar outcome; stronger evidence is never desired nor sought. However, whenever you depart in the *least* from the similarity of the cases, you diminish the evidence in proportion. You may finally reduce it to a very weak analogy, clearly liable to error and uncertainty. After having experienced the circulation of the blood in human creatures, we do not doubt that it takes place in Titius & Maevius.[1] However, given its circulation in frogs and fishes, it is only a *presumption*, though a strong one from analogy, that it also takes place in human beings and other animals. This analogical reasoning is much weaker still when we infer the circulation of sap in vegetables from our experience that blood circulates in animals. Indeed those who hastily followed that imperfect analogy were found mistaken by more accurate experiments.

If we see a house, Cleanthes, we conclude with the greatest certainty that it had an architect or builder; this being precisely that species of effect we have experienced from that species of cause. But surely you will not claim that the Universe bears such a resemblance to a house that we can infer

---

1 ie that it is universal among humankind.

a similar cause with the same certainty, or that this analogy is entire and perfect. The difference is so striking that the best you can manage here is a guess, a conjecture, a *presumption* concerning a similar cause. How *that* will be received in the world, I leave you to consider.

CLEANTHES It would surely be very badly received! I should be deservedly criticised and scorned if I admitted that the proofs of the Deity amounted to no more than a guess or conjecture. But is the whole adjustment of means to ends in a house *so* poor a resemblance to that in the Universe? The system of final causes or purposes in things? The order, proportion and arrangement of every part?

The steps of a stair are plainly designed so that human legs may use them in mounting and this inference is certain and infallible. Human legs are also designed for walking and mounting. This inference, I admit, is not altogether certain because of the dissimilarity you point out. But does it therefore deserve *only* the title of presumption, or conjecture?

DEMEA Good God, where are we? Zealous defenders of religion *admitting* that the proofs of a Deity fall short of perfect evidence! Philo, I depended on your assistance in proving the adorable mysteriousness of the divine nature. Do you agree with all these extravagant opinions of Cleanthes – for what other name can I give them? I disapprove of such principles being advanced and supported by such an authority, in front of so young a man as Pamphilus here?

PHILO You don't seem to grasp that I am arguing with Cleanthes in his own way. I hope to eventually reconcile him to our opinion by showing him the dangerous consequences of his tenets. But I see that what bothers *you* most, Demea, is the case that Cleanthes has made for the argument *a posteriori*. Finding that argument likely to escape you and vanish into air, you think it is so disguised that you can scarcely believe it is being set in its true light. Now, however much I may dissent in *other* respects from his principles, I must admit that Cleanthes has fairly represented that argument. I shall try to state the matter so as to remove your reservations.

Were we to attempt to understand the Universe without considering anything *already* known and experienced, we would be absolutely incapable of success; nor could we give preference to any one state or situation of things above another. Since nothing we clearly conceive could be reckoned impossible, or implying a contradiction, every figment of imagination would be upon an equal footing. Neither could we assign any accurate reason as to why we should adhere to particular idea or system, while rejecting others equally possible.

Again, after opening our eyes and contemplating the world as it really is, it would be impossible at first to assign the cause of any *one* event, much less the whole scheme of things, the Universe. We might set our fancy a-rambling and bring in an infinite variety of reports and representations. These would all be possible, but all being *equally* possible, we could never give a satisfactory reason for preferring any one to the rest. It is experience, *alone*, that can point out the true cause of any phenomenon.

Now, Demea, according to this line of reasoning it follows – indeed it is tacitly accepted by Cleanthes–that the order, arrangement, or adjustment of final causes is not *of itself* any proof of design, but only so far as it has been *experienced* to derive from that principle. For aught we can know *a priori*, matter may contain *within itself* the source, or wellspring, of order. The same goes for mind. There is no more difficulty in conceiving that the elements, from an internal unknown cause, may fall into their most exquisite arrangement, than there is in conceiving that ideas in the great *universal* Mind, also fall into that arrangement from a similar internal and unknown cause. The equal possibility of both these suppositions is admitted.

However, according to Cleanthes we find by experience that there is a difference between them. Throw several pieces of steel together without shape or form; they will never arrange themselves into a watch. Without an architect, stone, mortar and wood will never erect a house. However, by an unknown and inexplicable process, we see the ideas in a human mind so arrange themselves as to form the *plan* of a watch or house. Experience, therefore, proves that there is an original principle of order in *mind*–but not in matter. From similar effects we infer similar causes. The adjustment of means to ends is the same in the universe as in a machine of human contrivance. The causes, therefore, must resemble each other.

I must admit that I too was scandalised from the beginning with this asserted resemblance between the Deity and human creatures. It implies such degradation of the supreme Being as no sound theist could endure. Therefore with your assistance, Demea, I shall endeavour to defend what you correctly call 'the adorable mysteriousness of the divine Nature' and shall refute this reasoning of Cleanthes – provided he concedes that I have made a fair representation of it.

When Cleanthes had agreed to this, Philo, after a short break, proceeded as follows:

PHILO Cleanthes, I shall not argue with you at present that *all* inferences concerning fact are founded on experience. All experimental reasoning is founded on the supposition that similar causes prove similar effects, while similar effects imply similar causes. But observe, I entreat you, with what *extreme* caution all accurate thinkers proceed when transferring experiments to 'similar' cases. Unless the cases are *exactly* similar, we may not repose perfect confidence in applying their past observation to any particular phenomenon. Every alteration of circumstances occasions a doubt concerning the outcome. It requires *new* experiments to prove conclusively that the new circumstances are of no moment or importance. A change in bulk, situation, arrangement, age, condition of the air, or surrounding bodies; any of these particulars may be attended with the most unexpected consequences. Unless the objects are very familiar to us, it amounts to the highest temerity to confidently expect, after *any* of these changes, an outcome similar to that previously observed. Here more than anywhere, the slow, deliberate steps of philosophers are distinguished from the precipitate march of the general population. They, encouraged by the smallest similarity, are incapable of discernment or consideration.

Cleanthes, do you really believe that you preserved your usual composure and philosophy in that great step you took in comparing houses, ships, furniture and machines, to the Universe? From their similarity in *some* circumstances, you inferred a similarity in their causes. Thought, design, intelligence, of the sort we find in human beings and other animals, is only *one* of the springs and principles of the Universe. So also are heat or cold, attraction or repulsion and a hundred others that fall under daily observation.

It is through an active cause that we find some particular *parts* of Nature producing alterations in other parts. But can a conclusion be transferred *from* parts to the whole with any validity? Does the great disproportion not disbar all comparison and inference? From observing the growth of a hair, can we learn anything concerning human procreation? Would the manner of a leaf's blowing, even though perfectly known, give us any instruction concerning the vegetation[1] of a tree?

However, if we agree that we might make the operation of one part of Nature upon another the foundation of our judgement concerning the *origin* of the whole (something that can never be admitted), why select so

---

1 The power of growing and maturation (of a plant). OED.

minute, so weak and so narrow a principle as the reason and design of animals upon *this* planet? What peculiar privilege has this little agitation of the brain we call thought, that we must make *it* the model of the whole Universe? Our partiality in our own favour does indeed present it on all occasions–but sound philosophy ought to guard carefully against so natural an illusion.

Thus I will not admit that the operations of a part can afford us any justifiable conclusion concerning the origin of the whole. Similarly, I will not allow any one part to form a rule for any other part if the latter be remote from the former. Are there any reasonable grounds to conclude that the inhabitants of other planets possess thought, intelligence, reason, or anything similar to human faculties? Nature having extremely diversified its manner of operation in this small globe, can we imagine that she continuously copies herself throughout so immense a Universe?

And if, as seems likely, thought is confined merely to *this* narrow corner (and even here has so limited a sphere of action) with what propriety can we assign it as the original cause of *all* things? The narrow views of a peasant who makes domestic economy* the rule for the government of kingdoms is a pardonable sophism by comparison!

Let us *assume*, however, that thought and reason resembling the human variety were to be found throughout the Universe, its activity elsewhere vastly greater than it appears in this globe. I still cannot see why the operations of worlds *already* constituted, arranged and adjusted, can be extended to an embryonic world still advancing towards that constitution and arrangement.

By observation, we know somewhat of the economy,* action and nourishment of a finished animal. But it is with great caution that must transfer that observation to the growth of a foetus in the womb and with yet more caution to the formation of a sperm in the loins of its father. Nature, we find even in our limited experience, possesses an infinite number of springs and principles that incessantly reveal themselves on every change of her position and situation. Without the *utmost* temerity, we cannot claim to know what new–and presently unknown–principles would govern Nature in a new and unknown situation such as the formation of the Universe. A *very* small part of this great system, and over a very short time, is very imperfectly revealed to us. From *this* do we pronounce decisively concerning the origin of the whole?

---

* Economy: *Organisation and arrangements.* SJ

An admirable conclusion! Only at *this* time and at *this* minute earthly globe, do stone, wood, iron and brass, have an order or arrangement due to human art and contrivance. Therefore the Universe could not originally attain its order and arrangement without something similar to human art. But is one part of Nature a rule for another part remote from the former? Is it a rule for the whole? Is a very small part a rule for the Universe? Is Nature in one situation a certain rule for Nature in another situation vastly different from the former?

Can you criticise me, Cleanthes, if I here imitate the prudent caution of Simonides[1] in the famous story?

On being asked by Hiero[2] what God was, he requested a day to think about it; and then two days more; and continually prolonged the term without ever bringing in his definition or description.[3]

Could you even criticise me if I had answered at first that I did not know and was also aware that this subject lay vastly beyond my faculties? You might cry, '*Sceptic. Mocker!* ' as much as you pleased, but in many more familiar subjects I have found imperfections and even contradictions in human reason. Hence, I should never expect success *from* the feeble conjectures of human reason on a subject so sublime, so remote from the sphere of our observation.

When two species of objects have always been observed to be conjoined together I can infer, by custom, the existence of one wherever I see the existence of the other. This I call an argument from experience. But how this argument can have validity in the present case where the objects are single, individual, without parallel or specific resemblance, is difficult to explain.

---

1 Simonides of Keos (556–468 BCE). Said by Plato to be 'wise and divinely inspired' he was one of the nine canonical lyric poets of ancient Greece. He invented four letters of the alphabet and also the *epinician* or victory ode, two of the latter being to the Athenians after Marathon and to Leonidas, King of Sparta, after Thermopylae. He spent his last years in Sicily at the court of the tyrant Hiero of Syracuse.

2 Hiero I, Tyrant, ie ruler, of Syracuse 478–466 BCE. His defeat of the Carthaginians in Sicily greatly increased the power of Syracuse. Though despotic, Hiero was a liberal patron of literature. The poets Pindar, Simonides and his nephew Bacchylides were among those who repaid his hospitality with elegant verse.

3 M. Tullius Cicero, *De Natura Deorum*, 1.60. Hiero required his answer next day, but Simonides begged two days and, on each further request, redoubled the number. Ddemanding an explanation, Hiero received the famous answer: *quia quanto diutius considero tanto mihi spes videtur obscurior* (Because the longer I meditate on it, the more obscure it appears).

And will anyone tell me with a straight face that an orderly Universe *must* arise from some thought and art like the human, simply because *we* have experience of it? To verify this reasoning we would require experience of the origin of worlds—and it is surely not sufficient that we have seen ships and even cities arise from human art and contrivance...

Philo was proceeding in this vehement manner, one as it seemed to me some-where between jest and earnest, when he observed signs of impatience in Cleanthes and immediately stopped short.

CLEANTHES What I had only to suggest was that you do not abuse terms, or use popular expressions to subvert philosophical reasoning. You know that the common people often distinguish between reason and experience. Even where the question relates only to a matter of fact and existence, it is found when that reason is properly analysed that it is only a species of experience. To prove by experience the origin of the Universe from mind is not more contrary to common speech than to prove the motion of the Earth from the same principle. And a critic might raise exactly the same objections to the Copernican system you have raised against my reasoning. Have you *other* earths, they might say, that you have seen to move? Have...

PHILO Yes! We *have* other earths. Is the moon not another earth we see turning round its centre? Is not Venus another earth, where we observe the same phenomenon? Are not the revolutions of the sun also a confirmation, from analogy, of the same theory? Are not all the planets 'earths', each orbiting the Sun? Are the satellites orbiting Jupiter and Saturn not moons that move round the Sun along with their planets? These analogies and resemblances, together with others I have not mentioned, are the sole proofs of the Copernican system. It is down to you to consider whether you have any analogies of the same kind to support your theory.

In reality, Cleanthes, the modern system of astronomy is now so accepted and has become so essential a part of our earliest education that we are rarely scrupulous in examining the reasons upon which it is founded. It has now become a matter of mere curiosity to study the first writers on that subject. They had the full force of prejudice to encounter and were obliged to adjust their arguments on every side in order to render them popular and convincing. But if we peruse Galileo's famous *Dialogues concerning the system of the World*,[1] we shall find that great genius, one of the most sublime that ever lived, first endeavouring to prove that there was no foundation for the distinction commonly made between elementary and celestial substances. The Schools, proceeding from the illusions of sense, had carried this distinction very far, pronouncing celestial substances to be incorruptible, unalterable, impassable and assigning all the opposite qualities to the former.

Galileo, however, beginning with the moon, proved its similarity to the earth in every particular. These included its convex figure; its natural darkness when not illuminated; its density; its distinction into solid and liquid; its varying phases; the mutual illuminations of the earth and moon; their mutual eclipses; the irregularities of the lunar surface etc After many instances of this kind with regard to all the planets, it was plain that these bodies became proper objects of experience and that the similarity of their nature enabled us to extend the same arguments and phenomena from one to the other.

In this cautious proceeding of the astronomers, Cleanthes, you may read your own condemnation; or rather you may see that your subject exceeds all human reason and inquiry. Can you claim to show *any* similarity between the fabric of a house and the generation of a Universe? Have you ever seen Nature in any situation resembling the first arrangement of the elements? Have worlds ever been formed before your eyes–and have you had sufficient time to observe the whole progress of the phenomenon from the first appearance of order to its final consummation? If you have, cite your experience and deliver your theory.

PART III

CLEANTHES What an air of probability the most absurd argument may acquire in the hands of someone of ingenuity and invention!

Philo, are you not aware that it became necessary for Copernicus and his first disciples to *prove* the similarity of terrestrial and celestial matter? This was because several philosophers, blinded by old systems and supported by

---

1 Actually *Dialogue concerning the Two Chief World Systems* (*Dialogo sopra i due massimi sistemi del mondo* (1632). In it, 'Salviati' argues for the Copernican heliocentric system against 'Simplicio' who is for Ptolemaic geocentricity. It led to Galileo's 1633 conviction by the Inquisition on 'grave suspicion of heresy'. The work was on the *Index of forbidden Books* for 200 years; its author placed under house arrest for eight years. In 1990, Pope John Paul II absolved Galileo of his sin. The *Dialogo* was one of Hume's inspirations for the present work.

some observed appearances, had *denied* this similarity? Also, are you not aware that it is unnecessary for theists to *prove* the similarity of the works of Nature to those of Art, such similarity being self-evident and undeniable? The same matter and a similar form. What more is required to show an analogy between their causes and hence ascertain the origin of *all* things from divine purpose and intention? Your objections, I tell you frankly, are no better than the abstruse trivial objections of those philosophers who denied *motion*[1] and hence ought to be refuted in the same manner: by illustrations, examples and instances, rather than by philosophical argument.

Suppose, therefore, that an articulate Voice was heard in the clouds, one much louder and more melodious than any reachable by human art. Suppose also that this Voice were simultaneously heard by every nation and in its own language and dialect. Suppose that its words not only delivered accurate sense and meaning, but also some instruction altogether worthy of a benevolent Being superior to humankind. Could you hesitate for even a moment concerning the *cause* of this Voice? Must you not instantly ascribe it to some design or purpose? Yet I cannot see how all the same objections – if they merit that appellation – that challenges the system of theism, may not also be produced against this inference.[2]

Might you not say that *all* conclusions concerning fact were founded on experience? That when we hear an articulate voice in the dark and thence infer a human being, it is only the resemblance of the *effects* that leads us to conclude that there is a similar resemblance in the *cause*? But you might say that *this* extraordinary voice, by its loudness, extent and capacity in all languages, bears so little analogy to any human voice, that we have *no* reason to suppose any analogy in their causes: and consequently that its rational, wise, coherent speech was generated you know not whence, by some accidental whistling of the winds and not from any divine reason or intelligence? You can clearly see your own objections in these petty oppositions. I hope you also see clearly that they cannot possibly have more force in the one case than in the other.

---

1 Probably a reference to Zeno of Elea (490–430 BCE) whose nine *Paradoxes* are preserved in Aristotle's *Physics*. They seek to show that motion is an illusion, the most famous being that of Achilles and the Tortoise. They were discussed by Simplicius of Cilicia (490–560 CE), the 'Simplicio' of Galileo's *Dialogi*. Zeno's arguments are early examples of *reductio ad absurdum*, or proof by contradiction, used by Hume in Section x, 'On Miracles' in his *Enquiry into Human Understanding*.

2 Hume's 'Voice' has a precedent in Bishop Berkeley. *Alciphron*, 4.15 where Euphranor says: 'A common Man... would probably be convinced of the Being of a God by one single sentence heard... from the Sky.'

However, to bring the case still nearer the present one of the Universe, I shall make two suppositions that do not imply any absurdity or impossibility. Suppose that there were a natural, universal, invariable language, common to every individual of the human race; suppose also that books were *natural* productions, sustaining themselves like animals and vegetables by descent and propagation. Several expressions of *our* emotions contain a universal language. All animals have a natural speech that, however limited, is intelligible to their own species. And since there are both infinitely fewer parts and less arrangement of parts in the finest composition of eloquence than in the coarsest organised body, the propagation of an *Iliad* or an *Aeneid* is an easier supposition than that of any plant or animal.

Suppose, therefore, that you enter your library, thus peopled by *natural* volumes containing the most refined reason and exquisite beauty. Could you possibly open one of them and *doubt* that its original cause bore the strongest analogy to mind and intelligence? When it reasons and discourses; when it expostulates, argues and enforces its views and topics; when it appeals sometimes to the pure intellect, sometimes to the affections; when it collects, disposes, and adorns every consideration suited to the subject, could you *persist* in asserting that all this, in its basis, had really no meaning?

Could you assert that the first formation of this volume in the loins of its original parent did *not* proceed from thought and design? Your obstinacy, I know, does not reach that degree of firmness—even your scepticism and recklessness would be embarrassed at so glaring an absurdity.

Philo, if there is any difference between this supposed case and the real one of the Universe, it is all to the advantage of the latter. The anatomy of an animal affords many stronger instances of design than the perusal of Livy[1] or Tacitus.[2] Any objection you raise in the former case, by carrying me back to so unusual and extraordinary a scene as the origin of worlds, that same objection has place on the supposition of our vegetating library. Choose your party then, Philo, without ambiguity or evasion. Either assert that a rational volume is no proof of a rational cause, or admit a similar cause in all the works of Nature.

---

1 Titus Livius Patavinus (59 BCE–17 CE) anglicised to Livy. Roman historian from Padua. Author of *Ab urbe condita libri*, 'Books from the Foundation of the City,' covering Rome's history from its foundation in 753 BCE to the reign of Augustus.
2 Gaius Cornelius Tacitus (56–117 CE). Senator of Rome and historian of her Empire. His *Annals* and *Histories* cover Rome from the death of Augustus in 14 CE to that of Domitian in 96 CE. He was the Son-in-law and biographer of Julius Agricola, the Roman general responsible for the conquest of Caledonia.

Let me here observe also that this religious argument, instead of being weakened by the scepticism you affect, acquires instead force from it and becomes more firm and undisputed. To exclude all argument or reasoning of *every* kind is either affectation or madness. The declared purpose of every reasonable sceptic is: to reject only abstruse, remote and highly complex arguments; to adhere to common sense and the plain instincts of Nature and to agree wherever any reasoning strikes the mind with such force that one cannot reasonably prevent it. Now, the arguments for natural religion are plainly of *this* kind – and nothing but the most perverse and obstinate metaphysics can reject them.

Consider the anatomy of the eye. Survey its structure and function. Tell me, from your own responses, if the idea of a contriver does not immediately break in upon you with a force like that of sensory experience. The most obvious conclusion, surely, is in favour of design. It requires time, reflection and study to summon up those frivolous, though abstruse, objections that can support infidelity. Who can behold the male and female of each species, the similarity of their parts and instincts, their emotions and the whole course of their lives before and after conception, without being aware that the propagation of the species is intended by Nature? Millions upon millions of such instances present themselves through every part of the Universe and no language can convey a more intelligible and irresistible meaning than the astonishing adjustment of final causes. What degree of blind dogmatism must one have attained, to reject such natural and convincing arguments?

In literature we may meet with some beauties that seem contrary to rules. They gain our affections and stimulate the imagination in opposition both to precepts of criticism and the authority of established masters of the art. And if, as you claim, the argument for theism is contradictory to the principles of logic, its universal and irresistible influence clearly proves that there may be arguments of a similarly irregular nature. Whatever objections may be raised, an *orderly* world – just like a coherent and articulate speech – will still be received as incontestable proof of design and intention.

It sometimes happens, I concede, that the religious arguments do not have their proper influence on someone ignorant, rough and poorly raised. This is not because the arguments are obscure and difficult, but because people of that sort never ask themselves questions about them. Whence arises the amazing structure of an animal? From the copulation of its parents; and whence those parents? From *their* parents. A few such removes and the objects recede to such a distance that they are lost in darkness and confusion; nor is that kind of person motivated by curiosity to trace them further. This is neither dogmatism nor scepticism, but stupidity; a state of mind very different from your sifting, inquisitive disposition, my ingenious friend.

You can trace causes from effects and can compare the most distant and remote objects, but *your* greatest errors do not arise from barrenness of thought and invention. They derive from too luxuriant a *creativity* whose profusion of unnecessary scruples and objections suppresses your natural good sense.

Hermippus, here I could observe that Philo was a little embarrassed and confounded. But while he hesitated in delivering an answer, Demea broke in upon the discourse and spared his blushes.

DEMEA Cleanthes, your example is familiar, being drawn from books and language. I admit that it has much more force on that account; but in this very circumstance is there not also danger? May it not render us presumptuous by making us imagine that we fully *know* the Deity – and have some adequate idea of its nature and attributes? When I read a book I enter into the mind and intention of the author. In a sense I *become* the author for that instant, with an immediate conception of the author's ideas and imagination when writing. But surely, we can never make such a close approach to the Deity. Its ways are not our ways. Its attributes are perfect but incomprehensible. The book of Nature contains a great and inexplicable riddle that is beyond any intelligible discourse or reasoning.

As you know, the ancient Platonists were the most religious and devout of all pagan philosophers. Yet many of them, particularly Plotinus,[1] expressly declare that neither intellect nor understanding is to be ascribed to the Deity. They declare that our most perfect worship of it consists *not* in acts of veneration, reverence, gratitude or love, but in a certain mysterious self-annihilation, a total extinction of our faculties. These ideas are, perhaps, too far stretched. However, this still must be acknowledged: that by representing the Deity as so intelligible, comprehensible and so *similar* to the human mind, we are guilty of the grossest and most narrow partiality – since we thus make *ourselves* the model of the whole Universe.

---

1 Plotinus (*c.*204–270 CE) from Lycopolis ('wolf town') in Egypt. Generally regarded as the founder of 'Neoplatonism,' a term coined by 19th century European scholars. He was one of the most influential philosophers of antiquity after Plato, whose positions he defended in the 54 treatises constituting his *Enneads*.

All the sentiments of the human mind: gratitude, resentment, love, friendship, approbation, blame, pity, emulation and envy, have a plain reference to the state and situation of humankind. They are calculated to preserve the existence and promote the activity of such a being in such circumstances. Therefore it seems unreasonable to transfer such sentiments to a supreme Existence or to suppose it to be motivated by them. Besides, the phenomena of the Universe will not support us in such a theory. All our ideas, derived as they are from our senses, are admittedly false and illusive. They cannot therefore be supposed to have a place in a supreme Intelligence. The ideas of internal sentiment added to those of the external senses, compose the whole furniture of human understanding. We may thus conclude that none of the materials of thought are in any respect similar between the human mind and the divine Intelligence. Now, as to the *manner* of thinking; how can we make any comparison between them, the human and the divine, or suppose them to resemble each other in any way?

Human thought is fluctuating, uncertain, fleeting. It runs in streams of ideas that build upon one another. To remove these characteristics would be to annihilate its essence. In that case, to apply to it the names of thought or reason would be an abuse of terms. At least, if it appears more pious and respectful (as it really is) to retain these terms when mentioning the supreme Being, we should acknowledge that their meaning in *that* context is totally incomprehensible. The infirmities of our nature do not permit us to reach *any* ideas that correspond in the least to the inexpressible sublimity of the divine attributes.

PART IV

CLEANTHES Demea, it seems strange that you, so sincere in the cause of religion, should so strenuously maintain the mysterious, incomprehensible nature of the Deity, insisting that it does *not* resemble human beings. I readily agree that the Deity possesses many powers and attributes of which we can have no comprehension. However if our ideas, so far as they go, are invalid or inadequate and hence do not correspond to its real nature, what is worth debating on this subject? Is a name without any meaning, of such mighty importance? Or how do you mystics who maintain the absolute incomprehensibility of the Deity, differ from those sceptics or atheists asserting that the ultimate origin of *everything* is unknown and unintelligible? Their boldness must be very great if they claim to assign, with certainty, any *other* specific and intelligible origin to the Universe, having rejected the production by a Mind; a mind, moreover, resembling the human, for I know of no other kind!

Also, their consciences must be very rigorous indeed if they refuse to call the universal unknown cause a God or Deity and to bestow on it as many sublime eulogies and meaningless epithets as you shall require of them.

DEMEA Who could imagine that Cleanthes–the calm, philosophical *Cleanthes*–would attempt to refute his antagonists by fixing a nickname on them? That instead of reasoning, he would stoop to invective and declamation like common bigots and inquisitors of the age. Or does he not realise that these topics are easily refuted and that 'Anthropomorphite' is just as invidious – and implies just as dangerous consequences–as the epithet of 'Mystic' with which he has honoured us?

Cleanthes, consider what you assert exactly when you represent the Deity as similar to a human mind and understanding. What is the human Soul? It is an amalgam of various faculties, passions, sentiments and ideas united into one self or person, but still distinct from each other. When it reasons, the ideas that are the parts of its discourse, arrange themselves into a certain form or order preserved entire for not so much as a moment, but immediately giving place to another arrangement. New opinions, new passions, new affections and new feelings arise that continually diversify the mental scene and produce the greatest variety and in the most rapid succession imaginable. How is this compatible with that perfect immutability and simplicity all true theists ascribe to the Deity?

Within the same action, say they, it sees the past, present and future. Its love and hatred, its mercy and justice are one single operation. It is entire in every point of space and complete in every instant of duration. No succession, no change, no acquisition, no diminution. What it is carries no implication of any shadow of distinction or diversity. What it is at this moment it always has been–and always will be–without *any* new judgement, sentiment, or operation. It stands fixed in one simple, perfect state. You can neither say, ever, with justification that this particular act of it *differs* from any other, nor that a particular judgement or idea has been *recently* formed and will be succeeded by any different judgement or idea.

CLEANTHES I readily accept that those who maintain the perfect simplicity of the supreme Being, to the extent in which you have explained it, are complete Mystics, and liable for all the consequences of their opinion, as I have set out. They are, in a word, Atheists – though without knowing it! For though the Deity admittedly possesses attributes of which we have no comprehension, yet we should never ascribe to it attributes absolutely *incompatible* with the intelligent nature essential to it. A Mind whose acts, sentiments and ideas are *not* distinct and successive; one that is *entirely* simple and immutable, is a mind having no thought, no reason, no will, no sentiment, no love and no hatred. In a word, it is no Mind at all! It is an abuse of terms to give it that appellation; we might as well speak of 'limited extension' without shape, or of 'number' without composition.

PHILO Pray consider those you inveigh against. You are honouring with the appellation of 'Atheist' almost all the sound, orthodox *divines* who have addressed this subject. By your reckoning, in the last analysis you yourself will be found to be the world's only sound theist! But if idolaters be atheists, as I think may be asserted correctly, as well as Christian theologians, what becomes of the widely admired argument that God must exist because so many across the world and across time have believed it?[1]

Because I know you are little swayed by names and authorities, let me show you the inconveniences of your anthropomorphism more distinctly. I shall prove that there is no basis for imagining a plan of the world formed in the Divine mind and consisting of distinct ideas, differently arranged, but in the same *manner* as the plan of a house forms in the head of an architect.

I accept that it is not easy to see what is gained by this supposition, whether we judge the matter by reason or by experience. We are still obliged to mount higher, in order to find the *cause* of this Cause which you class as satisfactory and conclusive.

If reason, and I mean *abstract* reason, derived from inquiries *a priori* is not entirely mute with regard to all questions of cause and effect, at least it will venture to pronounce a judgement. It will pronounce that a mental world, or universe of ideas, requires a cause just as much as does a material world, or a universe of objects. If similar in its arrangements it must require a similar cause. For what is there in this subject that should occasion a *different* conclusion or inference? In the *abstract* view they are entirely alike and no difficulty attends the one supposition not common to both.

Again, when we force experience to pronounce sentence on these subjects that lie beyond her sphere, she cannot perceive any material difference, relevant to this question, between these two kinds of worlds. She finds them

---

1 Often called the '*consensus gentium*' (agreement of the peoples) argument. The near universality of religion in human cultures has been taken as evidence for the existence of God.

to be governed by similar principles and to depend upon an equal variety of causes in their operations. We have specimens in miniature of both of them. Our own mind resembles the one–a vegetable or animal body the other. Let experience, therefore, judge from these samples. With regard to its causes, nothing seems more delicate than thought and as these causes never operate in two persons in the same manner, so we never find two persons who think exactly alike. Nor indeed does the same person think exactly alike at any two different periods of time. A change of age, of body disposition, of weather, food, or company, books or passions; any of these particulars, or others more minute, are sufficient to alter the extraordinary machinery of thought and to communicate to it very different movements and operations. As far as we can judge, animals and vegetables are not more delicate in their motions, nor do they depend upon a greater variety or a more remarkable adjustment of mechanisms and principles.

How, therefore, shall we satisfy ourselves concerning the cause of that Being whom you suppose the Author of Nature or, according to your system of Anthropomorphism, the ideal, supernatural world into which you copy the material?[B] Have we not the same reason to copy that ideal world into *another* ideal world, or new intelligent principle? But if we stop and go no further, why go so far? Why not stop at the material world? How can we satisfy ourselves without going on *ad infinitum*? After all, what satisfaction is there in that infinite progression?

Let us remember the story of the Indian philosopher and his elephant.[1] It was never more applicable than to the present subject. If the material world rests upon a similar ideal world, that ideal world must rest upon some other–and so on without end. It would therefore be better never to look *beyond* the present material world.[2] By supposing it to contain the principle of its order within itself, we are really asserting it to *be* God and the sooner we arrive at *that* divine Being, the better. When you go *one* step beyond the mundane system you only excite an inquisitive desire that is impossible to satisfy.

---

1 Hume may be alluding to the Hindu sage and poet Valmiki (fl. *c.*500 BC) who describes four world-bearing elephants: Viru-paksha, Maha-padma, Saumanas and Bhadra, themselves borne by a giant turtle. *The Ramayana* 1.41
2 Locke had suggested that if Valmiki, 'had but thought of the word *Substance*, he needed not... an Elephant to support [the world] and a Tortoise to support his Elephant. *Essay Concerning Human Understanding*, 2.13

To say that the different ideas that compose the rational thinking of the Supreme Being fall into order by themselves and through their own nature, is to talk without precise meaning. If it has a meaning, I would dearly like to know why it is not just as good sense to say that the parts of the material world fall into order by themselves and through their own nature. Can the one opinion be intelligible while the other is not?

We have, indeed, experience of *ideas* that fall into order by themselves and without any known cause. But I am sure we have a much larger experience of *matter* that does the same. For example, all instances of procreation and growth where an accurate analysis of the cause exceeds human comprehension.

We have also experience of particular systems of thought and of matter that have *no* order: of the former in madness; of the latter in decay. Why then should we think that order is more essential to one than the other? And if a cause is required in both, what do we gain by copying the universe of objects into a similar universe of ideas? The very first step that we take leads us on *forever*. It would therefore be wise for us to limit all our inquiries to the present world without looking further. No satisfaction can ever be attained by these speculations so far beyond the bounds of human understanding.

Among the Peripatetics,[1] Cleanthes, it was usual when the cause of any phenomenon was demanded, to have recourse to their 'powers' or hidden qualities. They would say, for instance, that bread nourishes through its nutritive *power*, just as senna[2] purged by its *power* of purgation. However, it has been discovered that this subterfuge was nothing but a cloak for ignorance. These philosophers were really saying the same thing as the sceptics, or the unlettered, who confessed ignorance of the cause of these phenomena. In like manner, when asked what produces order in the ideas of the Supreme Being, can any reason be assigned by you Anthropomorphites *other* than that it is a rational power—and that such is the *nature* of the Deity? But it may be difficult to determine why a similar answer will not be equally satisfactory in accounting for the order of the *world*, without having recourse to any such intelligent Creator as you insist. You can only say that such is the nature of material objects, all originally possessed

---

1 Lit. Those who walk about. A collective term for the followers of Aristotle, who taught and discussed while perambulating the Lyceum, his school in Athens.
2 The laxative senna contains a number of anthraquinone derivatives found in plants of the genus *Senna*. Ingested, they irritate the lining of the bowel, causing purgation.

of a *power* of order and proportion. These are only more learned and elaborate ways of confessing our ignorance, nor has the one hypothesis any real advantage above the other except in conforming more closely to common prejudices.

CLEANTHES You have displayed this argument with great force. You also seem unaware how easy it is to answer it! Philo, even if in common life I assign a cause for any event, is it any objection that I cannot assign the cause of that cause–and answer every new question that may arise, perhaps in an endless series? What philosophers could possibly submit to such as rigid rule? I will tell you. It is those philosophers who confess ultimate causes to be totally unknown. They realise that the most highly abstract principles into which they trace the phenomena are still as inexplicable to them, as these phenomena themselves are to the laity.

The order and arrangement of Nature; the remarkable adjustment of final causes; the plain use and intention of every part and organ; all these bespeak in the clearest language an intelligent cause or Author. The heavens and the earth join in the same testimony. The whole chorus of Nature raises *one* hymn to the praises of its Creator. You alone, or almost alone, disturb this general harmony. You raise abstruse doubts, cavils and objections. You ask me, what is the cause of this cause? I know not. I *care* not. That concerns me not. I have found a Deity–and here I stop my inquiry. Let those who are wiser or more enterprising go further.

PHILO I claim to be neither; and for that very reason I should perhaps never have attempted to go so far. This is especially as I am aware that I must be content to finally arrive at that same answer that might have satisfied me *without* all this trouble from the beginning. If I am still to remain in utter ignorance of causes and can give an *absolute* explanation of nothing, I shall never regard it as an advantage to momentarily shove aside a difficulty that, as you acknowledge, must immediately recur in full force. Naturalists indeed, rightly explain particular effects by more general causes that themselves might ultimately remain totally inexplicable. But they surely *never* thought it satisfactory to explain a particular effect by a particular cause that could be no more to be accounted for, than by that effect *itself*. An ideal system, arranged by itself and without a precedent design, is not a whit more explicable than a material one attaining its order in a like manner. Neither is there any more difficulty in the latter supposition than in the former.

PART v

PHILO (continuing): Cleanthes, to show you still more difficulties in your Anthropomorphism, please undertake a new survey of your principles. Like effects prove like causes.[1] This is the experimental argument and, as you say, the *sole* theological argument. Now, it is certain that the more similar the effects seen and the more similar the causes inferred, the stronger is the argument. Every departure on either side diminishes the probability and renders the experiment less conclusive. You cannot doubt the principle–and neither ought you to reject its consequences.

> All the new discoveries in astronomy proving the immense grandeur and magnificence of the works of Nature are, according to what I call the *true* system of theism, additional arguments for a Deity. But, according to your hypothesis of *experimental* theism they become so many objections, by distancing the effect still further from all resemblance to the effects of *human* art and artifice. For, if Lucretius, following the old system of the world, could exclaim:[2]

> *Quis regere immensi summam, quis habere profundi*
> *Indu manu validas potis est moderanter habenas?*
> *Quis pariter coelos omnes convertere et omnis*
> *Ignibus aetheriis terras suffire feraces?*
> *Omnibus inque locis esse omni tempore praest ?*

> Who has the power to rule the totality of the immeasurable,
> To hold with a steady hand the giant reins of the boundless deep?
> Who has the power both to direct the multitude of the heavens,
> To heat fertile lands with unearthly fires;
> And to be present in all places and at all times?

Cicero reckoned this reasoning sufficiently strong to put it into the mouth of his Epicurean:[3]

> *Quibus enim oculis animi intueri potuit vester Plato fabricam illam tanti operis, qua construi a Deo atque aedificari mundum facit? quae molitio? quae ferramenta? qui vectes? quae machinae? qui ministri tanti muneris fuerunt? quemadmodum autem obedire et parere voluntati architecti aer, ignis, aqua, terra potuerunt?*

---

1 Hume again paraphrases Sir Isaac Newton's *Philosophiae Naturalis Principia Mathematica* 'Therefore to the same natural effects we must, as far as possible, assign the same causes.' *Rules of Reason in Philosophy*, II.
2 Titus Lucretius Carus, *De rerum natura* II. 1095–9
3 *De natura deorum* (on the nature of the gods) I.8.
   Cicero's 'Epicurean' among the three Roman discussants is Gaius Velleius, a Senator.

What power of mental vision enabled Plato, your master, to visualise the vast and elaborate process he discerns God to have adopted in the building of the universe? What constructional engineering was employed? What tools, levers, machines? What agents contracted such vast works? And how were air, fire, water and earth constrained to obey and then execute, the will of the architect?

I suggest that if this argument had any force in former ages, how much greater must it have at present, with the bounds of Nature infinitely enlarged and such a magnificent scene opened to us? It is thus even *more* unreasonable to generate our idea of so limitless an Origin from our experience of the narrow productions of human invention and design.

The discoveries by microscopes,[1] as they open a new universe in miniature, are still objections according to you, but positive arguments according to me. The further we push our researches of this kind the more we are led to infer that the universal Cause must be vastly different from Humankind and from *any* object of human experience and observation.

CLEANTHES And what say you to the discoveries in anatomy, chemistry and botany? These surely are not objections as they only reveal new instances of art and contrivance. It is still the image of Mind reflected on us from innumerable objects.

PHILO Add 'a mind like the human.'

CLEANTHES I know of no other.

PHILO And the liker the better?

CLEANTHES To be sure...

PHILO Now, Cleanthes, take note of the consequences! First, by this method of reasoning you renounce all claims to infinity in *any* of the attributes of the Deity, since a cause ought only to be proportioned to its effect–and the effect, so far as we can tell, is not infinite.[2] Thus what claims have we, upon your suppositions, to ascribe that attribute to the divine Being?

You will still insist that by removing it from all similarity to human creatures, we surrender to the most arbitrary hypotheses and at the same time weaken all proofs of its existence.

---

1 Johann Faber (1574–1629) is credited with the term 'microscope' (Gk. small-seeing) for the instrument termed 'occhiolino' (It. 'little eye') in 1625 by his friend Galileo.

2 That we should proportion our belief to the evidence is an important precept of Humean reasoning. See *Enquiry concerning Human Understanding* (1748), 6.4, Selby-Bigge/Nidditch edition, pp. 57–9.

Secondly, according to your theory you have no reason to ascribe perfection to the Deity, even in its *finite* capacity. Nor may you suppose it free from error, mistake, or incoherence in its undertakings. There are many inexplicable difficulties in the works of Nature. If we accept, *a priori*, a perfect Author to be proved, these problems are easily solved and only *seem* to become difficulties due to our narrow capacity and hence inability to trace infinite relations.

However, according to your method of reasoning, these difficulties all become real and perhaps will be claimed as new instances of *likeness* to human art and contrivance. You must acknowledge that, at least from our limited view, it is impossible for us to tell whether this system contains any great faults or deserves considerable praise, when compared to other possible or even real systems.

If the *Aeneid* were read to a peasant, could he or she pronounce that poem to be absolutely faultless? Could the peasant, never having seen any *other* work, even assign its proper rank among the productions of the human intellect?

But even if this world *were* a perfect production, it would still remain uncertain whether all the excellences of the work could be justly ascribed to the worker. If we survey a ship, what an exalted idea must we form of the ingenuity of the carpenter who framed so complicated, useful and beautiful a machine? And what surprise must we feel, when we find in the carpenter a stupid mechanic who imitated others. The carpenter had simply copied an art; one that had been gradually improving through a long succession of ages and after multiple trials, mistakes, corrections, deliberations and controversies?

Many *worlds* might have been botched and bungled throughout an eternity before our present system emerged. Much labour might have been lost, many fruitless trials made and a slow, continued improvement carried on over infinite ages in the art of world-making.

In such subjects, who can determine where the truth lies? Indeed, who can conjecture where the *probability* lies amidst a great number of hypotheses that may be proposed–and a still greater number that may be imagined?

Moreover, what shadow of an argument can your hypothesis produce to prove the *unity* of the Deity? A great number of people join in the building a house or a ship, in rearing a city or in framing a commonwealth. Why may not *several* deities combine in contriving and framing a world? This is showing much greater similarity to human affairs. By sharing the work among several we limit much further the attributes of each.[1] We get rid of that vast power and knowledge that must be presumed in a *sole* Deity and that, according to you, can only serve to weaken the proof of its existence. And if such foolish, vicious creatures as human beings can often unite in framing and executing one plan, how much more those deities – or demons – whom we may suppose to be, by several degrees, *more* perfect!

To multiply causes without necessity is indeed contrary to what I call true philosophy.[2] However, this principle does not apply to the present case. Were *one* prior Deity proved by your theory, one possessed of every attribute requisite to the production of the Universe it would be needless I admit–though not absurd–to suppose any *other* existent deity. But while it is still a question whether all these attributes are united in one individual or divided among several independent beings, on the basis of what phenomena in Nature can we claim to decide the controversy?

Where we see a body rise in a set of scales we may be sure that there is, in the opposite scale, however concealed from sight, a counterpoising weight at least equal to it. However, it is still open to doubt whether that weight is an *aggregate* of several distinct bodies, or one singular united mass. And if the required weight very much exceeds anything ever seen conjoined in any *single* body, the former supposition becomes still more likely and natural. An intelligent Being of the vast power and capacity necessary to produce the Universe exceeds all analogy – and even comprehension.

But further, Cleanthes, humans are mortal. They renew their species by reproduction, a function common to all living creatures. The two great sexes of male and female, says Milton, *animate* the world.[3] Why must this activity, so universal, so essential, be excluded from those numerous and limited deities? Behold, then, the theogony[4] of ancient times brought back today!

---

1 Hume (as Philo) here adduces the Division of Labour, set out by his friend Adam Smith in his *Enquiry into the Nature & Causes of the Wealth of Nations* (1776).

2 Hume again paraphrases Newton's *Principia*: 'We are to admit no more causes of natural things, than such as are both true and sufficient to explain their appearances.' *Rules of Reasoning*, 1. 3 The principle that neither causes nor kinds of entities should be multiplied without necessity, also often described as the simplicity principle and commonly attributed to William of Ockham (1287–1347). It is popularly known as 'Ockham's razor'.

3 John Milton, *Paradise Lost*, VIII.151

4 The origins of the Gods. See Hesiod, *Theogony*.

Why not become a *complete* Anthropomorphite? Why not assert the Deity, or deities, to be corporeal; to have eyes, a nose, mouth, ears *et cetera*? Epicurus maintained that since no-one had ever seen reason *except* in a human figure, hence the gods also must have a human figure.[1] According to you, this argument, severely and deservedly ridiculed by Cicero, becomes solid and philosophical.

In a word, Cleanthes, one who follows your hypothesis is able perhaps to assert – or at least conjecture – that the Universe sometime arose from something like design. However, beyond that position we can ascertain nothing. We are left afterwards to fix every point of theology through the utmost freedom of imagination and speculation. This world, for all anyone knows, is faulty and imperfect compared to a superior standard, only the first rough attempt of some infant Deity who later abandoned it, ashamed of its lame performance. It is perhaps the work only of some dependent, inferior deity and is the object of derision by its superiors: it is possibly the production of the old age and dotage of some superannuated Deity and ever since its death, it has run on chaotically from the first impulse and active force it received.

Demea, you are rightly showing signs of horror at these strange suppositions, but these and a thousand more of the same kind are Cleanthes's suppositions, not mine. From the moment the attributes of the Deity are supposed finite, all these are plausible. For my part, I cannot think that, in any respect, so wild and unsettled a system of theology is preferable to – none at all...!

CLEANTHES I absolutely disown these suppositions! However, they do not horrify me, especially when proposed in your rambling way. On the contrary, they give me pleasure when I see that even by indulging your imagination to the utmost, you never get rid of the hypothesis of *design* in the Universe. At every turn you are obliged to have recourse to it. To this concession I adhere unshakeably–and this I regard as a sufficient foundation for religion.

PART VI

DEMEA It must indeed be a flimsy fabric indeed that can be erected on so tottering a foundation. While we remain uncertain whether there is one Deity, or many; whether it, or they, to whom we owe our existence, are perfect or

---

1 In *Epicurus's Morals, translated from the Greek by John Digby Esq.* (1712), we find Epicurus's Maxim I: 'The Gods are unperceivable [*sic*] to our senses... their form is that of Men by reason of the perpetual flux of images that affect the [human] Mind.'

imperfect, subordinate or supreme, dead or alive, what trust or confidence can we place in them? What devotion or worship can we address to them – and what veneration or obedience can we pay them? To all the *purposes* of life, the theory of religion becomes altogether useless. Even with regard to its speculative consequences, its uncertainty – according to you – must render it totally precarious and unsatisfactory.

PHILO To render it still *more* unsatisfactory, another hypothesis occurs to me; one that acquires an air of probability from the method of reasoning Cleanthes insists on, namely: 'Like effects arise from like causes.'

This principle he supposes to be the foundation of *all* religion. But there is another principle of the same kind. It is no less certain and is derived from the same source of experience, *viz.* that where several known circumstances are observed to be similar, the unknown will also be found to be similar. Thus, if we see the limbs of a human body we conclude that it is accompanied by a human head, although hidden from us. If we see a small part of the sun through a chink in a wall, we conclude that if the wall was removed we would see the whole. In short, this method of reasoning is so obvious and familiar, that no objection can be made to its validity.

Now, if we survey the Universe as far as it falls under our knowledge, it bears a great resemblance to an animal, or an organised body, and seems actuated with a similar principle of life and motion. Continuous circulation of matter in it produces no disorder. Continuous decay in every part is incessantly repaired. The subtlest of interactions and dependencies are perceived throughout the entire system. In performing its proper duties, each part or member operates both for its own preservation and for that of the whole. The world, therefore, I infer to be an animal and the Deity is the soul of the world, actuating it – and actuated by it.

You have too much learning, Cleanthes, to be at all surprised at this opinion. You know it was maintained by almost all the theists of antiquity and dominates their discourses and arguments.[1] For although sometimes the ancient philosophers reason from final causes[C] as if they thought the world the *workmanship* of God, yet it appears rather to have been their favoured notion to consider the world to be the *body* of God, to whom its

---

1 For example, in his dialogue *On the Nature of the Gods*, Cicero has the Epicurean Velleius quote Plato's *Timaeus*, saying: *mundum deum esse et caelum et terram et animos...* 'The Earth, the Heavens, the Stars, the Land and our Souls... are God.' *De Natura Deorum*, 1.12.33

organisation renders it subservient. And since it must be admitted that, since the Universe resembles more a human *body* than the *works* of human art and contrivance, if our limited analogy could ever be justly extended to the whole of Nature, the inference would seem to favour the ancient rather than the modern theory.

There are also many other advantages in the former theory that recommended it to the ancient theologians. Nothing was more repugnant to all their notions than mind *without* body, because nothing could be more repugnant to common experience. A *purely* spiritual substance was beyond their senses or comprehension, being something of which they had observed not one single instance in Nature. Mind *and* body they knew because they sensed both; and in both they likewise perceived order, arrangement, organisation and internal machinery. It could only seem reasonable to transfer this experience to the Universe, supposing the divine mind and body to be *also* coeval, both of these having a naturally inherent and inseparable order and arrangement.

Here therefore, Cleanthes, is a new species of Anthropomorphism on which you may deliberate and a theory seemingly free of any major difficulty. You are surely far too unbiased by philosophical prejudices to find any more difficulty in supposing an animal *body* to be, either intrinsically and of itself (or from unknown causes), possessed of order and organisation – than in supposing a similar order in *mind*. But the common prejudice that body and mind ought *always* to accompany each other ought not to be entirely neglected. This is because it is founded on common experience, the only guide you profess to follow in all these theological inquiries. But if you assert that our limited experience is an unequal standard by which to judge the unlimited extent of Nature, you entirely abandon your own hypothesis. You must thenceforward adopt our 'mysticism', as you call it, and admit the *absolute* incomprehensibility of the divine Nature.

CLEANTHES I admit that this theory had never occurred to me, though it is a pretty natural one. However, I cannot readily give an opinion without longer examination and reflection.

PHILO Very careful and thoughtful. Were I to examine any system of *yours*, I should not have *half* that caution and reserve in raising objections and difficulties! However, if anything occurs, oblige us by proposing it.

CLEANTHES Why, then, it seems to me that although the world in many ways resembles an animal body, yet the analogy is defective in many circumstances. The most salient of these are: no organs of sense; no seat of thought, or reason; no one precise origin of motion and action. In short, the world would seem to bear a stronger resemblance to a *vegetable* than to an animal – and your inference would be equally inconclusive in favour of the Soul or Mind of the world.[1]

But in the next place, your theory seems to imply the *eternity* of the world and that is a principle that I think can be refuted by the strongest reasons and probabilities. Let me suggest an argument to support this that I believe has not been insisted on by any writer. Those who reason from the *recent* origin of arts and sciences, though their inference is forceful, may perhaps be refuted by considerations of the nature of human society. This is in such continual revolution, between ignorance and knowledge, liberty and slavery, riches and poverty, that it is impossible for us, from our limited experience, to predict accurately what events may or may not be expected.

Ancient learning and history seem to have been in great danger of perishing entirely after the *inundation* of barbarous nations. Had these convulsions continued longer, or been more violent, we should probably not know what had happened in the world a few centuries before us. Indeed, were it not for the superstition of the Popes, who preserved Latin jargon to support the appearance of an ancient and universal Church, that tongue would have been utterly lost. Had that happened, the totally barbarous Western world being would not have been fit to receive the Greek language and learning conveyed to them after the sack of Constantinople.[2]

With learning and books extinguished, even the mechanical arts would have fallen considerably into decay. As a result it can be easily imagined that tradition, or fable, might ascribe to them a much *later* origin than the true one. Hence this popular argument against the eternity of the world seems a little precarious.

---

1 Because in Cleanthes's view, only animals can possess mind.
2 In 1453, by the Ottoman Sultan Mehmet II. Greek scholars fled west, taking works of classical literature with them to Florence and other centres of Renaissance learning.

But here is what appears to be the foundation of a better argument. Lucullus was the first to bring cherry trees from Asia to Europe,[1] although in many European climates that tree thrives so well that it grows wild in the woods without cultivation. Is it possible that throughout a whole eternity, no European had ever crossed into Asia and thought of transplanting so delicious a fruit into their own country? Or if the tree *had* been transplanted and propagated even once, how could it ever afterwards perish? Empires may rise and fall; liberty and slavery succeed each other; ignorance alternate with knowledge, but the cherry tree will still remain in the woods of Greece, Spain and Italy and will never be affected by the revolutions of human society.

It is not two thousand years since vines were transplanted into France, though there is no climate in the world more favourable to them. It is not three centuries since horses, cows, sheep, swine, dogs, and corn were introduced into America. Is it possible that during the revolutions of a whole eternity, there never arose a Columbus who might open the communication between Europe and that continent? We might as well imagine that all men would wear stockings for ten thousand years, and never have the sense to think of garters to tie them.

All these seem convincing proofs of the youth, or rather infancy, of the world. It seems to be founded on more constant and steady principles than those by which *human* society is governed and directed. Nothing less than a total convulsion of the elements will ever destroy all the European animals and vegetables now to be found in the Western world.

PHILO And what arguments have you against such convulsions? Strong and almost incontestable proofs may be discovered across the whole earth that, for many ages, every part of this globe was covered with water. And though order were supposed inherent in matter and inseparable from it, yet matter may be susceptible of many great revolutions through aeons of time. The incessant changes to which every part of the world is subject, seem to intimate some such general transformations. However, at the same time it

---

1 Lucius Licinius Lucullus is said by Servius Honoratus to have first brought the tree bearing the sweet cherry (*Prunius avium*), back to Rome. This was in 72 BCE after his campaign against King Mithridates of Pontus in Asia Minor, modern Turkey. Lucullus was a friend of Antiochus of Ascalon, an Academic sceptic who broke with the historical Philo's sceptical Academy for being too radically sceptical. He features in Book II of the first version (the *Priora*) of Cicero's *Academica*, his text on Academic scepticism and known as 'the Lucullus.'

is observable that all the changes and decay we have experienced are only *passages* from one state of order to another. Matter can never *rest* in total deformity and confusion. What we see in the parts, we may infer for the whole – at least that is the method of reasoning on which you rest your whole theory.

Were I obliged to defend any particular system of this nature – something I should never willingly do – I reckon none more plausible than that ascribing to the world an eternal *inherent* principle of order, although attended with great and continual revolutions and alterations. This at once solves all difficulties. If this solution, by being so general, is not entirely complete and satisfactory, it is at least a theory that sooner or later we must turn to, *whatever* system we embrace.

How could things be *as they are* unless there were somewhere an original and inherent principle of order, either in thought or in matter? It matters little to which of these we give the preference. Chance has no place in any sceptical or religious hypothesis. Everything is stably governed by steady and inviolable laws. And were the inmost essence of things laid open to us, we should then discover a dimension of the world of which, at present, we can have no idea. Instead of *admiring* the order of natural beings, we should clearly see that, down to the smallest detail, it was impossible for them ever to have any *other* disposition.

Were any one inclined to revive the ancient pagan theology, it maintained, as we learn from Hesiod, that this globe was governed by thirty thousand deities who arose from the unknown powers of nature.[1] Cleanthes, you would naturally object that nothing is to be gained by this hypothesis and that it is as easy to suppose all humans and animals (beings more numerous but less perfect), to have sprung immediately from a similar origin. Push the same inference a step further and you will find that a numerous *society* of deities is just as explicable as one universal Deity with the powers and perfections of that whole society.

So, on your own principles you must accept all these systems: Scepticism, Polytheism and Theism, to be on a similar footing. You must also accept that none of them has any advantage over the others.

You may thence learn the fallacy of your principles...!

---

1 Hesiod, *Works and Days*, l. 246

PART VII

PHILO In examining the ancient system of the soul of the world, a new idea suddenly strikes me. If correct, it will come close to subverting your reasoning, destroying even the first inferences in which you repose such confidence. If the Universe bears a greater likeness to animal bodies and to vegetables than to the works of human art, it is more probable that its cause resembles the cause of the former than that of the latter. Hence its origin ought rather to be ascribed to something like the way plants and animals reproduce through procreation and growth, than to reason or design. Your conclusion, even according to your own principles, is thus lame and defective.

DEMEA Please open up this argument. I cannot understand it clearly in the concise format expressed.

PHILO As you have heard, our friend Cleanthes asserts that since no question of fact can be proved *other* than by experience, the existence of a Deity is incapable of proof from any other medium. The world, says he, resembles the works of human contrivance and therefore its cause must also resemble that of the human. Here we may remark that the operation of one very small part of Nature, Humanity, upon another very small part – the inanimate matter within its reach – is the rule by which Cleanthes judges the origin of the whole!

He measures objects so widely disproportioned by the same individual standard. But to withdraw all objections drawn from this topic, I affirm that there are other parts of the Universe *apart* from the machines of human invention, bearing an even greater resemblance to the fabric of the world.

Consequently, they afford a better conjecture concerning the universal origin of this system. These other parts are animals and vegetables. The world plainly resembles more an animal or a vegetable, than it does a watch or a knitting-loom. Hence it is more probable that its cause resembles the cause of the former.

The cause of the former is animal generation or vegetative growth. The cause of the world, therefore, we may conclude to be something similar, or analogous, to such procreation or power of growth.

DEMEA But how is it *conceivable* that the world can arise from anything similar to these?

PHILO Very easily. Just as a tree sheds seed into neighbouring fields and thus produces other trees, so the *great* vegetable the world, or this planetary system, produces within itself certain seeds that grow and develop into new worlds when scattered into the surrounding chaos. A comet, for instance, is the seed of a world.[1] After it has been fully ripened by passing from star to star, it is finally tossed into the unformed elements that everywhere surround this universe and immediately sprouts up into a new system.

Let us, for the sake of variety – for I see no other advantage – suppose this world to be an animal and a comet the egg of this animal. Just as an ostrich in the sand lays an egg that, without further intervention, hatches to produces a new animal, so…

DEMEA I see. But what wild, arbitrary suppositions! What data do you have to support such extraordinary conclusions? And is this slight, imaginary resemblance of the world to a vegetable or an animal sufficient to establish the same conclusion with regard to both? Should objects in general so widely *different*, be a standard for each other?

PHILO Right! This is the matter I've been insisting on all along. I still assert that we have *no* data upon which to establish any system of the origin of the Cosmos. Our experience, so imperfect in itself and so limited in extent and duration, can provide us with *no* probable conjecture concerning the whole of things. But if we must fix on *some* hypothesis, then by what rule ought we to determine our choice? Is there any other rule than the greater similarity of the objects compared? And does a plant or an animal, springing from botanical growth or procreation, not bear a stronger resemblance to the world, than any artificial machine arising from reason and design?

DEMEA But what *is* this power of growth and of procreation you speak about? Can you explain their functions and describe the fine internal structure they depend on?

---

1 Or of Life on Earth. The organic material now identified in comets augmented the organic budget of the Earth during its proto-history where it may have contributed to the origin of life. See Henkel, T. and Lyon, IC, *Proceedings* of the 44th Lunar and Planetary Science Conference, Houston, Texas. (2013).

PHILO I can as much explain that as Cleanthes can explain the operations of reason, or anatomise the internal structure on which *that* depends. But without any such elaborate descriptions; when I see an animal I infer that it sprang from procreation with as great a certainty as you conclude a house to have been raised by design. The words procreation and reason denote only certain powers and energies in Nature whose *effects* are known, but whose *essence* is incomprehensible. No one of these principles more than the other has the privilege for being made a standard to the whole of Nature.

In reality, Demea, it may reasonably be expected that the larger the view we take of things, the better will it lead us to conclusions concerning such extraordinary and magnificent subjects. In this little corner of the world there are only four principles: reason; instinct; procreation and power of growth that are similar to each other and are the causes of similar effects. How many other principles might we naturally imagine in the immense extent and variety of the Universe, were we able to travel from planet to planet and from system to system, to examine each part of this mighty fabric? Any one of the four principles above mentioned – and a hundred others lying open to our conjecture – might afford us a theory of the origin of the world.

It is a palpably egregious prejudice to confine our view entirely to that principle by which *our* own minds operate. Were this principle more intelligible, on that account such a partiality might be somewhat excusable. But in its *internal* fabric and structure, reason is just as *little* known to us as instinct, or the power of growth. Even Nature, that vague, indeterminate word to which we humans refer everything, is not *more* inexplicable in the last analysis. The effects of these principles are all known to us from experience but the *principles* themselves and their manner of operation, are totally unknown. Nor is it *less* intelligible, or *less* confirmed by experience, to say that the world arose by growth from a seed shed by another world, than to say that it arose from a divine reason or contrivance, according to the sense in which Cleanthes understands it.

DEMEA But if the world *had* a vegetative quality and could sow the seeds of new worlds into the infinite Chaos, this power would be an additional argument for design in its author! For how could so wonderful a faculty arise except from design? Or how can order spring from anything that does not *perceive* the very order it bestows?

PHILO You need only look around you to satisfy yourself with regard to this question. A tree bestows order and organisation on the sapling that springs from it without *knowing* the order. The same goes for an animal in respect of its offspring or a bird on its nest. Instances of this kind are even more frequent in the world than the order that arises from reason and contrivance. To say that all this order in animals and vegetables proceeds ultimately from design is begging the question. Neither can that great point be ascertained other than by proving, *a priori*, both that order is, by its *nature*, inseparably attached to thought – *and* that it can never of itself, or from original unknown principles, belong to matter.

But further, Demea, this objection you advocate can never be made use of by Cleanthes without renouncing a defence he has already made against one of my objections. When I inquired concerning the *cause* of that supreme Reason and Intelligence into which he resolves everything, he told me that the impossibility of satisfying such inquiries could never be accepted as an objection in any field of Philosophy.

'We must stop somewhere,' says he; 'nor is it ever within the reach of human capacity to explain ultimate Causes, or show the most basic connections of any objects. It is sufficient if our steps, so far as we go, are supported by experience and observation.'

Now, it is undeniable that procreation and growth, as well as reason, are experienced to be principles of order in Nature. If I rest my system of universal origins on the former, as I do in preference to the latter, this is my choice. The matter seems entirely arbitrary. When Cleanthes asks me the cause of my great vegetative or generative faculty, I am equally entitled to ask him the cause of his great reasoning principle.

These questions we have agreed to withhold on both sides. It is chiefly in *his* interest, on the present occasion, to stick to this agreement. Judging by our limited and imperfect experience, generation has some privileges above reason. Every day we see the latter arise from the former, but never the former from the latter.

Compare the consequences on both sides. The world, I say, resembles an animal. Therefore it *is* an animal, and therefore it arose from procreation. I confess that the steps are wide; and yet there is a small degree of analogy in each step.

The world, says *Cleanthes*, resembles a machine. Therefore it is a machine and therefore arose from design. The steps are here equally wide, and the analogy less striking. And if he insists on carrying my hypothesis a step further and inferring design or reason *from* the great principle of generation (on which I insist) I may, with better authority, use the same freedom to push *his* hypothesis further and infer a divine generation, or theogony, from his principle of reason. I have at least some faint shadow of experience, the most that can ever be attained in the present subject. Reason, in innumerable instances, is observed to arise from the principle of generation – and *never* to arise from any other principle.

Hesiod and all the ancient mythologists were so struck with this analogy that they explained the origin of Nature from an animal birth and copulation.[1] Plato too, so far as he is intelligible, seems to have adopted some such notion in his *Timaeus*.[2]

The Brahmins assert that the world arose from an infinite spider that spun this whole complicated mass from within its bowels. It later annihilates the whole, or any part of it, by absorbing it again and resolving it into its own essence. Here is a species of Universal origin that appears to us ridiculous because a spider is a little animal whose operations we are never likely to take as a model of the whole Universe. But here is yet a new species of analogy, even in our globe. Were there a planet wholly inhabited by spiders – which is entirely possible – this conclusion would appear *there* to be as natural and irrefragable as that in *our* planet, ascribing the origin of everything to design and intelligence, as explained by Cleanthes. It will be difficult for him to give a satisfactory reason why an orderly system may not be spun from the *belly* as well as from the brain!

CLEANTHES Philo, I must confess that of all men living, your task of raising doubts and objections suits you best. It seems natural and unavoidable to you, your fertility of invention being so great. I am not ashamed to confess that I cannot immediately, or regularly, solve the abstruse difficulties you continuously present even though in general I can clearly see their fallacy and error.

I don't doubt that you yourself are in the same position and do not have the solution so ready as the objection, while you must be aware that common sense and reason are entirely against you. Such whimsies as you have delivered may puzzle us – but can never convince...

PART VIII

PHILO What you ascribe to my creativity is entirely down to the nature of the subject. In subjects falling within the narrow compass of human understanding there is commonly only one conclusion that carries probability

---

1 Hesiod, *Theogony*, 116–232.
2 In Plato's dialogue, the eponymous Timaeus of Locri asks Socrates: 'In the likeness of *what* animal was the world made?' *Timaeus*, 30. Tr. B. Jowett; *cf.* 30c-31b, 32b-34b, 92c.

or conviction. To a person of sound judgement, all other possible conclusions appear absurd and unrealistic. But in such questions as we are *presently* about, a hundred contradictory views may preserve a kind of imperfect analogy. Here, the creative mind has full scope to exert itself. I believe that without any great mental effort I could rapidly propose other systems of the origin of the Cosmos. Each of these would have some faint appearance of truth, although it is a thousand, indeed a million to one against either yours or any one of mine *being* the true system.

For instance, what if I should revive the old Epicurean hypothesis? This is commonly, and I believe *correctly*, reckoned the most absurd system yet proposed.[1] However, I do not know whether, given a few alterations, it might not bear a faint appearance of probability. Instead of supposing matter to be infinite, as Epicurus did, let us suppose it finite. Since a finite number of particles is susceptible of a finite number of re-arrangements, it must happen, over an eternity of time, that every possible order or position must be tested an infinite number of times. Therefore, *this* world with all its events, even the most minute, has been produced and destroyed previously and will *again* be produced and destroyed without bounds or limitations. No one who has a conception of powers infinite in comparison to powers finite, will ever challenge this determination.

DEMEA But this supposes that matter can acquire motion *without* any voluntary agent or first mover.

PHILO And where is the difficulty in that? Every event *prior* to human experience is equally difficult and incomprehensible, while every event *after* experience is equally easy and intelligible. In many instances, motion begins in matter without any known voluntary agent: from gravity; from elasticity and from electricity. In these cases to always suppose an unknown voluntary agent is mere hypothesis – a hypothesis, moreover, attended by no advantage. The beginning of motion in matter *itself* is as conceivable *a priori* as is its communication from mind and intelligence.

---

1 Lucretius, *De Rerum Natura* 1. 958–1051. In a letter to the historian Herodotus, Epicurus proposes that 'there are infinite Worlds; both like, and unlike, this...' See: *Epicurus, the extant Remains*, ed. Cyril Bailey (Oxford, 1926). Nietzsche, under the rubric of what he calls 'the eternal recurrence', considers the possibility of the universe being formed and destroyed repeatedly over the infinite expanse of time on the basis of just the same reasoning; see *The Gay Science* #341. This was probably the first adumbration of the theory of the 'Multiverse', proposed in 1895 by the US philosopher William James, brother of novelist Henry.

Besides, why may not motion have simply been propagated through all eternity and the same, or nearly the same, amount of it be still persist in the Universe? As much is lost by the composition of motion, as is gained by its resolution.[1] Whatever the causes are, it is certainly a fact that matter is – and always has been–in continual agitation as far as human experience or tradition reaches. In the entire Universe at present, there is probably not one particle of matter at *absolute* rest.

Also, this very consideration on to which we have stumbled in the course of the argument, suggests a new hypothesis of Universal origin that is not absolutely absurd or even improbable. Is there a system, an order, an *economy* of things, by which matter can preserve the perpetual motion seemingly so essential to it while still maintaining constancy in the *forms* that it produces? There certainly is such an economy and this is actually the case in the present world. The continual motion of matter, therefore, given less than infinite possibilities of rearrangement, must produce this economy or order that, by its very *nature* when established, will support itself for many ages, if not for eternity. But wherever matter is so poised, arranged and adjusted as to continue in perpetual motion and yet preserve constancy in the forms, its situation must necessarily have all the same *appearance* of art and contrivance that we observe at present.

All the parts of each form must have a relation to each other, and to the whole. The whole *itself* must have a relation to the other parts of the Universe: to the element in which the form subsists; to the materials with which it repairs its waste and decay; and to every other form, either hostile or friendly.

A defect in any of these particulars destroys the form. The matter of which it is composed is again set loose, and is thrown into irregular motions and fermentations until it arranges itself into some other regular form.

If no such form be prepared to receive it, and if there exists a great quantity of this corrupted matter in the Universe, then the Universe *itself* is entirely disordered. Whether it be the feeble embryo of a world that is thus destroyed, or the rotten carcass of one in old age and infirmity, chaos ensues. Such chaos will then subsist until finite, though innumerable, changes at last produce some forms whose parts and organs are so adjusted as to support those forms amid a continued succession of matter.

---

1 An adumbration of the 'Law of conservation of Energy' itself a principle of the 1st Law of Thermodynamics. This states that the total Energy of an isolated System is constant, despite internal changes. Energy cannot be destroyed; only redistributed or changed in form.

Suppose, for we shall endeavour to vary the expression, that matter were thrown into any position by a blind, unguided force. It is evident that this first position must be the most confused and disorderly imaginable and have no resemblance to works of human contrivance. These, along with symmetry of parts, reveal an adjustment of means to ends and a tendency to self-preservation. If the actuating force ceases after this operation, matter must remain forever in disorder, an immense chaos without any proportion or activity. But suppose that the actuating force, whatever it be, still *continues* in matter. This first position will immediately give place to a second, in all probability just as disorderly as the first; and so on through many successions of changes and cycles. No particular order or position continues unaltered for a moment. The original force, still remaining in activity, gives a perpetual *restlessness* to matter. Every possible situation is produced and then instantly destroyed. If a glimpse, or dawn, of *order* appears for a moment, it is instantly hurried away and negated by that never-ceasing force actuating every particle of matter. Thus the Universe proceeds for many ages in a continued succession of chaos and disorder.

But is it not possible that it might settle down at last, without losing its inherent motion and active force, yet preserving a uniformity of appearance amidst the continual motion and fluctuation of its parts? This we find to be the case with the Universe at present. Every individual is perpetually changing; as also is every part of every individual – and yet in appearance, the whole remains the same. May we not hope for such a position, or rather be *assured* of it from the eternal revolutions of unguided matter. Might not *this* account for the Universe's apparent wisdom and contrivance?

Contemplate the subject a little. We shall find that this adjustment, if attained by matter, of a *seeming* stability in the forms, together with a real, perpetual revolution or motion of parts, affords a plausible – if not a true – solution of the difficulty.

It is in vain, therefore, to insist upon the uses of the parts in animals or vegetables and their remarkable adjustment to each other. I would fain know how an animal could survive *unless* its parts were so adjusted. Do we not find that it immediately perishes whenever this adjustment ceases and that its matter, in corrupting, acquires some new form? It happens indeed that the parts of the world are so well adjusted, that some regular form immediately lays claim to this corrupted matter and, were it not so, could the *world* survive? Must it not dissolve, as does the animal, passing through new positions and situations till in great, but finite succession, it falls at last into the present, or some such, order?

CLEANTHES It is just as well that you told us that this hypothesis was suggested suddenly in the course of the argument! For had you had time to examine it, you would have soon have perceived insuperable objections. No form, you say, can subsist unless it possesses the powers and organs requisite for its subsistence. New orders or economies must be tried without intermission till at last some stable order is arrived at, able to support and maintain itself. But according to this hypothesis, whence *arise* the many conveniences and advantages that all humans and animals possess? Two eyes, two ears, are not *absolutely* necessary for the survival of the species.

The human race might have been propagated and preserved without horses, dogs, cows, sheep and those innumerable fruits and products that we enjoy. If no camels had been created for human use in the sandy deserts of Africa and Arabia, would the world have been dissolved? If there were no lodestone[1] empowered to give its wonderfully useful direction to the compass needle, would human society or indeed humanity itself have been immediately extinguished? The maxims of Nature are in general very frugal, yet instances of this kind are far from rare. Any one of them is a sufficient proof of design, the *benevolent* design that gave rise to the order and arrangement of the Universe.

PHILO At least, you may safely infer that, so far, the foregoing hypothesis is incomplete and imperfect. This I shall not hesitate to admit. But can we ever reasonably expect greater success in any attempts of this nature? Can we ever hope to erect a system of universal origin liable to *no* exceptions and containing *no* circumstance repugnant to our own limited and imperfect experience of the analogy of Nature? Your theory itself cannot surely aspire to any such advantage, even though you have run into Anthropomorphism, in order to better preserve conformity with common experience.

Let us once more put it to trial. In all instances we have ever seen, ideas are copied from real objects and are thus *ectypal*,[2] or archetypal, to express myself in learned terms. You reverse this order and give *thought* the precedence. In all instances, thought has no influence upon matter, except where that matter is so conjoined with it as to have an equal and reciprocal influence upon it.

---

1 Old English 'lead stone.' The naturally magnetic mineral magnetite, first described in the 6th century BCE by the Greek philosopher Thales of Miletus in modern Turkey. Lodestones were found at the nearby city of Magnesia, hence 'magnet'.

2 Alongside of the archetypal knowledge of God, found within Himself, there is also ectypal knowledge given by revelation. The latter relates to the former as a copy to the original, and thus does not possess the same perfection. Louis Berkhof, *Systematic Theology*, 35.

No animal can immediately move anything *except* the components of its own body and indeed the equality of action and reaction seems to be a universal Law of Nature.[1] But your theory implies a contradiction to this experience.

These instances; of mind failing to influence matter, together with many more that it would be easy to collect, particularly the very *idea* of a mind or eternal system of thought. In other words, an animal without descendants and immortal. These instances, I say, may teach all of us caution in condemning each other. They may also let us see that, as no such system ought ever to be accepted from a slight analogy; neither ought any to be rejected through a small incongruity. That is an inconvenience from which we can justly pronounce no one to be exempted.

All religious systems are subject to great and insuperable difficulties. Each disputant triumphs in turn in an offensive war, exposing the absurdities, barbarities and pernicious tenets of the antagonist. But all of them prepare, on the whole, a complete triumph for the sceptic who tells them that no system ought ever to be embraced with regard to such subjects and for this plain reason – that no absurdity ought *ever* to be assented to with regard to *any* subject.

Here, a total suspension of judgement is our only reasonable resource. As is commonly observed, every attack upon theologians is successful–in contrast to their every defence. Consequently, the victory will be complete for those who, together with all humanity, remain permanently on the offensive, having no fixed station or an abiding city they are ever obliged to defend.

PART IX

DEMEA But if so many difficulties attend the argument *a posteriori*, had we not better adhere to that simple and sublime argument *a priori*? By offering us infallible demonstration, it cuts off immediately all doubt and difficulty. By this argument, too, we may prove the infinity of the Divine attributes that I fear can never be ascertained with certainty in any other way. For how can an infinite cause be proved by an effect that for all we know, is either finite–or *may* be so? It is difficult, if not absolutely impossible, to deduce the unity of the *divine* nature merely from contemplating the works *of* Nature. Nor will the uniformity alone of the Plan, even if accepted, give us any assurance of that attribute. Whereas the argument *a priori*...

---

1 Also a Law (the 3rd) of Motion.
  See I. Newton, *Philosophiae Naturalis Principia Mathematica* (1687).

CLEANTHES Demea, you seem to be reasoning that those advantages and conveniences in the abstract *a priori* argument were full proofs of its solidity. However, I think it is first proper to determine on *what* argument of this nature you choose to advance. From this argument *itself*, rather than from its useful consequences, we shall assess what value we ought to assign it.

DEMEA The argument that I would advance is the common one. Whatever exists must have a cause or reason for its existence, since it is impossible for anything to produce itself, or be the cause of its own existence. Therefore, in mounting from effects to causes, either we must go on tracing an infinite succession without reaching any ultimate cause at all, or we must have recourse to some ultimate cause that is *necessarily* existent.

Now, the first supposition is absurd and may be proved as follows: in the infinite chain of succession of causes and effects, each single effect is determined to exist by the power and efficacy of the cause immediately preceding it. But the whole eternal chain or succession, taken together, is not determined or caused by anything and yet it is evident that *it* requires a cause or reason, just as does any object that begins to exist in time. Still reasonable is the question of why *this* particular succession of causes existed from eternity and not any other succession, or indeed no succession at all. If there is no *necessarily* existent being, any supposition that can be formed is equally possible. Nor is there any more absurdity in *nothing* having existed from eternity, than there is in that succession of causes that actually constitutes the Universe. What *was* it, then, that determined *something* to exist rather than nothing and bestowed that existence, that *being*, on a particular possibility, exclusive of the rest? External causes, there are supposed to be none. Chance is a word without a meaning.

Was it *nothing*? But that can never produce anything! We must, therefore, have recourse to a necessarily existent Being, who carries the reason of its existence *within* itself and that cannot be supposed *not* to exist without an express contradiction. There is, consequently, just such a Being; and that is the Deity.

CLEANTHES Though I know the initiating of objections to be his chief delight, I shall not leave it to Philo to point out the weakness of this metaphysical reasoning. It seems to me both ill-grounded and of little value to the cause of true piety and religion. I shall now show the fallacy of it myself.

I begin by observing that there is an evident absurdity in claiming to demonstrate, or to prove, a matter of fact by any *a priori* argument. Nothing is demonstrable unless the contrary implies a contradiction. Nothing that is distinctly conceivable implies a contradiction. Whatever we conceive as existing we can also conceive as non-existent. There is no being, therefore, whose non-existence implies a contradiction. Consequently there is no being, whose existence is demonstrable. I propose this argument as entirely decisive and I am willing to rest the whole controversy upon it.

It is claimed that the Deity is a *necessarily* existent being. This necessity is explained by asserting that if we knew its *whole* essence or nature, we should perceive it impossible for it *not* to exist; just as it is impossible for twice two not to be four. But it is evident that perception of its *whole* essence can never happen while our faculties remain as at present. It will still be possible for us, at any time, to conceive the non-existence of what we formerly conceived to exist. The mind can never be required to suppose any object to remain *always* in being – in the same manner as we are required to always conceive twice two to be four. Therefore the words 'necessary existence' have no meaning, or none that is consistent, which is the same thing.

But further, why may not the material Universe *itself* actually be the necessarily existent Being, according to this claimed explanation of necessity? We dare not affirm that we know *all* the qualities of matter. For all we know, it may contain some qualities that, if known, would make its non-existence appear as great a contradiction as that twice two *is* five. I find only one argument employed to prove that the material world is not the necessarily existent Being and that this argument is derived from the contingency[1] both of the matter and the form of the world. 'Any particle of matter,' said Dr Clarke, 'may be conceived to be annihilated and any form may be conceived to be altered. Such an annihilation or alteration, therefore, is not impossible.'[2]

---

1 'Contingency' in this context is the contrasting term to 'necessity.' While 'necessary' being cannot possibly be otherwise (and cannot *but* exist), it is possible for contingent being to exist in other ways or to not exist entirely. Cleanthes observes that it is possible for the material components of the world to be different, perhaps by there being a different set of physical elements. They may also have a different size or shape, perhaps because of differences in their mass, the dimensions of space, or the law of gravitation. In short, the *a priori* argument here is that the existence of contingent being requires the existence of necessary being.

2 Dr Samuel Clarke (1675–1729). British philosopher and theologian. Cleanthes quotes from his *A Demonstration of the Being and Attributes of God* (1705).

But it seems profoundly biased not to perceive that the same argument extends equally to the Deity, in so far as we have any conception of it; and that the mind can at least imagine it to be non-existent, or its attributes to be altered. There *must* be some unknown, inconceivable qualities that can make its non-existence appear impossible, or its attributes unalterable. No reason can be assigned as to why these qualities may not belong to matter. As they are completely unknown *and* inconceivable, they can never be proved incompatible with it.

Add to this, that in tracing an eternal succession of objects it seems absurd to inquire for a general cause or first Author. How can anything that exists from eternity have a cause, since that very relationship implies a priority in time and a beginning of existence?

Also, in such a chain or succession of objects, each part is caused by that preceding it and causing that which succeeds it. Where then is the difficulty? But the *whole*, you say, lacks a Cause. I answer that the uniting of these parts *into* a whole, like the uniting of several distinct countries into one kingdom, or several distinct members into one body, is performed merely by an arbitrary act of the mind and has no influence on the *nature* of things. Were I to show you the particular causes of each individual in a collection of twenty particles of matter, I should think it very unreasonable if should you then ask me the cause of that whole twenty. This is sufficiently explained in explaining the cause of the parts.

PHILO Cleanthes, although your presented reasoning may well excuse me from raising further difficulties, yet I cannot forbear insisting still upon another topic.

It is observed by arithmeticians that multiples of 9 always contain either 9 itself, or some lesser multiple of 9, if you add the digits composing any such multiple. Thus, from 18, 27 and 36, you make 9 by adding 1+8, 2+7 and 3+6. Similarly, 369 is the product of 9x41; and 3+6+9 = 18; still a product, albeit lower, of 9.[1]

To the superficial observer, such a wonderful a regularity may be admired as the effect either of chance or design. However, a skilful algebraist concludes it to be the work of necessity and demonstrates that it *must* always result from the very nature of these numbers.

---

[1] Pierre Bayle, *Nouvelles de la république des lettres*, août (August) 1685.

Is it not probable, I ask, that the whole system of the Universe is conducted by a similar necessity, though no *human* algebra can furnish the key to solving the difficulty? And instead of admiring the order of natural beings, could we penetrate into the intimate nature of bodies, might we not clearly see why it was absolutely impossible they could ever be *otherwise*?

How dangerous it is to introduce this idea of *necessity* into the present question – and how naturally does it present an inference directly opposite to the religious hypothesis!

Dropping all these abstractions, however, and confining ourselves to more familiar topics, I shall venture to add the observation that the argument *a priori* has seldom been found very convincing, except to people of a metaphysically inclined mind accustomed to abstract reasoning. They, finding through mathematics that the understanding frequently leads to truth through obscurity – and *contrary* to first appearances – have transferred the same habit of thinking to subjects from which it ought to be absent. Others, even of good sense and most inclined to religion, always feel some deficiency in such arguments, though they are not perhaps able to explain distinctly where it lies. This is certain proof that humans always did – and always will – derive their religion from sources *other* than this species of reasoning.

PART x

DEMEA I admit that it is my opinion that each human being somehow feels the truth of religion within the breast. It is from a consciousness of their ignorance and their misery rather than from any reasoning, that people are led to seek protection from that Being upon whom they, and all Nature, are dependent. Even the best times of life are so anxious, or so tedious, that *futurity* remains the object of all our hopes and fears. We incessantly look forward. We endeavour, by prayers, adoration and sacrifice, to appease those unknown Powers whom we find by experience to afflict and oppress us. Wretched creatures that we are! What *resource* remains for us amidst the innumerable ills of life, were not religion able to suggest methods of atonement to appease those terrors incessantly agitating and tormenting us?

PHILO I am indeed persuaded that the best and indeed the only method of bringing everyone to a due sense of religion, is by accurate representations of the misery and wickedness of people. For that purpose, eloquence and strong imagery are more necessary than reasoning and argument. For is it necessary to *prove* what everyone feels? No. If possible, it is only necessary to make us *feel* it more intimately and sensibly.

DEMEA The people indeed are sufficiently convinced of this great and melancholy truth. The miseries of life; human unhappiness; the general corruptions of our nature; the unsatisfactory enjoyment of pleasures, riches or honours; these phrases have become almost proverbial in all languages. Who can doubt the truth of what *all* people declare from their own immediate feelings and experience?

PHILO On this point the learned are perfectly agreed with the uneducated. In all writings, both sacred and profane, the topic of human misery has been emphasized with the greatest eloquence that sorrow and melancholy could inspire. Poets abound in such images, speaking as they do from sentiment *without* a system, their testimony having thus more authority. From Homer down to Dr Young,[1] that whole inspired tribe have always been aware that no other representation of things would match the feeling and observation of each individual.

DEMEA As to authorities, you need not seek them. Look around Cleanthes's library here. Excepting authors in sciences such as chemistry or botany, who have no occasion to treat of *human* life, there is scarcely a writer who has not responded to human misery with a complaint about personal experience of it. And far as I recollect, not one author has ever been so extreme in expression as to deny it.

PHILO Excuse me; Leibniz[2] *has* denied it. He is perhaps the first who advanced so bold and paradoxical an opinion. At least, he was the first to make it essential to his philosophical system. The sentiment had been maintained by Dr King[3] and some few others before the German Leibniz; though by none of so great a fame.

---

1 Dr Edward Young (1683–1765). Author of *Night Thoughts* (1742), a long, rambling poetic treatment of the sublime. It influenced Edmund Burke and his work on aesthetic theory.
2 Gottfried Wilhelm Leibniz (1646–1716). German mathematician and one of the three great 17th century rationalist philosophers with Descartes and Spinoza. Hume is probably referring to Leibniz' *Theodicy* (1710).
3 Dr William King (1650–1729). Anglican Archbishop of Dublin. His *De Origine Mali*, 'On the Origin of Evil' (1702) was critically appraised by Leibniz who published it as an Appendix to his *Theodicy*.

DEMEA And by being the first, might he not have been *aware* of his error? For is this a subject where philosophers can claim to have made discoveries, especially in such recent times? Can anyone hope by a simple denial – for the subject hardly requires reasoning – to contradict united human testimony, founded as it is on sense and consciousness? And why should anyone claim exemption from the lot of all other animals? Believe me, Philo, the whole earth is cursed and polluted. Perpetual war rages amongst all living creatures. Necessity, hunger and want stimulate the strong and courageous while fear, anxiety and terror agitate the weak and infirm. The first entrance into life gives anguish to the new-born infant and to its wretched parent. Weakness, impotence and distress attend each stage of life that ends in agony and horror.

PHILO Observe too, Nature's own weird strategies for embittering the life of every living being. The stronger prey upon the weaker, keeping keep them in fear and anxiety. The weaker often prey upon the stronger, vexing and molesting them without respite. Consider that innumerable race of insects; either those bred on the bodies of animals or those that fly about, thrusting stings into them. These insects have others still smaller tormenting *them*. Thus on each hand, in front and behind and above and below, every animal is surrounded by enemies seeking its misery and destruction.[1]

DEMEA Humans alone seem to be a partial exception to this rule. By uniting with their fellows, they can easily master predatory lions, tigers and bears of greater strength and agility.

PHILO On the contrary, it is here that the uniform and equal maxims of Nature are *most* apparent. It is true that human beings, allied with their fellows, surmount all *real* enemies and become masters of the animal world. However, do not people, at the same time raise up *imaginary* enemies, demons of their unbridled imagination, who haunt them with superstitious terrors and blast every enjoyment of life? People imagine that their pleasures become, in the *spirits'* eyes, a crime; that their food and repose give supernatural beings umbrage and offence; that their very *dreams* furnish new materials for anxious fear; and that even death, their refuge from every other ill, presents only the dread of endless and innumerable woes.

---

1 In Dean Swift's *On Poetry*, we find: 'A flea / Hath smaller fleas that on him prey / And these have smaller Fleas to bite 'em / And so *ad infinitum...*'

The wolf no more molests the flock than superstition molests wretched mortals. Moreover, Demea, consider this very 'fellowship' by which we surmount wild beasts, our natural enemies. What new enemies does *it* not raise to us? What woe and misery does it not occasion? *Humans* are the greatest enemy of humankind. By oppression, injustice, contempt, contumely, violence, sedition, war, calumny, treachery and fraud, people torment each other. Humanity would dissolve society itself, were it not for the dread of still greater ills that would follow people's separation, one from another.

DEMEA These external insults from animals, by fellow humans and from all the elements that assault us, form a frightful catalogue of woes. They are, however, nothing in comparison to those that arise *within* us from the disturbed condition of our minds and bodies. How many lie under the lingering torment of disease? Hear the pathetic enumeration of the great poet.[1]

> Intestine stone and ulcer, colic-pangs,
> Demoniac frenzy, moping melancholy,
> And moon-struck madness, pining atrophy,
> Marasmus, and wide-wasting pestilence.
>
> Dire was the tossing, deep the groans: DESPAIR
> Tended the sick, busiest from couch to couch.
> And over them triumphant DEATH his dart
> Shook: but delay'd to strike, tho' oft invok'd
> With vows, as their chief good and final hope.

The disorders of the *mind*, though more hidden, are perhaps no less dismal and vexatious. Who passes through life without cruel inroads from these tormentors: remorse, shame, anguish, rage, disappointment, anxiety, fear, dejection and despair? How many have scarcely ever felt any *better* sensations? Labour and poverty, so abhorred by everyone, are the certain lot of the great majority. Even those few privileged persons who enjoy ease and opulence, never reach contentment or true happiness. All the good things of life *united* would not make a very happy man; but all the *ills* united would make a wretch indeed. Almost any one of those ills – and who can be free from every one – indeed, often the absence of *one* good – and who can possess all – is sufficient to render life unacceptable.

---

1 John Milton, *Paradise Lost*, XI. 484–93

Were strangers to suddenly drop into this world, I would show them its ills: a hospital full of disease; a prison crowded with malefactors and debtors; a battlefield strewn with corpses; a fleet foundering in the ocean, or a nation languishing under tyranny, famine or pestilence. To show them the gay side of life and give a notion of its pleasures, where should I conduct them? To a ball, to an opera, to Court? They might reasonably think I was only showing them a *diversity* of distress and sorrow.

PHILO There is no avoiding such striking instances except by apologising, thus further aggravating the charge. I ask; why has all humanity, in all ages, complained incessantly of the miseries of life? They have no valid reason, says someone: these complaints arise only from their discontented, whining, anxious disposition.

I reply, can there possibly be a more certain foundation of misery than such a wretched attitude of mind?

But says my antagonist, if they were really as unhappy as they claim, why do they remain in life? *Not satisfied with life, afraid of death.*[1]

This, I say, is the secret chain that holds us. We are *terrified*, not bribed, into the continuance of our existence.

The antagonist may insist that it is only a false fragility, indulged in by a few refined spirits, that has spread these complaints among humankind. And what is this fragility, I ask, that you criticise? Is it anything other than a greater sensibility to all the pleasures and pains of life? If the man or woman of a delicate and refined temper, by being so much more *alive* than the rest of the world, is only so much more *unhappy*, what judgement must we form in general of human life?

Let people remain at rest, says my adversary, and they will be comfortable. They are the willing makers of their own misery.

No! I reply. An anxious languor follows their repose, just as disappointment, vexation and trouble follow their activity and ambition.

CLEANTHES I can observe something of what you mention in others, but I confess I feel little or nothing of it myself. I hope it is not as common as you describe.

---

1 Matthew Prior (1664–1721): 'this wearied flesh draws fleeting breath /
Not satisfied with Life, afraid of Death.' *Solomon on the Vanity of the World*, 3.
A common human *cri de coeur*: cf. 'I'm tired of livin', but feared of dyin'...'
Oscar Hammerstein III, 'Ol' Man River', in *Showboat* (1927).

DEMEA If you don't feel human misery yourself, I congratulate you on so happy an exception. Others, seemingly the *most* prosperous, have not been ashamed to vent their complaints in the most depressing ways. Let us consider that great, fortunate emperor, Charles v,[1] who, tired of human grandeur, consigned all his dominions into the hands of his son. In his last speech on that memorable occasion, he avowed publicly that his greatest prosperities had been mixed with so many adversities that he had *never* enjoyed satisfaction or contentment. He sought shelter in the retired life, but did it bring him greater happiness?[2] If we believe his son's account, repentance commenced on the very *day* of his resignation.

Cicero's fortunes rose from small beginnings to the greatest lustre and renown.[3] Yet, what complaints of the ills of life are contained in his letters to friends and in his philosophical discourses! And appropriately to his own experience, he introduces Cato, the great, fortunate Cato,[4] protesting in old age that were he offered the present of a new life, he would reject it.[5]

Ask yourself, ask any of your acquaintances, whether they would live over again the last ten or twenty years of their life. No! they say –, but the *next* twenty will be better!

> *And from the dregs of life, hope to receive*
> *What the first sprightly running could not give.*[6]

Such is the greatness of human misery that it even reconciles contradictions; and we thus complain simultaneously of the shortness of life – *and* of its vanity and sorrow!

PHILO Cleanthes, is it possible that after all these reflections – and infinitely more that might be suggested – you still persevere in your Anthropomorphism and assert moral attributes to the Deity? You assert its justice, benevolence, mercy and rectitude to be of the same nature as in Humanity. The Deity's *power*, we accept, is infinite. Whatever it wills is executed. But

---

1 Holy Roman Emperor from 1519 until 1556 when he voluntarily abdicated in favour of his younger brother Ferdinand I and his son Philip II.
2 Hume paraphrases the statement of Charles v in the relevant entry in Bayle's *Dictionary*, 2.
3 Marcus Tullius Cicero, Rome's greatest orator, was born in modest circumstances at Arpinum in 106 BCE. Just over 40 years later, he was Consul. In 43 BCE he was brutally murdered by agents of Mark Antony, one of his political adversaries.
4 Marcus Porcius Cato (234–149 BCE), soldier, republican statesman and Stoic moralist. He is best known for his opposition to Julius Caesar's ascendency and for committing suicide after Caesar's victory over republican forces at the Battle of Thapsus in 46 BCE.
5 Cicero, *De Senectute*, 'On old Age', XXIII
6 John Dryden, *Aureng-Zebe*, (1676) Act IV. 1

neither humans, nor any other animal, are happy; therefore the Deity does not *will* their happiness. The Deity's *wisdom* is infinite. It is never mistaken in choosing the means to any end. But the course of Nature does not tend towards human or animal felicity and Nature therefore is not established for *that* purpose. Through the whole compass of human knowledge, *no* conclusions are more certain and infallible than these. In what respect, then, do the Deity's benevolence and mercy resemble the benevolence and mercy of human beings?

Epicurus's old questions are *still* unanswered:

> Is the Deity willing to prevent evil, but not able? Then it is impotent.
> Is the Deity able, but not willing? Then it is malevolent.
> Is the Deity both able *and* willing? Then, whence Evil?[1]

Cleanthes, you ascribe – I believe justly – a purpose and intention to Nature. But what, I beseech you, is the *object* of all that elegant artifice and machinery displayed by Nature in all animals? It is *solely* the preservation of individuals and the propagation of the species?[2] It seems enough for her purpose, if a species is simply able to *survive* in the Universe, without any care or even concern for the happiness of individuals. She deploys no resource for this purpose; no machinery in order merely to give pleasure or ease; no fund of pure joy and contentment; no indulgence without some want or necessity accompanying it. At best, the few such phenomena are overbalanced by opposite phenomena of still greater importance.

Our sense of music, harmony, and indeed beauty of all kinds gives satisfaction *without* being absolutely necessary for the preservation and propagation of the species. But on the other hand, what racking pains arise from gout, gravel,[3] depression toothache, rheumatism, where the injury to the animal machinery is either small or incurable? Mirth, laughter, play and frolic seem gratuitous satisfactions that have no further function: spleen, melancholy, discontent and superstition are pains of the same nature. How then does the Divine benevolence *display* itself to you anthropomorphites?

---

1 Absent from Lucretius, the great Epicurean *trilemma* is quoted by Lucius Lactantius (*c.*240–*c.*320 CE) adviser to Constantine I, in *A Treatise on the Anger of God*, 13.
2 Hume here anticipates evolutionary theory. Later biological theorists including TH Huxley and Charles Darwin were admirers of Hume, principally for his naturalistic positioning of human beings among animal species, not distinct from them in some metaphysical way.
3 Nephrolithiasis. (Kidney and/or bladder stones.)

Only we Mystics, as you were pleased to call us, can account for this strange mixture of phenomena by deriving it from attributes infinitely perfect, yet incomprehensible.

CLEANTHES (smiling): Have you at last betrayed your intentions, Philo? Your long agreement with Demea did indeed surprise me, but I now see that all the while you were erecting a concealed battery against *me*. However, I admit that you have now entered upon a subject worthy of your noble spirit of opposition and controversy. If you can make the present point and *prove* humankind to be unhappy or corrupted, there is an end of all religion. For to what purpose establish the *natural* attributes of the Deity, while the *moral* ones remain doubtful and uncertain?

DEMEA Cleanthes, you take umbrage very easily at the most innocent and generally accepted opinions amongst the devout. Nothing can be more surprising than to find a topic like this, the wickedness and misery of people, charged with no less than atheism and profanity. As for all pious divines and preachers who have covered this fertile subject, have they not given an easy solution to any difficulties attending it?

This world is but a *dot* in comparison with the Universe![1] This life is but a *moment* in comparison with eternity. Hence the present evil phenomena are to be rectified in other regions and in some *future* period of existence. The eyes of humanity, being then opened to a larger* views of things, see the whole connection of general Laws. They will trace with adoration the benevolence and rectitude of the Deity through all the mazes and intricacies of its Providence.

CLEANTHES No. *No*! These arbitrary suppositions can *never* be accepted. They are contrary to matters of visible and uncontroverted *fact*. Can any cause be known *except* from its known effects? Can any hypothesis be proved except from *observable* phenomena? To erect one hypothesis upon another is building entirely in the air! The utmost we ever attain by these conjectures and fictions is to ascertain the bare *possibility* of our opinion. We can *never* establish its reality upon such terms.

The only means to support Divine benevolence and it is one that I willingly embrace, is to deny absolutely the misery and wickedness of humanity. Your representations are exaggerated; your melancholy views mostly

---

* *Wider; more extensive.* SJ
1 Hume, as Demea, anticipates *Pale Blue Dot* (1990) by Prof. Carl Sagan.

fictitious; your inferences contrary to fact and experience. Health is more common than sickness; pleasure than pain and happiness than misery. And for every single vexation we meet with, we attain a hundred enjoyments.

PHILO Accepting your position, which is still extremely doubtful, you must concede that if pain is indeed less *frequent* than pleasure, it is infinitely more violent and durable. One hour of it is often outweighs a day, a week, a *month* of our common insipid enjoyments; and how many days, weeks and months, are passed in the most acute torments? Pleasure is scarcely ever able to reach ecstasy and rapture. It never continues for any time at its highest pitch and altitude. The spirits evaporate, the nerves relax, the fabric is disordered and the enjoyment quickly degenerates into fatigue and uneasiness. But pain often, good God *how* often, rises to torture and agony. And the longer it continues, it becomes still more genuine agony and torture. Patience is exhausted, courage languishes and melancholy seizes us. Nothing terminates our misery except the removal of its cause, or that other event,[1] the sole cure of all evil; the event that from our natural folly we regard with still greater horror and consternation.

But to move on from these topics, most obvious, certain and important as they are, I must admonish you, Cleanthes. You have turned the controversy in a most dangerous direction, unaware that you are introducing total scepticism into the most essential articles of both natural and revealed theology. What? No method of fixing a just foundation for religion unless we accept the essential happiness of human life? No foundation for it unless we assert, even in *this* world, an afterlife to be eligible and desirable, despite all our present pains, infirmities, vexations and follies?

This is contrary to everyone's feeling and experience. It is contrary to an authority so well established that nothing can subvert it. No decisive proofs can ever be produced against this authority; and neither is it possible for you to compute, estimate, or even *compare* all the pains and all the pleasures in the lives of all people and animals. By your resting the whole system of religion on a point that from its very nature must always be uncertain, you thus tacitly confess that that system *itself* is equally uncertain.

However, conceding to you what will never be believed, at least what you can never possibly *prove* – that animal or at least human happiness exceeds its misery – you have still done nothing. For this is not what we expect from infinite power, infinite wisdom and infinite goodness. Why is

---

1 Death.

there any misery *at all* in the world? Not by chance, surely. From some cause, then? Is it from the *intention* of the Deity? But it is perfectly benevolent. Is this contrary to its intention? But it is almighty. Nothing can shake the solidity of this reasoning, so short, so clear, so decisive. That is, unless we assert that these subjects exceed all *human* capacity and that *our* common standards of truth and falsehood are not applicable to them. This is an argument I have advocated all along, but that you have rejected from the start with scorn and indignation.

However, I will be content to withdraw from this intrenchment[1] for you can never force me out of it. I will admit that pain and misery in humanity is compatible with infinite power and goodness in the Deity, even in your sense of these attributes.

In what way is your position advanced by all these concessions? A mere possible compatibility is not sufficient. You must establish these pure, unmixed and uncontrollable attributes of the Deity from the present mixed and confused phenomena – and from these alone. An ambitious undertaking! Were the phenomena totally pure and unmixed they would, being finite, be insufficient for that purpose. How much more so where they are also so jarring and discordant!

Here, Cleanthes, I find myself comfortable in my argument. Here I triumph. Formerly, when we argued concerning the natural attributes of intelligence and design, I needed all my sceptical and metaphysical subtlety to elude your grasp. In many views of the Universe and particularly of its parts, the beauty and fitness of final causes strike us with irresistible force that all apparent objections are what I believe they *really* are; mere cavils and sophisms. Nor can we then imagine how it was ever possible to attach any weight to them.

However, there is *no* view of human life, or of the condition of humanity, from which we can infer *moral* attributes of a Deity. By the eyes of faith *alone* can we reveal and learn of infinite benevolence, conjoined with infinite power and infinite wisdom. It is your turn now to tug the labouring oar[2] and advance your philosophical subtleties against the dictates and tide of plain reason and experience.

---

1 'Retrenchment' altered to 'intrenchment' by DH's nephew Prof. David Hume.
2 Philo quotes from John Dryden's translation of Vergil's *Aeneid*, v. 189 *Nunc, nunc insurgite remis hectorei socii...* 'Now, my friends, Hector's followers heretofore / Exert your vigour; tug the laboring oar...'

PART xi

CLEANTHES I admit that the frequent repetition of the word 'infinite,' as we find in all theological writers, savours more of panegyric than of philosophy. Any purpose of reasoning and even of religion would be better served with more accurate and more moderate expressions. The terms: admirable; excellent; superlatively great; wise and holy, are sufficient to fill the human imagination. Anything beyond, apart from leading us into absurdities, has no influence on our affections or sentiments.

Thus if we abandon all *human* analogy in the present matter, as seems your intention, Demea, I am afraid we abandon all religion and retain no conception of the great Object of our adoration. If we preserve the human analogy, we must find it impossible to reconcile evil in the Universe with infinite attributes. Much less can we ever *prove* the latter from the former.

But supposing the Author of Nature to be *finitely* perfect, though far exceeding humankind, a satisfactory account may then be given of natural and moral evil. Every morally objectionable phenomenon may thus be explained and adjusted. A lesser evil may then be chosen in order to avoid a greater, while inconveniences may be endured in order to reach a desirable end. In a word, benevolence – regulated by wisdom *and* limited by necessity – may produce *just* such a world as the present.

You, Philo, so prompt at raising opinions, reflections and analogies, I would gladly hear at length and without interruption, your opinion of this new theory. If it deserves our attention we may afterwards and at leisure, reduce it into form.

PHILO My sentiments are not worth being made a mystery. Without ceremony, therefore, what occurs to me on the present subject is this. Let us imagine creatures of very limited intelligence and *external* to the Universe. This, they are assured, is the production of a very good, wise and powerful Being, however finite. Such creatures would conjecture a *very* different notion of it from what we actually experience. Nor would they ever imagine, when informed of the attributes of the Cause, that this *life* could be so full of vice, misery and disorder.

Now suppose those creatures brought *into* the world, still assured that it was the workmanship of a sublime, benevolent Being. They might perhaps be surprised at the disappointment, but would not retract their former belief if founded on solid argument, since such limited intelligence must be aware of its own ignorance. It must admit that there may be *many* solutions for those phenomena forever escaping their comprehension.

But now suppose – and this is actually the case with human beings – that these external creatures had not been *antecedently* convinced of a supremely benevolent, powerful intelligence, but had been left to generate such a belief from the appearances of things. This entirely alters the case. Now they will *never* find reasons for such a conclusion. They may be fully aware of the narrow limits of their understanding, but this will not help to form an inference concerning the *goodness* of superior powers. They must form that inference from knowledge, not from ignorance. The more you exaggerate their weakness and ignorance, the more diffident you make them and the more suspicious that such subjects lie beyond their faculties. You are obliged, therefore, to reason with them merely from *known* phenomena and to drop all arbitrary suppositions or conjectures.

Suppose I were to show you a house or a palace where not one apartment was convenient or agreeable. The windows, doors, fires, passages, stairs and the whole organisation of the building were the source of noise, confusion, fatigue, darkness and the extremes of heat and cold. You would certainly criticise the structure without further examination. The architect would in vain display his subtlety, seeking to prove to you that if this door or that window were altered, *greater* ills would ensue. What he says may be strictly true. The alteration of one particular, while the other parts of the building remain, might only augment the inconvenience. But in general you would still assert that, had the architect both skill and good intentions, a plan of the *whole* might have been formed with the parts adjusted to remedy all or most of these inconveniences. His ignorance, or even *your* own ignorance of such a plan, will never convince you of the impossibility of it. If you find inconveniences and deformities in a building, you will always, without entering into detail, condemn the architect.

In short, I repeat the question. Is the world, considered in general and as it appears to *us*, different from what humankind, or a similarly *limited* being, would expect from a very powerful, wise, and benevolent Deity? It must be strange prejudice to assert the contrary. And from that, I conclude that however consistent the world may be, to admit certain suppositions and conjectures with the *idea* of such a Deity, can never infer its *existence*.

The consistency is not absolutely denied, only the inference. Conjectures, especially where infinity is excluded from the Divine attributes, may perhaps be sufficient to prove a consistency but can never be *foundations* for any inference.

There seem to be four circumstances upon which depend all, or the greatest part, of the ills that molest sentient creatures. It is also possible that all these circumstances may be necessary and unavoidable. We know so little beyond common life, or even *of* common life that, with regard to the organisation of a Universe, there is no conjecture however wild that may not be correct. Neither is there any, however plausible, that may not be erroneous.

In this deep ignorance and obscurity, human understanding must be sceptical, or at least cautious. We should not accept any hypothesis whatsoever, much less one unsupported by any appearance of probability. Now, this I assert to be the case with regard to all the causes of evil and the four circumstances on which it depends. None of these four appears to human reason to be in any way necessary or unavoidable; nor can we suppose them to be so without the utmost flights of imagination.

The *First Circumstance* that introduces evil is that feature of the animal creation, by which pains as well as pleasures excite creatures to action, making make them vigilant in the great work of self-preservation. Now, to human understanding, pleasure alone in its various degrees seems sufficient for this purpose. All animals might be constantly in a state of enjoyment but, if urged by any necessity of nature such as thirst, hunger or weariness they might feel, instead of pain, a diminution of pleasure prompting them to seek whatever is necessary for their subsistence. Humans pursue pleasure as eagerly as they avoid pain – at least they appear to have been so constituted. It seems, therefore, clearly possible to carry on the business of life without any pain.

Why then is every animal susceptible of the sensation of pain?

If animals can be free from it for an hour, they might enjoy a perpetual exemption from it – and it would require an equally particular design of their organs to produce that feeling, like that required to endow sight, hearing, or any of the senses. Shall we conjecture that such a contrivance was necessary without any appearance of reason? Shall we build on that conjecture as on the most certain truth?

But a capacity of pain would not *alone* produce pain, were it not for the *Second Circumstance, viz.* the conducting of the world by general laws – and this seems in no wise necessary to a very perfect Being. It is true that were everything conducted by individual volition, the course of Nature would be perpetually derailed and no-one could employ reason in the conduct of life. But might not *other* particular volitions remedy this inconvenience? In short, might not the Deity exterminate *all* ill wherever it were to be found and produce *all* good without any preparation, or a long progress of causes and effects?

Besides, we must consider that according to the present arrangement of the world, the course of Nature, though supposed exactly regular, yet appears not so to us. Many events are uncertain and many disappoint our expectations. Health and sickness, calm and tempest, together with an infinite number of other occurrences whose causes are unknown and variable, have a great influence both on the fortunes of particular persons and on the prosperity of public societies. Indeed, all human life depends to a degree on such accidents. A Being, therefore, who knows the secret springs of the Universe might easily and by particular actions, turn all these accidents to the good of humanity and render the whole world happy, *without* revealing itself in any operation.

A fleet whose purposes were salutary to society might then always meet with a fair wind; good princes enjoy sound health and long life; persons born to power and authority might be accorded good tempers and virtuous dispositions. A few such events as these, regularly and wisely conducted, would change the face of the world. Furthermore, they would no more seem to disturb the course of Nature, or obstruct human conduct, than the present arrangement of things where the causes are secret, variable and compounded.

Some small adjustments to Caligula's brain in infancy might have converted him into a Trajan.[1] One wave, a little higher than the rest, by burying Caesar and his fortune in the bottom of the ocean, might have restored liberty to a considerable part of humankind.[2] There may, for all we know, be good reasons why Providence does *not* intervene in this manner – but they are unknown to us. Though the mere supposition that such reasons exist

---

1 Caligula ('little boot'), his childhood nickname among the legionaries in camps, was properly Gaius Julius Caesar Germanicus, Emperor 37–41CE. In his reign, well described in *Flaccus* by the historical Philo, he became ungovernably deranged, made his horse Incitatus a Consul and was assassinated. In contrast, Trajan, properly Caesar Nerva Traianus, Emperor 98–117CE, was an outstanding general and politician.
2 In 69 BCE, on an Aegean voyage to Rhodes to study under the *rhetor* Apollonius Molon, Caesar and his ship were taken by Cilician pirates off the island of Pharmacusa. See: Suetonius. *Julius Caesar*, 4

may be sufficient to save the conclusion concerning the Divine attributes, yet surely it can never be sufficient to *establish* that conclusion. If everything in the Universe is conducted by general laws and if animals be rendered susceptible of pain, it scarcely seems possible that some ills will not arise in the various shocks of matter and the various concurrence and opposition of general laws.

However, these ills would be very rare were it not for the *Third* Circumstance I propose, *viz.* the great *frugality* with which powers and faculties are distributed to every particular being. So well-adjusted are the organs and capacities of all animals and so well fitted to their preservation that, as far as history or tradition reaches, there appears not to be any single species that has yet been extinguished in the Universe.[1] Every animal has the requisite endowments; but these endowments are bestowed with so scrupulous an economy that any considerable diminution must entirely destroy the creature. Wherever one power is increased, there is a proportional abatement in the others. Animals that excel in swiftness are commonly defective in force. Those possessing both are either imperfect in some of their senses, or are oppressed with the most craving wants. Humankind, whose chief excellence is reason and sagacity, is the most needful and the most deficient of all in *bodily* advantages; being without clothes, without arms,[2] lodging, or any convenience of life except what we owe to our own skill and industry.

In short, Nature seems to have calculated *exactly* the necessities of her creatures and, like a rigid master, afforded them powers or endowments little more than those barely sufficient to supply those necessities. An indulgent parent would have bestowed a large stock in order to guard against accidents and secure the happiness and welfare of the creature in any unfortunate concurrence of circumstances. Every track through life would not have been so surrounded with precipices whereby the least departure from the true path, whether by mistake or necessity, would inevitably involve us in misery and ruin. Some reserve, some fund, would have been provided to ensure happiness; and the powers and the necessities would not have been given so rigid a structure.

The Author of Nature is inconceivably powerful. Its force is supposed great, if not altogether inexhaustible. There is no reason, as far as we can judge, to make it observe this strict frugality in its dealings with its creatures.

---

1 The Dodo was then (1776) still alive and the dinosaurs unknown.

2 Hume presumably means natural weaponry, ie physical (as opposed to oratorical) fangs, claws or venom.

It would have been better, were its power extremely limited, to have created fewer animals and to have endowed these with more faculties for their happiness and preservation. A prudent builder never undertakes a design beyond the stock required to finish the work.

In order to cure most of the ills of human life, I require not that human beings should have the wings of the eagle, the swiftness of the stag, the force of the ox, the arms of the lion or the scales of the crocodile. Much less do I demand the sagacity of an angel or cherubim. I am content to take an increase in one single power or faculty. Let humanity be endowed with a greater propensity to industry and labour, a more vigorous spring and activity of mind and a more constant bent to business and application. Let the whole species possess by *nature* a diligence equal to that which many individuals attain by habit and reflection – and the most beneficial consequences, without any relief of ill, would be the immediate and necessary result.

Almost all the moral as well as the natural evils of human life arise from idleness. Were our species exempt from this vice or infirmity by the original constitution of their frame, then the perfect cultivation of land, the improvement of arts and manufactures and the precise execution of every office and duty, would immediately follow. People at once might fully reach that state of society that is so imperfectly attained by the best regulated government. But since the capacity for hard and thoughtful work is the most valuable power of all, Nature, conforming to her usual maxims, seems determined to bestow it on people with a very sparing hand. Nature prefers rather to punish humans for *deficiency* in it, than to reward them for their attainments. Nature has so assembled the human frame that only extreme necessity can oblige people to labour. Nature employs all people's *other* desires to overcome, at least in part, this lack of diligence and to thus endow them with some share of a faculty of which she has deprive them naturally. Here our demands may be accepted as very humble and hence more reasonable.

If we required the endowments of superior intelligence and judgement, of a more delicate taste of beauty, of a kinder personality inclined towards good will and friendship, we might be told that we impiously seek to break the order of Nature. We might also be advised that we wanted to exalt ourselves into a higher rank of being, that the endowments we require, being unsuitable to our present state and condition, would only be harmful to us. But it is hard, I dare to repeat, it is *hard,* to be placed in a world so full of wants and necessities, where almost every being and element is either our foe or refuses assistance, that we should *also* have to struggle with our own temper. Hard it is that we should be deprived of that very faculty that can alone be a defence against these multiplied evils.

The *Fourth Circumstance* from which arises the misery and ills of the Universe is the inaccurate workmanship of all the sources and principles of the great machine of Nature. It must be acknowledged that there are few parts of the Universe that do not seem to serve some purpose and whose removal would not produce a visible defect and disorder in the whole. The parts all hang together and none can be altered without affecting the rest to a greater or lesser degree. But at the same time it must be observed that none of these parts or principles, however useful, are so accurately adjusted as to keep precisely within those bounds in which their utility consists. All of them are apt to run to one extreme or the other on every occasion. One would imagine that this grand production had not received the *final* touches of the Maker, so inadequately finished is every part and so coarse the strokes with which it is executed. Thus, winds are required to convey the atmosphere and gaseous effluents along the surface of the globe and to assist mariners in navigation. But how often, by rising into tempests and hurricanes, do they become pernicious? Rains are necessary to nourish all the plants and animals of the earth, but how often are they defective and how often excessive? Heat, requisite for all life and vegetation,[1] is not always found in due proportion to requirement.

The health and prosperity of an animal depend on the mixture and secretion of the humours and juices of the body, but the parts perform their proper function irregularly. What is more useful than all the passions of the mind: ambition; vanity; love and anger? But how often in society do they break out of their bounds, causing the greatest convulsions? There is nothing advantageous in the Universe that does not frequently become pernicious by its excess or deficit. Nature has not guarded with the requisite accuracy against disorder or confusion. This irregularity is never perhaps so great as to destroy any *species*, but is often sufficient to involve its *individuals* in ruin and misery.

On the concurrence, then, of these four circumstances depends all, or at least the greatest part, of natural evil. Were all living creatures incapable of pain, or were the world administered by particular volitions, evil never could have gained access to the Universe. Were animals endowed with a large stock of powers and faculties beyond what strict necessity requires, or

---

1 From Lat. *Vegetatio*, Power of growth.

were the several sources and principles of the Universe so accurately framed as to always preserve the just temperament and medium; there would have been very little ill in comparison of what we feel at present.

What then shall we conclude on this occasion? Shall we say that these circumstances are not necessary and might easily have been altered in the construction of the Universe? This decision seems too presumptuous for creatures so blind and ignorant. Let us be more modest in our conclusions. Let us allow* that if the goodness of the Deity – I mean a goodness like that of humankind – could be established on any tolerable reasons *a priori*, these phenomena, however untoward, would not be sufficient to subvert that principle. Indeed they might easily, in some unknown manner, be reconcilable to it. But let us continue to assert that this goodness is not *antecedently* established, but must be inferred from observable phenomena. Hence there can be no grounds for such an inference while there are so many ills in the Universe that might so easily have been remedied, so far as our human understanding may judge. I am sceptic enough to admit that the bad appearances, despite all my reasoning, may be compatible with such attributes as you suppose. Surely, however, they can never *prove* these attributes. Such a conclusion cannot result from scepticism. It must arise from the phenomena themselves and from our confidence in the arguments we deduce from these phenomena.

Look round the Universe. What an immense profusion of beings, animated and organised, sentient and active! You admire this prodigious variety and fecundity. But inspect a little more *narrowly* these living existences, the only ones worth regarding. How hostile and destructive are they to each other! How insufficient, all of them, for their own happiness! How contemptible or odious to the spectator! The whole presents nothing but the idea of a blind Nature impregnated by a great vivifying principle and pouring forth her maimed and abortive children without discernment or parental care!

Here the Manichaean system[1] occurs as a proper hypothesis to solve the difficulty. No doubt, in some respects it is very specious, but has more probability than the common hypothesis, by giving a plausible account of the strange mixture of good and ill appearing in life. But on the other hand, if we consider the perfect uniformity and agreement of the parts of the Universe,

---

* To allow: *to accept; to admit as fact.* SJ

1 Developed by the Persian prophet Manes (aka Mani, *c.*216–247 CE), it was a syncretic, dualistic philosophy, combining elements of Gnostic, Zoroastrian and Christian thought. It divides the world between good and evil principles or deities; matter being as intrinsically evil and mind as intrinsically good. The world is the site of war between the two opposing deities.

we shall not discover in it any marks of combat between a malevolent with a benevolent being. There is indeed an opposition of pains and pleasures in the feelings of sentient creatures, but are not all the operations of Nature carried on through an opposition of principles: hot and cold, moist and dry, light and heavy?

The true conclusion is that the original Source of all things is entirely *indifferent* to all these principles. It has no more regard to good above ill than to heat above cold, or to drought above moisture, or to light above heavy.

Four hypotheses may be framed concerning the originating causes of the Universe:

That such causes are endowed with perfect goodness.
That they have perfect malice
That they have both goodness and malice
That they have neither goodness nor malice

Mixed phenomena can never prove the two former unmixed principles, while the uniformity and steadiness of general laws seem to oppose the third. The fourth, therefore, seems by far the most probable.

What I have said concerning natural evil will apply to the moral variety with little or no variation. We have no reason to infer that the *rectitude* of the Supreme Being resembles human rectitude any more than that its *benevolence* resembles the human. Indeed, it will be thought that we have still greater cause to exclude from it those moral sentiments we humans feel. This is because moral evil, in the opinion of many, is much more predominant above moral good, than natural evil above natural good.

But even though this should not be accepted and though the virtue in humanity should be acknowledged much superior to the vice, yet so long as there is *any* vice in the universe, it will much puzzle you Anthropomorphites how to account for it. You must assign a cause for it, without having recourse to the first or originating Cause. But as every effect must have a cause, and that cause another, you must either carry on the progression *ad infinitum*, or rest on that original Principle, the ultimate cause of all things…

DEMEA Hold, *Hold*, Philo! Whither does your imagination hastily carry you? I joined in alliance with you in order to prove the incomprehensible nature of the divine Being and refute the principles of Cleanthes who would measure everything by human rule and standard. But I now find you running into all the topics of the greatest libertines and infidels, and betraying that holy cause you seemingly espoused. Are you secretly a more dangerous enemy than Cleanthes himself?

CLEANTHES Are you so *late* in perceiving it? Believe me, Demea, your friend Philo has been amusing himself at the expense of both of us from the very beginning! Also, the injudicious reasoning of our everyday theology has given him a far too useful handle of ridicule. The total infirmity of human reason; the absolute incomprehensibility of the divine Nature; the great and universal misery; the still greater wickedness of humanity. Surely these are strange topics to be so fondly cherished by orthodox divines and teachers. In ages of ignorance, these principles may safely be espoused and perhaps no view of things promotes superstition *more* than that which encourages the blind amazement, the diffidence and the melancholy of Human kind. But at present...

PHILO Blame not so much the *ignorance* of these reverend gentlemen. They know how to change their style with the times! Formerly, it was a most popular theological topic to maintain that human life *was* vanity and misery and to exaggerate the ills and pains that beset humanity. But of late we find divines beginning to retract this position. They maintain, though still with some hesitation, that there are more goods than evils, more pleasures than pains, even in *this* life. When religion was based entirely upon temper and education, it was thought proper to encourage melancholy; indeed when depressed, humankind never has such ready recourse to superior powers. But as humanity has now learned to form principles and to draw consequences, it is necessary to change the artillery and to deploy arguments that will withstand at least *some* scrutiny and examination. This variation is the same – and from the same *causes* – as that which I formerly remarked with regard to Scepticism.

Thus to the last, did Philo continue his spirit of opposition and censure of established opinions. But I could observe that Demea did not at all relish the latter part of the discourse. Soon after, on some pretence or other, he left the company.

PART XII

After Demea's departure, Cleanthes and Philo continued their conversation:

CLEANTHES I am afraid our friend will have little inclination to revive this topic of discourse while *you* are in the company. Truth to tell, Philo, I would rather reason with either of you separately on such a sublime and interesting subject. Your spirit of controversy, plus your abhorrence of common superstition, carries you to strange lengths in argument. You spare *nothing*, not even whatever is sacred and venerable to you!

PHILO I confess that I am less cautious on the subject of natural religion than on any other. This is because I know that on that topic I can never corrupt the principles of anyone of common sense. I also know that no one who regards *me* as a man of common sense will ever mistake my intentions. Cleanthes, you in particular with whom I live in intimacy, *you* know that despite the freedom of my conversation and my love of unusual arguments, no one has a deeper sense of religion. No-one more profoundly adores the divine Being, revealed to reason in the inexplicable construction and artifice of Nature. A purpose, an intention, a design, strikes home to the most cavalier, the most stupid thinker. No-one can be so hardened in absurd systems as to consistently reject it.

That Nature does nothing in vain (that is, *without* reason) is a maxim established in all the schools, simply from contemplation of the works of Nature – and without any *religious* purpose. From a firm conviction of this truth, an anatomist observing a new organ or canal would never be satisfied till its function and intention had also been discovered. One great foundation of the Copernican system is the maxim that Nature acts by the simplest methods, choosing the best and most fitting means to any end. Astronomers, without thinking of it, often lay this strong foundation of piety and religion. The same thing is observable in other parts of philosophy. Thus all the sciences lead us, almost insensibly, to acknowledge a first intelligent Author; and as they do not *directly* profess that intention, their authority is often so much the greater.

It is with pleasure that I hear Galen[1] reason concerning the structure of the human body. Human anatomy, says he,[2] reveals more than 600 different muscles. Whoever carefully examines them will find that in *each* of them Nature, in order to attain the desired end, must have balanced at least ten different requirements: proper shape; correct magnitude, right disposition of the several ends; upper and lower position of the whole; the due insertion of the several nerves, veins, and arteries. Thus in human muscles alone, more than 6000 views and intentions must have been formed and executed.

---

1 Aelius Galenus of Pergamon (129–c.200 CE) Roman, but of Greek stock. Physician, surgeon and philosopher. The greatest medical researcher and writer of antiquity.
2 *De formatione foetus* (Hume). Properly, *De Foetuum Formatione Libellus* (A little book on the formation of foetuses) 4.691 *et seq.*

The bones he calculates to be 284 in number and in the structure of *each*, the distinct purposes are above forty. What a prodigious display of artfulness, even in these simple and homogeneous parts! But if we also consider skin, ligaments, vessels, glands, humours, the several limbs and members of the body, how must our astonishment rise in proportion to the number and intricacy of parts so artificially adjusted.

The further we advance in such researches, the more we discover new examples of art and wisdom. We catch sight also, at a distance, of further scenes beyond our reach; in the fine internal structure of the parts; in the efficiency of the brain and in the fabric of the seminal vessels. All these artifices are repeated in every species of animal with wonderful variety and with whatever exact propriety suited the intentions of Nature in defining the various species. If the scepticism of Galen could not survive such striking appearances when these natural sciences were still imperfect, what pitch of determined obstinacy must have been attained by any modern philosopher doubting a supreme Intelligence?

Could I meet with one of this species (who, I thank God, are very rare), I would ask:

> Supposing there were a divine Being that did not reveal itself directly to our senses, could this Being possibly give *any* stronger proof of its existence than the whole face of Nature? What indeed could such a Being do *except* copy the present arrangement of things and render its artifices so plain that no stupidity could mistake them? The Being could also afford glimpses of still greater artifices, demonstrating its prodigious superiority above our narrow understanding, as well as concealing a great many from such imperfect creatures.

> Now, according to all the rules of correct reasoning, a fact must pass undisputed when it is supported by all the arguments its nature admits, even though these arguments are not in themselves either numerous or forcible. How much more, in the present case, where human imagination cannot compute their number and no understanding can even *estimate* their cogency?

CLEANTHES I shall add to what you have advocated so well. One great advantage of theism is that it is the *only* system of universal origins that can be rendered intelligible and complete while preserving throughout a strong analogy to what we see and experience every day. The comparison of the Universe to a machine of human construction is obvious and natural. Justified by so many instances of order and design in Nature, it must surmount all unprejudiced reservations and receive universal approval. Whoever attempts to weaken this theory cannot claim to succeed by establishing any alternative one that is precise and well defined. It is sufficient here for an aspiring sceptic to raise doubts and difficulties and, by remote and abstract views of things, reach that suspension of judgement that is the limit of a sceptic's wishes in this matter. But, besides the fact that this state of mind is in itself unsatisfactory, it can never be steadily maintained against such striking appearances as we continually encounter in the religious hypothesis. Due to the force of prejudice, human nature is capable of adhering to a false, absurd system with obstinacy and perseverance. But I think that it would be absolutely impossible to maintain or defend *any* system in opposition to a theory supported by strong and obvious reason, by natural propensity and by early education.

PHILO So little do I regard this 'suspension of judgement'[1] to be possible in the present case, that I suspect that a word dispute enters into this controversy more than is usually imagined. It is evident that the works of Nature bear a great analogy to the productions of art. According to all rules of good reasoning, we ought to infer, if we argue at all concerning them, that their *causes* have a proportional analogy. But as there are also considerable differences, we have reason to suppose a proportional difference in the causes. In particular, we ought to attribute a much higher degree of power and energy to the supreme Cause than any we have ever observed in humankind. Here, then, the existence of a Deity is plainly ascertained by reason. If we frame a question as to whether, on account of these analogies, we can properly call the Deity a Mind, or an Intelligence, then despite the vast difference we may reasonably suppose between the *divine* and *human* minds, what is this only a mere verbal controversy?

Since none can deny the analogies between the effects, to restrain from inquiry into the causes is scarcely possible. From this inquiry, the legitimate conclusion is that the causes have also an analogy. If we are not content with calling the first and supreme cause a God or Deity, but desire to vary the expression what can we use? Surely 'Mind', or 'Thought', to which the Deity is rightly supposed to bear a considerable resemblance.[2] All people of sound reason are disgusted with the verbal disputes abounding in philosophical

---

1 Sceptical thinkers, especially those in the tradition of Pyrrhonian scepticism, advocate 'suspension of judgment' or *epochē* in relation to matters of philosophical dogma, especially metaphysical dogma. Christian Pyrrhonians, however, such as Montaigne (1533–92) and Pierre Charron (1541–1603), argued that religious belief should *not* be subject to *epochē*.

2 This conjecture echoes the original Greek of John 1.3. θεὸς ἦν ὁ λόγος. 'God was the *Logos*' meaning, 'Immanent cosmic rationality; pure intelligence.' Lampe, GWH (ed.) *A Patristic Greek Lexicon* (Oxford: OUP, 1969).

and theological inquiries. The only remedy for this abuse is clear definitions and also precision in those ideas that enter the argument. Equally, there must be strict and uniform use of those terms employed.

However, there is a species of controversy that, from the very nature of language and of human ideas, is involved in perpetual ambiguity. This species concerns the *degrees* of any quality or circumstance. Neither by any precaution nor by any definitions can it be enabled to reach a reasonably certain or precise conclusion. We may argue to all eternity, whether Hannibal was a great, or a very great, or a superlatively great man. We may argue over what degree of beauty Cleopatra possessed or to what degree of praise Livy or Thucydides is entitled, without bringing the controversy to any determination. The disputants may here agree in their sense and differ in the terms, or *vice versa*; yet never be able to define their terms, so as to understand each other's meaning. This is because the *degrees* of these qualities, like quantity or number, are not susceptible of the exact measurement that can set standards or criteria of judgment in the controversy. The slightest inquiry will reveal that the theism dispute is of this nature and is consequently merely verbal – or perhaps, if this is possible, still *more* incurably ambiguous.

I ask the theist if he or she concedes that there is a great and (because it is incomprehensible) *immeasurable* difference between the human and the divine mind? The more pious, the more readily the theist will assent to this and the more disposed to magnify the difference. Theists will even assert that the difference is of a nature that cannot be too much magnified.

I next turn to the atheist who, I assert, is only nominally so and can never possibly be an atheist in a serious way. I ask whether, from the coherence and apparent sympathy in all the parts of this world, there be not a certain degree of analogy among all the operations of Nature? I ask the atheist whether in every situation and in every age the rotting of a turnip, the generation of an animal and the structure of human thought are not energies that probably bear some remote analogy to each other? It is impossible for the atheist to deny it and it will be readily acknowledged. Having obtained this concession, I push the atheist still further, asking if it is not probable that the Principle that first arranged, and still maintains, order in this Universe bears also some remote, inconceivable analogy to the other operations of Nature, including human mind and thought. However reluctantly, the atheist will have to assent.

Where then, I cry to *both* antagonists, is the subject of your dispute? The theist admits that the original Intelligence is very different from human reason, while the atheist concedes that the original Principle of Order bears some remote analogy to it.

Gentlemen, will you quarrel about the degrees? Will you enter into a controversy capable neither of any precise meaning, nor consequently of any resolution? If you prove so obstinate, I should not be surprised to find you insensibly changing sides with the theist exaggerating the *dissimilarity* between the Supreme Being and frail, imperfect, variable, fleeting and mortal creatures, while the atheist magnifies the *similarity* among all the operations of Nature in every period, situation and position.

Consider then, where the real point of controversy lies and, if you cannot lay aside your disputes, endeavour at least to cure yourselves of your animosity.

And here, Cleanthes, I must also acknowledge that as the works of Nature have a much greater analogy to the effects of human art and contrivance than to our benevolence and justice, we have reason to infer that the *natural* attributes of the Deity have a greater resemblance to those of humankind than have its *moral* attributes to human virtues. But what are the consequences? It is this alone; that human moral qualities are more defective than our natural abilities. Since the supreme Being is agreed to be absolutely and entirely perfect, whatever differs *most* from it departs *furthest* from the supreme standard of rectitude and perfection.

It seems evident that the dispute between sceptics and dogmatists is entirely verbal, or at least covers only the *degrees* of doubt or of assurance that we ought to indulge in all reasoning. Such disputes commonly are ultimately verbal and are thus incapable of precise resolution. No philosophical dogmatist denies that there are difficulties both with regard to the senses and to all science and that these difficulties are insoluble by regular, logical methods. No sceptic denies that, in spite of these difficulties, we lie under an absolute necessity of thinking, believing and reasoning on all kinds of subjects, even frequently *assenting* with confidence and security.

Hence the only difference between these sects, if they merit that name, is that the sceptic, from habit, caprice or inclination, insists most on the difficulties, the dogmatist, for similar reasons, on the necessity.

These, Cleanthes, are my honest sentiments on this subject. As you know, they are sentiments that I have always cherished and maintained. But equal to my veneration for true religion is my abhorrence of vulgar superstition. I confess that I indulge a peculiar pleasure in pushing superstitious ideas sometimes into absurdity, sometimes into impiety. Despite their great aversion to the latter above the former, all bigots, as you well know, are commonly equally guilty of both!

CLEANTHES My inclination lies, I admit, in a contrary direction. Religion, however corrupted, is still better than no religion at all. The doctrine of a future state, an afterlife, is so strong and necessary a security to morals that we ought never to abandon or neglect it. If, as we daily observe, *finite* temporal rewards and punishments have a great effect, how much a greater must be expected from such as are *infinite* – and eternal?

PHILO If common superstition is so salutary to society, why does all history abound with accounts of its pernicious consequences in public affairs? Factions, civil wars, persecutions, subversions of government, oppression, slavery; these are the dismal results of its influence over the human mind. If the religious spirit is ever mentioned in any historical narrative we are sure to meet with an account of miseries attending it. No periods of time can be happier or more prosperous than those in which it is never regarded, or heard of!

CLEANTHES The reason for this is obvious. The proper office of religion is to regulate the hearts of men and women, humanise their conduct and infuse a spirit of temperance, order and obedience. As its operation is silent, and only *enforces* the motives of morality and justice, it is in danger of being overlooked and confused with these other motives. When it distinguishes itself and acts as a *separate* principle over us, it has departed from its proper sphere and has become only a camouflage for faction and ambition.

PHILO And so will all religion, excepting the philosophical and rational kind. Your reasonings are more easily avoided than my facts. The inference is invalid that since *finite* and temporary rewards and punishments have influence, those that are *infinite* and eternal must have a greater influence. Consider, I beseech you, the attachment that we have to present things and the small concern that we entertain for objects so remote and uncertain. When divines are declaiming against common behaviour and conduct of the world, they always represent this principle as the strongest imaginable, as indeed it is. They describe almost all humankind as lying under the influence of it, sunk into the deepest lethargy and unconcern about their religious interests. Yet these *same* divines, when they refute their speculative antagonists, suppose the motives of religion to be so powerful that without them it would be impossible for civil society to subsist! They are not ashamed of so palpable a contradiction.

From experience, it is certain that the smallest grain of natural honesty and benevolence has more effect on people's conduct than the most pompous views suggested by theological theories and systems. *Natural* inclination works incessantly upon us. Constantly present in the mind, it mingles with every view and consideration, whereas *religious* motives, where they act at all, operate only by starts and bounds. It is thus scarcely possible for them to become habitual. The force of gravity, say physicists, is infinitely small in comparison with that of the least impulse.[1] However, it is certain that the smallest force of gravity will ultimately prevail above a great impulse since no strokes or blows can be repeated with such *constancy* as gravitational attraction.

Another advantage of inclination is that it engages on its side all the wit and ingenuity of the mind. When placed in opposition to religious principles, it seeks every method and art of eluding them. In this it is almost always successful. Who can explain the human heart, or account for those strange salves and excuses with which people justify themselves when they follow inclinations in opposition to their religious duty? This is well understood in the world and only fools ever repose less trust in someone because they hear that, through study and philosophy, they have entertained speculative doubts in theological subjects. And when we have to do with a person who makes a great profession of religion and devotion, has this not the effect of putting the prudent on their guard, lest they be cheated and deceived?

We must further consider that philosophers who cultivate reason and reflection, stand less in need of religious motives to keep them under the restraint of morals. In contrast, the common people, who alone may need religious motives, are utterly incapable of a religion so pure as to represent the Deity as being pleased *only* with virtue in human behaviour. Their recommendations to the Divinity are generally either frivolous observances, rapturous ecstasies, or a bigoted credulity. We need not go back into antiquity, or wander into remote regions, to find instances of this degeneracy. Amongst ourselves, some have been guilty of that atrociousness, unknown

---

1 Impulse here taken to be dynamic force. Gravity is indeed an extremely weak force; the gravitational pull of the *entire* Earth cannot prevent an athlete leaping two metres above it.

to the Egyptian and Greek superstitions, of declaiming in express terms against morality and representing it as a sure forfeiture of the Divine favour if the least trust or reliance is laid upon it.

But even though superstition or enthusiasm should not put itself in *direct* opposition to morality, the very diverting of the attention, the raising up of new and frivolous species of merit, the preposterous distribution of praise and blame, must have the following pernicious consequences. It must greatly weaken humanity's attachment to the natural motives of justice and humanity....

Likewise, such a principle of action being none of the familiar motives of human conduct, acts only at intervals on the temper. Thus it must be roused by continual efforts in order to render pious zealots satisfied with their own conduct and make them fulfil their devotional task. Many religious exercises are entered into with seeming fervour, while the heart feels cold and languid. In consequence, a habit of dissimulation is by degrees contracted; fraud and falsehood become the predominant principle. Hence comes the common observation that the highest zeal in religion *and* the deepest hypocrisy, rather than being mutually inconsistent, are commonly found united in the same individual character.

The bad effects of such habits, even in common life, are easily imagined. But where the interests of *religion* are concerned, no morality can be strong enough to restrain the enthusiastic zealot. The sacredness of the cause sanctifies every measure that can be utilised to promote it. Steady attention to so important an interest as eternal salvation tends to extinguish the benevolent affections and beget a narrow, contracted selfishness. And when such an attitude is encouraged, it easily escapes from all general precepts of charity and benevolence. Thus, the motives of vulgar superstition have no great influence on human conduct generally; nor are their operations favourable to morality in the circumstances where they predominate.

Is there any maxim in politics more certain and infallible, than that both the number and the authority of priests should be confined within very narrow limits; and that the civil Magistrate ought invariably to keep fasces and axes[1] out of such dangerous will hands? But if the spirit of popular religion is so *salutary* to society, a contrary maxim ought to prevail. The greater number of priests and their greater authority and riches will always augment

---

1 The fasces (rods) and axes, bound together, symbolised the civil authority and power of the Consuls in Republican Rome. The term fascism derives from the fasces.

the religious spirit. And though the priests have the guidance of this spirit, why may we not expect a superior sanctity of life, greater benevolence and moderation from persons who are set apart from religion but are continually inculcating it upon others and imbibing a greater share of it? How comes it, then, that the best that a wise Magistrate can propose regarding popular religions is, as far as possible, to conduct a holding operation, thus preventing its pernicious consequences for society? Every expedient that tried for so humble a purpose is surrounded with inconveniences. If only one religion is admitted among the subjects, there must be a sacrifice – and to an uncertain prospect of tranquillity–of every consideration of public liberty, science, reason, industry, and even the magistrate's independence. If several sects are indulged (the wiser maxim) there must be preserved a highly philosophical indifference to all of them and a careful restraint of the pretensions of the prevailing sect. Otherwise there can be expected nothing but endless disputes, factions, persecutions and civil commotion.

True religion, I accept, has no such pernicious consequences but we must deal with religion as it is commonly *found* in the world. I have nothing to do with the speculative tenet of theism that, being a species of philosophy, enjoys philosophy's beneficial influence, while lying under the philosophical inconvenience of being always confined to very few persons.

Oaths are requisite in all courts of justice, but does their authority arise from any popular *religion*? It is the solemnity and importance of the occasion, the regard to reputation and the reflection upon the general interests of society that are humankind's chief restraints. Custom-house oaths and political oaths are little regarded even by some who ascribe to principles of honesty and religion; and with us a Quaker's asseveration[1] is correctly put upon the same footing as the oath of any other person. I know that Polybius[2] ascribes the infamy of Greek faith to the prevalence of Epicurean philosophy, but I know also that Carthaginian faith had just as bad a reputation in ancient times. This is not to mention that Greek faith was infamous even

---

1 An 'asseveration' is a solemn affirmation to speak the truth, citing one's own conscience as a witness. It thus contrasts with the traditional oath citing God, both as witness of veracity and avenger of perjury. Quakers follow James 5.12, 'Let your yea be yea, and your nay be nay' and undertake to speak truth at all times. Swearing on the Bible to do so *in court* would thus imply a double standard. Since 1695, Quaker witnesses have been permitted to asseverate.

2 Polybius, *Histories*, 6.56. Here, he implies that the Epicurean denial of the Gods' ability to punish in Hades removes this potential sanction, leading to criminality. Polybius (*c.*200–*c.*118 BCE) was a Greek historian of the Roman Republic.

before the rise of Epicurean philosophy. Euripides, in a passage I shall point out to you, has delivered a remarkable stroke of satire against his nation with regard to this.[1]

CLEANTHES Take care Philo, take *care*! Push not matters too far. Do not allow your zeal against false religion to undermine your veneration for the *true* sort. Do not surrender this principle. It is the chief, the only great comfort in life – and our principal support' amid the attacks of adverse fortune. Genuine theism is the most agreeable reflection that it is possible for human imagination to suggest. It represents us as the workmanship of a Being perfectly good, wise and powerful, who created us for happiness. Also, having implanted in us immeasurable desires of good, the Being will prolong our existence for all eternity, placing us into an infinite variety of situations in order to satisfy those desires and render our happiness complete and durable. Next to such a Being itself, if the comparison is permitted, the happiest lot imaginable is that of being under its guardianship and protection.

PHILO These appearances are most engaging, most alluring. For the true philosopher, they are more than appearances. But it happens here, as in the former case, that with regard to the greater part of humankind, the appearances are deceitful; the *terrors* of religion commonly prevail above its comforts. It is agreed that we never have recourse to devotion so readily as when dejected with grief or depressed with sickness. Is this not evidence that the religious spirit is not nearly so allied to joy as to sorrow.

CLEANTHES But the afflicted find *consolation* in religion.

PHILO Sometimes. But it is natural to imagine that they will form a notion of unknown beings appropriate to their present gloom and melancholy when they start to contemplate them. Accordingly, we find fearsome images predominate in all religions. We ourselves, having employed the most exalted expressions to describe the Deity, fall into the flattest contradiction in affirming that the damned are infinitely greater in number to the elect.

I shall venture to affirm that there never was a popular religion that represented the state of departed souls in such a light as would render it *preferable* for humankind that there should be such a state. These fine models of religion are the mere product of philosophy. For as death lies between the eye

---

1 Philo probably has in mind Euripides' *Iphigenia in Tauris* (1205) where Iphigenia says contemptuously, πιστὸν Ἑλλὰς οἶδεν οὐδέν. 'Good faith is not to be found in Greece.' Tr. John Davie.

and the prospect of futurity, the event is so shocking to Nature that it throws a gloom on what lies beyond it and suggests to the generality of humanity the idea of Cerberus,[1] Furies, Devils, torrents of fire and brimstone.[2]

It is true that both fear and hope enter into religion because at different times both passions agitate the human mind, each of them forming a species of divinity suitable to itself. When one is in a cheerful disposition, one is fit for business, company and entertainment of any kind. People naturally apply themselves to these and think not about religion. But when melancholy and dejected, people have nothing to do but brood upon the terrors of the invisible world, thus plunging still deeper into affliction.

It may indeed happen that after one has thus engraved religious opinions deeply into one's thought and imagination, a change of health or circumstances may arrive. The restoration of good humour and the raising of cheerful prospects make one run to the other extreme of joy and triumph. But it must still be acknowledged that since terror is the *primary* principle of religion, it is the passion that always predominates, admitting only short intervals of pleasure. Furthermore, these fits of excessively enthusiastic joy exhaust the spirits and invariably prepare the way for equal fits of superstitious terror and dejection.

There is there no state of mind so happy as the calm and equable. But it is impossible to support this state when one thinks that he or she lies in profound darkness and uncertainty between an eternity of happiness and an eternity of misery. No wonder that such an opinion disjoints the normal frame of mind, throwing it into the greatest confusion. And though that opinion is seldom so steady in its operation as to influence *all* actions, it is apt to induce a considerable change in attitude to that gloom and melancholy so remarkable in devout people.

It is nonsensical to entertain fears or terrors upon account of any opinion whatsoever, or to imagine that by the freest use of our reason we run any risk hereafter. Such a sentiment implies both an absurdity and an inconsistency. It is an absurdity to believe that the Deity has human passions including one of the lowest, a restless appetite for applause. It is an inconsistency *not* to believe that since the Deity has this human passion, it has others also, in particular a disregard of the opinions of creatures so much inferior.

---

1 The ferocious three-headed hellhound tasked by Pluto with preventing escape from Hades. His capture was the twelfth and final Labour of Hercules.

2 The agents deployed by God to destroy Sodom & Gomorrah. See Genesis, 19. Brimstone is an archaic term for sulphur.

'To know God,' says Seneca,[1] 'is to worship'. All other worship is indeed absurd, superstitious, even impious. It degrades the Deity to the low condition of humanity, delighted as they are with entreaty, solicitation, presents and flattery. Yet such impiety is the smallest of which superstition is guilty. Commonly it depresses the Deity far *below* the condition of humankind; a capricious demon exercising power without reason or humanity!

Were that divine Being disposed to be offended at the vices and follies of the silly mortals who are the Deity's own workmanship, it would surely fare badly with the adherents of most popular superstitions. Only a very few of human race merit favour, namely the philosophical theists who entertain, or rather endeavour to entertain, suitable notions of its divine perfections. Similarly, the only persons entitled to its compassion and indulgence would be the philosophical sceptics, a sect almost equally rare. From a natural diffidence towards their own capacity, these suspend – or endeavour to suspend – all judgement with regard to such sublime and such extraordinary subjects.

Some maintain that the whole of natural theology resolves itself into one simple, though somewhat ambiguous, at least *undefined* proposition:

> That the Cause, or Causes, of order in the Universe probably bear some remote analogy to human intelligence.

If this proposition is incapable of extension, variation, or more specific explanation; if it affords no inference that affects human life, or can be the source of any action or forbearance; and if the analogy, imperfect as it is, can be carried no further than to human intelligence and cannot be transferred with any probability to the *other* qualities of the mind; if this *really* is the case, what can the most inquisitive, contemplative, and religious person do more than give a plain, philosophical assent to the proposition, believing the arguments establishing it exceed the objections lying against it?

Some astonishment indeed will naturally arise from the greatness of the object; some melancholy from its obscurity; some contempt for human reason's inability to give a more satisfactory solution to so extraordinary and magnificent a question.

But believe me, Cleanthes, the most natural sentiment a well-disposed mind will feel on this occasion, is this: a longing desire and expectation that Heaven would be pleased to *correct* this profound ignorance by providing

---

1 Lucius Annaeus Seneca, *Epistulae morales* CE *Lucilium* (Moral letters to Lucilius), 95. 50. *Primus est deorum cultus deos credere.* 'The prime aspect of divine worship is to believe in the Gods.' Philo reduces the polytheist Seneca to montheism.

some more particular revelation to humankind on the truth of the nature, attributes and operations of the divine Object of our faith. A person, seasoned with a fair sense of the imperfections of natural reason, will fly to revealed truth with the greatest avidity. In contrast, the haughty dogmatist, persuaded that a complete system of theology can be erected by the mere help of philosophy, disdains any further aid and rejects this assistance from beyond us.

To be a philosophical sceptic is, in a person of letters, the first and most essential step towards being a sound, believing Christian; a proposition that I would willingly recommend to the attention of young Pamphilus here. I hope Cleanthes will forgive me for intruding so deeply into the education and instruction of his pupil.

Cleanthes and Philo did not pursue their conversation much further. Since but nothing, *ever*, made a greater impression on me than all the reasoning of that day, I confess that upon a serious review of the whole, I can only think that Philo's principles are more probable than those of Demea[1], but that those of Cleanthes approach still nearer to the truth.

FINIS

---

1 *cf.* the conclusion of Cicero's *De natura deorum* ('On the Nature of the Gods'), a source-work for Hume. There, however, the Epicurean Velleius judges the principles of Balbus the Stoic more probable – but those of Cotta, the Academic, to be nearer to the truth.

Of Miracles

SECTION X: An Enquiry Concerning Human Understanding

PART I

In the writings of Dr John Tillotson there is an argument against the *real presence*[1] as concise, elegant and strong as any argument imaginable against a doctrine so nonsensical as to be little worthy of serious refutation. That learned prelate states that it is generally agreed that the authority of both Scripture and Christian tradition is founded solely on *testimony*.[2] The source of this evidence is those Apostles who were eyewitnesses to the miracles by which Christ demonstrated that his mission was divine.

Our evidence, then, for the truth of the Christian religion is thus *less* than the evidence for the truth of our own human senses. The latter truth was no greater among those first converts to our religion and clearly must diminish in passing from them to their disciples. Furthermore, no one can place as much confidence in the testimony of those disciples as in the immediate object of his or her own senses. Therefore, however clearly the doctrine of the *real presence* might be set out in Scripture, to accept it would violate correct reasoning, because a weaker body of evidence can never destroy a stronger. Thus, since both Scripture and the tradition on which it is supposed to be built, carry less evidence than sense, *real presence* thus contradicts sense – and therefore is nonsense. This is of course when the matter is considered purely as *external* evidence – rather than being brought home to us by the direct actions of the Holy Spirit.[3]

---

1 Transubstantiation is the translation of the bread and wine of the Eucharist into the 'substance' ie the *actual* flesh and blood of the Christ who is now a 'real presence.'

2 John Tillotson (1630–94). Anti-Catholic theologian. Archbishop of Canterbury 1691–4. Sermon XXVI: *A Discourse against Transubstantiation*, in *Works* (1715). He denied that transubstantiation had authority in either Scripture or apostolic literature.

3 Classic Humean irony. He did not believe in *any* direct action of any such Spirit.

Nothing is so convenient as a decisive argument of this kind, silencing the arrogance of bigotry and superstition, thus freeing us from their brazen and irrelevant pleadings. I flatter myself that I have discovered an argument of a similar nature. If valid, then at least to the wise and learned, it will serve as a permanent check to all kinds of superstitious delusion and will be useful as long as this world endures. I presume that throughout that time, accounts of miracles and prodigies will continue to appear in all sacred and secular histories.

Although experience is our *only* guide in reasoning over matters of fact, it must be acknowledged that this guide is not infallible and in some cases may lead us into error. For example, in our climate anyone who expects better weather in a week of June than in one of December is reasoning correctly and in line with experience, although occasionally they are bound to find themselves mistaken. They would, however, then have no cause to complain about experience, since that very experience commonly forewarns us of the uncertainty. This it does through the occurrence of contrary outcomes. We learn about these through diligent observation, for effects do *not* follow with identical certainty from their supposed causes.

Some outcomes are indeed found to be constantly conjoined to their causes in all countries and throughout all ages. Others, however, are found to be more variable and are sometimes the opposite of our expectations. Thus, in our reasoning concerning matters of fact, there are all imaginable *degrees* of assurance from the highest certainty to the lowest.[1]

The wise, therefore, *proportion* belief to the evidence.

In those conclusions founded on an infallible experience they expect the outcome with the highest degree of assurance; their past experience being regarded as proof of the outcome. In other cases, they proceed with more caution. They weigh the experiences of the opposite outcome and consider which side is supported by the greater number. They begin to incline to the latter side, though with proper sceptical caution, so that when eventually fixing judgement, the evidence for it will not exceed what we properly call *probability*.

---

1 This appeal to degrees of probability rather than perfect certainty is characteristic of Academic scepticism, a movement with which Hume associates his own work (eg *Enquiry concerning Human Understanding*, Section XII).

All probability, then, supposes a variety of experiential and observational results in which one side has been found to outweigh the other; the former's superiority being proportional to the preponderance of the evidence for it. A hundred experimental outcomes on one side, with fifty on the other, afford a doubtful expectation of any outcome, whereas a hundred identical outcomes with only one contradictory, beget a pretty strong degree of assurance. In all experiments having two opposite possible outcomes, we must balance the opposing results, deducting the smaller number from the greater to arrive at the precise magnitude of the superior evidence.

Let us apply these principles to the case in point – that of miracles. There is no species of reasoning more common, more useful and even necessary to human life, than that derived from human testimony and the reports of eyewitnesses and spectators. One might, perhaps, deny that this species of reasoning is founded on the relationship of cause and effect. I shall not argue over a word. It will be sufficient to observe that in any argument of this kind our assurance is solely derived from our observation of the veracity of human testimony – and from the degree to which the facts match witness reports.

It is a general maxim that no objects have any *detectable* connexion together and that all the inferences we can draw from one to another are founded merely on our experience of their constant and regular association. Clearly we ought not to make an exception to this maxim in the case of *human* testimony, whose connexion with any event seems, in itself, just as inconstant as any other. We would never repose any confidence at all in human testimony, had we not discovered by experience that human nature displays such qualities as: a memory tenacious to a certain degree; a common inclination to truth; a principle of probity; and a sensitivity to shame when detected in a falsehood. A delirious person, or one noted for falsehood and villainy, carries no authority.

Evidence derived from witnesses and human testimony is founded on past experience. It thus varies with that experience and is regarded either as a *proof* or a *probability* depending on whether the conjunction between any particular kind of report and the object of that report has been found to be constant – or variable.[1] There are a number of factors

---

1 Like demonstrable or deductively derived 'knowledge,' for Hume 'proof' in reasoning about matters of fact presents a kind of 'certainty', unlike mere 'probability' (see *Enquiry concerning Human Understanding*, Section 6, first footnote; and *A Treatise of Human Nature*, Book 1, Part 3, Section 11, paragraph 2).

to consider in all judgements of this kind, but the ultimate standard for adjudicating disputes over such judgements is always derived from experience and observation.

Where experience is *not* uniform on one side, it unavoidably leads to a degree of contrary judgement and to the same opposition and mutual cancelling-out of argument, as in every other kind of evidence. We frequently hesitate concerning the reports of others while we balance any contrary circumstances causing doubt or uncertainty.[1] When we discover evidential superiority on one side, we incline to that side – but with a diminution of assurance in proportion to the force of the contrary evidence.

In the present subject of *human* reports, inconsistency of evidence may be derived from several causes: from the opposition of contrary testimony; from the character or number of the witnesses; from the manner in which they deliver their testimony; or from a combination of all of these. We entertain a suspicion concerning any matter of fact when witnesses contradict each other; when they are but few or of a doubtful character; when they stand to gain from what they affirm; when they deliver their testimony either with hesitation or too emphatic assertion. There are many other particulars of the same kind that may diminish – or even destroy – the force of any argument derived from human testimony.

Suppose, for instance, that the fact that the testimony endeavours to establish involves the extraordinary and the marvellous.[2] In that case, the evidence undergoes a greater or lesser diminution in proportion to the degree to which the fact is more or less unusual. The reason why we place any credit in witnesses and historians is not derived from any connection we perceive, *a priori*,[3] between testimony and reality, but because we are *accustomed* to find a conformity between them.

When, however, the fact attested is one that has seldom fallen under our personal observation, here is a contest! It is a contest between two opposite experiences, one of which destroys the other as far as that other's force

---

1 Among the central strategies of Pyrrhonian sceptics was the ability of placing argument and evidence in opposition so as to 'balance' or cancel each other out (equipollence or *isosthenia*), producing thereby suspension of judgement or doubt (*epochē*). See Sextus Empiricus, *Outlines of Pyrrhonism*, Book 1, Chapters 3–5 (PH 1.3–5, 7–12).

2 These are increasing degrees of divergence from the expected course of events, but not yet amounting to the miraculous – in which the divergence is maximal.

3 *A priori*: by the exercise of pure reason, unalloyed with sensory perception. Knowing a truth *a priori* does not thus require empirical or experimental testing or confirmation.

goes, with the superior, or survivor, only operating on the mind through the *surviving* degree of its force. In this case, that very same principle of experience giving us a certain degree of assurance in the testimony of witnesses, also gives us a degree of assurance *against* the fact they are endeavouring to establish. From this contradiction there necessarily arises a counterpoise – a mutual destruction of belief and authority.

'I should not believe such a story, were it told me by Cato' was a proverbial saying in Rome, even during the lifetime of that philosophical patriot.[1] The sheer incredibility of a fact, it was admitted, would invalidate the word of even so great an authority.

The Indian prince reasoned justly when he refused to believe reports of frost.[2] It naturally required very strong testimony to obtain his acceptance of facts arising from a state of nature with which he was unacquainted; one bearing so little analogy to events within his constant and uniform experience. Though they were not *contrary* to his experience, they simply did not *conform* to it.

It is evident that no Indian could have experience that water did *not* freeze in cold climates. This is placing nature in a situation unknown to them; and it is impossible for them to tell *a priori* what will result from it. It is a new experiment, the consequence of which is always uncertain. One may sometimes conjecture from analogy what will follow; but this is still only conjecture. And it must be confessed that in the present case of freezing, the event follows contrary to the rules of analogy, and is such as a rational Indian would not look for. The operations of cold upon water are not gradual; whenever it comes to the freezing point, the water passes in a moment from the complete liquidity to perfect hardness.

Such an event, therefore, may be denominated *extraordinary* and requires a pretty strong testimony to render it credible to people in a warm climate. It is, however, still not *miraculous,* nor contrary to uniform experience of the course of nature in cases where all the circumstances are the same. The inhabitants of Sumatra have always seen water as fluid in their own climate

---

1 M. Porcius Cato (234–149 BCE) Roman Republican statesman and moralist, surnamed the Censor. Quoted in Plutarch's *Vita catonis maioris* (Life of Cato the Elder, XIX.4)

2 Borrowed by Hume from the Introduction to: *Analogy of Religion* (1736) by Joseph Butler. It first appeared in John Locke's *Essay on Human Understanding,* 4.15.

and the freezing of their rivers ought to be deemed a *prodigy*. They, however, never saw water in Muscovy[1] during the winter; and therefore cannot reasonably be positive on what would be the consequence there.

In order to increase the probability *against* the testimony of witnesses, let us suppose that the fact they affirm is truly miraculous, instead of being only marvellous. Let us further suppose that their testimony considered separately and of itself, amounts to an entire proof. In such a contest of proof against proof, the strongest must prevail but, again, with its force diminished in proportion to that of its antagonist.

A miracle is a violation of the laws of Nature.

Since a firm and unalterable experience has established these laws, the proof against a miracle is, from the very nature of the event, as total as any conceivable argument from experience. Why is it more than probable that we all must die; that lead cannot remain suspended in the air unaided; that fire consumes wood and is extinguished by water? It is because these events conform to the laws of Nature and a violation of these laws, ie a miracle, is required to prevent them. Nothing may be classed as a miracle if it occurs, *ever*, in the common course of Nature. It is no miracle that someone, seemingly in good health, should suddenly die because such a death, though unusual, has nevertheless been frequently observed.

It *is* a miracle, however, should a dead person come back to life, because such an event has never been observed in any age or country. There must, therefore, be a *uniform* experience against every miraculous event, since otherwise the event would not merit the very title of miracle. And since a uniform experience amounts to a proof, here from the very nature of the fact, is a direct and full proof against the existence of any miracle. Such a proof can only be destroyed – and the miracle thus rendered credible – through the existence of an opposite and *superior* proof.

Sometimes an event may not in itself *seem* to be contrary to the laws of Nature and yet, if real, it might by reason of some circumstances be termed a miracle because in fact it *is* contrary to these laws. Suppose a person, claiming divine authority, should command a sick person to be well; a healthy person to fall down dead; the clouds to pour rain or the wind to blow: in short, order many natural events that immediately follow the command. These might justly be esteemed miracles because in this case they really are contrary to the laws of Nature. If any suspicion remains that the event and command

1 Strictly the Moscow region; however, in Hume's day it stood for all the Russias.

concurred by *accident*, there is no miracle and no transgression of the laws of Nature. If this suspicion be removed, there evidently *is* a miracle. There is a transgression of these laws since nothing is more contrary to Nature than that a human voice, or command, should exercise such influence.

A miracle may be accurately defined as:

> A transgression of a Law of Nature by a particular volition of the Deity, or by the interposition of some invisible Agent.

A miracle may either be discoverable, or not. This does not alter its nature and essence. The raising of a house or ship into the air is a visible miracle. The raising of a feather when the wind lacks ever so little of the force required for that purpose is as real a miracle, though not so sensible with regard to us. The plain consequence is – and it is a general maxim worthy of our attention:

> That *no* testimony is sufficient to establish a miracle, unless the testimony be of such a kind, that its *falsehood* would be *more* miraculous than the fact it endeavours to establish.

> Even in such a case there exists a mutual destruction of arguments, with the superior only giving us an assurance proportional to that degree of force remaining after deducting the inferior.

When anyone tells me that they saw a corpse restored to life, I immediately ask myself if it is *more* probable that this person should either be actively deceiving me (or have *themselves* been deceived), or that the occurrence described could have really happened?

I weigh the one miracle against the other and, having ascertained where the superiority of evidence lies, I pronounce my decision, invariably rejecting the *greater* miracle. Only if the *falsehood* of my informant's testimony would be *more* miraculous than the event related then, and not till then, can they hope to command my belief or opinion.

PART II

In the foregoing reasoning we have supposed that the testimony upon which a miracle is founded may, just possibly, amount to proof – and that the falsehood of that testimony would *itself* be the genuine prodigy.[1] However, it is

---

1 An extraordinary event. From Lat. *Prodigium*, a remarkable thing.
  Often regarded by the ancients as an omen or portent.

easy to demonstrate that we have been far too liberal in these concessions and that a miraculous event has never been established – even on such full evidence.

Firstly, in all recorded history there is no miracle attested by the following:

A sufficient number of persons of such unquestioned good sense, education and learning, as to secure us against their mass delusion.

Persons of such undoubted integrity as to place them beyond all suspicion of any intention to deceive.

Persons of such credit and reputation as to have a great deal to lose if detected in falsehood.

Persons attesting acts performed so publicly and in so well known a part of the world, as to render detection unavoidable.

All the foregoing circumstances are requisite to give us full confidence in the testimony.

Secondly, there is a principle in human nature that, if carefully examined, severely diminishes the confidence we might have in the truth of any prodigy presented by human testimony. The maxim by which we commonly conduct our reasoning is this: that those objects of which we have *no* experience, resemble those of which we do – and an experience we have found to be most usual is always most probable. In a clash of arguments, we ought to give our preference to those founded on the greatest number of past observations. Although in following this rule we readily reject any fact that is unusual and incredible to an *ordinary* degree, yet in advancing farther, the rule is not always observed by the mind.

When anything is affirmed that is utterly absurd and miraculous, the mind is actually *more* ready to accept such a fact – and this is due to those very circumstances that ought to destroy its entire authority.

The sensations of surprise and wonder arising from miracles are agreeable emotions and give a perceptible tendency towards belief in the events from which they derive. This extends even to those who cannot enjoy this pleasure directly from the miracle and even to those who cannot believe reports of the miraculous event. They, however, love to partake of the satisfaction at second-hand, or vicariously, taking pride and delight in exciting the admiration of others.

With what greediness are the miraculous accounts of travellers received! Their descriptions of sea and land monsters; their reports of wonderful adventures, of strange people and uncouth manners. But if the spirit of *religion* joins the love of wonder, that spells the end of common sense. In these circumstances, human testimony loses all pretensions to authority. A religionist may be a fanatic,[1] imagining that they actually see what has no actual reality. They may know their narrative to be false yet, with the best intentions in the world, they persevere with it for the sake of promoting so holy a cause. Even where this delusion is absent, vanity and self-interest, excited by such a strong temptation, operate with equal force. They also operate more powerfully on the fanatic than on the rest of humanity in *any* other circumstance. Auditors may not have, indeed commonly *do* not have, sufficient judgement to examine the fanatic's evidence critically. What judgement they do have they renounce on principle when faced with subjects so sublime and mysterious. Even were they willing to retain and employ their judgement, the regularity of its operations would be disturbed by passion and a heated imagination. Their credulity increases the impudence of the advocate of the miracle, which impudence in turn, overpowers their judgement.

Eloquence at its highest pitch leaves little room for reason or reflection. By addressing itself entirely to the imagination or the emotions, it captivates willing hearers and subdues their understanding. Happily, this pitch is seldom attained. Whatever influence a Cicero[2] or a Demosthenes[3] could scarcely exert over a Roman or Athenian audience, every Capuchin[4] or an itinerant or stationary teacher can exert to a higher degree over the generality of humanity by engaging such gross and elemental passions.

There is a strong human propensity to believe the extraordinary and the marvellous. This is proved by the many instances of forged miracles, prophecies and supernatural events. In all ages these have been detected either by contradictory evidence, or have revealed themselves by their absurdity. Logically, such forgeries ought to beget suspicion over *all* reports of this kind, for a degree of suspicion is our natural way of thinking, even with the commonest and most credible events.

For instance, there is no kind of report that arises so easily and spreads so quickly as those concerning marriages, especially in country places and provincial towns. Two young persons of equal similar background cannot

---

1 *Struck with* [exclusively] *religious frenzy.* SJ
2 M. Tullius Cicero (106–43 BCE). Roman republican statesman, orator and writer.
3 Demosthenes (384–322 BCE). Greatest of the Athenian orators.
4 Capuchin: Member of the Order of the Friars Minor Capuchin. Founded in 1520, they were sensationalist preachers among the poor. From It. *Capuccio*, a hood.

see each other twice without the neighbourhood immediately joining them together. With so interesting a piece of news, the intelligence is spread by the pleasure of the telling of it, from the propagating of it, and of being the first reporters of it. This is so well known that no-one of sense gives credence to such reports until confirmed by firmer evidence. Is it not these same passions – and others still stronger – that incline the generality of humankind to believe in and report all *religious* miracles with the greatest vehemence and assurance?

Thirdly, a strong presumption against all the truth of miraculous reports is that they are chiefly observed among ignorant and barbarous nations. If a civilized people has given credence to any of them, that people will be found to have received them from ignorant and barbarous ancestors who handed them down with the inviolable endorsement and authority attending received[1] opinions. When we peruse the earliest histories of all nations we are apt to imagine ourselves transported into some new world. Here the whole construction of Nature is disjointed, every element performing in a different manner from that observed today. Battles, revolutions, pestilence, famine and death are never the result of the natural causes we experience now. Prodigies, omens, oracles and judgements completely obscure the few natural events intermingled with them. The former grow thinner with every page as we advance towards the enlightened ages and we soon learn that there is nothing mysterious or supernatural about them. Everything flows from the constant human susceptibility for the marvellous[2] and, although this inclination may at intervals receive checks from sense and learning, it can never be thoroughly extirpated from human nature.

'It is strange,' the judicious reader is apt to say upon the perusal of these wonderful historians, 'that such prodigious events never happen in *our* days.'

However, I hope it is not thought strange that people should lie in all ages. You must surely have seen instances enough of that frailty. You must have yourself heard many such marvellous reports that are treated with scorn by the wise and judicious and have finally been abandoned even by the commonality. Be assured that those famous lies that have spread and flourished to such a monstrous height arose from identical beginnings. However, having been sown in a more fertile soil, they eventually shot up into prodigies almost equal to those to which they relate.

---

1 *Generally accepted and agreed.* SJ
2 *Strange; Astonishing.* SJ

It was a wise policy for that false prophet Alexander,[1] once so famous but now forgotten, to begin his swindle in Paphlagonia. There, Lucian tells us, the people were extremely ignorant, stupid and ready to swallow even the grossest delusion.[2] People at a distance who are gullible enough to think the matter at all worth enquiry, have no opportunity of receiving better information. The stories come to them magnified by a hundred circumstances. Those duped are industrious in propagating the pretence, while the wise and educated are generally content simply to deride its absurdity without establishing the particular facts necessary for a specific refutation.

Thus the impostor Alexander was enabled to proceed from his ignorant Paphlagonians to enlist adherents even among Greek philosophers and also men of the most eminent rank and distinction in Rome. Indeed he so far engaged the attention of that sage emperor Marcus Aurelius[3] as to make him entrust the success of a military expedition to his deceptive prophecies.[4]

The advantages of starting an imposture among an ignorant people are great. Even though the delusion is too gross for the generality of them (sometimes the case, though seldom) it has a much better chance of succeeding in remote areas than if first appearing in a city renowned for arts and knowledge. The most ignorant and unsophisticated of barbarians carry the report abroad while none of their countrymen have a wide enough correspondence, sufficient credit or authority, to contradict and beat down the delusion. Human partiality for the marvellous now has full opportunity to display itself. Thus a story, universally exploded in its place of origin, goes on to pass for absolute certainty at a thousand miles distance. Had Alexander fixed his residence at Athens, the philosophers of that renowned mart of learning would have immediately broadcast their opinions of the matter

---

1 Alexander of Abonoteichus, in Paphlagonia, part of modern Turkey. fl. 150–170 CE. A notorious charlatan and fraudster, he dealt in 'prophecy.'

2 Lucian of Samostata (c.125–post 180 CE) Syrian rhetorician, essayist and satirist much admired by Hume. He nailed Alexander as a fraud in his *Alexander, Oracle – monger & false Prophet*.

3 Marcus Aurelius (121–180 CE). Roman Emperor from 161– 80 CE and Stoic philosopher. Author of *Meditations* (Τα εἰς ἑαυτόν) lit. 'Thoughts to himself.'

4 The expedition was during the war with the Marcomanni (c.160 CE). Alexander declared that victory required the throwing of two live lions into the Danube. This was done. The campaign was a disaster for Rome. Alexander's trembling excuse was that of the Delphic oracle to King Croesus of Lydia after his failed invasion of Persia; ie that he had not specified *which* side would be victorious.

throughout the whole Roman Empire. Their criticism, supported by great authority and displayed with all the force of reason and eloquence, would have fully opened eyes. It is true that Lucian, passing by chance through Paphlagonia, had the opportunity to perform this good office. However, much as it may be wished, it does not always happen that every Alexander runs into a Lucian ready to detect and expose his deceits.

I may add a *fourth* reason diminishing the authority of prodigies. There is no testimony for any of them that is not *opposed* by an infinite number of witnesses. Not only does a miracle destroy the credit of testimony, the testimony also destroys itself. To illustrate this, let us reflect that in matters of religion whatever is different is actually *contrary*. It is hence impossible for the religions of ancient Rome, of Turkey, of Siam, and of China to be established on any solid foundation. Every miracle claimed to have been wrought in any of these religion – and all of them *abound* in miracles – seeks, as its direct purpose, to establish its own particular system of faith. It thus has the same force, though more indirectly, to overthrow every *other* system. In destroying a rival system it likewise destroys the credit of those miracles upon which that system was established. Consequently, all the prodigies of different religions are to be regarded as refutations, with the *evidences* for these prodigies, whether weak or strong, being regarded as mutually destructive.

According to this method of reasoning, when we believe any miracle of Mahomet or his successors, we have for our authorisation merely the testimony of a few Arabians. On the other hand, are we to respect the authority of Titus Livius[1], Plutarch[2], Tacitus[3], in short all the authors and witnesses, be they Grecian, Chinese or Roman Catholic, who have related any miracle in their own particular religion? I say that we are to regard their testimony in just the same light as if they had mentioned that Mahommedan miracle and had, in express terms, contradicted it with the same certainty of the miracle they themselves report. This argument may appear over-subtle and refined. However, in reality it is no different from the reasoning of a judge who finds that the credibility of two witnesses accusing a third of a crime, is destroyed by the testimony of two others affirming that, at the relevant time, the accused was two hundred leagues distant.

---

1 T. Livius – anglicised to Livy. (59 BCE–17 CE) Roman historian. Author of *Ab urbe condita* – 'From the foundation of the City' (of Rome)
2 Plutarch (AD *c.*46–*c.*120). Greek biographer, historian and moral philosopher.
3 C. Cornelius Tacitus. Historian of the early Roman Empire. Son-in-law of Cn. Julius Agricola, victor over the *Caledonii* at 'Mons Graupius' somewhere in north-east Scotland.

One of the best attested miracles in all secular history is that which Tacitus reports of the Emperor Vespasian[1] who cured a blind man in Alexandria by means of his spittle – and a lame man by the mere touch of his foot. These two men were obedient to the god Serapis,[2] who had enjoined them, in a vision, to resort to the Emperor for these miraculous cures. The story may be seen in the *Historia* of that fine historian Tacitus, where every circumstance seems to add weight to the testimony.[3] It might be displayed at large with all the force of argument and eloquence, were anyone now bothered to advocate that exploded and idolatrous superstition.

The Emperor Vespasian was a man of gravity, solidity, age, probity and true greatness. Through the whole course of his life he conversed in a familiar manner with his friends and courtiers and never affected those extraordinary airs of divinity assumed by Alexander the Great and Demetrius.[4]

Tacitus, a contemporary writer noted for candour and veracity, was perhaps the greatest and most penetrating genius of all antiquity. So free was he from credulity that he actually lies under suspicion of atheism and profaneness. We may confidently presume that the persons on whose authority he related the miracle were of established character for judgement and veracity since they were eye-witnesses of the fact. They also reconfirmed their testimony even after the Flavian family had been stripped of Imperial power and could no longer give any reward as the price of a lie:

> *Utrumque, qui interfuere, nunc quoque memorant,*
> *postquam nullum mendacio pretium.*[5]

To all of which, if we add the public nature of the events reported, it would appear that no stronger evidence could be *imagined* for so gross and so palpable a falsehood.

---

1 T. Flavius Vespasianus (AD 9–79). Emperor 69–79 CE. He had commanded *Legio* II *Augusta* in Britannia during the Claudian invasion of 43 CE.
2 Serapis: Egyptian god. His cult, centred on the *Serapaeum* of Alexandria, was syncretic, ie it sought to unite Greek and Egyptian religious practices.
3 Tacitus, *Historia*: IV.81
4 Alexander proclaimed himself the son of Zeus.
  Demetrius I, King of Macedon (336–283 BCE). Known as Πολιορκητής (Poliorcetes), the Besieger. He was worshipped as a tutelary divinity titled Σωτήρ (Soter) the Preserver.
5 'Both of those still living who were present, still relate the event – even after the disappearance of any possible reward for mendacity.' Tr: DWP

There is also a memorable story related by Cardinal de Retz that may well deserve our consideration.[1] When that intriguing politician fled into Spain [c.1654] to avoid the persecution of his enemies, he passed through Saragossa, the capital of Aragon. In the Cathedral there he was shown a man who had served seven years as a door-keeper and was well known to everybody in town that had ever worshipped in that church. For a long time he had been noted to be lacking a leg, but recovered that limb by the rubbing of holy oil upon the stump. The Cardinal assures us that he saw him with two legs.

This miracle was vouched by all the Canons of the church and the whole population of the town was appealed to for confirmation of the fact. By their zealous devotion the Cardinal found them to be thorough believers in the miracle. Here the relater, de Retz, was also contemporary with the supposed prodigy and was of a sceptical and scandalously freethinking character, as well as of great genius. The miracle was of so *singular* a nature as to scarcely permit a counterfeit while the witnesses were numerous – all of them being, in a manner, spectators of the fact to which they gave their testimony.

On this occasion, what adds mightily to the force of the evidence and may double our surprise, is that the Cardinal himself who relates the story seems not to give any credit to it. Consequently he cannot be suspected of any connivance in the holy fraud. He considered, reasonably, that in order to reject a fact of this nature it was not required to be able to accurately disprove the testimony. Nor was it necessary to track its falsehood through all the circumstances of knavery and credulity that had produced it. He knew that since this was usually impossible even at a *short* distance of time and place, it remained extremely difficult even where one had been actually present, due to the bigotry, ignorance, cunning and roguery of a great part of humanity. Like a rational judge, therefore, he concluded that such a body of evidence carried falsehood upon its very *face* and that a miracle supported by any human testimony was more properly a subject for derision than for argument.

Never, surely, were more miracles ascribed to one person than those recently said to have been wrought in France. These occurred upon the tomb of Abbé François de Pâris, the famous Jansenist,[2] regarding whose

---

1 De Retz, J. *Œuvres complètes du Cardinal de Retz*, Vol. IV (Paris, 1887)
2 Followers of Cornelius Otto Jansen (1585–1638) His theology emphasised original sin and predestination, but also an element of free will. The latter was seen as an attack on the Jesuits and on Papal power. Jansenism's central tenets would be condemned as heretical by Innocent X in 1653 and the sect was outlawed in 1730.

sanctity the people were so long deluded. The curing of the sick, the restoration of hearing to the deaf and sight to the blind were everywhere talked
of as the customary effects of that holy sepulchre.[1] But what is even more
extraordinary, many of the miracles were immediately confirmed upon the
spot and in the presence of judges of unquestioned integrity. They were
further attested by witnesses of credit and distinction in a learned age –
and in the world's most eminent Metropolis. Nor were the Jesuits ever able
distinctly to refute or detect them, despite being a learned body supported
by the civil magistrate and determined enemies of the Jansenists in whose
favour these miracles were allegedly performed.

Nor is this all, for an account of them was published and dispersed
everywhere. This book was written by Mons. Montgeron a counsellor or
judge of the *parlement* of Paris, a man of figure and character who was also
a martyr to the cause – and is now [1748] said to be in a dungeon somewhere on account of his book.[2]

There is another book in three volumes giving an account of many of
these miracles and accompanied by very well written prefatory discourses.[3]
Running through the whole of these, however, is a ridiculous comparison
between the miracles of our Saviour and those of the Abbé. It is asserted
that the evidence for the latter is equal to that for the former: as if human
testimony could ever be put in the balance with that of God himself, who
directed the pen of the inspired writers. Indeed, if these writers were to be
considered merely as human testimony, the French author is very moderate
in his comparison since he might, with some appearance of reason, claim
that the Jansenist miracles much surpass the other in evidence and authority. The following circumstances are drawn from authentic papers, inserted
in the above-mentioned book.

---

1 Cemetery of St Médard, 12th Arrondissement, near the Jardin des Plantes.
2 Louis Basile Carré de Montgeron (1686–1754). He published *La verité des miracles operés
   par l'intercession de M. de Paris* (1739) – and was promptly arrested. Hume was right; the
   'dungeon' was that of the Bastille whither de Montgeron had been consigned by *Lettre de
   cachet*. He never regained his freedom.
3 *Recueil des Miracles de l'Abbé Pâris*. (1731). An anonymous compendium of evidence
   supporting 'miracles' resulting, allegedly, from touching the Abbé's tomb.

Many of the miracles of Abbé Pâris were attested immediately by witnesses before the Officiality, or Bishop's court, at Paris under the eye of Cardinal Noailles,[1] whose character for integrity and intellect was never contested even by his enemies.

His successor in the archbishopric[2] was an enemy to the Jansenists and, for that reason, promoted to the See by the court. Yet twenty-two rectors or *curés* of Paris pressed him with infinite earnestness to examine those miracles they asserted to be known to the whole world and to be indisputably certain: But he wisely forbore.

The Molinist party had tried to discredit these miracles in one instance, that of Mlle le Franc.[3] Their proceedings were not only most irregular in many respects, particularly in citing only a few of the Jansenist witnesses (with whom they tampered); but also, I say, they soon found themselves overwhelmed by a cloud of new witnesses. These were one hundred and twenty in number, most of them persons of credit and substance in Paris, who gave oath for the miracle. This was accompanied with a solemn and earnest appeal to the *parlement* which was, however, forbidden by authority to meddle in the affair.

It was at last observed that where people are heated by zeal and enthusiasm,[4] there is no degree of human testimony so strong as may not be procured by them for the greatest absurdity. Those who will be silly enough as to examine the affair by that medium and seek particular flaws in testimony, are almost sure to be confounded. It would be a miserable imposture indeed that did not prevail in that contest.

All who have been in France about that time[5] have heard of the reputation of Mons. Heraut, the *Lieutenant de Police,* whose vigilance, penetration, activity and extensive intelligence have been much talked of. This magistrate, who by the nature of his office is almost absolute, was vested with

---

1 Louis Antoine de Noailles (1651–1729). Archbishop of Paris, defended Jansenists against the French government and the Papacy. Clement XI's Bull *Unigenitus* (1713) condemned Jansenism.

2 Charles-Gaspard-Guillaume de Vintimille du Luc (1655–1746)

3 In 1730, Mlle Anne Le Franc was said to have been cured of blindness and paralysis by touching the tomb of Abbé Pâris at St Médard.

4 'Enthusiasm', suggesting excessive emotion, is an important critical term in Hume and is not far in contemporary usage from what may be termed 'fanaticism' or 'zealotry.'

5 This included Hume himself who arrived to study in France in 1734.

full powers for the purpose of suppressing or discrediting these miracles. He frequently seized the witnesses immediately and examined the subjects of them: yet never could he satisfactorily determine anything against them.

In the case of Mademoiselle Thibaut,[1] he sent the famous Dr De Sylva to examine her and his evidence is very odd. The physician declares that it was impossible she could have been so ill, as was attested by witnesses. This was because it was impossible that, in so short a time, she could have recovered as perfectly as he found her. Like a person of sense, he reasoned that it was due to natural causes. The opposite party, however, told him that the whole *was* a miracle and that *his* evidence was the best proof of it.

The Molinists were in a sad dilemma. They dared not assert the absolute insufficiency of human evidence, to prove a miracle. They were obliged to say, that these miracles were wrought by witchcraft and the devil. But they were told that this was the tactic used by the Jews of old.

No Jansenist was embarrassed to account for the cessation of the miracles when the churchyard was shut up by the King's edict. It was the *touching* of the tomb, that produced these extraordinary effects; and so when no one could approach it, no effects could be expected. God, indeed, could have thrown down the walls in a moment; but it is master of its own abilities and works and it not in our power to account for them. God did not throw down the walls of *every* city, like those of Jericho on the sounding of the rams horns, nor break up the prison of every apostle, like that of St Paul.

No less a man than the Duc de Chatillon, a duke and peer of France and of the highest rank and family, gives evidence of a miraculous cure performed upon a servant of his, who had lived several years in his house with a visible and palpable infirmity.

I shall conclude by observing that no clergy are more celebrated for strictness of life and manners than the secular clergy of France, particularly the Rectors or *Curés* of Paris, who bear testimony to these impostures. The learning, genius, and probity of these gentlemen and the austerity of the nuns of Port-Royal[2] have been much celebrated all over Europe. Yet they all give evidence for a miracle wrought on the niece of the famous Pascal whose sanctity of life, as well as extraordinary intellect, is well known.

---

1 In 1731, an elderly stroke victim, Mlle Marguerite Thibaut, was allegedly cured of her paralysis and dermatological conditions by the Abbé's tomb.
2 A famous Jansenist monastery close to Paris.

Racine gives an account of this miracle in his famous history of Port-Royal,[1] fortifying it with all the proofs that a multitude of nuns, priests, physicians and worldly persons, all of them of undoubted credit, could bestow upon it. Several *literati*, particularly the Bishop of Tournay, thought this miracle so certain, as to employ it in the refutation of atheists and freethinkers. The Queen-Regent of France[2] who was extremely prejudiced against the Port-Royal, sent her own physician to examine the miracle. He returned an absolute convert. In short, the supernatural cure was so incontestable that for a time it saved that famous monastery from the ruin threatened by the Jesuits.

Had it been a fraud, it would have certainly been detected by such sagacious and powerful antagonists and would have hastened the ruin of the contrivers. Our divines, who can build up a formidable castle from such despicable materials; what a prodigious fabric they could have reared from these and many other circumstances I have not mentioned! How often would the great names of Pascal, Racine, Arnaud, Nicole, have resounded in our ears? But if they are wise, they had better adopt the miracle as being worth a thousand times more than all the rest of the collection. Besides, it may serve very much to their purpose. For that miracle was really performed by the touch of an authentic holy prickle, of the holy thorn, that had composed the holy crown, that... *&c*

Where shall we find such a large number of circumstances agreeing to the corroboration of one fact? And what do we have to counter such a cloud of witnesses, except the *absolute* impossibility or miraculous nature of the events they relate? In the eyes of all reasonable people, surely this alone will be regarded as a sufficient refutation.

Does it follow that just because human testimony sometimes has the utmost force and authority, for instance when it relates the battles of Philippi[3] or Pharsalus,[4] that *all* kinds of testimony must, in *all* cases, have equal force and authority? Suppose that the Caesarean and Pompeian factions had both claimed the victory in these battles and that the historians of each party had each ascribed the advantage to their own side. How could humankind, at

---

1 J. Racine. *Abrégé de l'Histoire de Port-Royal* (1767)
2 Anne of Austria, daughter of Philip III of Spain; Regent to her son, Louis XV.
3 Philippi, in Macedonia. The scene in 42 BCE of the defeat of M. Brutus and C. Cassius by the Caesarean forces under Mark Antony and Octavian.
4 Pharsalus, in Thessaly, Greece. Site in 48 BCE of the decisive defeat of Pompey by Julius Caesar.

this distance, determine between them? The inconsistency is equally strong between the miracles related by Herodotus[1] or Plutarch[2] and those delivered by Mariana,[3] Bede,[4] or any other monkish historian.

The wise will take a very sceptical view of any report favouring an enthusiasm of the reporters, whether it magnifies their country, their family, themselves, or in any other way chimes with their natural inclinations and propensities. But what greater temptation is there than to appear as a missionary, a prophet, an ambassador from *heaven*? Who would not brave many dangers and difficulties, in order to attain so sublime a character? If, through vanity and a heated imagination, someone has first become a convert and entered seriously into the delusion, would they then hesitate to utilise pious frauds in support of so holy and meritorious a cause? The tiniest spark may here kindle into the greatest flame because combustible material is always ready and waiting for it. The listening populace, Lucretius' *avidum genus auricularum*,[5] hears greedily and without examination whatever confirms superstition and promotes wonder.

In all ages, how many stories of this nature have been detected and exploded in their infancy? How many more have been celebrated for a time and have afterwards sunk into neglect and oblivion? Where such reports fly about, the solution to the phenomenon is thus obvious. We are only judging in accordance with regular experience and observation when we account for a miracle by the known and natural principles of human credulity and delusion. Shall we accept a miraculous violation of the most established laws of Nature, rather than resort to a natural explanation?

I need not mention the difficulty of detecting a falsehood in any private or even public history at the place where it is said to have happened. Much more difficult is its detection when the scene is removed to a distance, be it ever so small. Even courts of law, with all the authority, accuracy and judgement they can deploy, often find themselves at a loss to distinguish between truth and falsehood in the most recent actions. But the matter never comes to any conclusion if left to the common method of altercation, debate and flying rumours, especially when human passions have been engaged on either side.

---

1 Herodotus. (*c*.490–*c*.425 BCE) Greek historian of the Persian Wars.
2 Plutarch (*c*.46–*c*.120 CE). Greek biographer, historian and moral philosopher.
3 Juan de Mariana (1536–1624). Spanish Jesuit historian and political philosopher.
4 The Venerable Bede (672–735CE) of Jarrow. Monk, theologian and historian. Author of *Historia ecclesiastica gentis anglorum* (*The Ecclesiastical History of the English People*).
5 Lucretius, *De Rerum Natura*, iv.594; *humanum genus est avidum nimis auricularum*. 'The human race is far too ready to believe what it hears.' Tr: DWP.

In the infancy of new religions, the wise and learned commonly regard the new faith as too insignificant to warrant their attention or regard. Afterwards, when they would willingly expose the fraud in order to *undeceive* the deluded multitude, the season is now past and the reports and witnesses whose testimony might clear up the matter are perished beyond recovery. No means of fraud detection now remain, save those that must be drawn from the reporters' actual testimonies themselves. These means of detection, though always sufficient for the judicious and *insightful*, are commonly too subtle to enter the comprehension of the generality of humankind.

Upon the whole, then, it appears that no testimony for *any* kind of miracle has ever amounted to a probability, much less to a proof. But even supposing it *did* amount to a proof, it would be opposed by another proof derived from the very *nature* of the fact it would endeavour to establish. It is experience and experience *only*, that gives authority to human testimony and it is that same experience that assures us of the immutable laws of Nature. Therefore, when these two kinds of experience conflict, all we can do is to subtract one from the other, the assurance furnished by the remainder allowing us to embrace an opinion on one side or the other. However, according to the principle explained above, such a subtraction amounts to an entire annihilation when applied to all popular religions. Therefore we may establish it as a maxim that *no* human testimony can have such force as to prove any miracle – and make it a sound foundation for religious Faith.

I beg that the above limitations may be noted when I assert that a miracle can never be proved sufficiently to act as the foundation of a Faith. On the other hand, I admit that there may possibly be miracles – violations of the usual course of Nature – of such a kind as actually to admit proof from human testimony. However, I suspect it will be impossible to find any such in the entire historical record.

Thus, suppose all authors and in all languages agree that beginning on the first of January 1600 there was a total darkness over the whole earth for eight days. Suppose that the tradition of this extraordinary event is still strong and lively among the people and that all travellers who return from foreign countries bring us the same traditional accounts without variation or contradiction. It is evident that our present philosophers, instead of doubting the fact, ought to receive it as certain and ought to search for causes whence it might be derived. The decay, corruption, and dissolution of Nature is an event rendered probable by so many analogies, that any phenomenon tending towards that catastrophe comes within the reach of human testimony – *provided* that such extends among numerous witnesses whose testimony is also uniform.

However, suppose that all the historians of England should agree as follows: that on the first of January 1600, Queen Elizabeth died; that both before and after her death she was seen by her physicians and the whole court, as is usual with persons of her rank; that her successor was acknowledged and proclaimed by Parliament; and that after being interred for a month she reappeared, resumed the throne, and governed England for three years. I must confess that I should be surprised at the concurrence of so many odd circumstances, but I should still have not the least inclination to believe such a miraculous event. I should not doubt her *alleged* death and of those other public circumstances that followed it. I should only assert that it had been fabricated and that it neither was, nor possibly could be, real. In vain would you raise the objection that to deceive the world in an affair of such consequence would be difficult, indeed well nigh impossible. You would cite the wisdom and solid judgement of that renowned Queen and the little or no advantage she could reap from so poor an artifice. All this might astonish me, but I would still reply that human knavery and folly are such *common* phenomena that I should rather believe the most extraordinary events to arise from their collusion, than accept so gross a violation of the laws of Nature.

However, what if this miracle were to be ascribed to a new system of *religion*? Humanity, in all ages has been so imposed on by ridiculous stories of that kind that the very claim itself would constitute proof positive of fraud. Indeed, it would be sufficient to make all people of sense reject the fact without farther examination. Though the Being to whom the miracle is ascribed in this case is almighty, upon that account the miracle does not become a whit more probable. This is because it is impossible for us to *know* the attributes or actions of such a Being, other than from our experience of its handiwork in the usual course of Nature. We are thus still reduced to past observations, obliged to compare instances of the violation of *truth* in human testimony, with those of the violation of Nature's *laws* by miracles. This we do in order to judge which of them is most likely and probable. Since violations of truth are more common in testimony regarding religious miracles than in any other matter of fact, this greatly diminishes the authority of the former testimony. It also directs us to form a general resolution never to lend any attention to such testimony, *whatever* the specious pretence with which it is cloaked.

Lord Bacon[1] seems to have embraced the same principles of reasoning:

> 'We ought,' says he, 'to make a collection or particular history of all monsters and prodigious births or productions – in a word, of everything new, rare, and extraordinary in Nature. But this must be done with the most severe scrutiny, lest we depart from truth. Above all, every relation must be considered as suspicious if it depends in any degree upon religion, as in the prodigies cited by Livy. And no less so, everything that is to be found in the writers on natural magic or alchemy or suchlike, all of who seem to have an unconquerable appetite for falsehood and fable.'[2]

I am the better pleased with the method of reasoning described here, since I think it may serve to confound those dangerous friends, or disguised enemies, of the Christian religion who have undertaken to defend it by the principles of human reason. Our most holy religion is founded on faith, *not* on reason. To subject it to a trial that it is unfitted to endure, is a sure method of rendering it vulnerable. To illustrate this further, let us examine those miracles related in scripture and so as not to lose ourselves in too broad a field, let us confine ourselves to those found in the Pentateuch.[3] We shall examine these according to the principles of avowed Christians, not as the word or testimony of God himself, but as the production of a mere human writer and historian.

Here, then, we are first to consider a book presented to us by a barbarous and ignorant people, written in an age when they were even more so and, in all probability, long after the facts it relates. Such facts are corroborated by no concurring testimony and resemble those fabulous accounts that every nation gives of its origin. Upon reading this book, we find it full of prodigies and miracles.

It gives accounts of a state of the world and of human nature entirely different from the present; of our fall from that state; of human longevity extended to nearly a thousand years; of the destruction of the world by a deluge; of the arbitrary choice of one people (the countrymen of the author) as the favourites of heaven and of their deliverance from bondage by the most astonishing prodigies imaginable.[4]

---

1 Francis Bacon, 1st Viscount St Albans (1561–1626). English statesman, philosopher, scientist and jurist. Chancellor to King James I.
2 Bacon, *Novum Organum*. Vol. 14, ed. Montagu, B. (London: W. Pickering, 1831), p138.
3 Pentateuch; from Gk., 'the five–volumed'. The first five books of the Old Testament.
4 The Mosaic deliverance of the Children of Israel from Egypt; Exodus *passim*.

I desire anyone to lay hand upon heart and, after a serious consideration, declare whether they actually think that the falsehood of such a book, supported by such a testimony, would actually be *more* extraordinary and miraculous than all the miracles it relates.

However, according to the criteria of probability we have established above, such proof of falsehood would be necessary to render the miracles credible. What we have said of miracles may be applied without any variation to prophecies. Indeed, all prophecies *are* real miracles. It is only as such that they can be admitted as proofs of any revelation. If it did not exceed the capacity of human nature to foretell future events, it would be absurd to employ any prophecy as an argument for a divine mission or authority from heaven.

Thus we may conclude overall that not only was the Christian religion first attended by miracles, but even today cannot be believed by any reasonable person *without* one. Mere reason is insufficient to convince us of its veracity. Whoever is moved by faith to assent to it must be conscious, in their own person, of a *continuing* miracle that, subverting all the principles of their reason, gives them the determination to believe what is *absolutely* contrary to custom and experience.

Of A Particular Providence and of A Future State

SECTION XI: **An Enquiry concerning Human Understanding**

I was recently engaged with a friend who loves sceptical paradoxes. In conversation, he advanced many opinions with which I totally disagreed, but that were interesting and bore some relation to the chain of reasoning in this *Enquiry*.[1] I shall here copy them from memory as accurately as I can – and submit them to your judgement.

Our conversation began with my admiring the singular good fortune of philosophy, which requires, above all other privileges, *absolute* liberty. It flourishes, above all, through argument and the free divergence of opinions. It received its first birth in classical Greece in a country and in an age of freedom and toleration. There, even in its most extravagant ideas, it was never cramped by creeds, concessions or penal statutes. With the exceptions of the banishment of Protagoras[2] and the death of Socrates,[3] the latter event resulting partly from other motives – there are scarcely any instances in ancient history of the bigoted hostility to heterodoxy with which the present age is so infested.

The philosopher Epicurus,[4] for example, lived to an advanced age at Athens in peace and tranquillity. Epicureans were even permitted to be conferred with priestly status and to officiate at the altar in the most sacred

---

1 Hume, David. *Philosophical Essays concerning Human Understanding* (London: A Millar, 1748). Later retitled, *An Enquiry concerning Human Understanding*.
2 Protagoras of Abdera; fl. fifth century BCE. Sophist, philosopher, and friend of Pericles. Expelled from Athens for atheism. He had said truthfully, if incautiously, 'I have no means of *knowing* if the Gods exist – or not.'
3 Socrates (470–399 BCE). Athenian moral philosopher. Teacher of Plato. Condemned to death for impiety, he was required to drink Hemlock (*Conium maculatum*). There may have been, as Hume's remark suggests, political motives for his prosecution, as he associated with the anti-democratic faction and with men, such as Alcibiades, seen as enemies of Athens.
4 Epicurus (341–270 BCE) founder of 'The Garden', a philosophic ashram. He advocated atomism, hedonism and atheism to achieve αταραξια (ataraxia) or calmness of mind. He and his disciple, the Roman poet Lucretius, author of *De Rerum Natura* (*On the Nature of the Universe*) were much admired by Hume.

rites of the established religion.[1] Marcus Aurelius, wisest of all the Roman Emperors, gave public encouragement through salaries and pensions distributed equally to the professors of every sect of philosophy.[2]

It will easily be conceived how necessary such treatment was to philosophy in her early youth. Today, when in contrast she may be supposed more hardy and robust, she bears with great difficulty the inclemency of the seasons. Their harsh winds of calumny and persecution blow upon her.

My friend said:

> You admire as the singular good *fortune* of philosophy, those freedoms following from the natural course of things and that should be standard in every age and nation. The obstinate bigotry you complain of as fatal to philosophy, is really her own offspring!
>
> Bigotry, after allying itself with superstition, separates itself entirely from the philosophical parent and becomes her most inveterate enemy and persecutor.
>
> Speculative religious dogmas are the present causes of such furious disputes. They could not possibly have been conceived, far less accepted, in the early stages of human history. Humankind, then wholly illiterate, formed an idea of religion appropriate to their limited understanding. Their sacred tenets were composed chiefly from folk tales – themselves the objects of traditional belief – rather than from argument or disputation. After the first alarm arising from the novelty of the paradoxes and positions advanced by philosophers, the latter seem to have lived throughout antiquity in *harmony* with established superstitions. They also seem to have partitioned humankind between them; philosophy claiming all the learned and the wise, leaving superstition to the commonality and the illiterate.

I said:

> It seems that you are leaving politics entirely out of the question. Don't you think that a wise magistrate could reasonably be hostile towards certain tenets of philosophy; for example those of Epicurus denying a divine existence and consequently a providence and an afterlife.[2] These tenets would seem

---

1 Lucian of Samostata, *The Drinking Party or Lapithae*, 9

2 Not quite all. Lucian, in his maliciously witty dialogue Ευνυχοσ (the Eunuch) says that only four: the Platonists, Epicureans, Stoics and Aristotelians were funded by Marcus Aurelius, Roman Emperor 161–180 CE and Stoic philosopher.

2 Epicurus was a deist: ie he did not deny the existence of gods, but did reject their providence, or engagement in human affairs. He also held that the soul was not immortal; it died with the body and hence there was no afterlife.

to loosen the ties of morality and might be reckoned pernicious to the peace of civil society.

He replied:

I know that in fact persecutions never resulted from calm reason or from the *experience* of any pernicious consequence of philosophy. They arose entirely from emotion and prejudice. But what if I should go farther and assert that Epicurus could easily have defended his doctrines had he been accused before the people by any of the sycophants[1] or informers of those days. He could also have demonstrated that his principles of philosophy were just as salutary as those of the adversaries zealously trying to expose him to public hatred and jealousy?

I said:

I would like you to test your eloquence upon so extraordinary a topic. Make a speech for Epicurus! Make a speech that might not satisfy the *mob* of Athens, if you will allow that polite city to *have* a mob, but that would satisfy the more philosophical part of his audience.'[2]

He replied:

The matter would not be difficult under these conditions. Very well. I shall imagine myself Epicurus while you represent the Athenians. I shall deliver such an address as will fill the *entire* urn with white beans, with not a single black one to gratify the malice of my adversaries!'[3]

'Very well, *proceed!*'

'Athenians, I come to justify here in your Assembly what I maintain in my School; for I find myself assailed by furious antagonists, instead of reasoning with calm and dispassionate enquirers. Your deliberations, that *should* be dealing with questions of the public good and the interests of the Commonwealth, are being diverted to speculative philosophy! These splendid but perhaps fruitless enquiries are replacing your more familiar, useful activities. However, as far as I can, I will prevent this abuse.

---

1 At Athens; a litigant who, for personal gain, brought a malicious prosecution on a trumped-up charge.

2 Hume may have been inspired by Pierre Bayle's imagined debate at Athens between the atheist Straton, 3rd *Scholarch* (Director) of Aristotle's Lyceum – and Stoic theists. See Bayle's *Continuation des Pensées diverses* (1705).

3 Greek jurors voted by placing coloured beans in an urn: black for condemnation, white for acquittal. This *may* have been the origin of Pythagoras' enigmatic and famously terse injunction, Κυάμων ἀπέχεσθαι (Abstain from beans...)

We shall not argue here about the origin or the government of worlds. We shall restrict ourselves to enquiring; to what extent such questions concern the public interest? If I can persuade you that they are entirely *unrelated* to the peace of society and the security of government, I hope that you will presently send us back to our Schools.[1] There we may examine, at leisure, the question that is both the most sublime and the most speculative in all Philosophy.[2] Philosophers of religion, not satisfied with the traditions of your forefathers and the doctrines of your priests – with which I myself willingly concur – indulge in a rash curiosity. They examine how far they can establish religion upon the principles of *reason*. As a result they excite, rather than satisfy, the doubts naturally arising from diligent and scrupulous enquiry. They begin by painting, in the most magnificent colours, the order and beauty and wise arrangement of the Universe. They then ask if such a glorious display of intelligence could arise from the fortuitous concourse of atoms; could *chance* produce what the greatest genius can never sufficiently comprehend?

I shall not examine the justice of this argument. I shall accept that it is as solid as my antagonists and accusers can desire. It is sufficient if I can prove by this very reasoning that the question is entirely *speculative*. When I deny a providential Deity and an afterlife in my philosophical statements, I can also prove that I do not undermine the foundations of society. Indeed, I shall advance principles that my opponents must admit as solid and satisfactory within their own fields of interest.

You then, my accusers, have acknowledged that the chief or *sole* argument for a divine Existence – which, incidentally, I have never questioned – is derived from the *order* of Nature. Where signs of intelligence and of design appear, you think it improper to assign its cause either to chance or to the blind and unguided *force* of matter. You concede that this is an argument from effects back to causes. From the orderly nature of the work, you *infer* that there must have been a project and also forethought in the workman. However, if you cannot *establish* this point, you must concede that your conclusion fails – and you cannot *then* claim to establish any conclusion of a latitude greater than the actual phenomena of Nature will justify. These are your concessions; I now desire you to mark the consequences.

---

1 Philosophical seminaries such as the Academy of Plato or the Lyceum of Aristotle.
2 ie Does religious belief and observance have a basis in reason?

When we infer any particular cause from an effect, we must proportion the one to the other. We can never ascribe to the cause, any qualities *other* than those exactly sufficient to produce that effect. A body of ten ounces rising in a pair of scales may serve as proof that the counterweight exceeds ten ounces, but can *never* afford a reason as to why it exceeds an hundred. If the cause assigned for any effect is insufficient to produce it, we must either reject that cause – *or*, add to it such qualities as will give it a force truly proportional to the effect.

However, if we ascribe *further* qualities to the cause, or affirm it capable of producing *other* effects, we are indulging in pure conjecture. We are, arbitrarily, supposing the existence of causal qualities and energies without reason or authority.

The same rule holds, whether the cause in question is brute unconscious matter – or a rational intelligent Being. If the cause is known *only* by the effect, we never ought to ascribe to that cause any quality *beyond* that precisely requisite to produce that effect. Nor can we, by any rule of valid reasoning, return back from the cause and infer from it any *other* effects beyond those by which it is directly known to us. No one, merely from the sight of one of Zeuxis's pictures, could know that he was *also* a sculptor or architect and an artist no less skilful in stone and marble than in colours.[1] We may *only* safely conclude that a workman is possessed of those talents and taste displayed in the particular work before us. The cause must be proportioned to the effect. If we then proportion the cause exactly and precisely, we shall never find in it any qualities that point further, or even provide an inference concerning any *other* design or performance. Such qualities would be beyond those precisely requisite for producing the effect presently being examined.

Accepting, therefore, the Gods to be the authors of the existence or *order* of the Universe, it follows that they possess that precise degree of power, intelligence and benevolence that appears in their workmanship. But nothing further can *ever* be proved unless we call in exaggeration and flattery to remedy the defects of argument and reasoning. In so far as attributes appear to be present, we may conclude that these attributes exist. However, the supposition of any *further* attributes is mere hypothesis.

---

1 Zeuxis of Heraclea (modern Basilicata, S. Italy) fl. 5th century BCE. Greek painter famous for his *trompe l'oeil* works. Birds were said to fly down to peck at his painting of grapes.

Even more hypothetical is the supposition that in distant regions of space, or periods of time, there has been, or ever will be, a *more* magnificent display of these attributes and a scheme of administration more suitable to such imaginary virtues. We can never mount up from the effect eg the Universe, to the cause, Jupiter,[1] and then descend again to infer any *new* effect from that cause. To do so would suggest that the presently observed effects, on their own, were not entirely worthy of the glorious attributes we ascribe to that Deity. Where knowledge of the cause is being derived *solely* from the effect, they must be precisely adjusted to each other. The former can never refer to anything further, or be the foundation of any new inference and conclusion.

You observe certain phenomena in Nature. You seek a cause or author. You imagine that you have found it. You afterwards become so enamoured of this offspring of your brain that you imagine it impossible that it cannot produce something greater, more perfect, than the present scheme of things, so full of ill and disorder. You forget that this superlative intelligence and benevolence are entirely *imaginary*, or at least without any foundation in reason. You forget that you have no grounds to ascribe to the Gods *any* qualities other than those observed to have been *actually* exerted and displayed in their productions. Therefore, philosophers, let your gods be *trimmed* to the present appearances of Nature. Do not presume, by arbitrary suppositions, to alter these appearances in order to fit them to the attributes you wish to ascribe to your Deities.

Athenians, when priests and poets, supported by your authority, talk of a golden or silver age preceding the present state of vice and misery, I hear them with attention and with reverence.[2] But when this is advocated by philosophers claiming to disregard authority and to cultivate reason, I do not pay them the same submission and pious deference. I ask instead; who *carried* them into the celestial regions? Who *admitted* them into the councils of the gods? Who *opened* to them the book of fate from which they rashly affirm that their Deities have executed, or will execute, any purpose beyond what has actually appeared?

If they tell me that they have mounted the steps by the gradual ascent of reason and by drawing inferences from effects to causes, I will still insist that they have augmented that ascent of reason with the wings of imagination. Otherwise, they could not thus change their direction of inference, arguing

---

1 Hume means Zeus, given that the present audience is Greek.
2 *See* Hesiod, *Works and Days*, 109 ff.

now from causes to effects and presuming that a *more* perfect production than the present world would be more appropriate to such perfect beings as the Gods. They forget that they have no reason to ascribe to these celestial beings *any* perfection, or indeed *any* attribute, other than that found in the present world.

From hence comes all the fruitless activity to account for the ill appearances of Nature and to save the honour of the Gods, while acknowledging the reality of the evil and disorder with which the world abounds.

We are told that obstinate and intractable qualities of matter, or the observance of general Laws – or some such reason – is the *sole* cause controlling the power and benevolence of Zeus. He was thus obliged to create humankind and every observable creature with attributes so imperfect and so unhappy. These attributes, it seems *a priori*, are taken for granted in their broadest latitude. And upon that supposition, I admit that such conjectures may perhaps be accepted as plausible solutions of those ill phenomena of evil and disorder. But *still* I ask; why take these attributes for granted? Why ascribe to the cause any qualities *apart* from what actually appears in the effect? Why torture your brain to justify the course of Nature upon suppositions that, for all you know, may be entirely imaginary, with no traces of them observable *within* that very course of Nature?

The religious hypothesis, therefore, must be considered only as *one* particular means of accounting for the visible phenomena of the Universe. But no rational enquirer will ever presume to infer from it any single fact, or alter, or add to those phenomena in any single particular. If you believe that the appearances of things *prove* such causes, then you may validly draw an inference concerning the existence of these causes. In such complicated and sublime subjects, everyone should be allowed the liberty of conjecture and argument.

But here you ought to stop. For if you then come backwards, arguing *from* your inferred causes that any *other* effect has existed, or will exist in the course of Nature, more fully displaying particular attributes, be warned! You have departed from the method of reasoning attached to the present subject. You will have certainly added something to the attributes of the cause, *beyond* what appears in the effect. Otherwise you could never, with acceptable sense or propriety, add anything to the effect, in order to render it *more* worthy of the cause.

Where, then, is the alleged odiousness of that doctrine I teach in my School – or rather examine in my Garden?[1] Do you find anything in this whole question of the *least* concern to the security of good morals, or the peace and order of society?

You say that I deny a Deity, a supreme Governor of the world, guiding the course of events, punishing the vicious with infamy and disappointment while rewarding the undertakings of the virtuous with honour and success. But surely I do not deny the very *course* of events that lie open to every one's inquiry and examination. I acknowledge that in the present order of things, virtue is attended with more peace of mind than vice and meets with a more favourable reception from the world. I am aware that, according to the past experience of humanity, friendship is the chief joy of human life and moderation the only source of tranquillity and happiness.

I never balance between the virtuous and the vicious course of life, being persuaded that to a well-disposed mind every advantage is on the side of the former. And what can you say more, all your suppositions and reasoning accepted? You tell me, indeed, that the present disposition of things results from intelligence and design. But *whatever* it proceeds from, that very disposition, upon which depends our happiness or misery and consequently our conduct and deportment in life, is *still the same*. It is still open to me, as well as to you, to regulate behaviour by experience of past events. Given that a divine Providence is accepted and that a supreme distributive Justice exists in the Universe, you affirm that I ought to expect some more particular reward of the good – and punishment of the bad – *beyond* the ordinary course of events. I find in this the very same fallacy I have been endeavouring to detect! You persist in imagining that if we grant that divine Existence for which you so earnestly contend, you may safely infer *consequences* from it. You are thus seeking to add something to the order of Nature, as we experience it, by arguing from attributes *you* ascribe to your Gods! You seem to have forgotten that all your reasoning on this subject can only be drawn from effects to causes and that consequently every *reverse* argument, ie deducing from causes to effects, has to be grossly fallacious and specious. For it is impossible for you to know anything about the cause beyond what you have previously *not* inferred but rather *discovered* to the full – through its observed effect.

---

[1] The school of Epicurus at Athens was known as 'The Garden' from its ambience.

But what must a Philosopher make of those thinkers who, instead of making the present scheme of things the sole object of their contemplation, go so far as to *reverse* the whole course of Nature? They seek to render this life merely a passage to something *farther*; a porch leading to a greater and vastly different building; a prologue serving only to introduce an afterlife and give it more grace and propriety. Whence, do you think, such philosophers derive their idea of the Gods? Surely from their own conceit and imagination!

For if they derived it from *observable* phenomena, it would never point to anything farther, but would require to be exactly adjusted *to* those phenomena. It may be freely allowed that the Divinity may *possibly* be endowed with attributes we have never seen exerted – and may *possibly* be governed by principles of action that we cannot determine to be satisfied. But this is still mere possibility, mere hypothesis. We can never have reason to *infer* any attributes, or any principles or purposes of action in the Divinity, except those we *know* to have been exerted and fulfilled.

Are there any signs of a distributive Justice in the world? If you answer in the affirmative I will conclude that since justice here exerts itself, it is satisfied. If you reply in the negative, I conclude that you have then no reason to ascribe justice, in our sense of it, to the Gods. If you hold a position midway between affirmation and negation – saying that the justice of the gods presently exerts itself in part but not in its full extent – I answer that you have no reason to give it any *particular* extent, but only so far as you presently *see* it exerting itself.

Athenians, I thus bring the dispute, to a summary judgment with my antagonists. The course of Nature lies open to my contemplation as well as to theirs. The train of events *experienced* by humanity is the great standard by which we all regulate our conduct. Nothing else can be appealed to, either in the field or in the Senate. Nothing else ought ever to be heard of in the school, or in the study. It would be in vain were our limited understanding to break through those boundaries, that are too narrow for our fond imagination. When we argue from the course of Nature, inferring a single intelligent Cause that first bestowed, and still preserves, *order* in the Universe, we are embracing a principle both uncertain and useless. It is uncertain because the subject lies entirely beyond the reach of human experience. It is useless because our knowledge of this cause is derived entirely from the course of Nature. Hence we can never, according to the rules of proper reasoning, return back from the cause with any *new* inference. Neither can we make additions to the common and experienced course of Nature and thereby establish any new principles of conduct and behaviour.'

His harangue being finished, I said:

'I notice that you follow the oratorical stratagems of the demagogues of old. Pleased as you were to make me represent the Athenians, you curried my favour by embracing those principles to which, as you well know, I have a particular attachment. You make *experience* – as indeed you should – the only standard of our judgement concerning this and all other questions of fact. However, I am in no doubt that starting from the very same experience to which you appeal, it may be possible to refute the reasoning you put in the mouth of Epicurus. If you saw, for instance, a half-finished building surrounded with heaps of brick, stone, mortar and all the instruments of masonry, could you not *infer* from these effects that it was a work of design and contrivance? And from this inferred cause could you not return again to infer new additions to the effect, concluding that the building would soon be finished and receive all the further improvements that art could bestow upon it?

If you saw upon the seashore the print of one human foot, you would conclude that someone had passed that way and had also left the imprint of the other foot, though now effaced by the incoming tide. Why then do you refuse to admit the same method of reasoning with regard to the order of Nature? Think of the world itself and present life only as an imperfect building from which you can infer an intelligence so superior that it can leave nothing imperfect. Why not then infer a more finished scheme or plan that will receive its completion in some distant point of space or time? Are not these methods of reasoning exactly similar? Why embrace the one while rejecting the other?'

He replied:

'The infinite difference between these subjects is sufficient foundation for the following difference in my conclusions. In works of *human* art and contrivance it *is* allowable to advance from the effect to the cause and, returning back from the cause, to form new inferences concerning the effect. This is done through examination of the alterations that the effect has probably undergone, or may still undergo. What is the foundation of this method of reasoning? Simply this; human beings we *know* by experience. With their motives and designs we are acquainted. Their projects and inclinations have an assured connexion and coherence according to the laws Nature has established for their government. Therefore, when we find that any work has resulted from human skill and industry, we may, having *prior* acquaintance with the nature of the animal, draw a hundred inferences concerning what may be expected. These inferences will all be founded on experience and observation.

However, were we to know humanity only from a *single* work or production, it would be impossible for us to argue in this manner. In that case, our knowledge of all the qualities we ascribe to humankind would be derived from that sole production and it would be impossible for them to point to anything farther, or be the foundation of any new inference. Considered alone, a footprint in the sand can only prove that it was produced by some figure attached to it. But the print of a *human* foot proves from our other prior experiences, that there was probably another foot which also left its impression, though later effaced. Here we may mount from the effect to the cause and, descending again *from* the cause, infer alterations in the effect. But this is not a continuation of the same simple chain of reasoning. We can muster, in the *human* case, a hundred other experiences and observations concerning the *usual* overall figure and limbs of that species of animal. Without these, this method of argument would be fallacious and spurious.

The case is not the same with our reasoning from the works of Nature. The Deity is known to us *only* by its productions. This is a single Being, unrepresented by any *other* type or general kind from whose known attributes or qualities we can, by analogy, infer any attribute or quality. To the degree that the Universe shows wisdom and goodness, we infer wisdom and goodness. To the extent that it shows a particular degree of these attributes, we infer a particular degree, precisely proportional to the effect we are examining. But by any rules of logical reasoning we can never be authorised to infer or suppose *farther* degrees of those attributes, let alone any further attributes themselves. Now, without licence of supposition it is impossible for us to argue from the cause, or infer any alteration in the effect, beyond what we have directly observed. Greater good produced by this Being must still indicate a greater degree of goodness, while a more impartial distribution of rewards and punishments must proceed from the Being's greater regard to justice and equity. Every supposed addition to the works of Nature makes an addition to the attributes of the Author of Nature. Consequently, being entirely unsupported by any reason or argument, such attributes can *never* be more than mere conjecture and hypothesis.

In general, I think it may be established as a maxim that where any cause is known *only* by its particular effects, it must be impossible to infer any *new* effects from that cause. This is because the qualities required to produce these new effects must either be different, superior, or of more extensive operation, than those producing the original effect by which the cause is known to us. We can thus never have any reason to suppose the existence of these qualities. To say that the new effects result only from a continuation of the *same* energy known from the first effects, will not remove the difficulty. Even granting this to be the case, the very continuation and exertion of a similar energy (for it cannot be identical) in a different period of space and time, is a very arbitrary supposition. There cannot be any traces of it in those effects from which all our knowledge of the cause is *originally* derived. Let the inferred cause be exactly proportioned, as it should be, to the known effect; and it is impossible that it can possess any qualities from which *new or different* effects can be inferred.

The great source of our mistakes in this subject and of the unbounded freedom of conjecture in which we indulge, is due to our tacitly putting *ourselves* in the place of the supreme Being. We conclude that the Being will invariably display the same conduct that we ourselves, in that situation, would have embraced as reasonable and preferable. However, apart from the fact that the ordinary course of Nature may convince us that almost everything is regulated by principles and maxims *very* different from ours; it is obviously contrary to all the rules of analogy to extrapolate from human intentions and projects, to those of a Being *so* different and so much superior.

In human nature, there is a certain coherence of experience of designs and inclinations. When, from any fact, we have discovered any intention of any person, it may be reasonable from experience to infer another. We may then draw a long chain of conclusions concerning their past or future conduct. But this method of reasoning can have no place with regard to a Being *so* remote, incomprehensible and bearing far less analogy to *any* other being in the Universe than does the sun to a wax candle. This is a Being that reveals itself only by faint traces or outlines. Beyond these we have no authority to ascribe to it *any* attribute or perfection.

Any attribute we imagine to be a superior perfection may actually be a defect. And were it indeed a superior perfection, to ascribe it to the supreme Being in whose works it appears to have been *incompletely* exerted, savours more of flattery and panegyric than of accurate reasoning and sound philosophy. Therefore, all the philosophy in the world *and* all the religion – which is after all nothing but a species of Philosophy – will never be able to take us beyond the usual course of our experience. Neither can it give us measures of conduct and behaviour different from those reflected in everyday human life. No *new* fact can ever be inferred from the religious hypothesis; no event foreseen or foretold; no reward or punishment expected or dreaded beyond what is *already* known by practice and observation. So my apology for Epicurus will still appear solid and satisfactory and the *political* interests of society will be seen to have no relation to philosophical disputes in metaphysics and religion.'

I replied:

'There is still one circumstance you seem to have overlooked. Although I shall accept your premises, I must deny your conclusion. You conclude that religious doctrines and reasoning can have no influence on life, because they *ought* to have no influence. You fail to consider that common humanity does not reason in the manner you do. They draw many consequences from belief in a divine Existence. They suppose that the Deity will inflict punishments on vice and bestow rewards on virtue *beyond* what appears in the ordinary course of Nature. It does not matter whether this reasoning is valid or not since its influence on their life and conduct will still be the same. Those, like Epicurus, who attempt to disabuse them of such prejudices may, for all I know, be rational thinkers – but I cannot accept them to be good citizens and politicians. They release people from one *restraint* upon their passions, thus making more easy and more likely, infringement of the laws of *society*.

After all, I may perhaps agree with your general conclusion in favour of liberty, though upon different premises from yours. I think the State ought to tolerate every principle of philosophy, there being no instance of any government's political interests suffering by such indulgence. There is no fanaticism among philosophers – their doctrines are not very attractive to the people. Conversely, any restraint put upon their reasoning would have dangerous consequence to the sciences and even to the State, by paving the way for persecution and oppression in other areas where the general population *are* more deeply interested and concerned.

However, with regard to your main topic there occurs to me a difficulty. I shall put it to you without insisting on it in case it leads into an argument too refined and delicate. In a word, I much doubt whether it is possible for a cause to be *known* only by its effect as you have supposed all along, or to be of *so* unusual and particular a nature as to have no parallel, or similarity, with any other observed cause or object. It is only when two species of objects are found to be *constantly* conjoined that we can infer the one from the other. Were an effect observed that was both entirely unique and unrelated to any known kind of thing, I do not see that we could form any conjecture or inference concerning its cause. If experience, observation and analogy are indeed the only guides we can reasonably follow in inferences of this nature, then both the effect *and* the cause must bear a similarity and resemblance to known effects and causes regularly found conjoined.

I leave it to your own reflection to pursue the consequences of this principle. I shall just observe that since the antagonists of Epicurus always suppose the Universe – itself an *effect* quite singular and unparalleled – to be the proof of a Deity, itself a *cause* no less singular and unparalleled, your reasoning on that supposition seems at least to merit our attention.

There is, I admit, difficulty as to how we can ever return from the cause to the effect and, reasoning from our ideas of the former, infer any alteration to the latter – or any addition to it.'

FINIS

Of Superstition and Enthusiasm

'That the corruption of the best things produces the worst' has grown into a maxim.[1] It is frequently demonstrated, among other instances, by the pernicious effects of superstition and enthusiasm[2] both of which are corruptions of true religion. These two species of *false* religion, while both pernicious, are yet of a very different and even of a contrary nature.

The human mind is subject to certain unaccountable terrors and apprehensions. These may result either from an unhappy state of private or public affairs, from ill health, from a gloomy and melancholy disposition, or from the concurrence of all these. In such a state of mind there is dread of infinite and unknown evils from equally unknown agents. Where *real* objects of terror are lacking, the soul, responding to its own prejudice and its dominant inclination, finds *imaginary* ones to whose power and malevolence it sets no limits.

As these enemies are both invisible and unknown, the methods taken to appease them are equally unaccountable. They consist of ceremonies, observances, self-denials, sacrifices and presents. They also involve practices, however absurd or frivolous, recommended by folly, or dishonesty, to a blind and terrified credulity. The true sources of superstition therefore are: weakness; fear; melancholy; together with ignorance.

However, the human mind is also subject to inexplicable elevations and confidence. These arise from prosperous success, luxuriant health, strong spirits, or a bold and confident disposition. In such a state of mind, the imagination swells with great, but confused, conceptions to which no *earthly* beauty or enjoyments can correspond. Everything mortal and perishable is banished as unworthy of attention. Free and full range is given by the imagination to the invisible regions or world of spirits. Here, the soul is at liberty to indulge itself with every conception best suited to its present taste and disposition. From this arise raptures, transports and surprising flights of fancy.

---

1 A maxim of Henry, Lord Bolingbroke, in: *A Dissertation upon Parties* (1735)
2 Fanaticism. '*Violence of passion*' SJ

With confidence still increasing, these inexplicable raptures, without rational foundation and apparently beyond the reach of our ordinary faculties, are attributed to the direct inspiration of that divine Being who is the object of devotion. Shortly, the inspired person comes to regard himself as a distinguished *favourite* of the Divinity. When frenzy, the summit of fanaticism, supervenes, every whimsy is consecrated with human reason and even morality being dismissed as fallacious guides. The fanatic is thus delivered, blindly and without reserve, to supposed spiritual possession and to inspiration from above. The true sources of enthusiasm, therefore, are hope, pride, presumption and a warm imagination – together with ignorance.

These two species of false religion might give rise to many speculations but I shall at present confine myself to a few reflections concerning their different influence on government and society. My first reflection is:

> That superstition is favourable to priestly power, whereas enthusiasm is contrary to it, to a degree equal, or even greater, than sound reason and philosophy.

As superstition is founded on fear, sorrow and depression of spirits, it presents people to themselves in such despicable colours that, in their own eyes, they appear unworthy to approach the divine presence. They thus naturally have recourse to any other person whose sanctity of life – or perhaps impudence and cunning – have led to that person being supposed *more* favoured by the Divinity. If a man, it is to him that the superstitious entrust their devotions. To his care they recommend their prayers, petitions, and sacrifices. It is through him that they hope that their addresses will be rendered acceptable to their incensed Deity. Hence the origin of Priests. These, consequently, may be justly regarded as an invention of a timorous and abject superstition. Ever unsure of itself, it does not dare to offer up its own devotions. In ignorance, it thinks it may only recommend itself to the Divinity through the mediation of his supposed friends and servants.

Superstition is a considerable ingredient in almost all religions, including the most fanatical. Only philosophy is able to conquer such imaginary terrors. As a result, priests are to be found in almost every sect of religion – and the stronger the superstition, the higher the authority of the priesthood.

Enthusiasts, on the other hand, may be observed to have been free from the yoke of ecclesiastics and have expressed great *independence* in their devotion, being contemptuous of forms, ceremonies and traditions. The Quakers[1] are the most egregious, though at the same time the most innocent

---

1 The Quakers: Founded in England by George Fox, a Dissenter, in 1647. Quakers believe that there is Deity in each human who is thus of unique worth. They seek religious truth in inner experience, regarding conscience as the basis of morality. They reject ritual and priests, regarding such as obstructions between the believer and God.

enthusiasts ever known. They are perhaps the only sect never to have admitted priests. The Independents,[1] of all the English sects, approach nearest to the Quakers in both their fanaticism and freedom from priestly bondage, while the Presbyterians[2] follow at an equal distance in both particulars. In short, this observation is founded in experience – and will also appear to be founded in reason. This follows if we consider that since enthusiasm arises from a presumptuous pride and confidence, it thinks itself sufficiently qualified to approach the Divinity *direct*, without any human mediator. Its rapturous devotions are so fervent that it even imagines itself actually approaching the Deity through contemplation and inward converse. Thus does enthusiasm ignore all those outward ceremonies and observances for which priestly assistance appears so necessary to the superstitious. The fanatic consecrates *himself*, bestowing on his own person a sacred character far superior to that which institutions with their forms & ceremonies can confer on any other person.

My second reflection with regard to these species of false religion is:

That religions which partake of enthusiasm are, on their first appearance, more furious and violent than those which partake of superstition; but within a short time become more gentle and moderate.

The violence of this species of religion, when excited by novelty and animated by opposition, is shown in innumerable examples; the Anabaptists[3] in Germany; the Camisards[4] in France; the Levellers[5] and other fanatics in England and the Covenanters[6] in Scotland. Enthusiasm being founded

---

1 The Independents: During the English civil war (1641–5) the Puritan MPs of the Long Parliament split broadly into two factions: the Independents and the Presbyterians. The former advocated separation of Church and State, each congregation to be independent of *all* civil and ecclesiastical organisatons. The latter favoured a State religion on Presbyterian principles.
2 The Presbyterians: From Gk. Πρεσβύτερος (presbyteros) or 'Elder.' To this communion DH's family adhered as the Established Church of Scotland. Parish ministers and elders are chosen by their congregations. There no higher clergy, even the 'Moderator' ie Chairman, of the Kirk's General Assembly of ministers and elders being replaced annually.
3 Anabaptists: A 16th century central European sect rejecting infant baptism and participation in civil government. Only repenting adults might be baptised. The present-day Amish, Hutterites and Mennonites are their spiritual descendants.
4 Camisards were French Protestants (Huguenots) from the Cévennes who revolted (1702–15) against the Catholic persecutions following the loss of their religious freedom by Louis XIV's 1685 revocation of the Edict of Nantes.
5 Levellers: Members of a political movement on the Parliamentary side during the English Civil War. They advocated popular sovereignty, extended suffrage, equality before the law and religious tolerance.
6 The Covenanters were adherents to either The Solemn League and Covenant (1643) or the earlier National Covenant (1638) which sought to promote, by civil and military means, the Presbyterian system of Church governance.

on strong spirits and a presumptuous boldness of character, it naturally begets the most extreme resolutions. This is especially after it becomes sufficiently strong to inspire the fanatic with divine delusions and revelations, together with contempt for the common rules of reason, morality, and prudence.

It is thus enthusiasm which produces the cruellest disorders of human society. However, its fury is like that of thunder and tempest, exhausting itself in short order and leaving the air calmer and more serene than before. When the first fire of enthusiasm is spent, all fanatical sects sink naturally into the greatest laxity and coolness in sacred matters. This is because among them there is no group endowed with sufficient authority to support the religious spirit. There are no rites, no ceremonies and no holy observances which may enter into the common train of life and thus preserve the sacred principles from oblivion.

Superstition, on the contrary, steals in gradually and insensibly, rendering people tame and submissive. It is acceptable to rulers and seems inoffensive to the people. But this is only until the priests, having firmly established their authority, become the tyrants and disturbers of human society. This they do through their endless contentions, persecutions, and religious wars. How smoothly the Roman Catholic Church advanced in her acquisition of power; but into what dreadful convulsions did she throw all Europe in order to maintain it! Our schismatics, on the other hand, who were formerly such dangerous bigots have now become free thinkers, while the Quakers appear to be closely approaching the *literati,* the disciples of Confucius in China[1] who are the only organised body of deists[2] in the Universe.

My third observation on this head is:

That superstition is an enemy to civil liberty, and enthusiasm a friend to it.

---

1 Confucianism is a complex system of moral and political philosophy derived from the writings and teachings of the Chinese philosopher K'ung-fu-tzu, Master K'ung' (551–478 BCE), anglicised to Confucius.

2 Deists believe that while an engineering intelligence, or god, may have created the Universe, it is uninvolved in human affairs. They reject revealed religion and all its appurtenances such as a priesthood, miracles and an afterlife.

The groaning of superstition under the dominion of priests, while enthusiasm *destroys* ecclesiastical power, sufficiently accounts for the present observation. This is not to say that enthusiasm, being the disease of bold and ambitious tempers, is naturally accompanied with a spirit of liberty. Superstition, on the contrary, by rendering people tame and abject, *fits* them for slavery. We learn from English history that during the civil wars the Independents and the Deists, although the most opposite in their religious principles, were yet united in their political ones. Both were passionate for a Commonwealth. And since the origin of Whig and Tory,[1] the leaders of the Whigs[2] have either been Deists or professed latitudinarians[3] in their principles, ie friends to toleration and indifferent to any particular Christian sect.

On the other hand, all the sectaries who have a strong tincture of enthusiasm, have always without exception concurred with the Whig party in defence of civil liberty. The resemblance of their superstitions long united the High Church Tories and the Roman Catholics in support of royal prerogative[4] and kingly power, although experience of the tolerating spirit of the Whigs seems to have recently reconciled the Catholics to that party.

The Molinists[5] and Jansenists[6] in France have a thousand unintelligible disputes, not ten of which are worthy of reflection by a person of sense. However, what principally distinguishes these two sects – and alone merits our attention – is the different *spirit* of their religion. The Molinists, directed as they are by the Jesuits, are consequently great friends to superstition, rigid observers of external forms and ceremonies, devotees of tradition and the authority of priests.

---

1 The 'Party of Court', traditionally monarchist and conservative. Originally a term of abuse; from the Middle Irish *toraidh*, an outlaw.
2 The 'Party of Parliament' traditionally democratic and reformative. Also originally a term of abuse; from the Scots *whiggamor*, a cattle driver.
3 Toleration of variation in diocesan Church governance. Dominant in the 18th century Church of England.
4 The right of the monarch to govern, for which God was cited as the ultimate authority.
5 The religious doctrine seeking to reconcile an interventionist ie a provident God with human free will. After Luis de Molina (1535–1600) a Spanish Jesuit theologian.
6 Followers of Cornelius Otto Jansen (1585–1638) His theology accepted original sin and predestination, but also an element of free will. This was seen as an attack on Jesuits and on Papal power. Jansenism's central tenets were condemned as heretical by Innocent x in 1653.

The Jansenists, enthusiasts and zealous promoters of passionate devotion and of the inward life, are little influenced by authority. They are, in a word, only half Catholic. The consequences conform exactly to the foregoing reasoning. The Jesuits are the tyrants of the people and the slaves of the Court, while it is the Jansenists who keep alive those small sparks of the love of liberty still to be found in the French nation.

Of Suicide

One considerable advantage that derives from Philosophy is the sovereign antidote it provides to superstition and false religion. All other remedies against that pestilent distemper are ineffective or at best uncertain. Plain good sense and the ways of the world, sufficient as they are for most purposes of life, are ineffectual here.

Both history and daily experience furnish instances of persons who, throughout their lives, have crouched in slavery to the grossest superstitions despite endowments of the strongest capacity for business and affairs. Even gaiety and sweetness of temper, that infuse a balm into every *other* wound, afford no remedy to so virulent a poison. We may particularly observe this among the fair sex who, despite being richly endowed by Nature, find many joys blasted by this importunate intruder.

However, superstition is effectually excluded when philosophy has gained possession of the mind. One may affirm that her triumph over *this* enemy is more complete than over most of the vices and imperfections of human nature. Love and anger, ambition and avarice, all have their roots in those tempers and emotions that even the soundest reason is rarely able to correct. Superstition, however, being founded on *false* opinion, will immediately vanish when true philosophy has inspired more accurate impressions of superior powers. The contest is here more evenly balanced between the disease and the medicine –and nothing can hinder the efficacy of the latter, except *its* being false and artificial.

It will be superfluous here to magnify the merits of philosophy by presenting the pernicious tendencies of superstition, the vice philosophy cleanses from the mind. The superstitious, says Cicero, are miserable in every field of life and in its every incident. Even sleep itself, banishing the *other* cares of unhappy mortals, brings new terrors to them. On examining their dreams, they find prognostications of future calamities in those visions of the night.[1]

---

1 M. Tullius Cicero; *De Divinatione* (On Divination) II. 72.

I may add that although death alone can put a full stop to their misery, the superstitious dare not fly to this refuge. Instead, they prolong a miserable existence through the vain fear of offending their Maker by using the power of self-destruction; a power actually *endowed* to them by that beneficent Being. The gifts of both God and Nature are ripped from us by this cruel enemy.

Despite the fact that this one action would remove us from pain and sorrow, superstition's threats still chain us to the hated and miserable existence to which it is the chief contributor. It is observed by those reduced to attempting suicide by the calamities of life, that if friends' well-meaning actions deprive them of this type of death, they seldom venture upon another, unable to summon sufficient resolution a second time.

So great is our horror of death, that when it approaches in any form *other* than that to which a person has reconciled the imagination, it acquires new terrors and overcomes his or her feeble courage. But when the menaces of *superstition* are added to this natural timidity, no wonder it deprives people of all power over their lives. Indeed, many of our greatest pleasures and enjoyments are also torn from us by this inhuman tyrant.

Let us endeavour here to restore humans to their native liberty by examining all the common arguments *against* suicide, showing that according to all the ancient philosophers, it may be free from the imputation of guilt or blame. If suicide is criminal, it must be a transgression of our duty either to God, our neighbours, or ourselves. To prove that suicide is no transgression of our duty to God, the following considerations may suffice.

In order to govern the material world, the almighty Creator has established general and immutable laws by which all bodies from the greatest planet to the smallest particle of matter are maintained in structure and function. To govern the animal world, God has endowed all living creatures with bodily and mental powers. They are also endowed with senses, emotions, appetites, memory and judgement by which they are both impelled and regulated within their destined course of life. These two distinct principles of the material and animal world continually encroach upon each other and mutually retard, or accelerate, each other's operation.

The powers of humans and all other animals are also restrained and directed by the nature of their environment. In turn, the modifications and actions of that environment are themselves incessantly altered by human and animal activity. Humankind is stopped by rivers in its passage over the earth while rivers, properly directed, supply power to machines in human service. But though the provinces of the material and animal powers are not kept entirely separate, no discord or disorder results from this. On the contrary, it is from the union, mixture and contrast of the various powers of inanimate bodies and living creatures that there arises that sympathy, harmony and proportion that affords the surest argument of supreme Wisdom.

The intervention of the Deity does not appear *directly* in any operation, but rather governs everything by general and immutable Laws established from the beginning of time. In one sense, all events may be pronounced the actions of the Almighty, proceeding as they do from those powers with which it has endowed its creatures. A house that collapses under its own weight is not brought to ruin by divine providence any more than one destroyed by human hands. Similarly, the human faculties are less divine workmanship than the result of the laws of motion and gravitation. When the passions play, when the judgment dictates, when the limbs obey, they do so as an operation of God. It is upon these animate principles, as well as upon the inanimate, that the government of the Universe is established.

Every event is equally important in the eyes of that infinite Being who takes in, at one glance, the most distant regions of space and the remotest periods of time. There is no event, however important to us that it has *exempted* from the general Laws that govern the Universe, or that it has peculiarly reserved for its own immediate action and operation.

The revolution of states and empires depends upon the smallest caprice or passion of individuals, while the very lives of humans are shortened or extended by the smallest accident of air or diet, sunshine or tempest. Nature, however, still continues her progress and operations – and if general Laws are ever broken by particular wishes of the Deity, it is in a manner that entirely escapes human observation. While the elements and other *inanimate* parts of Creation proceed regardless of the particular interest and situation of humanity, the latter are left to their *own* judgment and discretion when faced with the various shocks of matter. Here they may employ every endowed faculty in order to provide ease, happiness or preservation.

Consider a person who, tired of life and hunted by pain and misery, has bravely overcome all the natural terrors of death and made their escape from this cruel scene. What, I ask, can be the meaning of the principle that, by disturbing the order of the Universe, such a person has incurred the indignation of the Creator by encroaching on divine providence?

Shall we assert that the Almighty has reserved to itself in some unique manner the *disposal* of human lives, and has exempted such events from the general Laws by which the Universe is governed? This is plainly false since human lives depend upon the same laws as do the lives of all other animals, both being subject to the general Laws of matter and motion. The fall of a tower or the infusion of a poison will destroy a person just as easily as the meanest creature. A flood sweeps away without distinction, everything that comes within the reach.

Since, therefore, human lives are utterly dependant on the general Laws of matter and motion, is a person's disposing of his or her life to be reckoned a criminal encroachment upon these Laws, or a disturbance of their operation? This seems absurd. All animals trust to their own prudence and skill for their conduct in the world and have full authority, as far as is in their power, to alter all the operations of Nature. Without the exercise of this authority they could not subsist for a moment. Every human action, every human *motion* changes the arrangement of some parts of matter, diverting the general Laws of motion from their ordinary course. Putting these conclusions together, we find that human life *depends* upon the general Laws of matter and motion and that it is no encroachment on the office of providence to disturb or alter them. Consequently, everyone the free disposal of their own life – and may they not lawfully employ that power with which Nature has endowed them?

In order to *invalidate* the evidence leading to this conclusion, we must show why the particular human case is excepted. Is it because human life is of such great importance that it is improper for human prudence[1] to dispose of it? But the life of a person is of no greater importance to the Universe than that of an oyster. Even if it *were* of great importance, human nature has actually placed it in submission it to human prudence, thus requiring us, in *every* eventuality, to subject it to our will. Were the disposal of human life such a unique province of the Almighty that it would be an encroachment on its right for humans to dispose of their own lives, then it would be equally criminal to act for the *preservation* of life as for its destruction.

If I deflect a stone that is falling towards my head I disturb the course of Nature. I also invade the peculiar province of the Almighty by lengthening my life beyond the period that had been assigned it by the general Laws of matter and motion, A hair, a fly, an insect is able to destroy this mighty

---

1 Prudence: Wisdom applied to practice. SJ

human being whose life is of such importance. Is it then an absurdity to suppose that *human* prudence may lawfully dispose of what depends on such insignificant causes? It would be no crime for me to divert the Nile or the Danube from their courses, were I able to effect such a redirection. Where then is the crime of turning a few ounces of blood from their natural channel? Do you imagine that I fret at Providence or curse my creation, because I end my life, putting a full stop to an existence that would render me miserable if continued? Far be such sentiments from me.

I am only convinced of a matter of fact; one that you, reader, will acknowledge possible. This is that human life may be unhappy and that my existence, if prolonged, would become redundant. However, I thank Providence both for the good that I have already enjoyed *and* for the endowed power of escaping the ill that threatens me.

It is for you to be vexed at Providence if you foolishly imagine that you have no such power and hence must prolong a hated life loaded with pain, sickness, shame and poverty. Do you not teach that when any ill befalls me, even through the malice of my enemies, I ought to be resigned to Providence? Do you not teach that human actions are *just* as much the operations of the Almighty as the actions of inanimate objects? When I fall upon my own sword, therefore, I meet my death equally at the hands of the Deity as if it had been due to a lion, a precipice, or a fever. In every calamity that befalls me, the submission to Providence that you require surely does not exclude the operation of human skill and industry whereby I might avoid or even *escape* the calamity. Why may I not employ one remedy as well as another? If my life were not my own, it would be criminal for me to put it in danger, as well as to dispose of it. A person whom glory or friendship carries into the greatest dangers would no more deserve the appellation of *hero*, than another would merit *wretch* or *miscreant* for ending his life from the same or similar motives.

No being possesses any power or faculty that it does not receive from its Creator. Neither is there one whose action, however disorderly, can encroach upon the plan of the Creator's providence, or can disorder the Universe. Its operations are the Creator's works, equally as are whatever chain of events that action invades; and for that very reason whichever principle prevails, we may conclude it to be that most favoured by the Creator. Be it animate, or inanimate, rational or irrational, it is the same. Its power is still derived from the supreme Creator, and is equally comprehended in the order of its Providence. When the horror of pain prevails over the love of life or when a voluntary action anticipates the effects of blind causes, it is only a result of those implanted powers and principles. Divine Providence remains inviolate and is placed far beyond the reach of human injuries. It is impious, says the old Roman superstition,[1] to divert rivers from their courses, or invade the prerogatives of Nature. It is impious, says French superstition, to inoculate against smallpox, thus usurping the business of Providence by deliberately producing distempers and maladies.[2] It is impious, says a modern European superstition, to put an end to one's own life, thereby rebelling against our Creator.

So why is it *not* impious, say I, to build houses, cultivate the land, or sail upon the ocean? In all these actions we employ our powers of mind and body to produce an innovation in the course of Nature – and in *none* of them do we do more than simply that. All of these activities are therefore equally innocent, or equally criminal. However, you are placed by Providence in a particular station, like a sentinel. If you then desert your post without being recalled, you are equally guilty of rebellion against your almighty Sovereign, and will have incurred his displeasure.

I ask, why do you conclude that Providence has placed me in this station? For my part I find that I owe my birth to a long chain of causes, many of them dependent upon the voluntary actions of men and women. But Providence guided all these causes, and *nothing* happens in the Universe without its consent and co-operation. Hence my death, however voluntary, cannot happen without the consent of Providence. Thus whenever pain or sorrow overcomes my patience to make me tired of life, I may conclude that I am being expressly *recalled* from my station in life in the clearest terms. It is surely Providence that has currently placed me in this room. But may I not leave it when I think proper without the imputation of having deserted my post or station?

When I am dead, the atoms of which I am composed will still perform their function in the Universe. They will be just as useful in its grand fabric as they were when they were brought together to compose this individual

---

1 Tacitus, *Annales* I.79. The Roman Senate was debating diversions of the tributaries of the Tiber. (They decided against it.)
2 Inoculation, properly *vaccination* (Lat. *Vacca*, a cow) with cowpox virus induces antibodies conferring cross-resistance to smallpox. The 'business of Providence' is here the production of disease; its production by a human agency is hence impious.

creature. The difference to the whole will be no greater than between my being in a chamber and in the open air. The one change may be of more importance to me *personally* than the other – but not to the Universe.

It is a kind of blasphemy to imagine that any created being can disturb the order of the world, or invade the business of Providence. It supposes that the being possesses powers and faculties received *other* than from its Creator – and that are not subordinate to that Creator's government and authority. A person may disturb society, no doubt, and thereby incur the displeasure of the Almighty. But the overall government of the world is placed far beyond his reach and violence. And how is it made manifest when the Almighty is displeased with those actions that disturb Society? It is by principles that it has implanted in human nature. These fill us with sentiments of remorse if we ourselves have been guilty of such actions – and with blame and disapproval if we observe them in others. So let us now examine, according to the method proposed, whether suicide belongs to this species of action and is a breach of our *duty* to our neighbours and to society.

A person who retires from life does no harm to society and merely ceases to do good. If this be an injury to society, it is one of the most miniscule kind. All our obligations to do good to society seem to imply something recipro-cal. I receive the benefits of society and therefore ought to promote its inter-ests, but when I withdraw myself *altogether* from society, can I be bound any longer? However, while accepting that our obligations to do good are perpetual, they have certainly some limits. If I am not obliged to do a small good to society at the expense of a great harm to myself, why then should I prolong a miserable existence, because of some frivolous advantage that the public may thereby receive from me?

I may lawfully resign any office on account of age and infirmities and employ my time in both insuring against these calamities and in alleviating, as far as possible, the miseries of my future life. Why, then, may I not cut short these miseries by an action that is no *more* prejudicial to society?

But suppose that it is no longer in my power to *promote* the interest of society. Suppose that I am a burden to it and that my life hinders some other person from being more useful to society. In that case my resignation of life would be not only innocent, but actually laudable. Most people who lie under any temptation to abandon existence are in some such situation, while those who have health, power or authority, have commonly better reason to be in humour with the world.

Suppose someone engaged in a conspiracy against the public interest, is arrested on suspicion, threatened with the rack[1] and, aware of his own weakness, knows that the secret will be extracted. Could such a person serve the public interest better than by putting a quick end to a miserable life? This was the case of the famous and brave Filippo Strozzi of Florence.[2]

Again, suppose a malefactor is justly condemned to a shameful death. Can any reason be imagined why he should not anticipate his punishment and save himself all the anguish of thinking of its dreadful approach? He invades the business of Providence no more than did the magistrate who ordered his execution and his voluntary death is equally advantageous to society by ridding it of a pernicious member.

Suicide may often be consistent with advantage and with our duty to ourselves. This cannot be questioned by anyone who accepts that age, sickness or misfortune may render life a burden worse than death itself. I believe that no-one ever threw away life while it was worth keeping. Such is our natural horror of death that trivial motives will never reconcile us to it. Where a person's health or fortune perhaps did not appear to require the remedy of suicide, we may at least be assured that anyone who having recourse to it without *apparent* reason, was cursed with incurable depression of spirit or gloominess of temper. This must have been of sufficient degree to poison all enjoyment, rendering him as miserable as one loaded with the most grievous misfortunes.

If Suicide is reckoned a crime, it is only cowardice that can impel us to it. If it is no crime, both prudence and courage should motivate us to rid ourselves of an existence that has become a burden. It is then the only way that we can be useful to society, by setting an example. If imitated, it would preserve for everyone their chance for happiness in life and would effectually free them from all danger of misery.

---

1 The Rack; an instrument of torture forcing the victim's limbs to be progressively extended, leading to severe tendon and joint injury and excruciating pain.

2 Filippo Strozzi (1488–1538). Florentine banker, politician and *condottiero*. He committed suicide while a prisoner of Cosimo de' Medici in the Fortress of San Giovanni Battista.

Of the Immortality of the Soul

By the mere light of Reason, it seems difficult to prove the Immortality of the Soul. The arguments for it are commonly either metaphysical, moral or physical. But in reality it is the Gospel alone that has brought its life and immortality to light.

I: Metaphysical Arguments

Arguments in this field are founded on the supposition that the soul is immaterial and that it is impossible for thought to belong to a material substance. But well-founded metaphysics[1] teaches us that the notion of substance itself is wholly confused and imperfect. Furthermore, we can have no idea of any substance other than as an aggregate of particular qualities, inherent within an unknown *something*. Therefore, both matter and spirit are, at bottom, equally unknown and we cannot determine what qualities may be inherent in the one or in the other.

Metaphysical arguments likewise teach us that nothing can be decided *a priori* concerning any cause or effect.[2] Since *experience* is the only source of our judgments of this nature, we cannot know from any other principle whether matter, by its structure or arrangement, may or may not be the cause of thought. Abstract reasoning cannot decide any question of fact or existence.

---

1 Metaphysics: The term first appears simply as a title applied to a book of Aristotle by a later Editor. Appearing in his collected works immediately *after* his book *On Physics*, it was thus entitled *Metaphysics* ie *after Physics*. It is that branch of philosophy that seeks to describe the fundamental principles underlying the nature of reality and to explain all that that exists.

2 *A priori* knowledge: that derived from the exercise of pure reason – rather than from experience.

If we accept that a spiritual substance, like the ethereal fire of the Stoics,[1] is dispersed throughout the Universe and is the only inherent subject of thought, we have reason to conclude, by analogy, that Nature uses it as she does that other substance, matter. She employs it as a kind of paste or clay, modifies it into a variety of forms and existences, dissolves each modification after a time and, from its substance, erects a new form. As the same material substance may successively compose the body of all animals, the same spiritual substance may compose their minds. Their consciousness, or that system of thought that they formed during life, may be continually dissolved by death; they being foreign to the new modification. The most positive asserters of the *mortality* of the soul never denied the immortality of its substance. And that an immaterial substance, as well as a material, may lose its memory or consciousness appears, in part, from experience if the soul is immaterial.

Reasoning from the common course of Nature and without supposing any new intervention of the Supreme Cause[2] (that always should be excluded from philosophy), what cannot be destroyed cannot be produced. The soul, therefore, if immortal, existed before our birth and if the former state of existence no wise concerned us, neither will the latter. Animals undoubtedly feel, think, love, hate, will, and even reason – though in a more imperfect manner than the human. Are their souls also immaterial and immortal?[3]

II: Moral Arguments

Let us now consider the moral arguments, chiefly those arguments derived from the *justice* of God, who is supposed to be greatly interested in the punishment of the vicious, and reward of the virtuous. However, these arguments are grounded on the supposition that God has attributes *beyond* those exerted in producing this, the sole Universe we know. Whence do we infer the existence of these attributes?

---

1 Members of the School founded in Athens, *c.*300 BCE by Zeno of Citium (in Cyprus), Stoicism taught that of the four elements, earth, air, water and fire, the latter was most closely associated with the *Logos*, the power controlling the Universe, itself cyclically consumed by ethereal fire, of which each human possessed a spark.
2 Divinity.
3 A valid point. The discovery in 2005 that the DNA of chimpanzees has 98.5 per cent identity with that of *H. sapiens*, led to the conjecture by an Anglican Archbishop that the chimpanzee also has a soul. This provoked the excellent newspaper headline: 'Chimpanzees have souls, says Primate...'

It is safe for us to affirm that whatever we know the Deity to have actually *done*, is for the best. But it is very dangerous to affirm that it must always do what *to us* seems best. In how many instances would this reasoning fail us with regard to the present world? But if any purpose of Nature is clear, we may affirm that so far as we can judge by natural reason, the whole scope and intention of created humanity is limited to the *present* life. Due to the original inherent structure of the mind and passions, with how little interest do humans ever look farther? What comparison either for consistency or efficacy can there be between so nebulous an idea and even the slenderest evidence for any matter of fact occurring in common life.

Unaccountable terrors do indeed arise in some minds with regard to futurity. However, these would quickly vanish again, unless artificially fostered by religious instruction and education. And what is the motive of those [priests] who foster them? It is simply to gain a livelihood and to acquire power and riches in this world. Their very zeal and industry, therefore, constitute an argument against them. What cruelty, what iniquity and what injustice for Nature to thus confine all our concern and all our knowledge to this *present* life, if there is another of infinitely greater consequence still awaiting us? Should such a barbarous deceit to be ascribed to a beneficent and wise Being?

Throughout all Nature, observe the *exact* proportion* with which the task to be performed is adjusted to the available performing powers. If human reason gives us a great superiority above other animals, our necessities are proportionally multiplied. Our whole time and whole capacity; comprising our activity, courage and passion are fully employed defending ourselves against the miseries of our present condition. Frequently, indeed almost always, they prove too slender for the business assigned them.

A pair of shoes, perhaps, has never yet been fashioned to the highest degree of perfection possible. Yet is it necessary, or at least very useful, that there should be politicians and moralists, even some geometricians, historians, poets and philosophers. The powers of humans are no more superior to their wants, considered merely in this life, than are those of foxes and hares compared to *their* wants and lifespan. The inference from parity of reason is therefore obvious.

---

* Proportion: *Adaptation of one to another; Symmetry; Harmonick degree*; SJ

On the theory of the soul's mortality, the inferiority of women's capacity is easily accounted for. Their domestic life requires no higher faculties either of mind or body. This circumstance vanishes and becomes absolutely insignificant, on the religious theory: The task of one sex is equal to the task required of the other. Hence their powers of reason and resolution ought also to have been equal, and both of them infinitely greater than at present.

As every effect implies a cause, that implies another, till we reach the first Cause of all – the Deity. Everything that happens is ultimately ordained by it and hence nothing can be the object of punishment or vengeance by it. By what rule are punishments and reward distributed? What is the divine standard of merit and demerit? Shall we suppose that human sentiments have a place *within* the Deity? How bold a hypothesis that is, when we have no conception of any *other* of its sentiments!

According to human reckoning, sense, courage, good manners, industry, prudence, genius etc., are essential parts of personal merit. Shall we therefore erect an Elysium[1] only for poets and heroes, as in ancient mythology? Why confine all rewards to one species of virtue? Punishment without any proper purpose is inconsistent with our ideas of goodness and justice and no end can be served by it after the whole scene is closed. According to *our* conceptions, punishment should bear some proportion to the offence. Why then, *eternal* punishment for the temporary offences of such frail creatures as humankind? Can anyone approve of the enraged Alexander's intention to exterminate a whole nation because they had seized Bucephalus, his favourite horse?[2]

Heaven and hell suppose two distinct species of humanity, the good and the bad. But the greatest part of humanity floats somewhere *between* vice and virtue. Were one to go around with the intention of giving a good supper to the righteous and a sound drubbing to the wicked, one would frequently be embarrassed in one's choice. One would find that the merits and the demerits of most men and women scarcely amount to the criterion of either goodness or wickedness. To imagine measures of approbation and

---

1 The Fields of Elysium: The ancient Greek heaven for those blessed by the Gods. Also the great avenue linking the Place de la Concorde and L'Arc de Triomphe in Paris.

2 Plutarch, *Life of Alexander*, 44.3. In August 330 BCE, while Alexander was campaigning in Hyrcania to the S. W. of the Caspian Sea, his charger Bucephalus ('ox-head' in Greek) was abducted by the Mardians, a barbarian mountain tribe.

blame that are different from the human confuses everything. For where else, except from our very own sentiments, do we learn that there are such things as moral distinctions?

Who has not met with personal provocation (or what good-natured person who *has*) could, from the sense of blame alone, inflict on crimes even the common, legal and frivolous punishments? And does anything steel the breast of judges and juries against the sentiments of humanity except reflections on necessity and the public interest?

Under Roman law, those who had been guilty of parricide and had confessed, were put into a sack along with an ape, a dog and a serpent and thrown into the Tiber. Death alone was the punishment of those who denied their guilt, however strong the evidence. An alleged parricide was tried before Augustus and condemned to death after conviction. However, that humane Emperor in putting the last question, gave it such a turn as to lead the wretch into a denial of his guilt. Said the Prince,

'You surely did *not* kill your father?'[1]

This leniency suits our natural ideas of right, even towards the greatest of all criminals. Indeed, even the most bigoted priest would approve of it naturally and without reflection, provided of course that the crime was *not* heresy or infidelity. Since the priest is hurt by these crimes in his *temporal* interests and advantages, he might not be altogether so indulgent to them.

The chief source of moral ideas is the reflection on the interest of human society. Ought these interests, so short and so frivolous, to be guarded by punishments eternal and infinite? The damnation of one person is an infinitely greater evil in the Universe than the subversion of a thousand million kingdoms. Nature has rendered human infancy peculiarly frail and mortal, as if to purposely refute the notion of a probationary state. Half of all humans die before they become rational creatures.

III: Physical arguments

Arguments from the analogy of Nature are strong for the *mortality* of the soul and these are really the only philosophical arguments that ought to be considered with regard to this question, or indeed any question of *fact*.

---

1 Suetonius: *De Vita Caesarum*: *Divus Augustus*, 33. 'Certe patrem tuum non occidisti.'

Consider any two objects so closely connected that all alterations seen in the one are attended with proportional alterations in the other. By all rules of analogy we ought then to conclude that when alterations produced in the former amount to its total dissolution, there should follows a total dissolution of the latter.

Sleep, a very small effect on the body, is attended with a temporary extinction or at least a great confusion in the soul. The weakness of the body and that of the mind in infancy are in exact proportion, just as is their vigour in manhood, their sympathic disorder in sickness and their joint gradual decay in old age. The one step further seems unavoidable; their common dissolution at death. The last symptoms that the mind perceives are disorder, weakness, insensibility and stupidity – forerunners of its annihilation. The further progress of these causes increases the same effects and, finally, totally extinguishes it.

Judging by the usual analogy of Nature, no form can survive when transferred to conditions very different from those in which it was originally placed. Trees perish in water, fish in air and animals when buried in the earth. Even so small a difference as that of climate is often fatal. What reason then to imagine that the immense alteration made on the soul by the dissolution of its body and its organs of thought and sensation, can happen *without* the dissolution of the whole? Everything is held in common between soul and body. The organs of the one are all organs of the other. Hence the existence of the one must be dependent on that of the other.

The souls of *animals* are accepted to be mortal. Since these bear so close a resemblance to human souls, the analogy from one to the other forms another very strong argument. Their bodies are not more resembling, yet no one rejects arguments drawn from comparative anatomy. Metempsychosis[1] is therefore the only system of this kind to which philosophy can so much as hearken.

Nothing in this world is perpetual. Every being, however solid in appearance, is in a state of continual flux and change. The world itself gives symptoms of frailty and dissolution. How contrary to analogy, therefore,

---

1 Metempsychosis; Gk: μετεμψύχωσις. The concept of the *intra-* or *extra*-species transmigration of the soul at, or after, death. Its principal early exponent was Pythagoras of Samos (*c.*570–495 BCE)

to imagine that one single form, the soul, seemingly the frailest of any and subject to the greatest disorders from the slightest causes, is immortal and indissoluble? How daring a theory is that? How lightly and how rashly entertained!

The existence of an infinite number of posthumous souls and the question of how to dispose of them, ought also to embarrass the religious theory. We are at liberty to imagine every planet in every solar system being peopled with intelligent, mortal beings; at least we can fix on no other supposition. For these, then, a new *universe* must be created, every generation, beyond the bounds of the present universe. Alternatively, one must have been initially so prodigiously wide as to admit this continual influx of beings. Ought such bold suppositions to be received by any philosophy – merely on the claim of a bare *possibility*?

When it is asked whether Agamemnon,[1] Thersites,[2] Hannibal,[3] Nero[4] and every stupid clown that ever existed in Italy, Scythia, Bactria or Guinea, is presently alive, can anyone think of arguments strong enough to answer so strange a question in the affirmative? In the absence of Revelation, the lack of arguments sufficiently establishes the negative.

> *Quanto facilius, certiusque sibi quemque credere,*
> *ac specimen securitatis antigenitali sumere experimento.*[5]

How much easier and safer to trust in oneself and to derive the concept of one's *future* tranquillity – from our experience of it *before* birth.

Our inability to sense our existence before birth seems, to natural reason, to be a proof of a similarly insensible state after our dissolution in death.'[6]

Were our horror of annihilation an *original* passion rather than derived from our general love of happiness, it would support the mortality of the soul. This is because Nature, that does nothing in vain, would never give us a horror of an impossible event. She may give us a horror against an *unavoidable* event, provided that our endeavours, as in the present case, are

---

1 King of Mycenae and leader of the Greek forces in the Trojan War.
2 Variously, a common soldier in Agamemnon's army; a servant in Shakespeare's *Troilus and Cressida* and, in Goethe's *Faust*, a victim of metamorphosis (into an egg).
3 The celebrated Carthaginian general (247–182 BCE) and inveterate enemy of Rome.
4 Roman Emperor (54–68 CE) Last of the Julio-Claudian dynasty.
5 C. Plinius Secundus (23–79 CE) *Naturalis Historia*, VII. 55.
6 In July 1776, the dying Hume would use this argument when challenged by James Boswell as to whether he was not fearful of a 'future state', ie an afterlife.

capable of postponing it. Death is unavoidable; yet the human species could not have been preserved without an aversion to death having been inspired by Nature.

All doctrines that are favoured by our emotions are to be suspected. These include the hopes and fears that obviously gave rise to the doctrine of the soul's immortality. It is an infinite advantage in every controversy, to be defending against the negative. If the question is beyond the commonly experienced course of Nature, this very circumstance is almost, if not altogether, decisive. What arguments or analogies can prove any state of existence that no-one ever saw and that in no way even resembles any ever seen? Who will repose trust in any pretended philosophy that is able to accept, upon that philosophy's *internal* testimony, so extraordinary a circumstance?

For that purpose, some new species of logic would be requisite, together with some new faculties of the mind that might enable us to comprehend that logic.

Nothing could set in a clearer light the infinite obligations that humanity has to divine revelation, since we find that no other medium could ascertain this great and important truth.[1]

FINIS

---

1 A classic Humean peroration in its ironical obeisance to revealed religion.

Endnotes

A By 'corporate' here Hume means Nature as a whole. Corporate providence is thus contrasted with 'particular' providence. Corporate providence is provided through the structure of Nature so that having created it, the Deity need not intervene in particular circumstances to ensure that things work out. There are, in other words, no miracles through corporate providence, except the miracle of the initial creation. Particular providence involves the deity intervening from time to time in particular circumstances to readjust and direct events to a favourable outcome.

B 'Ideal' in this context, contrasted with 'material', refers not to a moral exemplar to which one might aspire (eg an ideal society or an ideal husband) but rather to (the not wholly unrelated notion of) a different order of reality whose very being is not material (or composed of matter) but of mind, ideas, or mental substance. Philosophers who assert the existence of ideal reality commonly argue that its operations are governed by principles different from those governing material reality, usually by principles or logic or reason distinct from those of causation. (Cautionary note: the relationship between what is 'rational' and what is 'causal' is a difficult and much contested one in philosophy.

C The idea of 'final causes' is technical and refers to one of the four dimensions of explanation (Greek αἰτία, aitia, or 'cause') required by Aristotelian inquirers to properly comprehend an object of inquiry. The four causes include: the 'material' cause (the matter of which the object of explanation is composed); the 'formal' cause (the Aristotelian *Form* enmattered in the object); the 'efficient' or 'moving' cause (what circumstances bring the object into existence); and the 'final' cause (the natural end or state of completeness internal to the being of the object).

Thus a sapling may be composed of: various chemical compounds (material cause); organised into a tree (formal cause); as the result of some person, process, or accident planting the seed from which it sprung (efficient cause); and that is now on its way to growing into a mature oak (final cause), perhaps serving the planter's ornamental or commercial purpose. This latter is another kind of final cause, the sense used in Hume's passage here. Modern natural science has largely rejected formal and final causes in favour of modes of explanation exclusively material and efficient in character. See Aristotle, *Metaphysics*, Book v, 1013a.

Luath Press Limited

committed to publishing well written books worth reading

LUATH PRESS takes its name from Robert Burns, whose little collie
Luath (*Gael.*, swift or nimble) tripped up Jean Armour at a wedding
and gave him the chance to speak to the woman who was to be his wife
and the abiding love of his life. Burns called one of the 'Twa Dogs'
Luath after Cuchullin's hunting dog in Ossian's *Fingal*.
Luath Press was established in 1981 in the heart of
Burns country, and is now based a few steps up
the road from Burns' first lodgings on
Edinburgh's Royal Mile. Luath offers you
distinctive writing with a hint of
unexpected pleasures.
Most bookshops in the UK, the US, Canada,
Australia, New Zealand and parts of Europe,
either carry our books in stock or can order them
for you. To order direct from us, please send a £sterling
cheque, postal order, international money order or your
credit card details (number, address of cardholder and
expiry date) to us at the address below. Please add post
and packing as follows: UK – £1.00 per delivery address;
overseas surface mail – £2.50 per delivery address; overseas airmail –
£3.50 for the first book to each delivery address, plus £1.00 for each
additional book by airmail to the same address. If your order is a gift,
we will happily enclose your card or message at no extra charge.

Luath Press Limited
543/2 Castlehill
The Royal Mile
Edinburgh EH1 2ND
Scotland
Telephone: +44 (0)131 225 4326 (24 hours)
email: sales@luath. co.uk
Website: www. luath.co.uk